CANADIANA
Reprint Series No. 34

Colchester County

HISTORICAL

and

Genealogical Record

of the

First Settlers of Colchester County

by

THOMAS MILLER

Mika Publishing Company

Belleville, Ontario

1983

Third Printing 1983

Originally published in 1873
by A. & W. MacKinlay, Halifax, N.S.

Facsimile edition printed
by Mika Publishing Company
Belleville, Ontario
ISBN 0919302-45-9
1983

HISTORICAL

AND

GENEALOGICAL RECORD

OF THE

FIRST SETTLERS OF COLCHESTER COUNTY.

DOWN TO THE PRESENT TIME,

COMPILED FROM THE MOST AUTHENTIC SOURCES.

BY

THOMAS MILLER.

HALIFAX, N. S:

A. & W. MACKINLAY,

1873.

PREFACE.

THE Author of the following work being now about three score and ten years old, and nearly done with the affairs of this world, having some knowledge of the first settlement of Colchester, the names of the first settlers and their descendants, especially of the Townships of Truro and Onslow, as well as with *many* circumstances connected with the early settlement of the County, obtained by tradition and otherwise, was induced to note down, from time to time, some of them, in order that *his* children, and others who may come after, might know something about their forefathers, and the hardships they underwent in settling a new country.

It was his intention at first to write only about his own kindred; but, having begun, he was led on to mention nearly all the Grantees of the Townships of Truro, and some of Onslow and Londonderry, with their descendants, as far as he could gather information. By the persuasion of a number of his friends, he has been induced to place it before the public. In doing so, it is with a great amount of diffidence, knowing his want of fitness for the work—being illiterate and ill-qualified for the task.

If the dates in this work are not correct, the author here claims the forbearance of those interested, as he has expended a large amount of time and labour to get them as nearly correct as possible,

To all those who have given me information by letter or otherwise, I hereby tender my warm and hearty thanks for these favours.

THOMAS MILLAR.

TRURO, APRIL, 1873.

HISTORICAL AND GENEALOGICAL RECORD

OF THE

FIRST SETTLERS OF COLCHESTER COUNTY.

CHAPTER I.

On the second day of September, 1775, the French inhabitants of Cobequid Village (now Masstown) lying on the north side of the bay, and upper part of the Township of Londonderry, were engaged in their fields at their work, it being harvest time. With the afternoon tide three vessels were seen coming up the Bay. Two of them prepared to anchor, one opposite the Village, and the other at Lower Cobequid ; whilst the third ran further up the shore. Curiosity was rife. Who were they, and whither were they going? Their curiosity was still heightened by the appearance of a person in the garb of a curate, who informed them that the following notice was posted on the door of the Church: " To the inhabitants of the Village of Cobequid, and the surrounding shores, as well ancient as young men and lads ordering them all to repair to the Church the next day at three P. M., and hear what he had to say to them." Signed by John Winslow.

Meanwhile the Sailors landed, and were freely supplied with milk, eggs, and anything they wanted, by the farmers. Small parties of Soldiers landed, chatted with the people, examined their farms, or strolled to the uplands in search of partridges, and in the afternoon of the third day of September they joined the people as they repaired to the Church. The women had milked the cows, and prepared supper, but no one came from the Church. The moon rose, and the sisters strolled out and ran to the Church to ascertain the cause of their delay. When they arrived at the Church, to their great astonishment, they found it surrounded by armed Soldiers, who answered their inquiries by pointing their bayonets, and ordering them to go home. They met many of the women from the houses nearest the Church, all anxious and sad at the detention of their friends. At daybreak the following notice was read, which was stuck on the fence opposite the Church : "Cobequid, September 4th, 1775 . All Officers, Soldiers and Seamen employed in His Majesty's Service, as well as all His subjects, of what denomination soever, are hereby notified that all cattle, viz., horses, horned cattle, sheep, goats, hogs, and poultry of every kind, that was supposed to be vested in the French inhabitants of this Province, have become forfeited to His Majesty, whose property they now are ; and every person of what denomination soever, is to take care not to hurt, destroy, or kill any of the above named animals, nor to rob orchards, or gardens, or to make waste of anything in these districts, without special order given at my Camp, the day and place to be published throughout the Camp, and at the Village where the vessels lie. Signed by John Winslow, Lieut. Colonel Commanding."

When the people read this notice they were speechless with terror ; death stared them in the face. In the meantime three hundred men and boys found themselves close prisoners in their own Church. Some of the boys screamed aloud, some attempted to force the door, but they were overawed by the muskets of their guards. Day dawned at length over the wretched prisoners ; they wished to be allowed to return to their families for food ; this was refused, but their families were ordered to supply food to them. A few of these prisoners were sent out during the day to inform those that dwelt at a distance from the Church if they did not immediately surrender, their houses would be burnt and their nearest friends shot. One of these messengers attempted to escape ; he was shot, and his house and barn set on fire. Thus the work of destruction was commenced. About 200 married women, and upwards of 100 young women, besides children, were ordered to collect what they could of their apparel, and prepare to embark. In vain the men entreated to know whither they were going, but no answer was given. By noon, the 5th of September, the beach was piled with boxes, baskets and bundles ; behind them were crowds of weeping women and children ; children crying for their mothers, and mothers looking for their children ; sick men and bed-ridden women were carried by strong maidens, or tipped out of the carts which bore them to the spot. A little before high water the prisoners in the Church were ordered to form six deep and march to the place of embarkation ; they refused to obey this command. The troops were ordered to fix bayonets and advance on the prisoners. This act produced obedience, and they commenced their march. When they came to the beach and saw their property, their mothers, wives, children and sisters kneeling at each side of the road, one long, loud wail of anguish went up from them on account of being so suddenly torn away from their houses and homes, the place of their nativity, their flocks and fields, which were then covered with the crops of the season, with some of their wheat cut, and the remainder ready for cutting, and separated from their wives and families, leaving behind them their Church and the graves of their kindred, to be dispersed among strangers in a strange land,—among a people whose customs, laws, language and religion were strongly opposed to their own. The women were ordered the same afternoon to embark in another ship. About midnight all were on board, except one or two women who had escaped to visit their forsaken houses the next morning, and witness the sad havoc that had been made the night before by some of the British soldiers who remained, by setting fire to a number of the houses of the Village. Among these was their Chapel, of 100 feet in length and 40 feet in breadth, which contained a large heavy bell. This Chapel stood in a field which is now owned by Alexander Vance, near the house of Mr. Lightbody of Masstown. This place took its name from the fact that the French had their place of worship or Masshouse there. Mr. Vance informed the writer, that he had recently ploughed up some of the n elted metal of the bell, and the spot upon which it stood was pointed out by Mr. Thomas Fletcher, son of the late Thomas Fletcher, who was one of the first settlers in this place after the French were driven out.

The transport ship, with the men on board drifted down to the mouth of the Avon River, and there awaited the other vessel that had the women and children on board. At daybreak she was in sight, and they drif d down the Bay with the saddest freight on board that ever sailed out of the Cobequid Bay ; and as the vessels stood out to pass Blomedon, the third vessel that had run further up the Bay joined them, freighted with the French inhabitants who were gathered from the places now called Onslow, Truro, Clifton and Selma. With a favorable wind these miserable, houseless, homeless wanderers were soon borne out of sight of the place of their nativity ; night hid from their view forever the blue mountains of Cobequid.

It may here be mentioned that while the French inhabitants of Truro were hunted by the British soldiers as the partridge on the mount, some of them fled for a hiding place, and encamped in the woods up the Salmon River, in a deep valley of the brook that Mr. William Murray had his Mills on recently, and from this the brook took its name as French Village Brook.   One of the females who had escaped, or had been left behind on account of a boat being overloaded, returned that night to her former place of abode, and there remained during the night altogether unconscious.   In the morning, when she returned to consciousness, she was too weak to stand; it was some hours before she realized the full horrors of her situation.   After a time she was able to crawl to the door, and there the scene which surrounded her was fearful.   The first object she beheld was the Church, the beautiful Mass House, a blackened heap of ruins.   She was recalled to a sense of her forlorn situation by her cow which came to her, asking by her lowing to be milked.   She milked her cow and partook of some of the milk with a crust of bread, which revived her so much that she set out to see if she could find any one remaining in the Village; but there was no one to be found.   Cattle had broken into the fields and were eating the wheat; horses were running in droves through the fields.   On the evening of that day, cows and goats came up to their accustomed milking place, and lowed around the deserted dwellings; pigs yet fastened in the pens, squealed with hunger; and the oxen, waiting in vain for their master's hand to free them from the yoke, (for they were used in moving the goods to the vessels) were bellowing in the agony of hunger; they hooked and fought with each other, running through the marsh, upsetting the carts or tumbling into the ditches, until death put an end to their sufferings.   The pigs were rooting up the gardens.   She sat down on the doorstep beholding the desolation of the Village, when an Indian approached her and told her to come with him.   She enquired the fate of her people.   "Gone," said he, "all gone," pointing down the Bay, "the people everywhere are prisoners; see the smoke rise, they will burn all here to-night." He pointed up the Bay; two or three blazing fires attested the Indian's story as too true.   He assisted her in gathering some of the most valuable things that were left.   The Indian then piloted her to his wigwam, near the edge of the forest; here she found about a dozen of her people, the remnant left of what was once the happy settlement of the Village of Cobequid (now Masstown).   They waited about the woods on the north side of the Bay, for more than a month to see if any more stragglers could be found before they would start to go to Miramichi.   At length they were joined by about twenty of the French inhabitants who had escaped from Annapolis.   These persons informed them that the houses and crops in Annapolis were burnt by the soldiers who were sent up the River to bring them to the ships.   Some fled to the woods ; some, besides this party, crossed the Bay intending to go to Miramichi through the woods. After another week's travel they met with a party that had escaped from Shepoudie (now called Shubenacadie). From these persons they learned that about two hundred and fifty buildings were burned along the sides of this River, and that while they were firing the Mass House there, the Indians and French rallied and attacked the British Soldiers and killed and wounded about thirty of them, and drove the remainder back to their ships.

CHAPTER II.

As the most of our readers are already aware, Governor Cornwallis arrived in Halifax in the month of June, 1749, with a fleet of ships loaded with passengers, and other things which were necessary for the settlement of a new country. These ships were bearers of nearly 3000 souls. These persons set to work with vigour to clear off the bushes and erect houses for themselves and families to live in, and put themselves in a way to defend themselves from the attacks of the Indians and a few French settlers who were still remaining in the place. Mr. Anthony Elliott was in this company. He was in His Majesty's service as a Soldier. It is said Mrs. Elliott was the first WOMAN that sat foot on the shore on their arrival in Halifax. After Louisbourg and Quebec were taken by the British, Mr. Elliott and a number of others were discharged from His Majesty's service. In the spring of the year 1762 he removed, with his family and a number of others, from Halifax to Onslow. He settled on the farm on which James Crow, Esq., now resides, at the lower end of Onslow, where he spent the remainder of his days. He died there. His wife died there in 1813. He was a grantee of the Township of Onslow. This grant is dated February 21st, 1769.

Nancy, their eldest daughter, was married to Thomas Stevens. They had four sons and one daughter. She was married again to John Read, in 1815. Mr. Read died in 1818, and she was married again to Thomas Hunt in 1822. Elizabeth, the second daughter of Mr. and Mrs. Elliott, was married to John Carr.

William Elliott, their only son, was born in Onslow, February 7th, 1763. His wife, Patience Miller, was born May 15th, 1770.

They were married April 8th, 1791.   He inherited his father's farm, where he spent the whole of his life.   He died May 14th, 1842, aged 79 years.   His wife died in July, 1846, aged 76 years.   Sarah, the eldest daughter of William and Patience Elliott, was born December 28th, 1791.   She was married to Enoch Stevens.   They had five sons and one daughter.   Mary, their second daughter, was born May 19th, 1793.   She was married to John Copeland.   They removed to Canada.   She died there April, 1866, aged 43 years. Isaac Elliòtt, their eldest son, was born February 18th, 1795.   He was married to Mary Erralds, of Falmouth.   They had two sons and four daughters.   Phœbe, their third daughter, was born March 18th, 1798.   She was married to Samuel Crowel.   They had two sons.   She was married again to William Rude.   She removed to Boston, U. S., and was married there to Henry Brewel.   Elizabeth Elliott, their fourth daughter, was born July 25th, 1800.   She was married to John Erralds.   They had three sons and four daughters. Jemima Elliott, their fifth daughter, was born September 26th, 1804. She was married to Robert McLeod.   They had five sons and two daughters.   They removed to Pictou.   William, the second son of William and Patience Elliott, was born June 28th, 1807.   He was married to Jane, daughter of James and Sarah Blair, in 1835.   They had five sons and two daughters.   Mrs. Elliott died in 1848.   He was married again to Eleanor, daughter of Samuel and Margaret Yuill, of Clifton, July 25th, 1848.   They had three sons and three daughters.   He inherited the farm that was owned by his father and his grandfather.   He then exchanged his farm for another further up the Chiganois River, where he now resides.   Hannah Elliott, their sixth daughter, was born December 23rd, 1809.   She is living unmarried. Anthony Elliott, third and youngest son, was born 'uly 13th, 1811. He married Isabella McKinley.   They had five sons and five daughters, who now reside in New Annan.

Margaret, the fourth daughter of Anthony Elliott, Senr., and Jemima, was born Nov. 3rd, 1773.   She was married to James Good, of Shubenacadie.   They had six sons and four daughters.   She died January 24th, 1848, aged 83 years.   Mr. Good died October 12th, 1852, aged 91 years.   Mary Elliott, their third daughter, was born April 6th, 1769.   She was married to William Joyce, December 1792. They had three sons and four daughters.   Mr. Joyce was a Cooper by trade.   He was Jail keeper in Truro for a considerable length of time.   After this he built a house on the same place that Mr. Stephen

Archibald now resides, near the Court House, where he spent the remainder of his days. On May 8th, 1833, he was riding on an ox cart loaded with hoop poles, and as he was coming down the hill, passing the house in which Mr. Robert H. Cummings now resides, the oxen turned suddenly off the road and upset the cart. It fell upon him and fractured his skull. He was taken up dead. He was 64 years old at the time. His wife died July 24th, 1834, aged 66 years.

Rachel Elliott, their fifth daughter, was born September 22nd, 1771. She was married to John Herron. They had three sons.

Eleanor, the sixth daughter of Anthony Elliott, Senr., and Jemima, was married to Richard Perry about 1798. They had three sons and four daughters. She died about 1827. Mr. Perry died in 1855, aged 86 years.

CHAPTER III.

Matthew Staples was another who came with Governor Cornwallis to Halifax in the year 1749. He remained in Halifax about 13 years, working at the trade of Blacksmith. He obtained a grant of 1000 acres of land, before the Township of Onslow was granted. His land was laid out adjoining the Chiganois River on the east side, north of Mr. Anthony Elliott's farm, which is now included in the Township of Onslow. He removed to this farm in 1762 (being the same spring that a number of others settled in the same neighborhood). He had his house and shop on the west side of the road, near the Chiganois River, southwest of Mr. Timothy Barnhill's house. At this place he spent the remainder of his days. He died there about the year 1771. He was married shortly after he removed to Onslow to a lady who had been married twice before. Her maiden name was Sidney Homes. She was married first to David Marshall. Elizabeth Marshall, their eldest daughter, was born in 1752. She was married to John Crowe, of Onslow, in 1776. They had five sons and two daughters. She died at Onslow May 11th, 1838, aged 86 years. Her husband died October 6th, 1825, aged 77 years. Rachel Marshall, their second daughter, was born in England in 1754. She was married to a Mr. Green. They removed to England, where they both died some time ago. Mr. Marshall died. She was married again to William Cook. Rebecca Cook, their only daughter, was married to David, the second son of the Rev. David Smith, of Londonderry. They had four sons. James Cook, their only son, died a bachelor. William Cook was drowned at Port au Pique. His widow was married to Matthew Staples about the year 1766.

John Staples, their eldest son, was born in 1767. He was married to Jane, daughter of John and Joanna Cutten, of Onslow, Oct. 7th, 1791. He inherited that part of his father's farm which is now owned by Messrs. Barnhills. He sold this farm about the year 1820, and removed further up the Chiganois River, and settled on the farm that his son Ephraim now resides upon, where he spent the remainder of his days. He died July 25th, 1855, aged 87 years. His first wife died April 3rd, 1802. He was married again to Catherine, daughter of William and Mary Blair, of North River, May 30th, 1803. His second wife died January, 1830, aged 48 years.

Sarah, the eldest daughter of John and Jane Staples, was born August 4th, 1792. She was married to George, son of Aaron Crow, of Onslow, January 16th 1816. They had four sons and four daughters. Mrs. Crow died January 15th, 1857.

Esther Staples, their second daughter, was born Dec. 3rd, 1793. She was married to Henry Wilson, April, 1814. They had three sons and two daughters. She died April 9th, 1824.

Hannah Staples, their third daughter, was born Dec. 15th, 1795. She was married to Jabish Rude, Nov. 24th, 1814. They had nine sons and four daughters. Mr. Rude died Dec. 23rd, 1869, aged 76 years.

Elizabeth Staples, their fourth daughter, was born May 7th, 1798. She was married to James Wilson, Nov. 22nd, 1815. They had eight sons and five daughters. She died April 19th 1872, aged 74 years.

Rachel Staples, their fifth daughter, was born January 4th, 1800. She was married to Aaron Crow, of Onslow, February 3rd, 1819. They had eight sons and four daughters. She died April 2nd, 1872, Aged 72 years. Mr. Crow died Dec. 23rd, 1852.

Jane, the eldest daughter of John and Catherine Staples, was born June 8th, 1804. She was married to Joseph Crow, Dec. 28th, 1828. They had six sons and six daughters. She died April 29th, 1853, aged 49 years. Mr. Crow died January 3rd, 1868, aged 76 years.

Matthew, the eldest son of John and Catherine Staples, was born August 15th, 1805. He was married to Elizabeth, daughter of Saml. and Letitia Rude, Nov. 14th, 1828. They had three sons and five daughters. He reclaimed his farm from the forest, lying on the cross road between Debert and Chiganois Rivers, upon which he now resides.

William, the second son of Samuel and Catherine Staples, was born January 17th, 1807. He was married to Sarah, daughter of Samuel and Letitia Rude, Dec. 14th, 1828. They had four sons and five daughters.

John Staples, their third son, was born April 21st, 1808. He was married to Rachel, daughter of Samuel and Letitia Rude, January, 1830. They had one son and five daughters.

Alex. Staples, their fourth son, was born April 21st, 1813. He was married to Mary Ann, daughter of Samuel and Letitia Rude, May 12th, 1842. They had three sons and eight daughters. Mrs. Rude died April 7th, 1870.

Ephraim Staples, their fifth son, was born August 1st, 1815. He was married to Rachel, second daughter of Matthew J. and Rebecca Archibald, of Truro, July 4th, 1839. They had three sons and four daughters.

Mary Staples, their second daughter, was born June 27th, 1811. She died 1861, aged 50 years.

Catherine Staples, their third daughter, was born January 20th, 1820. She was married to Joseph Henderson Nov., 1867.

James Staples, their sixth son, was born March, 1824. He was married to Matilda, daughter of William and Sarah Blair, of Onslow, ———, 1853. They had one son and five daughters.

William, the second son of Matthew Staples, Senr., was born in 1769. He was married to Susan Wilson of Masstown, Dec. 20th, 1807. He inherited half of his father's farm, where he continued to reside until his death, Dec. 8th, 1854, aged 84 years. His wife died August 17th, 1862, aged 82 years.

Mary Staples, their eldest daughter, was born Dec., 1808. She died when young.

James C., the eldest son of William and Susan Staples, was born Sept. 25th, 1810. He was married to Sarah, daughter of John and Isabell Baird, of Onslow Mountain, Dec., 28th, 1841. They had four sons and three daughters.

Eliza Staples, their second daughter, was born Nov. 9th, 1812. She was married to John Morrison, of Debert, July, 1835. They removed to the United States.

Mary Staples, their third daughter, was born January 4th, 1815.

She was married to Samuel A. Fulton, of Economy, February, 1839. They had one son.

William, the second son of William and Susan Staples, was born February 18th, 1819. He was married to Mary McCabe of Greenfield, March 23rd, 1848. They had one daughter. He inherits a part of what was his father's farm.

Jane Staples, their fourth daughter, was born January 4th, 1817. She was married to George Davis Sept. 12th, 1863. They removed to the United States.

Wilson Staples, their third son, was born April 19th, 1821. He was married to Margaret Ann, daughter of John and Elizabeth Deyarmond, January 7th, 1864. He inherits the homestead.

John H. Staples, their fourth son, was born August 30th, 1824. He was married to Elizabeth Rodenberry, of Boston, Mass., where they now reside.

CHAPTER IV

In the fall of the year 1759, about 20 men came up the Bay of Fundy from New England, to Truro and Onslow, to make preparations for a settlement. The most of these men had been in Nova Scotia a few years before, assisting in subduing and driving out the old French settlers, and the taking of Louisbourg. These men erected small houses on the same place that Truro Village now stands, and other parts of the neighbourhood. They returned to New England to spend the winter; and in the spring of the year 1760, they returned again to Nova Scotia with their families, and commenced the settlement of the country with that vigour and perseverance that but few of the present day possess. There was a large quantity of manure lying at the place where an old French barn had stood, on the south side of the Salmon River, at the head of the tide. This enabled them to raise potatoes the first year. In July of this year, they applied to the Governor and Council for aid to cut out a road between the several lakes lying between Fort Sackville (now Bedford) and the Shubenacadie River. The Council replied that provisions would be furnished to the men while employed at the work, and that was all they could do.

On July 12th, 1761, it was enacted, that Cobequid be included in the County of Halifax. On August 7th, 1761, the Council directed writs to be issued for the election of members to represent the Townships of Onslow and Truro in the General Assembly of the Province, but we cannot ascertain that any election took place until the year 1765, when James Brenton, Esq., was returned to represent Onslow, and Charles Morris, Jr., to represent Truro. Mr. Morris, being returned for Kings County at the same time, accepted the latter, and Truro was unrepresented until 1766. On June 5th, 1766, David Archibald, Esq., took his seat in the Assembly to represent Truro.

These first settlers endured a considerable amount of hardship for the first few years. In the fall of the year 1760 all the women excepting one returned to New England to spend the winter. In the Spring of the year 1761 they returned to Truro and Onslow with a considerable number of other settlers. On October 9th, 1761, Colonel Alexander McNutt, Agent of the British Government, arrived in Halifax with upwards of three hundred settlers from the North of Ireland ; they were landed on the 15th of October, on what is now called McNab's Island ; they remained about Halifax during the following winter, and endured a considerable amount of hardship. They were sent out by the British Government, and scantily supplied with provisions. In the Spring of the year, 1762 some of them went to Horton, some to Windsor, some to Londonderry, some to Onslow, and others to Truro. On April 17th, 1762, Governor Belcher recommended to the House of Assembly to aid the inhabitants of Truro and Onslow, with provisions and seed grain, as they were very much in need of both. The house declared it impossible on account of the heavy debt that was on the Province. More settlers continued to arrive in Nova Scotia, and the fertile intervals of Truro and Onslow attracted their attention ; also the valuable marsh and upland lying on the two sides of Cobequid Bay.

In the year 1763 there were sixty families in Truro, and in 1765 there were about seventy. This year they obtained a grant from Government of the whole of the Township of Truro in one grant. It contains about eighty thousand acres of land. There is no reserve in this grant of mines or minerals. It is granted to about seventy persons, in " Rights." Some having but half a Right, some one Right, some a Right and a half, and others two Rights. This Grant is signed by Governor Wilmot, dated October 31st, 1765.

Alexander Miller (grandfather of the writer) was one of these grantees. He was the youngest son of Alexander Miller who emigrated from Belfast, Ireland, with his wife and several children, about the year 1718. He settled first in Saco, Maine. A few years after he purchased a large tract of land near what is now Portland, Maine, where he settled and continued the remainder of his life. About the year 1740 he loaded a vessel with boards and sailed in her for Boston to dispose of the cargo. The vessel was last seen near Wood Island ; it was supposed that all on board were lost. After this the family removed to Londonderry, New Hampshire. Alexander Miller, Senior, had four sons and one daughter. About this daughter we have not been able to ascertain anything.

James, the eldest son of Alexander Miller, Senior, was born in Belfast, Ireland, in the year 1712. He was brought by his parents to New England, when he was six years old. He married Mary Alexander, for a second wife. They removed to Belfast, Maine, and arrived there May 20th, 1770. He was the first settler in that City. One of the principal streets is called Miller Street. He died there in the year 1794, aged 82 years.

James, the eldest son of James Miller and Mary Alexander, was married to Betsey Nismoth, of Belfast, Me. They had five sons and two daughters. He occupied lot No. 38 (now known as the Frothingham Place) for a term of years. He then removed with his family to the Western Country, where a number of his descendants still reside. He died there in the year 1840. His wife died about the year 1849.

Robert, another son of James Miller, Senr., occupied lot No. 37. He resided on High Street in the City of Belfast, U. S. He was one of the most respected in that city. He died a bachelor, in the year 1827.

Alexander, the third and youngest son of James Miller, died when he was young.

David, another son of James Miller, Senior, was married to Mary Boyes, of Londonderry, N. H. They had two sons and five daughters. They resided in the house that stands on the farm now known as the Griffin Farm in Northport, Maine. Samuel B., son of David Miller, lived a bachelor, and died May, 1842. Captain James Miller, the other son of David, was born at Northport, Maine, December 16th, 1787. Early in life he chose the occupation of a sailor. His sound health and strong body admirably fitted him for his calling. Many an incident in his history from boyhood to old age, very definitely indicate the man, as he was well known to be, most active and robust. One day, when he was quite a boy, he was returning home from Belfast, he cut a limb of a willow tree for a walking stick, at the Nismith place, now the Reed Farm ; when he arrived home, he stuck down his walking staff into the soft ground ; it took root, and grew to be a large tree, under the shade of which many weary travellers between Belfast and Camden have rested. During the years that he followed the sea, he sailed with many of the residents of Northport and Belfast, Maine. Gradually he advanced from the boy before the mast to the master mariner, coasting along *our* shores to the Provinces, West Indies and Europe. As an instance of his presence of mind and courage, the like of which very few men excel, may be known by what he did when about 22 years of age. He was on a voyage to England, and they had rough weather. In the English Channel a man fell overboard, February 21st, 1809 ; quick as thought James Miller passed a loose end of a rope around his body, and jumped over the railing of the ship after the man ; he grasped him and both were dragged by the rope on board the ship again. He might have been identified by the mark of that rope for some time after. He was married February 23rd, 1830, and occupied the Robert Miller house on High Street, corner of Miller Street, being a joint owner with his brother, of that and other property. Having left the sea his attention was directed to the cultivation, improvement, and sale of land and other property in the city. Several of the streets were projected by him. He and his brother erected a store on the site of the present Post Office. He always felt an interest in all the maritime affairs of the day, and he was owner of several vessels. He built Commercial Street Wharf, which he disposed of to Sanford, of the Independent Line of Steamers. He lost his wife, May 1st, 1861 (a Christian woman). After that time he appeared greatly saddened and seemed to grow old much faster than in former year. As he had no children of his own, he has been very kind to the children of others—a father to the fatherless— giving good advice to all, which he was able to do from his long experience with his fellow men He was charitable to the poor, no one ever left his house hungry or in distress if it was in his power to relieve them. Although he was strong and vigorous, yet the strong man was brought down. In January, 1871, he took a bad cold, and from that time he gradually failed in health. On July 6th, 1872, the once strong man was worn down, and quietly passed to rest on the morning of that day, being eighty-four years and six months old. The

2

name of Captain James Miller will ever be remembered by those who knew him, for his kindness, patience, and charitable labours.

The foregoing are extracts from the obituary notice in the *Progressive Age*, paper, of Belfast, Me., July 26th, 1872.

Samuel, the second son of Alexander Miller, Senior, was married to Margaret Turner of Londonderry, N. H. They had two sons, and ten daughters. They settled in Petersborough, N. H., where they spent the remainder of their lives.

Joseph, another son of Alexander Miller, Senior, settled in Sullivan, Maine, where he left a numerous posterity.

Alexander, the fourth and youngest son of Alexander Miller, Senr., was born in New England in the year 1725. He was married to Nancy Anderson, of New England, about the year 1749. He was one of the first company that came to Truro in the fall of the year 1759, and came again *with their families* in the Spring of the year 1760. It may here be observed that his aged mother, who had been long a widow, and in a poor state of health, would not consent to stay in New England with any of her sons, but came to Nova Scotia with her youngest son, Alexander, as her attachment was strong towards him. She died about eight or ten days after they arrived in Truro, and was the first person who was interred in the Truro Cemetery, the exact spot being now unknown. It is said that when they erected the Church, eight years after, it was found necessary to place it over the grave. Alexander Miller's house lot was on the west side of the Parade. He built his first house on the same place where the Court House now stands, and lived in it fifteen years. He built his next house on his front wood lot, near the place that Mr. John L. Doggett now resides. At this time it was considered quite a distance in the woods. At this place he spent the remainder of his days, and died April 9th, 1791, aged 66 years. His widow died March 28th 1807. It was he and his brother-in-law, Captain John Morrison, (grandfather of Thomas F. Morrison, M.P.P.) who built the first mill which was started in Truro after it was settled by the British. This Mill was built at the same place the Mills now stand near the house of Mr. John McClure. The French had some kind of a Mill at the same place ; there was a millstone found in the bottom of the brook. The writer has now in his possession a copy of an interesting letter written by Alexander Miller to his brother James, who resided then in Belfast, Province of Maine, ated at Truro, June 24th, 1786. He states in this letter how well he had prospered in worldly things since he settled in Truro. That he was now owner of 1650 acres of good land, 31 head of cattle, 3 horses, and 14 sheep ; and that his son Isaac had 500 acres of land, and Samuel had 250 acres ; and that his son Samuel had helped to kill eleven moose the winter before. His son James had not returned home having been absent more than eight years. He had a letter from him, dated at Cork, Ireland, May 9th, 1785. He informed him by this letter that he was married to a woman in Cork, and that he was bound for Holland as first mate of a brig. Alexander Miller sympathized with his brother James on account of the sufferings of him and family during the time of the American Revolution. He states to him the critical situation that he was placed in at one time in Truro between the two parties. For entertaining some of his American friends, he and his two sons had to take to the woods and remain there until the soldiers went off. He also states that the winter before the snow was three feet deep along the side of the Bay, and back about ten miles it was five feet deep, and that it went off that Spring with the heat of the sun. The grain that had been sowed about six weeks before the date of the letter was but then coming through the ground. He and his wife join in thanking God for His many mercies. This letter contains a great deal more about family affairs that might be interesting to connections, but which we do not copy.

Isaac, the eldest son of Alexander and Nancy Miller, was born in New England in the year 1750, and was brought by his parents to Nova Scotia when he was ten years old. He was married to Elizabeth, daughter of Adam and Janet Dickey, Dec. 12th 1781. He settled on what was his father's land, and built his house on the east side of the Mill Brook, in the field that is now owned by Mr. William Sutherland. He owned all the interval and meadow lying on both sides of this brook, with a considerable upland. In the fall of the year 1809, there were quite a number of Indians encamped on his farm, on the upland, west of the interval, now called the Indian Hill. Some of the Indians had borrowed an axe from him. One evening, a little before sunset, he unyoked his team from the plough in his interval, and walked up the hill to the Indian's camp to see about his axe, as he had not heard any noise of the Indians during the day. When he approached the camps, all was stillness. Almost the first thing he saw was his axe, lying outside the door covered with blood. He went into the camp, and there he found an Indian lying with a cloth spread over him. When he removed the cloth, he was very much astonished at seeing the head nearly severed from the body, which had evidently been done with *his* axe. He was so struck with awe, that he left the place in haste to give notice to the neighbours. It appeared that all the Indians, except this one and his squaw, had left the day before. His squaw was suspected for committing the fatal deed. It was said that her attachment was stronger to another Indian than it was towards her husband. She was pursued by a constable and a number of others, and taken prisoner at Stewiacke, brought back to jail, and was tried in the court at Truro. The verdict of the jury was, *not guilty*, as there was no positive proof of her guilt. The late George S. Dickey was one of the men who went after her. She was taken from among a large number of Indians; but there was no resistance offered by them towards the company that took her. Mr. Miller sold out his farm in Truro in the spring of the year 1816. He removed with his family to Lower Stewiacke, and purchased a farm from William Pollock, Senr., and his son Samuel, being the same farm that Mr. John Teas and son now reside upon, north of the railroad station, and on the north side of the River. He died there Nov. 4th, 1825, aged 75 years. His wife died in Truro December 20th 1803, aged 40 years.

Mary Miller, their eldest daughter, was born Nov. 7th 1782. She was married to Samuel, the youngest son of James and Mary Dunlap, February 11th, 1813. They had three sons and four daughters. She died January 12th, 1861, aged 78 years. Mr. Dunlap died March 2nd, 1850, aged 68 years.

James Miller, their eldest son, was born ———, 1784. He died when young.

Janet Dickey Miller, their second daughter, was born August 8th, 1785. She was married to William Frieze, of Maitland, Jan'y 14th, 1809. They had five sons and four daughters. She died Dec. 25th, 1844, aged 59 years. Mr. Frieze died January 14th, 1843, aged 68 years.

Nancy Anderson Miller, their third daughter, was born March 30th, 1787. She was married to Andrew Yuill, of Clifton, Dec. 1st, 1814. They had three daughters. She died April 15th, 1822, aged 35 years.

James, the second son of Isaac and Elizabeth Miller, was born January 17th, 1790. He followed land surveying. When he was a young man, he was engaged surveying in the County of Pictou, and there became acquainted with Miss Jane McGill, of the West River. They were married February 14th, 1816. He settled at Lower

Stewiacke, and remained there for about ten or twelve years. He then sold out and removed to Halifax, and remained there until the fall of the year 1834, when he removed to New Glasgow, and shortly after lost his health. He died there Dec. 5th, 1836, in the 47th year of his age. His widow died there June 3rd 1872, aged 75 years.

Elizabeth, the eldest daughter of James and Jane Miller, was born May 2nd, 1817. She was married to John Ray in Halifax. They removed to the United States. They had two sons and two daughters. Mr. Ray died there. She was married again.

Ann Miller, their second daughter, was born March 18th, 1819. She now resides in New Glasgow, Pictou.

John Miller, their eldest son, was born January 21st, 1821. He was married to Hannah, daughter of Robert McConnell and Marian Smith, his wife, Dec. 25th, 1848. He settled at New Glasgow, where he carries on business as a flour and bread merchant. His first wife died March 18th, 1869. He was married again to Elizabeth, the third daughter of Andrew and Nancy Yuill, of Clifton, June 27th, 1871.

Frederick, the eldest son of John and Hannah Miller, was born March 17th, 1850. James Miller, their second son, was born June 29th, 1851. William Miller, their third son, was born May 28th, 1857. Christiana Miller, their eldest daughter, was born May 10th, 1860. Jane Miller, their second daughter, was born June 12th, 1862. Hannah Miller, their third daughter, was born March 5th, 1869.

David, the second son of James and Jane Miller, was born March 10th, 1823. He went to reside with his uncle, William McGill, in 1834, and continued with him while he lived. He now inherits what was his uncle's farm. He was married to Sarah, daughter of Robert McConnell and Marian Smith, his wife, June 2nd, 1848. Isaac Miller, their eldest son, was born March 13th, 1849. Jane Miller, their eldest daughter, was born February 28th, 1851. Caroline Miller was born May 12th, 1853. Amelia Miller, born Sept. 28th, 1857. William McGill Miller was born February 12th, 1859. Anne Miller was born March 19th 1862. Frank Miller was born May 12th, 1869.

Nancy, the third daughter of James and Jane Miller, was born March 4th, 1825.

Rebecca, the fourth daughter of James and Jane Miller, was born April 18th, 1827. She was married to James Stewart on March 18th, 1847. They had four sons and four daughters. They are settled at Brookfield.

Alexander, the third son of Isaac and Elizabeth Miller, was born in Truro, February 15th, 1792. He removed to Lower Stewiacke with his father and family in 1816. He removed again to the State of Maine in the spring of the year 1824. He died there a bachelor, January 20th, 1861, aged 69 years.

Rebecca Crowe Miller, their fourth daughter, was born in Truro, January 8th, 1794. She removed to the State of Maine, and resided with her brother Alexander during the remainder of his life. Shortly after his death, she returned to Truro. She died at Clifton unmarried, October 12th, 1866, aged 72 years.

Eleanor Miller, their fifth daughter, was born Nov. 6th, 1797. She had poor health, and was subject to fits. She died at Stewiacke February, 1822, aged 24 years.

Adam Miller, their fourth son, was born May 21st, 1799. He was married to Sarah, the eldest daughter of William and Louisa Hamilton, of Brookfield, March 12th, 1829. They have resided in Upper Stewiacke since about the year 1840.

Nancy, the eldest daughter of Adam and Sarah Miller, was born February 28th, 1830. She was married to Thomas Robison, Halifax, January 4th, 1868.

Sarah Ann, their second daughter, was born October 18th, 1831. She was married to John Henderson Archibald April 5th, 1853. They inherit her father's farm at Upper Stewiacke.

Louisa Miller,, their youngest daughter, was born September 14th, 1837. She was married to Henry Brown, of Halifax, October 17th, 1865. They had two daughters.

Elizabeth, the youngest daughter of Isaac and Elizabeth Miller, was born in Truro, July 13th, 1801.

James, the second son of Alexander and Nancy Miller, was born in New England in 1753, and was brought by his parents to Truro in 1760. He left home when young, to follow the sea, and was pressed to serve on board of a ship of war for some time; and, after being released, he returned home. In April 1778, he left home again to follow his calling as a mariner. Some time after this, he was in charge of a brig, which laid in the Port of Cork, Ireland, during the winter; and he there made the acquaintance of Miss Eleanor Mahon, and they were married in the year 1783.

Nancy, their eldest daughter, was born in Cork December 16th, 1784. She was married to Stephen, son of Robert and Susan Johnston, of the Lower Village of Truro, July 27th, 1811. They had three sons and three daughters. She died in Upper Stewiacke, Nov. 25th, 1870 ; and her husband died Dec. 26th, 1856, aged 69 years.

James and Eleanor Miller had two sons, who died young, in Ireland. He continued to follow the sea as captain. Upon one occasion he met with Captain Wm. Cock on the street in the city of London ; and, as Capt. Cock said himself, " He never was gladder in his life to see any person than he was when he met Captain James Miller." In the year 1792, he returned home with his wife and daughter, then eight years old, and settled for a while on the farm on which John Barber now resides, near the mouth of the Shubenacadie River, where their two sons, Alexander and James, were born. He had John Nelson hired to work his farm ; and he continued to go to sea until his wife died in the year 1796. He was married again to Elizabeth, daughter of William and Dolly Putnam, widow of James Smith of Upper Stewiacke in 1797, and had three sons and one daughter.

Alexander, the eldest son of Captain James and Eleanor Miller, was married to Margaret McLeod, of Cape Breton, October 15th, 1836. They had four sons and two daughters, whose names are John, Alexander, James, Charles, Eleanor, and Nancy. James, their third son is married to Miss Agnes Reynolds and has removed to the United States. They have one son and two daughters. Alexander married Melvina Cummings. Alexander Miller fourth died in Cape Breton, June 10th, 1844. His widow is married to Abraham Newcomb of Musquodoboit. James the second son of Captain James Miller, was married to Margaret McDonald. They had three sons and one daughter. James the eldest of these three was lost at sea. The names of the other two are John and Alexander. The daughter's name is Eleanor. Mrs. Miller died, and he married again to Jane Maples. They removed to Margaree, Cape Breton, and had three sons and three daughters.

Joseph, the eldest son of Capt. James and Elizabeth Miller, was born 1798. He was married to Ann Shipley, of Cumberland County, in 1830, and had two sons and two daughters. Their names are James, Prescott Isaac, Elizabeth, and Ann. Elizabeth is married to Joseph Atkinson, and has a family of children in Boston, Mass. Ann, the second daughter of Joseph and Ann Miller, is married to Henry Lyford, and has a family of children in Boston, Mass. Joseph Miller removed from Antigonish, where he was born and brought up, to the United States in the year 1836, and about three years after, as he was driving along the road in a stage waggon, with a number of others, in the State of Florida, he was shot by the Indians, who were concealed in ambush. He left a widow and four young children.

Elizabeth, the only daughter of Capt. James and Elizabeth Miller, was born in Antigonish in 1800. She removed to Boston, Mass., some time ago, and was married to Mr. ———— Sheffield. She died July 4th, 1859.

David, the second son of Capt. James and Elizabeth Miller, was born in Antigonish in 1802, he removed to the United States, and was married there to Martha Floid, of Boston. They have three sons and two daughters.

Charles, the youngest son of Capt. James and Elizabeth Miller, was born at Antigonish in 1804. He was married to Elizabeth Smith, and had five sons and four daughters. He died suddenly some time ago, and left a widow with nine young children. His second son, William, is now a member of the Senate of the Dominion of Canada. His eldest son, James, died in the United States. His third son, Daniel, died a bachelor. Capt. James Miller, after he was married to his second wife, removed to Antigonish, where he reared his family and spent the remainder of his days. He carried on farming, milling and land surveying. He died November 10th, 1825, and his wife died a few years after him.

Jane, the eldest daughter of Alexander and Nancy Miller, was born about two years before they came to Nova Scotia. She was married to David Archibald, second son of Samuel Archibald and Eleanor Taylor, December 1st, 1778, and had seven sons and two daughters. Samuel, the third son of Alexander and Nancy Miller, was born in Truro in the year 1761. He was married to Elizabeth Davidson, February 3rd, 1791. (Her father, James Davidson, lived in a house that stood on the same spot that William Nelson's house now stands, on the east of the Truro Cemetery.) Margaret Thomson Miller, their eldest daughter, was born December 2nd, 1791. She was married to Alexander, son of Alexander and Margaret Nelson, of Clifton, December 23rd, 1812, and had three sons and two daughters. She died October 1st, 1865. Mr. Nelson died about ten years before her. James Davidson Miller, their eldest son, was born March 2nd, 1795. He died a bachelor March 17th, 1858, aged sixty-three years. Sarah, the second daughter of Samuel and Elizabeth Miller, was born March 2nd, 1797. She died unmarried October 22nd, 1871, aged seventy-four years. Alexander, their second son, was born

August 25th, 1799. He died in March, 1800. Nancy, their third daughter, was born March 18th, 1801, and died January 18th, 1803. William, their third son, was born May 12th, 1804. He is living a bachelor. Eleanor T., their fourth daughter, was born July 22nd, 1806. She was married to Hugh Ross, and has two sons. She is now a widow, living near Elmsdale. Samuel, fourth son of Samuel and Elizabeth Miller, was born April 1st, 1808, and died December, 1830. Elizabeth, their fifth daughter, was born December 25th, 1811. She was married to John Frane December 18th, 1852, and has one son. Mary, their youngest daughter, was born June 5th, 1814. She is married to Robert Hall, and has three sons and three daughters. Samuel Miller lived and reared his family on the same farm on which the three sons of the late Samuel Forbes now reside, lying on the shore at Clifton. He died April 11th, 1837, aged seventy-six years, and his wife died October 18th, 1855, aged eighty-five years.

Sarah, the youngest daughter of Alexander and Nancy Miller, was born in Truro February 22nd, 1767. She was married to William, son of James and Elizabeth Johnson, of the Lower Village of Truro, November 15th, 1787. They removed to Upper Stewiacke, where they settled and reared their family. They had two sons and four daughters. Mrs. Johnson being in a bad state of health in the fall of the year 1820, was carried on her bed from Stewiacke to Truro, by two horses in a carriage, which was made for the purpose, and had a pair of shafts made long enough for one horse to walk after the other, and a place housed in for the bed between the horses, for the purpose of being attended by Dr. Suther, as there was no doctor at the time in Stewiacke. She died at the house of her brother, Alexander Miller, in Truro March 3rd, 1821. Her remains were taken to Stewiacke for interment. Mr. Johnson died at Stewiacke December 16th, 1830.

Alexander, the youngest son of Alexander and Nancy Miller, was born where the Court House now stands in Truro, April 22nd, 1769. He was married to Rebecca, daughter of Joseph Crowe, Senr., and Esther Barnhill, of Chiganoise, December 6th, 1792. Mrs. Miller died October 19th, 1793. He was married again to Rebecca, daughter of Thomas Baird and Margaret Barnhill, of Chiganoise (by the Rev. Duncan Ross, when he came first to this country), June 29th, 1795. He inherited his father's farm, and, having purchased the adjoining lot on the west from David Whidden, he removed his house across the road to the place on which David B. Fletcher's house now stands, in the year 1799, where he spent the remainder of his days. At the moving of his house Alexander Barnhill (father of John Barnhill) got his leg broken. He followed farming and land surveying. From the year 1820 to 1826 he owned a schooner and was engaged in trade, which proved to be very unprofitable to his worldly circumstances. He was an elder in the Presbyterian Church for thirty-one years, and most of this time he was clerk and treasurer of the Session. He was one of the first advocates of the Temperance cause in Truro, which commenced about the year 1828. And it may here be observed that the first funeral that was held in Truro (except it might have been at the very early settlement of the place) without the use of spirituous liquor, was the funeral of the late Ebenezer Archibald, which took place August 10th, 1829. The writer has in his possession the rules of the first Temperance Society which was formed in Truro, in the handwriting of John McCurdy, who was then teaching school in the school house which stood near Mr. Thomas Taylor's house. Mr. McCurdy was Secretary of the Society, Rev. John Waddell, President, Alexander Miller Vice-President, Alexander Kent, David Page, Senr., Charles Tucker, John J. Archibald and David Page, Junr., were the committee of management. These rules are dated January 10th, 1831. One of the rules of this Society was that it should meet quarterly, and at every meeting there should be an address given by some person to be appointed by the committee.

The following is the address given by the said Alexander Miller at one of the quarterly meetings held in the old Court House in the fall of 1832 :—

" I have been young and now am old, and have seen public opinion often changed in Truro. I am now standing near the spot where I first existed, as this house nearly touches the ground on which the house stood where I was born ; and on this green around here is where my feet trod in my early days. Nearly all my former acquaintances have left me, and I am becoming a stranger on the spot where I was born. And knowing that I must soon go the way that nearly all of my acquaintances have gone a little before me, I think it my duty to take notice of some of the changes that I have witnessed regarding the traffic in, and ·use of, ardent spirits, and the different changes in public opinion with regard to the same, together with the change that has taken place in my own opinion.

" In the first of my recollection, perhaps about the year 1773, there was one barrel of rum sold in the Upper Village of Truro ; and the next year one puncheon ; and the next two, and I believe the next year there were three puncheons sold, and so on it kept increasing until, in the year 1831, there were sixty puncheons sold in Truro. In these early days the people of Truro were famed for a sober, orderly, and hospitable people, but pretty much as trade increased and the use of ardent spirits increased, the people sank in reputation, and many of our old respectable people fell before the destroyer. The public opinion was then that ardent spirits was one of the good creatures of God, to be used, but not abused, and according as they believed they practised, and they went on in this way until the use of it became common, and was thought respectable. A person was not thought sociable or generous if he did not keep it to treat his friends, till alas, the many instances of the evils which have passed before us are enough to make us shudder. It is not worth while to mention them here, for they are too well known to us all. But we have reason to be thankful that a change of public opinion has, in some measure, taken place, and is still on the move ; and many who formerly considered it one of God's good creatures, to be used in moderation, consider it now the creature perverted from its original use to the service of the devil, and that it is a sin to tamper with it at any rate. Total abstinence is the only way of defeating the adversary, and from principles of christianity, philanthrophy, and true patriotism, a number have come forward and pledged themselves to total abstinence from the use of ardent spirits, and the immoderate use of all intoxicating liquors, under the name of the " Truro Temperance Society." About two years ago there were only eighteen persons found to embrace these principles. At the end of the first year the number stood 133, and at the end of the second year 175, belonging to what is called the " Old Society." Besides these, about 60 young men have espoused the cause and formed themselves into a society on the same principles, and are doing much good by co-operating with us. The young people taking the cause in hand, bids fair for the work being completed by the next generation.

" There is much against the work being accomplished by this generation, who have been brought up in what I call the old school, where moderate drinking was taught, believed in, and practised, until the appetite became so strong for the poison by habit, the understanding impaired, and the conscience lulled to sleep, and persons saying it is good for the body in a great many circumstances, and it would be wrong for us to deprive ourselves of this good, and so they drink on ; still they grow more attached to it, until final ruin ensues.

Now, the world is divided on these two great questions, whether ardent spirits is the good creature of God or not? These two great questions are to be determined by the Court of public opinion, and every person has a part to act in the decision. Therefore each one should endeavor to qualify himself as a Judge, to give an impartial opinion on this great and important subject. We must see that we are not prejudiced in the cause, and that we give due attention to have ourselves properly informed in the matter, and have none of the spiritous liquor mixed with our blood, nor so strongly wedded to its use that nothing but death can separate. When all are thus properly qualified to vote in this matter by having the understanding informed, the conscience enlightened and in lively exercise, then I have no doubt but the decision will be in favor of total abstinence principles. And if this was acted upon, the monster would soon be driven from this world, and man delivered from one of his greatest enemies. But should the Court of public opinion not take due pains to qualify itself on this question, and give but a partial decision, then the monster would still be permitted to den in our land, and go through it destroying its inhabitants. Then where will the responsibility lie? Will it not be upon those who have not done their duty in discouraging the use of it in every way that lay in their power? If all would come forward, the work would be done at once. Those who have come forward and done their duty have acquitted themselves. But awful must be the responsibility on those where it rests, not only to society in this world, but the responsibility that they are under to the great Judge at the last day.

"The cause of temperance admits of no doubt of its originating in Divine love, and it *will* progress, although there is so much opposition to the good cause, under so many false opinions that are abroad in the world. Of some of these false pretences I shall here take notice, such as the following : ' Some say that they would join the society only the members are a set of hypocrites. They pretend to abstain for a while and then drink worse than ever.' ' Others say that they like temperance very well, but they carry things too far, and those who are its most zealous friends say things that are so disgusting ; such as that ardent spirits are not the good creatures of God, but the perversion of them through the invention of men, under the instigation of the devil, and we cannot put up with such doctrine as to abstain altogether. But grant us the moderate use, and not the abuse, and we will join you.' ' Others say that they see no use in these societies ;

if a man has not religious principle enough to bind him, it will not be the signing of the pledge that will do any good to make him refrain.' Now, to these last we say that the religion of Jesus binds every one of his followers, and especially those who have been themselves guilty in countenancing any sin, and have been brought to an evangelical repentance of the same, and are sensible of the dishonor done to Christ and his cause. They that love him cannot stand by and see the spear thrust into his side without regret, and, out of love to him, make use of all rational means in their power to stem vice, especially this one of intemperance, which has done so much evil to the human race ; and what means would be so effectual as if all would come forward and assist in removing the temptation out of the way, by not countenancing the traffic or use of it. Now, I say from Christian principle that it is the duty of every one to come forward and make use of every means in his power to put a stop to the use of an article which has been proved to be of no use, but hurtful to the human constitution, from the testimony of hundreds of respectable physicians who have given their names to the world. Also, the evidence of thousands who have made the experiment ought to be conclusive evidence to those who have not as yet made the experiment ; and the responsibility rests on those who stand aloof from this great work. To those who plead for the moderate use, and not the abuse, I would say, look at the danger you are in and let conscience speak, and see if it will not tell you that it is presumption for you to follow a path which has conducted so many to ruin, for no man ever became a drunkard at once, and I would have you to examine and see if you are not trusting to your own strength, which it is to be feared will be your ruin, as it has been to many before you. I would ask those who are still wavering in opinion whether ardent spirits is one of the good creatures of God, or whether they have been preverted from their original use by the art of man, through the instigation or suggestion of Satan ? The tree is known by its fruit, and when we come to look and see the amount of evil and mischief the use of it produces, we must come to the conclusion at once that it is the work of the bad and not of the good spirit. Next, to those who say that the temperance people are all a set of hypocrites who only pretend that they abstain, but will drink as fast as those who make no pretensions—to these I would say not to be too hasty in judging the heart, which belongs only to God, who well knows the intentions of the heart. But it is to be regretted that there is so much truth in this remark—that so many have put their hand to the plough and have looked back, or, from want of resolution, have gone in the way of temptation, and have fallen before it. To such as have been sensible of their fall, and express a desire to continue in the good cause, looking for Divine assistance (being now by their fall made sensible of their own weakness), I would say bear with them, and admonish them in the spirit of meekness, and drop a tear of pity over those who are so far gone as to allow themselves to indulge in moderate or immoderate drinking, which is the road to misery. To those who have been enabled to sustain their pledge I would say endeavor to be firm and stand fast, taking good heed lest you fall; and go on steadily, depending on Him who can give strength to bring us all honorably through this world. It is much to be regretted that so many of those who were expected to come forward are still standing aloof and taking no part in this great work. It is recommended by your committee not to deal in stores where this traffic is carried on. Also, to petition the Legislature and the Court of Sessions to prohibit the use of strong drink in houses of entertainment."

Upon the foregoing recommendation, petitions were prepared, and signed by a large number of persons from the different parts of the County, to the Court of Sessions for the County of Colchester, January term 1833, asking the Court not to grant license to any person to sell spirituous liquors. Mr. William Creelman (father of the Hon Samuel Creelman) was the delegate and bearer of petitions from Upper Stewiacke. And when it was proposed to grant license, the foregoing named Alexander Miller rose in the court, and stated that he held in his hand petitions, signed by hundreds of respectable persons, asking the worshipful Court not to grant license for the sale of liquors, when the Judge, in a very peremptory manner, stopped him from saying anything in support of the prayer of the petition. And when the petitions *were* read and the vote taken, there was a majority of the Justices in favour of not granting licenses. With this decision the Judge appeared quite dissatisfied, and said to the Justices, " that he did not know what they meant by violating the laws of the Province in such a manner." Alexander Miller, 3rd, eldest son of the foregoing Alex. Miller and Rebecca Baird, his wife, was born in Truro, May 8th, 1796 (being the same day that Truro Village was burnt). He was married to Sarah, daughter of John Faulkner and Janet Moor, his wife. (Sarah being the widow of the late James Perkins who was drowned from a fishing boat at Five Islands, and left a young widow and one daughter. This daughter is now the wife of Robert Cummings, and has two sons and one daughter). Alexander Miller and Sarah Perkins were married Dec. 19th, 1822. They had three sons and two daughters.

James, the eldest son of Alexander and Sarah Miller, was born in Truro, March 4th, 1824. He was married to Margaret, daughter of Samuel and Margaret Forbes, of Clifton, May 24th, 1851, and had two daughters. Sarah, their eldest daughter, was born Feb. 11th, 1853. Ermina, their other daughter, was born August 12th, 1855. James Miller was a Colporteur and School teacher. He died suddenly at the Folley, Londonderry, Feb. 10th, 1858, in the 34th year of his age. Nancy, the eldest daughter ef Alexander and Sarah Miller, was born December 5th, 1824. She died unmarried Dec. 29th, 1862.

Robert, the second son of Alexander and Sarah Miller, was born January 4th, 1828. He was a house-joiner, and removed to New Hampshire, U. S.; and was married there to Sarah Blanchard, of Watertown, Mass., U. S., Feb. 29th 1851, and died March 7th, 1852, aged 23 years. Elizabath, the second daughter of Alexander and Sarah Miller, was born June 10th, 1830. She was married to Isaac Miller October 24th, 1859, and removed to California, where he had his arm broken, and some time after, the arm was taken off; and he returned to Truro in a bad state of health, and died on Nov. 13th, 1864, in the 40th year of his age. Elizabeth was married again to William Dickson, of Onslow, June 20th, 1865, and had one son and one daughter.

Alexander, the youngest son of Alexander and Sarah Miller, was born October 15th, 1832. He works at cutting and engraving monuments. He was married to Sarah Ann, daughter of John J. and Mary Archibald, Nov. 25th, 1856. Agnes, their eldest daughter, was born April 11th, 1859, Mary Jane, their second daughter, was born August 7th, 1861, and died August 30th, 1863. Andrew, their son, was born February 16th, 1863, and died Dec. 18th, 1865. Jannie Blanchard, their third daughter, was born December 31st, 1867. The above named Alexander Miller, 3rd, died May 31st, 1855, aged 59 years.

Margaret, the eldest daughter of Alexander and Rebecca Miller, was born May 24th, 1797. She was married to James M. McCurdy, of Onslow, October 25th, 1814. They removed to Musquodoboit in March, 1816, where they took their farm from the forest, erected comfortable buildings, and raised their numerous family. They had

eight sons and five daughters.   All their daughters and four of their
sons are dead.   Their son, George, and daughter, Elizabeth, died near
one time, and were both laid in one grave,   George was 20 years old
and Elizabeth 18.   Mrs. McCurdy died Oct, 11th, 1845.   Mr. Mc-
Curdy died March 30th, 1871.

Rebecca, the second daughter of Alexander and Rebecca Miller,
was born August 10th, 1798.   She was married to Joseph, eldest son
of John and Sarah Barnhill, of Chiganoise, Feb. 29th, 1816.   They
had five sons and two daughters.   She died June 1st, 1843, aged 45
years, and her husband died March 15th, 1869, aged 77 years.
Nancy, the third daughter of Alexander and Rebecca Miller, was born
May 21st, 1800.   She was married to James D. Baird, of Onslow,
July 13th, 1820.   They had six sons and two daughters.   Two sons
and one daughter died some time ago.   They removed to Pembroke,
Upper Stewiacke, in the spring of the year 1861, where she is still
living, but has been blind during the past ten or twelve years.   Mr.
Baird died June 2nd, 1871, aged 74 years.

Jane, the fourth daughter of Alexander and Rebecca Miller, was
born December 26th, 1801.   She was married to Alexander Nelson,
April 8th, 1823.   They had six sons and four daughters.   They
removed from Middle Stewiacke to Boston, Mass., in the year 1853.
Their son, William, was drowned in Stewiacke River July 20th, 1845,
when he was 12 years old,   Their sons Alex., Thomas and George,
all died near one time, in the year 1863, in the United States.   Their
daughter, Elizabeth, was married to Thomas West.   Mr. West died
December 12th, 1861, aged 29 years, and his wife, Elizabeth Nelson,
died March 27th, 1859, aged 22 years,

Thomas, the second son of Alexender and Rebecca Miller, was
born December 25th, 1803.   He was married in 1823, to Janet
Colvan, daughter of John and Jane Smith.   Rebecca, their eldest
daughter, was born March 1st, 1824, and was married to John H.
Archibald, of Harmony, January 29th, 1844.   They have one
daughter.

Jane, the second daughter of Thomas and Janet C. Miller, was
born March 26th, 1826.   She is married to John L. Archibald, of
Harmony, Nov. 17th, 1846.   They have six sons and one daughter.
Their names are among the Archibalds.

Daniel Cock, the eldest son of Thomas and Janet C. Miiler, was
born March 4th, 1829.   He was married to Olive Crowell March 4th,

1853. Colvan their eldest daughter, was born December 25th, 1853. Charles B., their eldest son, was born Oct. 25th, 1855.

Elizabeth Jane, their eldest daughter, was born Feb. 13th, 1857. Sarah was born Sept. 15th, 1858, and died Nov. 11th, 1859. Sarah Rebecca was born May 27th, 1860. Robert was born Sept. 22nd, 1861. Albert Edward was born August 18th, 1863. Clara Agnes, was born August 13th, 1865, and died May 5th, 1866. Mary Etta was born March 12th, 1867. William was born June 11th, 1868. Thomas was born March 6th, 1871.

Alison, the third daughter of Thomas and Janet C. Miller, was born April 5th, 1832. She was married to Edward Johnson, of Upper Stewiacke, Dec, 4th, 1855. They had four sons. Mr. Johnson died in Halifax, March 20th, 1864.

Christie, the fourth daughter of Thomas and Janet C. Miller, was born Feb. 5th, 1837. She was married to Robert Dinsmore October 13th, 1859. They have two sons and three daughters.

Mary, the fifth daughter of Thomas and Janet C. Miller, was born May 26th, 1840. She died unmarried August 22nd, 1859, in the 20th year of her age. William, their second son, was born January 8th, 1843, and died June 10th, 1843. William Alexander, their third son, was born June 21st, 1844. He left home April 2nd, 1867, and went to California. He was absent more than four years, and returned home May 9th, 1871. He was married to Olive, the youngest daughter of David T. and Eleanor Archibald, Dec. 18th, 1872.

Isaac Geddie, the fourth son of Thomas and Janet C. Miller, was born May 4th, 1847. He removed to the United States May 31st, 1870. He returned home January, 1872. John Smith, their fifth son, was born Dec. 6th, 1849.

Robert Smith, their youngest son, was born March 25th, 1853, and died July 24th, 1858. Mrs. Miller died January 23rd, 1873, in the 68th year of her age. Mary, the fifth daughter of Alexander and Rebecca Miller, was born Sept. 22nd, 1805. She was married to Robert Archibald. They had two sons ; both died young. She died Feb. 8th, 1855. Elizabeth, the sixth daughter of Alex. and Rebecca Miller, was born Jan. 23rd, 1807. She was married to Robert, son of Edward and Hannah Logan, January 22nd, 1828. Their family and deaths appear in the Logan family. Sarah, the seventh daughter of Alex. and Rebecca Miller, was born April 17th, 1809. She was married to William Logan January 8th, 1829, and had five sons and two daughters, who appear in the Logan family. Eleanor, the youngest daughter of Alexander and Rebecca Miller, was born July 13th, 1812. She was married to Daniel Hamilton, of Onslow, Feb. 14th, 1835. They had five sons and four daughters. On Nov. 5th, 1844, Mr. Hamilton was caught by his coat with the cogs of a wheel of a grist mill, and was drawn through between the cogs of the two wheels where there was a space of but two and a half inches. He was very much injured ; and had it not been that one cog came on each side of his back-bone, he would have been nearly cut in two.

CHAPTER V.

David Archibald, Esq., was the eldest of four brothers who settled in Truro. They arrived in Nova Scotia with a number of others on the 13th day of December, 1762. He was a leading man in society ; was the first Justice of the Peace who was settled in Truro ; was the first who represented Truro Township in Parliament. He first took his seat June 5th, 1766. His name stands first in the Grant of said Township, also to the call given the Rev. Daniel Cock, which was dated September, 13th, 1770. His name is also at the head of the list of elders of the Presbyterian Congregation. These were chosen in the summer of 1770. He had his front lands on the north side of Salmon River. His house stood near George McLeod's, on what is called Bible Hill. At one time a thief was brought before him for trial, and the sentence was, " That the thief should be tied to a cart and driven from the Hill across the River, down round the Parade, and back to the Hill again ; and that the driver should use the whip more freely on the thief than on the horse. Mr. Archibald was born in Londonderry, Ireland, September 20th, 1717. Elizabeth Elliott, his wife, was born June 10th, 1720. They were married May 19th, 1741. He died about 1795. His wife died October 19th, 1791, aged seventy-one years.

Samuel, the eldest son of David Archibald, Esq., and Elizabeth Elliott, his wife, was born in Londonderry, Ireland, November 11th, 1742. He was married to Rachel, second daughter of John Duncan and Rachel Todd, his wife, of Londonderry ; he settled at Little Dyke, and remained there until 1769. His eldest child was born there in 1767, and died young. It was buried on a small island near the shore. He exchanged farms with William Corbett, removed to Truro, and settled upon the Townsend Farm, so called, being the same upon which William C. Eaton, Esq., now resides. He was an active man in business and a good writer. He was Town Clerk of Truro from the year 1771, until the time of his death. He took his seat in the House of Assembly as representative of the Township of Truro on June 12th, 1775. He was again returned to represent Truro in 1777. He was very full of sport. On one occasion when a number of men were engaged dyking in the marsh, as it was the custom in those days, the men took their dram in the middle of the afternoon, and laid down to have a little rest. This time they all fell asleep ; he then took every man's spade and fastened each one of them down to the marsh by the cue of his hair pressed with their spades into the marsh.

In 1779 he started to go to the West Indies in a vessel with a cargo of boards and horses. When he was on his way down to the Bay, to go on board of the vessel, he rode up to John Smith's shop door, and said to him, " Come, Smith, let us have a parting drop," When Smith was about taking the parting drop with him, he snatched the bottle from him, and rode off, laughing, at the sport of playing a good trick on him. The bottle was filled with fish oil. While he was in the West Indies he received foul treatment from a British officer, and died there suddenly, leaving a widow and six young children to bemoan their sad bereavement. His widow was married again to Captain John McKeen, February 12th, 1783. They had one son. She died January 20th, 1814, aged 71 years. Mr. McKeen died in St. Mary's.

John Duncan, the eldest son of Samuel and Rachel Archibald, was born February 5th, 1769. He removed to Upper Stewiacke and commenced work on the farm on which the late George Hamilton afterwards lived and died. He died there a bachelor, May, 1792, aged 23 years. Elizabeth Elliott Archibald, their eldest daughter, was born in Truro, November 30th, 1770. She was married to Hugh, the eldest son of William Logan and Janet Moore, about the year 1793. They had three sons and four daughters. They settled in Upper Stewiacke. She died there.

David, the second son of Samuel and Rachel Archibald, was born in Truro, November 4th 1772. He went by the name of David the seventh, or Colonel David. He built the house in which Isaac Barnhill, Esq., now resides, at Onslow parade, in which he lived and died. He was married to Olivia, one of the twin daughters of Charles and Amelia Dickson, of Onslow, February 5th, 1801. He was an active man in business. He died November 23rd, 1814, aged forty-two years. His widow was married again to John Henderson (who was Sheriff of the District of Colchester) February 11th, 1819. They had one son. Mr. Henderson died July 8th, 1832. Mrs. Henderson died at Tatamagouche, February 7th, 1872, in the 88th year of her age.

Samuel George William, the eldest son of David and Olivia Archibald, was born in Onslow, May 31st, 1804. He was married to Maria Henderson, January, 1839. He died October 10th, 1871. George, their eldest son was born in 1840. Charles Archibald, the second son was born in 1842. He removed to Trinidad, where he was married had some family and died. Margaret Archibald, their eldest daughter, was born in 1844. Edward Archibald their third son was born in 1846. He removed to Newfoundland and died there. Rose Olivia Archibald, their second daughter, was born in 1848. David Archibald, their fourth son, was born in 1850. He died in Scotland in 1871. Maria Archibald, their third daughter, was born in 1852. Susan Amelia Archibald, their fourth daughter, was born in 1854. Rupert Archibald, their fifth son, was born in 1856.

Elizabeth, the eldest daughter of David and Olivia Archibald, was born in Onslow January 27th, 1706. She was married to Alexander McKenzie in 1827. They had five sons and three daughters. They settled at River John. She died there January 27th, 1870. Mr. McKenzie died March, 1868. Mary, the second daughter of David and Olivia Archibald, was born in Onslow January 27th, 1808. She was married to Hon. Alexander Campbell March 10th, 1825. They had four sons and four daughters. He settled in Tatamagouche, where he carried on a large business at shipbuilding and merchandise. He died suddenly April 13th, 1854, aged 59 years.

Charles Dickson Archibald, their second son, was born December 16th, 1809. He was lost at sea when he was a young man. William Henry Archibald, their third son, was born December 10th, 1811. He died April 10th, 1812. Thomas Dickson Archibald, their fourth son, was born April 8th, 1813. He was married to Susan, daughter of William Corbett and Isabell Davison. Their sons names are Edward, Thomas and Blowers. Their daughter's name was Emma. She died when twenty years old. Mrs. Archibald died and he was married again to Elizabeth Hughes. He settled in Sydney, C. B., where he carries on a large business, He was a member of the Legislative Council of Nova Scotia for a number of years. He is now a member of the Senate of Canada.

Rachel Todd, the second daughter of Samuel and Rachel Archibald, was born in Truro January 16th, 1775. She was married to Charles, the second son of Charles and Amelia Dickson, of Onslow, December 31st, 1799. They had five sons and six daughters. He was a carpenter by trade. He built the house in Onslow in which John B. Dickie, Esq , recently resided, and died there March, 1821, aged 45 years. His wife died in 1819, aged 44 years.

Samuel George William, the third son of Samuel and Rachel Archibald, was born in Truro, February 5th, 1777. He was left a poor fatherless boy when about three years old, and was taken by his grandfather and brought up until he was able to earn his own living. He went to Stewiacke and commenced improving on the same farm that his brother had been working on before his death. He continued at this work but a short time. He soon threw down the handspike that he was rolling the black logs with, and resolved to try some other way of obtaining a living. He commenced the study of law, and it was but a short time until he was admitted to the Bar. He commenced with that vigor which but few persons can bring into action. He soon became popular. In 1806 he was returned to represent the County of Halifax in the House of Assembly, and he continued to hold his seat for thirty years. He represented the County of Colchester from the year 1836 to 1841. On May 21st, 1817, he was appointed King's Counsel. On February 15th, 1825, he was unanimously chosen Speaker of the House of Assembly. He filled the office of Clerk of the Peace for a few years when he was a young man ; also, of Judge of Probate. He was appointed Solicitor General on April 11th, 1826. He was Attorney General for a number of years. In 1841 he was appointed to the office of Master of the Rolls. He was married to Elizabeth, daughter of Charles and Amelia Dickson, of Onslow, March 16th, 1802. Mrs. Archibald died in Halifax May 13th, 1830, aged 43 years. He was married again to Mrs. Joanna Brodley, August 1832. He died in Halifax January 28th, 1846, aged 69 years. His widow died in England.

Charles Dickson, the eldest son of S. G. W. and Elizabeth Archibald, was born in Truro October 31st, 1802. He was married to Bridget Walker in 1832. She was heiress of a large estate in Lancashire, England. He died in 1868. Elizabeth Archibald, their eldest daughter, was born in England in 1833. Charles William Archibald, their eldest son, was born in Truro, N. S., in 1838. They had three other daughters; their names are Juliel, Claria and Clarence.

John Duncan, second son of S. G. W. and Elizabeth Archibald was born March 27th, 1804. He was married to Annie Mitchell, of Halifax, January, 1830. He died in Truro July 27th, 1830.

Foster Hutchison Archibald, their third son, was born December 24th, 1806. He died in 1817.

George William, their fourth son, was born October 9th, 1808. He died April, 1822.

Edward Mortimer Archibald, their fifth son, was born May 10th, 1810. He was married to Catherine, daughter of Andrew Richardson, Esq., of Halifax, September 1834. He has filled the office of British Consul in New York for a number of years.

Elizabeth Archibald, their eldest daughter, was born January 19th, 1812. She died October 24th, 1831. Mary Archibald, their second daughter, was born January 1st, 1814. She was married to George Hill, of Halifax, August 29th, 1833. She died April 23rd, 1838. Rachel Dickson Archibald, their third daughter, was born April 22nd, 1815. She died in 1818.

Thomas Dickson Archibald, their sixth son, was born August 23rd, 1817. He was married to Sarah Smith, of England. They have three sons ; their names are George, Douglas, and William. Ellen, their daughter, is married to Capt. McNeill, of England. He is settled in London and practices at the Bar. In 1872 he was appointed as Baron of the Exchequer.

Samson Salter Blowers Archibald, their seventh son, was born in Halifax April 1st, 1819. He was married to Anovie, daughter of William and Isabell Corbett. They had two daughters. Mrs. Archibald died. He was married again to Margaret, daughter of Hon. Alexander and Mary Campbell, of Tatamagouche, October 10th, 1870. He is settled and carries on business at Sydney, Cape Breton.

Peter Suther Archibald, their eighth son, was born in Truro September 9th, 1820. He is a barrister, and Colonel of the Militia. He is living on the homestead. William George, their ninth son, was born in Halifax April 14th, 1822. Richard Archibald, their tenth son, was born September 9th, 1823. He died June, 1824. Jane Amelia, their fourth daughter, was born in Truro August 12th, 1826.

She died October 4th, 1838. Robert Dickson, their eleventh son, was born February 17th, 1828. He is dead.

Margaret, the third daughter of Samuel and Rachel Archibald, was born in Truro January 23rd, 1779. She died unmarried November 23rd, 1811, aged 32 years.

Robert, the second son of David Archibald, Esq., and Elizabeth Elliott, his wife, was born in Londonderry, Ireland, January 22nd, 1745. He was brought by his parents to New England about the year 1757. They removed again to Nova Scotia December 13th, 1769. He and his brother Samuel were grantees of the Township of Londonderry. They had their front land at Little Dyke. They resided there for some time, and buried two of their children on a small Island near the shore. Capt. John Morrison (grandfather of Thomas F. Morrison, M. P. P.) and William Corbet, were grantees of the Township of Truro. Morrison and Corbett exchanged farms with Samuel and Robert Archibald. Morrison and Corbet removed to Little Dyke, and the Archibalds removed to Truro. Robert Archibald, while in Truro, resided in a house which stood on the hill near the place that Capt. R. W. Miriam now resides. In his house the Town meetings were frequently held, as it was the lower house in the Upper Village. He was Town Clerk for a length of time, and on September 16th, 1780, he was appointed Justice of the Peace for what is now the whole of the counties of Colchester and Pictou. Charles Dickson, of Onslow, and Eliakim Tupper, of Truro, were in the same appointment. Mr. Archibald was Colonel of the Militia and land surveyor. He surveyed and divided a large part of Truro Township, and the whole of the Township of Onslow. 'He was Judge of the Court of Common Pleas. He removed to Musquodoboit in 1787, and settled on the farm on which his grandson, David Archibald, now resides. He travelled to Onslow to attend Court. (The Court was then held in the house of old Mr. Nichols, which then stood about forty rods below the Onslow Meeting House.) After he removed to Musquodoboit, he travelled to Halifax with his butter-tubs in a bag on the horse's back, and one article that he purchased in Halifax was a large Family Bible, and he carried it home in one of his butter-tubs in the end of the bag. The writer had the satisfaction of examining this bible on July 10th, 1871, and found it in good condition. It contained the record of his family ; also the record of his daughter Hannah's family, and was in the possession of his great-grandson, George McLeod, Esq., of Musquodoboit. He was

married to Hannah, the third daughter of William Blair and Jane
Barnes, of Onslow, April 2nd, 1767. Elizabeth, the eldest daughter
of Robert and Hannah Archibald, was born in Truro November 2nd
1768. She was married to Samuel Tupper, Esq., of Upper Stewiacke.
They had two daughters. Mrs. Tupper died in January, 1789.

Janet, the second daughter of Robert and Hannah Archibald, was
born in Truro October 29th, 1770. She was married to William, son
of John and Mary Logan. They had one son and one daughter.
Mr. Logan died, and his widow was married again to Alexander
McNutt Fisher, and had two sons and one daughter.

William Archibald, their eldest son, was born in Truro October
18th, 1772. He was drowned in Salmon River, near the head of the
tide, while engaged fishing salmon. He was about sixteen years old
at the time.

Capt. David, or David Archibald eighth, second son of Robert
and Hannah Archibald, was born in Truro April 2nd, 1775. He
removed, with his parents, to Musquodoboit, where he spent the
remainder of his days, upon the same farm on which his son David
now resides. He was married to Elizabeth Kent, of Musquodoboit,
February 25th, 1801. Alexander Kent Archibald, their eldest son,
was born in Musquodoboit, January 1st, 1802. He was married to
Janet Harvey, of Newport. They had four sons and three daughters ;
their names are David, James, Charles, Alice, Margaret, Alexander,
and Hannah. This family has removed from Musquodoboit.
Hannah, the eldest daughter of David Archibald and Elizabeth Kent,
his wife, was born May 9th, 1805. She was married to William J.
Lydiard. They have three sons and four daughters. They have all
removed to the United States. She died at Minnesota February
11th, 1873. Mary, the second daughter of David and Elizabeth
Archibald, was born January 6th, 1807. She was married to Dr.
George Harvey. They have four sons and four daughters. They
removed to Ohio, United States. Susan, their third daughter, was
born September 6th, 1809. She was married to Angus McInnis.
She died and left no family.

William, the second son of David and and Elizabeth Archibald,
was born August 26th, 1811. He was married to Diana Hutchison.
They had three sons and five daughters. They removed to Minnesota,
United States. Robert, their third son, was born June 6th, 1815.
He died a bachelor.

David, their fourth son, was born May 27th, 1818. He inherited the farm which was owned by his father and his grandfather. He was married to Margaret, daughter of Jonathan Archibald and Margaret Talbot October 31st, 1844. Frederick, their eldest son, was born September 6th, 1846. William, their second son, was born June 2nd, 1850. Samuel, their third son, was born January 23rd, 1853. David, their fourth son, was born December 14th, 1854. Margaret E., their eldest daughter, was born July 15th, 1858. Charles, their youngest son, was born November 11th, 1863. David Archibald, Esq., and his wife are both living.

Eliza M., the youngest daughter of David Archibald, eighth, and Elizabeth, his wife, was born July 1st, 1821. She was married to Hugh Dunlap, Esq., of Stewiacke, November 10th, 1847. They had one son and two daughters. Mrs. Dunlap died April 26th, 1854, aged 32 years.

Margaret Price, the third daughter of Robert and Hannah Archibald, was born in Truro September 18th, 1777. She was married to Hugh, son of John Archibald, of Musquodoboit. Their family appears among the descendants of John Archibald. Hannah, the fourth daughter of Robert and Hannah Archibald, was born in Truro February 2nd, 1780. She was married to Adams Archibald, Esq., of Musquodoboit January 22nd, 1802. Their family appears among the descendants of Matthew Archibald.

Sarah, the fifth daughter of Robert and Hannah Archibald, was born February 22nd, 1785. She was married to William, youngest son of William Logan and Janet Moor. They had three sons and six daughters, which appear among the Logans. Susan, the youngest daughter of Robert and Hannah Archibald, was born February 7th, 1787. She was married to William Guild, of Musquodoboit. Robert Archibald died in Musquodoboit October, 1812, aged 67 years. His son David died Nov. 1843, and his widow, Elizabeth, died December, 1841. Hannah Blair, the wife of Robert Archibald, died November 4th, 1834. William Guild, died January 25th, 1862, aged 77 years ; and Susan, his wife, died July 12th, 1854, aged 68.

John, the third son of David Archibald, Esq., and Elizabeth Elliott, his wife, was born in Londonderry, Ireland, August 18th, 1747. He came, with the rest of the family, to New England about the year 1757, and to Truro December 13th, 1762. He was one of the grantees of Truro Township. He lived, while in Truro, on his house lot in the Village, it being the same place on which Mr. Hiram Hyde now resides. He removed to Musquodoboit, and settled on the farm that Mr. John Tupper now resides upon, where he spent the remainder of his days. He was married to Alice Moor, sister of the late Hugh Moor, Snr., of Truro, June 2nd, 1768. David, their eldest son, was born in Truro March 19th, 1769. He was married to Letitia, daughter of John Barnhill and Letitia Deyarmond, of Chiganoise, August 9th, 1792. This David Archibald was David the fifth, or otherwise known by the name of David Barnhill. Letitia, the eldest daughter of David Archibald fifth, and Letitia Barnhill, his wife, was born June 9th, 1793. She was married to John Hollandsworth, and had two sons and six daughters. She died July 11th, 1863, aged 70 years. Alice, the second daughter of David and Letitia Archibald, was married to James Murphy in 1815. They had three sons and two daughters. She died August 9th, 1848, aged 54 years. Mr. Murphy died April 21st, 1868, aged 76 years.

John Barnhill Archibald, the eldest son of David and Letitia Archibald, was born in Musquodoboit October 1802. He was married to Mary, daughter of Thomas McCallum and Janet Logan March, 1824. Janet, the eldest daughter of John B. and Mary Archibald' was born May 18th, 1830. She was married to David Pearson October 30th, 1856. They have three sons and one daughter. David, the eldest son of John B. and Mary Archibald, was born November 24th, 1831. He removed to the United States, was married there, and has a family of children.

John Barnhill, the second son of John B. and Mary Archibald, was born June 24th, 1833. He was married to Margaret, daughter of William Irwin, of the Lower Village of Truro, October 28th, 1862. Franklin, the eldest son of John B. and Margaret Archibald, was born in Musquodoboit September 8th, 1863. Mary Eliza, their eldest daughter, was born April 24th, 1865. Henry Irwin and John, their twin sons, were born April 23rd, 1867. Sarah Irwin, their second daughter, was born April 27th, 1869. Margaret Ann, their daughter, was born April 14th, 1871.

Thomas, the third son of John B. and Mary Archibald, was born in the year 1835. He was lost at sea in the year 1856, when he was about 21 years old.

Phoebe Ann, the second daughter of John B. and Mary Archibald, was born January, 1837. She removed to the United States.

William, their fourth son, was born November 9th, 1838. He was married to Mary McFatridge February 8th, 1862. They have

one son.   John B. Archibald, Senr., died March 17th, 1844, aged 42
years, and his wife, Mary, died March 1st, 1841.

Margaret, the third daughter of David and Letitia Archibald, was
born September 1800.   She was married to David Holandsworth in
1825.   She died April 22nd, 1869, and left no family.

David, the second son of David and Letitia Archibald, was born
September 12th, 1804.   This David Archibald is known by the name
of David the sixteenth.   He was married to Christy Ann, daughter of
James Guild and Elizabeth Johnson November 1st, 1832.   Elizabeth,
their eldest daughter, was born March 24th, 1834.   She died October
6th, 1837.   Anne, their second daughter, was born December 4th,
1835.   She was married to William Kaulback December 24th,
1865, and has one son and two daughters.   Letitia, their third
daughter, was born May 10th, 1838.   She died December
6th, 1861.   Amèlia J., their fourth daughter, was born September
10th, 1840.   She was married to James McCurdy, of Clifton.
November 29th, 1858.   They have five sons and one daughter,
Mary Alice, their fifth daughter, was born April 24th, 1843.
William J., their only son, was born April 29th, 1847.   Jessie S.,
their youngest daughter, was born November 26th, 1852, and died
April 15th, 1853.

Ann, the fourth daughter of David and Letitia Archibald, was
born March 14th, 1808.   She was married to Robert Kaulback,
Postmaster of Middle Musquodoboit, November 13, 1834, and has
three sons and three daughters.   Rebecca, the fifth daughter of
David and Letitia Archibald, was born in 1810.   She was married to
Thomas Lord, of Lawrencetown.   They had one son and two
daughters.

Richard, the third son of David and Letitia Archibald, was born
in Musquodoboit June 15th, 1812.   He was married to Mary White
December 31st, 1835.   Susannah, their eldest daughter was born
October 25th, 1836.   She was married to Johnson Kaulback, March
15th, 1856, and had one daughter.   Mr. Kaulback died, and
she was married again to Whidden Pyke, September, 1865.   They
have two sons and two daughters, and have removed to the United
States.   Letitia, their second daughter, was born March 25th, 1839.
She died unmarried.   Alice, the third daughter of Richard and Mary
Archibald, was born March 11th, 1842.   She was married to
Benjamin O'Connell, May 1865.   They have three children.* David,
their only son, was born April 5th, 1846.

Hugh, the second son of John Archibald and Alice Moor, was born October 24th, 1770. He died January 7th, 1771.

Ann, the eldest daughter of John and Alice Archibald, was born in Truro March 28th, 1772. She was married to John Kennedy, of Middle Stewiacke, in the year 1795. They had five sons and two daughters. Mr. Kennedy died May 5th, 1817, and she was married again to David Dickey, of Musquodoboit (known by the name of Yankee David). She died October, 1858, aged 86 years.

Hugh, the third son of John and Alice Archibald, was born in Truro December 1st, 1773. He removed, with the rest of his father's family, to Musquodoboit, about the year 1790, and spent the remainder of his days there. He was married to Margaret Price, daughter of Robert Archibald and Hannah Blair, his wife, in the year 1797.

David the eldest son of Hugh and Margaret Price Archibald, was born March 17th, 1798. He was married to Mary Belyea, of New Brunswick. John, their eldest son, is married and has three children, William, the second son of David and Mary Archibald, was born May 3rd, 1836. He removed to the United States, and is married there and has one daughter. Margaret, the eldest daughter of David and Mary Archibald, was born in 1830. She is married to James Glencross, and has one son and three daughters. Martha Ann, their second daughter, was born in 1832. She was married to Robert Flake in 1852, and has two sons and five daughters. Hannah, their third daughter was born in 1834, was married to Thomas Cole in 1854, and has four sons and two daughters. Eliza, their fourth daughter, was born in the year 1838. Jane, their fifth daughter, was born in 1840. She was married to William Dickey in 1866, and has one son.

Janet, the eldest daughter of Hugh and Margaret Price Archibald, was born February 4th, 1800. She was married to Frederick Hurley in April 1830. They have four daughters. She is living with one of her daughters on the same farm on which her father and mother lived and died. Mr. Hurley died May 21st, 1849, aged 47 years. Alice, the second daughter of Hugh and Margaret Price Archibald, was born February 1802. She was married to John Hurley in 1822, and had four sons and one daughter. She died July 14th, 1855, aged 53 years. Hannah, their third daughter, was born in Musquodoboit in the year 1804. Adams, the second son of Hugh and Margaret Price

Archibald, was born in the year 1806. He died when about 25 years old.

William, their third son, was born in the year 1808. He was married to Christy McDougal in 1831. Miles, their eldest son was born in 1832. He removed to the United States. Catherine, the eldest daughter of William and Christy Archibald, was born in 1836. She was married to Mr. —— Woodworth, and has three sons and one daughter. Ann, the second daughter of William and Christy Archibald, was born in 1838. She was married to Benjamin Green in the year 1865, and has three sons. George, the second son of William and Christy Archibald, was born in 1840. He removed to New Brunswick, and married there in 1869, and has one son. Eliza, the third daughter of William and Christy Archibald, was born in 1843. She was recently married to Mr. —— Wetherby.

Eliza, the fourth daughter of Hugh and Margaret Price Archibald, was born in 1811. She was married to Samuel Taylor in 1838, and has four sons and one daughter. Margaret, the fifth daughter of Hugh and Margaret Price Archibald, was born in 1813. She was married to Michael Maher, and has four sons and two daughters.

James Archibald 4th, the youngest son of John Archibald, Senr., and Alice Moor, was born in Truro, Nov. 20th, 1775. He was married to Mary, daughter of David Fisher and Martha Dickey of Middle Stewiacke, January 7th, 1802.

David, their eldest son, was born June 17th, 1803. He was married to Sarah Brinton of Middle Stewiacke, June, 1823. Mary, the eldest daughter of David and Susan Archibald, was born October, 1824. She was married to Matthew Burris in 1858. Mr. Burris died, and she was married again to William Moor.

Alice, the second daughter of David and Susan Archibald, was born in 1826. She was married to James Smith in 1852, and they removed to the United States. Ann, their third daughter, was born in 1827. She was married to James Wisenor in 1850. They had six sons and seven daughters. Eliza, their fourth daughter was born in 1828. She removed to the United States, and is married there. Robert Dickey, the eldest son of David and Susan Archibald, was born in 1829. He removed to the United States, and is married there. Rebecca, their fifth daughter, was born in 1831. She removed to the United States, and is married there. Sarah, their sixth daughter, was born in 1833. She removed to the United States, and is married there. Hannah, their seventh daughter, was born in 1835. She removed to the United States, and is married there.

James William, the second son of David and Susan Archibald, was born in 1839. He was married to Margaret Ryan in June, 1869, and has removed to the United States. Esther, their eighth daughter, was born in 1837. She is deaf and dumb. Jane, their ninth daughter, was born in 1845. She removed to the United States, and was married there. Margaret, their tenth daughter, was born in 1850. She was married to Samuel Burris in February, 1866. David Archibald died at Shubenacadie.

John, the second son of James Archibald, 4th, and Mary, was born September 14th, 1806. He was married to Amelia, daughter of William Conley, June 8th, 1830. William Conley, their eldest son, was born March 10th, 1831. He was married to Jane Williamson of New Brunswick, September 21st, 1856. Curlenda, their eldest daughter, was born September 21st, 1857. Clara, their second daughter, was born March 27th, 1859. Alexander, the eldest son of William C. and Jane Archibald, was born February 21st, 1861. Ida, their third daughter, was born December 4th, 1862. Isaiah, their second son, was born October 2nd, 1864. Matilda, their fourth daughter, was born September 11th, 1866. Lymon, their third son, was born July 3rd, 1868. Agnes, their fifth daughter, was born March 16th, 1870.

Hugh, the second son of John and Amelia Archibald, was born at Pleasant Valley, February 3rd, 1833. He was married to Margaret, daughter of Robert Fisher, of Shubenacadie, July, 1855. Alexander, their eldest son, was born August 14th, 1857. Susan Amelia, their eldest daughter, was born April 13th, 1859. Leander, their second son, was born April 14th, 1861. William, their third son, was born February 27th, 1864. Matthew, their fourth son, was born May 24th, 1867.

Susan, the eldest daughter of John and Amelia Archibald, was born at Pleasant Valley, December 20th, 1836. She was married to William, son of John Green of Shubenacadie, Sept. 15th, 1859. They have three sons and two daughters.

Mary, the second daughter of John and Amelia Archibald, was born April 13th, 1839. She was married to Isaac Brinton, December, —, 1866.

Alice, their third daughter was born October 14th, 1844. She was married to William Wright, June 15th, 1869. They have one son.

John, their third son, was born January 3rd, 1846. He died September 23rd, 1870. Lucy, their fourth daughter, was born January 2nd, 1849. Daniel, their fourth son, was born January 11th, 1854.

Alice, the eldest daughter of James Archibald, 4th, and Mary, was born June 15th, 1808. She was married to David Green of Shubenacadie, February 7th, 1828. They had four sons and five daughters. She died September 17th, 1868, and Mr. Green was drowned in the Shubenacadie River, Nov. 25th, 1847.

Robert Dickey, the third son of James and Mary Archibald, was born December 2nd, 1809. He was married to Ann Neal in 1836. He died in 1838.

James, the fourth son of James and Mary Archibald, was born July 14th, 1814. He was married to Sarah Maynord, July, 1838. Daniel, the eldest son of James and Sarah Archibald, was born January 15th, 1841. He was marrried to Margaret McCollam, February 4th, 1870. Ruth, the eldest daughter of James and Sarah Archibald, was born June, 1842. She removed to the United States, and is married there. Amos, their second son, was born November, 1843. James, their third son, was born September 15th, 1845. The above named James, son of James Archibald, 4th, died October 6th, 1845.

Daniel, the fifth son of James and Mary Archibald, was born July 20th, 1816. He was married to Jane Tatten of New Brunswick, January, 1840. Mary, their eldest daughter, was born in 1842. She was married to Robert Guthrie of New Brunswick, in 1859. They have one son and four daughters. Alice, the second daughter of Daniel and Jane Archibald, was born in 1844. She was married to John Brown of Pleasant Valley, December 22nd, 1866, and has one son. Amelia, their third daughter, was born in 1846. She was married to Samuel Kennedy in November, 1863. They have two sons and one daughter. William James, the eldest son of Daniel and Jane Archibald, was born August 17th, 1849. George, their second son, was born in 1851. John, their third son, was born in June, 1853. Edward, their fourth son, was born in February, 1856. Clara, their youngest daughter, was born June 17th, 1859. Daniel Archibald, when he was a young man, removed to New Brunswick, where he was married, and all his children were born. He removed again, with his family, to Nova Scotia, and settled in Pleasant Valley in the year 1860. He died June 26th, 1868. His wife died October 15th, 1867.

Kennedy, a twin son of James and Mary Archibald, was born September 3rd, 1818. He was married to Mary, daughter of Simeon Whidden and Susannah Harris, December 22nd, 1840. Johnson, their eldest son, was born May 15th, 1841. He was married to Matilda Williamson of New Brunswick, November 17th, 1863. George, their eldest son, was born February 19th, 1866. Jessie, their eldest daughter, was born May 10th, 1868. George, the second son of Kennedy and Mary Archibald, was born July 20th, 1846. David, the third son of Kennedy and Mary Archibald, was born May 2nd, 1848. He was married to Mary Williamson of New Brunswick, August 1st, 1868. Lesley, their daughter, was born April 25th, 1869. Adams G., the fourth son of Kennedy and Mary Archibald, was born January 3rd, 1851. Janet, their eldest daughter, was born November 22nd, 1852. Ermina and Elmira, their twin daughters, were born November 1st, 1854. Eleazer, their fifth son, was born September 20th, 1856. John, their sixth son, was born October 28th, 1858. Peter Suther, their seventh son, was born November 1st, 1860.

Johnson, the other twin son of James and Mary Archibald, 4th, was born September 3rd, 1818. He was married to Abigail, daughter of the late Simeon Whidden, junr., and Susannah Harris, October 9th, 1845. Kennedy, the eldest son of Johnson and Abigail Archibald, was born October 30th, 1846. Mary Susan, their eldest daughter, was born August 17th, 1848. She was married to Daniel Millon, February 8th, 1870. Eleanor, their second daughter, was born October 27th, 1854. Sarah, their third daughter, was born September 17th, 1856. Jane, their fourth daughter was born June 28th, 1858. Edmon, their second son, was born June 17th, 1861. Alonzo, their third son, was born July 7th, 1864. James Archibald, 4th, after he was married, settled in Middle Stewiacke, and had a Grist Mill on the same brook on which the Mills now stand, and remained there until the year 1823, when he removed into the woods in Pleasant Valley, and commenced clearing a farm; being the same on which his two sons Kennedy and Johnson now reside. He spent the remainder of his days there, and died July 4th, 1834, aged 59 years. His wife died March 12th, 1854, aged 75 years.

Elizabeth, the second daughter of John and Alice Archibald, was born in Truro, November 24th, 1777. She was married to Johnson Kaulback of Musquodoboit. They had six sons and one daughter.

Mary, the third daughter of John and Alice Archibald, was born in Truro, December 10th, 1781. She was married to David McCollum,

Genealogical Record. 49

junr., of North River, Onslow, in 1803. They had six sons and six daughters. She died March, 1866. Mr. McCollum died January, 1858.

Alice, the fourth daughter of John and Alice Archibald, was born in Musquodoboit. She was married to Thomas Burgess. They had one daughter.

Margaret, the fifth daughter of John and Alice Archibald, was born in Musquodoboit. She was married to John Nelson. They had five sons and three daughters.

John and Alice Archibald had another daughter; her name cannot now be ascertained. The father, mother, and child were crossing the Musquodoboit river on horseback when an ice cake floating down the river struck the horse's hind legs and nearly threw him down. The mother, in the struggle, let the child fall and it was drowned.

Margaret, the eldest daughter of David Archibald, Esq., and Elizabeth Elliot his wife, was born in Londonderry, Ireland, December 15th, 1749. She came with the rest of the family when she was 8 years old to New England, and from thence to Nova Scotia, when she was about 13 years old. She was married to John Savage. She was his second wife; his first wife, Jane, died April 3rd, 1767, aged 24 years. To her memory a stone is standing in the Truro Cemetery, with the oldest date on it of all the stones now standing there. John Savage was one of the grantees of Truro Township, and was an active member of society. He was a land surveyor, and at one time he agreed with the proprietors of the Township to subdivide their back lands into one hundred acre lots; for this work he was to have twelve thousand acres off the south-west corner of the Township, extending down the Shubenacadie River four miles, and as far east as it would require to make up the complement. This work was never done by him, as he died shortly after. He was one of the seven elders of the Presbyterian Church who were chosen in the summer of the year 1770. He had one son by his second wife, Margaret Archibald, they called him David. Mr. and Mrs. Savage both died when their son David was quite young, and he was taken by his grandfather, David Archibald, Esq., and brought up with his other grandson, S. G. W. Archibald. This David Savage was married to Elizabeth Brydon, and they kept an Inn near the place where Mr. Tremain now resides. In the year 1800 they removed to the United States.

Ann, the second daughter of David and Elizabeth Archibald, was born in Londonderry, Ireland, March 12th, 1752. She came to Nova

4

Scotia when about 10 years old. She was married to William, the eldest son of John McKeen, Esq., and Martha his wife, October 3rd, 1771. They had five sons and four daughters. They appear among the McKeen's.

James, the fourth son of David Archibald, Esq., and Elizabeth Elliott his wife, was born in Londonderry, Ireland, April 19th, 1754. He was brought by his parents to New England, and thence to Nova Scotia. In the year 1780, after the sudden death of his brother Samuel, which took place on one of the West India Islands, he left home to go there to look after the vessel and cargo, which belonged to his late brother. He never returned. A few years ago there was a sea Captain by the name of Archibald, sailed into a port at one of the West India Islands. He found that the Custom House officer's name was Archibald also. This led to a conversation; he stated to the Captain that his grandfather was a white man from Britain, and that he settled and married on the Island, a long time ago. As was stated by the Captain to the writer, he was a portly good looking man, resembling some of the Archibalds in Nova Scotia. His complexion was a little dark, but he was a smart man for business.

Thomas, the fifth son of David and Elizabeth Archibald, was born in Ireland, May 17th, 1756. He was brought by his parents to New England when about one year old, and to Nova Scotia when he was about 6 years old. His name is among the grantees of the Township of Truro, although he was not quite ten years old at the date of the grant. He remained in Truro until he was about 21 years old. He then returned to New Hampshire. In 1783 he was among the graduates at Dartmouth College, being then 27 years old. On November 11th, 1789, he was ordained over a Church of Congregationalists in Acworth; this church contained but fifty-eight members at the time. He was dismissed from this congregation June 14th, 1794.

David, the sixth and youngest son of David and Elizabeth Archibald, was born in Londonderry, New Hampshire, September 27th, 1758. He was known by the name of clerk David, or David the 3rd. He inherited a large part of his father's farm on Bible Hill. He built the house in which Mr. George W. Hamlon now resides, south of the bridge. He built another house near the place that Mr. John Davison now resides. He sold this house, with a large part of his farm, to Mr. Robert Barry, about the year 1812. He built another house on the top of the hill, on the place that the Court House stood a few years ; north of the Metzler house. He carried on a considerable business at shipbuilding, which was not very profitable. He was married to Sarah, the eldest daughter of Matthew and Janet Archibald, January 29th, 1788. They had one son and three daughters. Mrs. Archibald died in the year 1797. He was married again to Hannah, the fourth daughter of Colonel Jonathan and Elizabeth Blanchard in the year 1799. He obtained a large tract of land on the St. Mary's River, on which now stands a large part of the Village of Sherbrooke. He removed to this place in July, 1815. He carried on there a considerable business at milling, lumbering and farming. He died there in the year 1823, aged 65 years. His widow died there about the year 1830, aged 56 years.

William Thomson Archibald, their only son, was born in Truro, Dec. 12th, 1788. He built a house near the place that Mr. William McLeod now resides, on the north side of Salmon river. On the night of November 12th, 1813, there was a great hurricane, which blew down this house, and a great many others about Truro and elsewhere. Shortly after this, he removed to St. Mary's, and was married there to Janet McDonald, Dec. 20th, 1814. Sarah, the eldest daughter of Wm. T. and Janet Archibald, was born Nov. 23rd, 1815. She was married to David, the eldest son of Isaac and Janet Archibald, of the Middle River of Pictou, Sept. 16th, 1840. They had four sons. She died May 3rd, 1847, aged 32 years. Martha, the second daughter of Wm. T. and Janet Archibald, was born June 22nd, 1817. She was married to Wm. McKeen Dec. 2nd, 1840. They had three sons and four daughters. She died July 19th, 1861, aged 44 years. Nancy, the third daughter of Wm. T. and Janet Archibald, was born May 26th, 1819. She was married to Thomas McKeen, of Cape Breton, in October, 1858. They had one son and one daughter. Mr. McKeen died March 9th, 1867. Margaret, the fourth daughter of Wm. T. and Janet Archibald, was born June 10th, 1821. She was married to William Crocket, of Middle River Pictou. They have one son and three daughters. Elizabeth, the fifth daughter of Wm. T. and Janet Archibald, was born May 20th 1823. She was married to Alex., the second son of Isaac and Janet Archibald, Sept. 19th, 1843. They had five sons and three daughters. Mrs. Archibald died May 21st, 1868. Mary, the sixth daughter of W. T. and Janet Archibald, was born July 14th, 1827. She was married to Donald Kennedy, of Sherbrooke, Dec. 27th, 1846. They have four sons and four daughters. Eleanor, their seventh daughter, was born March 14th, 1829.

She was married to Peter Crookshanks, in Nov., 1851. They had four sons and one daughter. Rebecca, their eighth daughter, was born Feb. 10th, 1831. She was married to Hugh Chisholm Dec. 20th, 1854. They had one son and one daughter. Janet, the ninth daughter of Wm. T. and Janet Archibald, was born Sept. 11th, 1833. She was marrid to Adam Dickman in Sept., 1854. They had three sons and three daughters. Hannah, their tenth daughter, was born Dec. 18th, 1834. David, the eldest son of Wm. T. and Janet Archibald, was born March 1st, 1836. He was married to Anne Coaley in Sept., 1864. Sarah Elizabeth, their eldest daughter, was born Oct. 9th, 1868. Margaret, their daughter, was born July 9th, 1871. James, the youngest son of Wm. T. and Janet Archibald, was born April 26th, 1839. He was married to Sarah Tate December 20th, 1863. Herbert, their eldest son, was born March 30th, 1865. Ada was born Nov. 2nd, 1866. William Thomson Archibald died January 9th, 1841, aged 52 years.

Elizabeth Elliot, eldest daughter of David and Sarah Archibald, was born in Truro, Nov. 8th, 1790. She was married to Hugh Mc-Donald, Esq., of St. Mary's, February 29th, 1816. They had four sons and three daughters. She died Nov. 20th, 1835. Janet, the second daughter of David and Sarah Archibald, was born in Truro August 21st, 1792. She was married to Isaac Archibald Dec. 1st, 1808. Nancy, the third daughter of David and Sarah Archibald, was born in Truro, in the year 1794. She was married to David A. Archibald, Oct. 31st, 1811. Sarah, the wife of David Archibald, 3rd, died in year 1797. He was married again to Hannah, daughter of Colonel Jotham and Elizabeth Blanchard, in the year 1799.

Sarah, the eldest daughter of David Archibald, 3rd, and Hannah Blanchard, was born in Truro, August, 1800. She was married to the Rev. Daniel McCurdy, June 3rd, 1832. They had two sons and two daughters. She died March 19th, 1870. Their sons and one daughter died some time ago. Mr. McCurdy died at Halifax, Jan'y, 1873. They are all buried at Wallace, Cumberland County. Rebecca S., the second daughter of David and Hannah Archibald, was born in Truro, March 3rd, 1802. She was married to John McDonald, of Stellary's, Dec., 1822. They had two sons and five daughters. She died Nov., 1840.

Edward, the eldest son of David, 3rd, and Hannah Archibald, was born in Truro, in the year 1804. When he was about seven or eight years old, attending Mrs. Janet Faulkner's school on the south side of

Salmon River, in returning home, as he was crossing the bridge, he dropped his book into the river. In his attempt to recover his book, he was drowned.

John Waddell, the second son of David, 3rd, and Hannah Archibald, was born in Truro, Dec. 20th, 1806. He was married to Anne Hughes, January 16th, 1841. Annette, their eldest daughter, was born November 8th, 1841. She died in the year 1842. Edward, their eldest son, was born May 16th, 1843. He died of croop, Feb'y 25th, 1845. Jane Walker, their second daughter, was born April 30th, 1815. She is married to James Parker Layton, of Wallace River, and has two daughters. Mr. J. P. Layton died in Sept., 1872. David William Archibald, their second son, was born August 20th, 1847. Josephine Rebecca, their third daughter, was born April 23rd, 1850. John Standley, their third son, was born Dec. 20th, 1852. He died May 14th, 1853. Charles Symonds Archibald, their youngest son, was born Dec. 23rd, 1855.

Jotham, the third son of David, 3rd, and Hannah Archibald, was born in Truro, December 28th, 1808. He removed with his parents to Sherbrooke, in July, 1815, where he now resides. He was married to Elizabeth McDaniel, Nov. 10th, 1838. Catherine, their eldest daughter, was born in 1839, and died in 1865. Mary Jane, the second daughter of Jotham and Elizabeth Archibald, was born July 13th, 1843. Henry McDaniel, their second son, was born September 6th, 1844. He is Married to Miss Elizabeth Bollong. David Campbell, the second son of Jotham and Elizabeth Archibald, was born January 1st, 1848. Freeman, their third son, was born July 4th, 1850. William, their fourth son, was born Nov. 10th, 1855.

Mary, the third daughter of David Archibald, 3rd, and Hannah Blanchard, was born in Truro, May 28th, 1812. She was married to David McCurdy, of Onslow, February 20th, 1832. They had four sons and two daughters.

Jane, the fourth daughter of David and Hannah Archibald, was born August 31st, 1816. She was married to Edward Patten, of New Brunswick, in the year 1838. They had one daughter. Mr. Patten died suddenly in California ; and she returned to Boston, and was married there to Mr. Foster. Mr. Foster died, and she is living a widow in Boston. Harriet, the youngest daughter of David and Hannah Archibald, was born in Sherbrooke, October 10th. 1819. She is now Matron in the Insane Asylum of Carleton, N. B.

Samuel Archibald, Senr., the second of the four brothers who removed from Londonderry, Ireland, to New England, about the year 1757, and thence to Nova Scotia, and arrived in Truro December 13th, 1762. He was born in the year 1719. He was married to Eleanor Taylor about the year 1743, fourteen years before they left Ireland. (She was born in the year 1724). They had six sons and four daughters before they came to Truro, and two daughters born in Truro. He was one of the grantees of Truro Township. He built his house on his house lot, being near the same place where his grand-son, David W. Archibald, now resides, where he spent the remainder of his days. He was one of the first elders of the Presbyterian congregation. He died July 15th, 1774, aged 55 years. This was the first breach made by death in the church session. His wife, Eleanor Taylor, died May 1st, 1781, aged 57 years.

Matthew, the eldest son of Samuel and Eleanor Archibald, was born in Londonderry, Ireland, in the year 1745, and came to Nova Scotia in the year 1762. He returned to New England, and was married there to Janet Fisher, in the year 1767. He returned with his wife to Truro, and settled and built his house on the north bank of the Salmon River, where he spent the remainder of his days. This house is standing yet, and is owned by the Rev. Dr. McCulloch. He carried on farming and tanning, at the same place where the tanyard now stands. He was part-owner of and attended the mills that stood on the south side of the river and east end of the village. He was eminently pious; and, from his careful use of the Bible, the hill took its name as " Bible Hill." He represented Truro in Parliament fourteen years, from the year 1785 to 1799; and he held the offices of Justice of the Peace and Coroner of the District of Colchester for a number of years before his death. He died January 18th, 1820, aged 75 years, and his wife died March 5th, 1843, aged 93 years.

The following is taken from the Halifax *Guardian* of March, 1843:—" Died at Truro, on Saturday, March 5th, 1843, Janet, widow of the late Matthew Archibald, Esq., aged 93 years. She was married when 17 years old ; and, shortly after, came to this Province, where she has left a large body of descendants. She had twelve children, one hundred grand children, two hundred and fifty great grand children, and twenty-three great great grand children—in all, three hundred and eighty-five. Of these, three hundred and twenty-three survive her. Mrs. Archibald exhibited, in her life and example, unobtrusive, but consistent piety. Her religion was her delight in her days of health, and in sorrow and sickness her consolation and support." I may here mention that she was one of the females who assisted raising the Truro meeting house-frame, in the spring of the year 1768.

Sarah, the eldest daughter of Matthew and Janet Archibald, was born in Truro, May 3rd, 1769. She was married to David Archibald, 3rd, January 29th, 1788. She had one son and three daughters, whose names appear in another place. She died in the year 1797, aged 28 years. Agnes, the second daughter of Matthew and Janet, Archibald, was born Nov. 26th, 1770. She was married to James McCurdy, of Onslow, Dec. 25th, 1788. They had seven sons and seven daughters. This was a remarkable family, as there was not a death in it until all the family were married and had families. Two of the sons were ministers of the Gospel, and the other five were all elected Elders of the Presbyterian Church. She died May 2nd, 1851, aged 81 years, and her husband died June 6th, 1854, aged 88 years.

Samuel Fisher, the eldest son of Matthew and Janet Archibald, was born in Truro October 3rd, 1772. He was married to Olivia Scott October, 1797. (She was daughter of Joseph Scott, who was Sheriff of the District of Colchester for a considerable length of time.) Mr. Archibald, shortly after he was married, removed to Musquodoboit, where he settled and spent the remainder of his days. He died May 14th, 1860, aged 87 years. The following is taken from the *Morning Chronicle*: " Died at Musquodoboit on the 14th day of May, 1860, Samuel Fisher Archibald, aged 87 years. Few men have passed through life more creditably than Mr. Archibald. He was distinguished for sound judgment and good sense ; he seldom said a foolish word or did a foolish action. His religion was not confined to the merit of dealing fairly with men, but he walked with God, and like old Simeon, was just and devout. For integrity and truth, he stood at the head of his class, and he was ready to engage in every good work. His house was the temple of hospitality. His usefulness was continued until late in life. His last days were soothed by the prayers of kind friends, and with the presence of his Maker. We hope he has joined that great congregation into which all the people of God will in due time be gathered." Sarah, the eldest daughter of Samuel F. and Olivia Archibald, was born October 24th, 1798. She died unmarried in October 1842, aged 44 years.

William, the eldest son of Samuel F. and Olivia Archibald, was born October 31st, 1800. He was married to Mary, daughter of Thomas Ellis and Elizabeth Deyarmond, his wife, July 25th, 1821.

Samuel, the eldest son of William and Mary Archibald, was born in Musquodoboit May 15th, 1822. He was married to Margaret Parker, March 1843, James, the eldest son of Samuel and Margaret Archibald, was born December, 1844. He died in 1867, aged 23 years. William, their second son, was born in the year 1846. He died 1852. William, their third son, was born October 5th, 1852. Joseph, their fourth son, was born December 15th, 1854. Caroline, their daughter, was born January 1857. Mrs. Archibald died June 24th, 1858. He was married again to Susan Parker in April, 1860. Margaret, their eldest daughter, was born 1861. Mary, their second daughter. was born 1863. Thomas, their son, was born 1865.

Thomas Ellis, the second son of William and Mary Archibald, was born June 22nd, 1824. He was married to Sarah, daughter of George and Eleanor Hamilton, January 18th, 1849. Elizabeth Archibald, their eldest daughter, was born March 28th, 1850. William Archibald, their eldest son, was born in 1851. Emma, their second daughter, was born in 1853. Mary, their third daughter, was born in 1855. She died young. George, their second son, was born 1857. Edward, their third son, was born in 1861. Minnie, their fourth daughter, was born 1864. This family removed lately to the United States.

Olive, the eldest daughter of William and Mary Archibald, was born October 14th, 1826. Elizabeth, their second daughter, was born April 9th, 1831. She died June 20th, 1851. Matthew, the third son, was born January 1st, 1829. He was married to Mary Sophia Bates January 17th, 1851. Sidney S. M. Archibald, their eldest son, was born July 1st, 1852. Mary Aubery, their eldest daughter, was born February 14th, 1854. Elizabeth, their second daughter, was born July 12th, 1856. Sarah, the third daughter of William and Mary Archibald, was born October 31st, 1833. She died December, 1837. George, the fourth son, was born August 16th, 1835. He was married to Lavinia, daughter of Daniel McKeen, September 8th, 1857. David McKeen, their eldest son, was born January 9th, 1858. Hedley Vicars, their second son, was born April 1861. Lambert Lewis, their third son, was born October, 1863. James Parker, their fourth son, was born September, 1867. Almira was born June, 1870.

John, the fifth son of William and Mary Archibald, was born September 1st, 1838. He was married to Isabel Moir, May 26th, 1865. Ralph Erskine, their sixth son, was born August 5th, 1840.

He was married to Elizabeth Hutchinson, August 3rd, 1863. Sophia Bates Archibald, their daughter, was born February, 1867. William H. Archibald, their eldest son, was born May, 1864. John H., their second son, was born March, 1869.

Isaac N., the seventh son of William and Mary Archibald, was born November 3rd, 1842. He 'was married to Anne McAuly, February 8th, 1868. James Parker, their eldest son, was born May, 1870. He died young. Lambert Edmund, their second son, was born 1871. Charles Blackie, the eighth son of Willian and Mary Archibald, was born August 24th, 1844. Mary Gladwin, his wife, was born January, 1852. They were married August 10th, 1871. James Bayne, the ninth son of William and Mary Archibald, was born July 3rd, 1847. He was married to Adela Alma Philips, of Illinois. Charles, their third son, was born in 1871. He died in 1872.

Matthew, the second son of Samuel F. and Olive Archibald, was born August 3rd, 1804. He was married to Jane Grant, May 3rd, 1838. Rev. Samuel Archibald, their eldest son, was born in Musquodoboit February 23rd, 1839. He was settled in Shelburne as Minister of the Presbyterian congregation there. Donald, the second son of Matthew and Jane Archibald, was born August 16th, 1840. He was married to Grizell McLaughland, of Middle Stewiacke, February 9th, 1865. He was elected May 16th, 1871, to represent the County of Halifax in the Local Parliament of Nova Scotia. George Parker, their son, was born December 8th, 1866. Samuel Melville, was born July, 1868. Rupert Foster, born January, 1870. Lewis Gordon, March, 1872. George Parker, the third son of Matthew and Jane Archibald, was born August 7th, 1842. He died January 14th, 1857. William, the fourth son of Matthew and Jane Archibald, was born in Musquodoboit May 9th, 1844. Alexander R., their fifth son, was born July 27th, 1846. Mary Jane, their daughter, was born September 20th, 1848. Sarah, their second daughter, was born March 11th, 1851. Janet, their third daughter, was born May 9th, 1853. Peter McGregor, their sixth son, was born March 12th, 1855. Janet, the second daughter of Samuel F. and Olive Archibald, was born September 16th, 1802. She was married to George Parker January 18th, 1831. Mary, the youngest daughter of Samuel and Olive Archibald, was born in Musquodoboit, June 24th, 1815. She was married to Matthew Burris, Esq., March, 1835. They had four sons and five daughters.

Matthew Taylor Archibald, the second son of Matthew and Janet, was born in Truro, November 17th, 1774. He was married to Jane Guild, of Musquodoboit, September 15th, 1801. Janet, their eldest daughter, was born May 21st, 1803. She was married to Alexander McCurdy in the year 1819, and had six sons and three daughters. William Guild Archibald, the eldest son of Matthew T. and Jane Archibald, was born in Musquodoboit, May 21st, 1805. He was married to Nancy, daughter of Ebenezer Archibald and Rebecca Christie, March 17th, 1830. Mary Ann, the eldest daughter of William G. and Nancy Archibald, was born in Musquodoboit October, 1836. She was married to Robert Read, October, 1856. They have three sons and two daughters. Ellen Jane, the second daughter of William G. and Nancy Archibald, was born January 1838. She was married to William H. Cumminger in the year 1857. Edward, the eldest son of William G. and Nancy Archibald, was born October, 1840. He was licensed to preach the Gospel, but is now teaching in Canada. John, their second son, was born September 15th, 1843. He is now a barrister in Montreal. Isaac, their youngest son, was born June 8th, 1846. He was married to Mary, only daughter of John McCurdy and Mary A. Tupper, Oct. 12th, 1871. Matthew T. Archibald's wife, Jane, died November 5th, 1808, and he was married again to Margaret Braydon July 5th, 1810. Their daughter, Jane Guild was born June 5th. 1811. She was married to William Guild, and had five sons and five daughters. Margaret, Matthew T. Archibald's second wife, died in the year 1815. He was married again to Mary Lord, July 29th, 1816. Matthew James, their eldest son, was born January 21st, 1819. He was married to Elizabeth Jane Braydon, December 6th, 1842. Matthew Taylor, the eldest son of Matthew James and Elizabeth Jane Archibald, was born in Musquodoboit October 13th, 1843. Emma Jane, their eldest daughter was born July 4th, 1845. She was married to Samuel Irvin, December 10th, 1868. Mary Lord, the second daughter of Matthew James and Elizabeth Jane Archibald, was born October 8th, 1847. William H., their second son, was born July 6th, 1850. Elizabeth Jane, their third daughter, was born May 29th, 1852. Hannah P., their fourth daughter, was born October 12th, 1854. Isaac Adams, the third son of Matthew James and Elizabeth Jane Archibald, was born July 6th, 1857. Sarah M., the youngest daughter of Matthew T. and Mary Archibald, was born January 24th, 1821. She was married to William Scott Hutchison, in November 1841. They had three sons and three daughters. Isaac Adams, the youngest son of Matthew T. and Mary Archibald, was born April 1st, 1823. He was married to Eliza McKenzie in October 1846. They removed shortly after they were married to the south sea Islands in company with Dr. John Geddie. They had seven children, and Mrs. Archibald died in Australia in September, 1867. Matthew Taylor Archibald died in Musquodoboit in November, 1839, aged 65 years, and his third wife died May 28th, 1863.

Adams, the third son of Matthew and Janet Archibald, was born in Truro April 18th, 1777. He was married to Hannah, the fourth daughter of Robert Archibald, Esq., and Hannah Blair, January 22nd, 1802. Eliza, their eldest daughter, was born May 1st, 1803. She was married to Angus McLeod February 14th, 1822. They had two sons and two daughters. Mrs. McLeod died July 24th, 1827, aged 23 years. Janet, the second daughter of Adams and Hannah Archibald, was born Nov. 14th, 1804. She was married to John, the fourth son of Samuel Tupper, Esq., and Rachael Dunlap, of Upper Stewiacke, March 2nd, 1830. They had three sons and one daughter. She died February 8th, 1843, aged 38 years, and her husband died July 26th, 1844, aged 40 years. Adams Archibald, Esq., died April 24th, 1857, aged 80 years, and his wife Hannah died June 10th, 1854, aged 75 years.

The following is taken from the *Morning Chronicle* of May 9th, 1857 :—" We have this day to record the death of Adams Archibald, Esq., of Musquodoboit. He was a man who taking him all in all, we may not see his like again for a long time to come. Few men were better known, or more generally respected in this Province, particularly in the Counties of Halifax and Colchester, and few men leave a greater blank in their community, than the subject of our notice. For more than fifty years Mr. Archibald occupied a prominent place in society ; during the greater part of this time he was in the commission of the Peace, and even as his eldest brother was known by the name of Deacon, so was he universally known as Squire Adams, and he was nearly as long connected with the Session of the Presbyterian congregation of Musquodoboit. He was a member of the Board of Commissioners of Schools for the eastern district of Halifax County ever since that body was organized. It will be generally admitted that the duties of these various and important offices were discharged with promptitude and effect, which had their origin in the uncommon force of character for which he was distinguished. In private life, and in ordinary business, the same peculiarity was manifested. When alive, he abhorred pretence or vain boasting, and it would be unseemly to insult his memory with any eulogy of his goodness however just. His brethern and friends know well that he démonstrated his faith by his works, and that he was behind none of them in those marks and proofs of genuine religïon, which only the grace of God can account for. He diéd old and full of days, having entered his 81st year, and good men carried him to his last resting place."

Ebenezer, the fourth son of Matthew and Janet Archibald, was born in Truro, April 13th, 1779. He was married to Rebecca, daughter of John Christie and Nancy Denny, his wife, April 12th, 1804. Nancy, their eldest daughter, whs born in Truro January 20th, 1805. She was married to William Guild Archibald, of Musquodoboit, March 17th, 1830. Their families appear among the descendants of Matthew T. Archibald.

Matthew, the eldest son of Ebenezer and Rebecca Archibald, was born January 29th, 1807. He was married to Margaret, daughter of James and Mary Johnson, of Pembroke, Upper Stewiacke, March 2nd, 1841. James William, their eldest son was born 1842. He died March 10th, 1862. Mary, their only daughter was born October 1st, 1844. Andrew Christie, their youngest son was born 1847. Mrs. Archibald died at Harmony, May 6th, 1851, aged 33 years. Mr. Archibald was married again to Nancy McKim, of Londonderry, May 5th, 1853. He died at Harmony October 15th, 1865, in the 59th year of his age.

Anne Waddell, the second daughter of Ebenezer and Rebecca Archibald, was born in Truro, March 8th, 1809. She was married to Samuel James, eldest son of John B. and Catherine Archibald, January 21st, 1836. Their family appears among the family of John B. Archibald.

John Christie, the second son of Ebenezer and Rebecca Archibald, was born in Truro, January 16th, 1812. He was married to Jane, daughter of William O'Brien, Esq., of Noel, October 27th, 1834. He removed to Kansas, and died there November 5th, 1866. Ebenezer, their eldest son was born in Truro December 3rd, 1835. He was married to Annie Wheaton March, 1869. Cathcrine, their eldest daughter, was born February 14th, 1870. Jane, the second daughter, was born January 24th, 1872. Julia Annie, the eldest daughter of John and Jane Archibald, was born February 15th, 1838. She was married to James H. Holmes of New York, October 10th, 1857.

Albert William, the second son of John Archibald, was born January 1st, 1840. Nancy, their second daughter, was born January 6th, 1842. She died January 29th, 1860. Clara Margaret, their third daughter was born December 31st, 1843. Frederick William, their eldest son, was born September 8th, 1845. He was married to Sarah C. Reid of Ohio, September 17th, 1871. Caleb P., their fourth son, was born May 18th, 1848. He was married to Kate Lamon of Virginia, February, 1872. Clarence L., their son, was born November 8th, 1872. Alice Jane, the youngest daughter of John and Jane Archibald was born October 1st, 1852.

Henry C., the third son of Ebenezer and Rebecca Archibald, was born May 22nd, 1815. He was married to Rebecca McCurdy, daughter of James M. McCurdy, January 31st, 1838 They removed to Grotten, Mass. After Mrs. Archibald's death, June 13th, 1854, he returned to Musquodoboit, and was married again to Mary Jane, daughter of Alexander and Janet McCurdy, June 12th, 1856. He died April 1st, 1859. Ebenezer Charles, his eldest son, was born March 7th, 1839. He died at Grotten, October 20th, 1861. Melville McCurdy, their second son, was born December 23rd, 1840. He died March 2nd, 1849. Margaret Jane was born September 5th, 1842, and died March 27th, 1846. Rebecca Ann, was born August 30th, 1844, and died July 24th, 1861. Margaret Agnes was born Sept. 14th, 1846 ; she died August 12th, 1852. Georgia Elizabeth was born September 25th, 1848, and died March 8th, 1849. Miriam was born March 20th, 1850. James William was born February 24th, 1852, and died January 10th, 1868. Henry Adams was born December 3rd, 1854, and died March 20th, 1854. Adams Tarbell, the only son of his second wife, was born July 8th, 1857.

Edward, the fourth son of Ebenezer and Rebecca Archibald, was born August 8th, 1818. He was married to Isabel, daughter of Robert O. Christie, November 27th, 1844. Edgar, their eldest son, was born September 1st, 1845. Margaret was born October 9th, 1857. Rebecca was born August 29th, 1860. Sarah, the youngest daughter was born November 7th, 1863.

Adams, the fifth son of Ebenezer and Rebecca Archibald, was born in Truro July 26th, 1822. He removed to Massachusetts, and was married there to Mary Ann Tarbell March 17th, 1853.

Charles, the youngest son of Ebenezer and Rebecca Archibald, was born September 22nd, 1827. He died when about four years of age.

Ebenezer Archibald died August 8th, 1829, in the fiftieth year of his age, and his widow died May 25th, 1854, aged 68.

Alexander Lackie, the fifth son of Matthew and Janet Archibald, was born in Truro, March 5th, 1788. He was married to Mary, daughter of William Fulton and Sarah Dunlap of Upper Stewiacke, December 13th, 1810.

Samuel George William Archibald, their eldest son, was born in Truro February 8th, 1812. He was married to Susannah, daughter of William and Lydia Fulton, of Wallace, February 24th, 1835. Alexander Lackie, the eldest son of S. G. W. and Susannah Archibald, was born in Truro January 3rd, 1836. Alexander L. Archibald was married to Nancy, the eldest daughter of David T. Archibald and Eleanor Taylor his wife, September 27th, 1859. Lilly Christianna, the eldest daughter of Alexander L. and Nancy Archibald, was. born in Truro April 12th, 1863. Josephine, their second daughter was born January 12th, 1866. William Fulton, the second son of S. G. W. and Susannah Archibald, was born in Truro December 17th, 1837. Rebecca Huestis, their eldest daughter, was born in Truro February 22nd, 1840. She was married to the Rev. John Haward July 26th, 1865. They have three daughters. Lydia, the second daughter of S. G. W. and Susannah Archibald, was born in Truro September 14th, 1841. She was married to James Leman January 12th, 1869. Stephen Fulton, their third son, was born May 3rd, 1843. He was married to Mary Cowperthwait October 18th, 1870. Joseph Howe, their fourth son, was born December 18th, 1844. He was married to Emily Dickson November 13th, 1867. Frederick, the eldest son of Joseph H. and Emily Archibald was born November 1869. Charles, their fifth son, was born March 4th, 1847. He died November 4th, 1847. Mary Jane, their third daughter, was born in Truro, February 2nd, 1849. Richard, their sixth son, was born in Truro, February 28th, 1851. Henry, their seventh son, was born August 15th, 1853. He died August 3rd, 1854. Ella, their fourth daughter, was born February 14th, 1855. George M., their eighth son was born August 18th. 1858.

Sarah, the eldest daughter of Alexander L. and Mary Archibald, was born January 26th, 1814. She was married to James, son of Alexander Kent, Esq., and Jane Christie his wife, January 10th, 1833. They had one son and five daughters. She died January 8th, 1847, aged 33 years.

Charles Frederick Augustus, the second son of Alexander L. and

Mary Archibald, was born in Truro December 22nd, 1817. He removed to the United States.

William, the third son of Alexander L. and Mary Archibald, was born December 20th, 1820. He was married to Elizabeth, daughter of Samuel Blair and Nancy Archibald his wife November 4th, 1845. Cecilia, their eldest daughter, was born August 13th, 1846. Peter, their eldest son was born March 21st, 1848. He is now an engineer on the Intercolonial Railroad. Leonard Carey and Bertha, being twins, were born March 28th, 1850. Leonard was married to Annie Lindsay January 7th, 1873. He is a merchant in Antigonish. Mary Agnes, their third daughter, was born March 25th, 1851. Jenny, their fourth daughter, was born March 6th, 1854. Clara, their fifth daughter, was born May 30th, 1860.

Alexander, the fourth son of Alexander L. and Mary Archibald, was born March 27th, 1825. This Alexander Archibald was one of the passengers on board the ill-fated vessel *Enterprise.*

Mary Jane, the second daughter of Alexander L. and Mary Archibald, was born in Truro January 5th, 1828. She removed to Boston, United States, and was married there to Charles Gay in the year 1855, and died in the year 1866, in November. Mary Fulton, the first wife of Alexander L. Archibald died September 8th, 1828 ; and he was married again to Christiana F., daughter of Daniel and Elizabeth Cock, March 29th, 1831.

Alfred Archibald, their eldest son, was born May 21st, 1833. He was married to Nancy McLain in the year 1857. Margaret, their eldest daughter, was born in September, 1858. Alexander Lackie Archibald, their eldest son, was born August 2nd, 1860. In August 1869, he was killed while raking hay ; being thrown from the horse, and drawn by the rake, over the field. The family were living at Cape John, in the County of Pictou, at the time. Joanna Archibald, their second daughter, was born in the year 1862. She died young. Annie, their third daughter, was born in the year 1864. She died young. Gordon, their second son, was born in the year 1866. Walter Henry, their third son, was born in the year 1868.

Walter, the youngest son of Alexander L. and Christianna N. Archibald, was born in Truro in the month of May, 1835. He was married to Olivia, daughter of James McCurdy and his wife of Onslow, in the month of August, 1859. Frank, their eldest son, was born in Truro March 21st, 1861. Alice, their eldest daughter, was born in the year 1863. Percy, their second daughter, was born in the year

1864.   Mary, their third daughter, was born January 1st, 1867. Walter Archibald and his family removed to the United States.

Alexander Lackie Archibald, whose descendants are the foregoing, was Major of the Militia.   He represented the township of Truro in the House of Assembly from the year 1830 to 1842, and from the year 1847 until 1851.   He carried on farming and tanning.   He built the house in which his son William now resides, where he reared his family, and died February 12th, 1859, aged 71 years.

John James, the sixth son of Matthew and Janet Archibald, was born July 22nd, 1790.   He was married to Mary, daughter of Isaac and Mary O'Brien, of Noel, in the County of Hants, October 13th, 1812.   Timothy O'Brien Archibald, their eldest son, was born in Truro August 9th, 1813.   He was married to Martha, daughter of Alexander and Jane Kent. of the Lower Village of Truro, January 1st, 1835.   Isaac, the eldest son of Timothy and Martha Archibald, was born in Truro in the month of February, 1838.   He started to go to British Columbia, and died on the voyage in the month of April, 1861, aged 28 years.   Clarissa, the eldest daughter of Timothy and Martha Archibald, was born December 27th, 1835.   She was married to John Ryan and they have three sons and three daughters. Barbara, their second daughter was born in the month of September, 1840.   She was married to Arthur Gladwin, of Musquodoboit, and had two sons.   She died in the year 1869.   Alexander Kent, the second son of Timothy and Martha Archibald, was born in the month of March, 1843.   Edward, their third son, was born December 25th, 1845.

Adams, the second son of John James and Mary Archibald, was born in Truro February 21st, 1815.   He was married to Mary Ann McConnell, of Tatamagouche, July 2nd, 1840.   They now reside at River John.

Rachel O'Brien, the eldest daughter of John J. and Mary Archibald, was born in Truro March 26th, 1817.   She was married to James Johnson, of Salmon River, February 24th, 1845.   They have two sons and four daughters.

Janet, their second daughter, was born May 6th, 1819.   She was married to Daniel McNutt, December 21st, 1841.   They have two sons and five daughters.

Margaret, the third daughter of John J. and Mary Archibald, was born August 2nd, 1821.   She was married to Isaac, the fourth son of John B. and Catherine Archibald in the month of November, 1840. They had four sons and two daughters.

Sarah Ann, their fourth daughter, was born April 9th, 1825. She was married to Alexander Miller November 25th, 1856. Their family is among the Millers.

Mary Elizabeth, their fifth daughter, was born December 11th, 1828. She is married to the Rev. Hector B. McKay, of River John. They had three sons and four daughters.

John McCurdy, the third son of John J. and Mary Archibald, was born in Truro, January 24th, 1833. He was married to Margaret, daughter of Isaac Christie and Susan Yuill, his wife, May 10th, 1855. Clarence, their eldest son, was born April 26th, 1856. He died April 28th, 1859. Mary, their second daughter, was born March 29th, 1859. Susan Jane, their third daughter, was born July 9th, 1866. John McCurdy Archibald died November 27th, 1865, aged 32 years.

John James Archibald died August 6th, 1864, aged 74 years, and his wife, Mary O'Brien, died October 30th, 1854.

Jonathan, the seventh and youngest son of Matthew and Janet Archibald, was born in Truro, July 1st, 1793. He was married to Margaret Talbot, of Truro, November 18th, 1813.

James, the eldest son of Jonathan and Margaret Archibald, was born in Truro, December 14th, 1815. He was married to Margaret, the eldest daughter of James Talbot and Mary Urquhart, his wife, January 14th, 1845. Mary, the eldest daughter of James and Margaret Archibald, was born in Musquodoboit, August 1st, 1846. Margaret, their second daughter, was born May 27th, 1848. Adams, the eldest son of James and Margaret Archibald, was born in Musquodoboit, October 17th, 1850. Eleanor, their third daughter, was born April 27th, 1852. James, their second son, was born January 1st, 1854. He died January 10th, 1861. Jonathan, their third son, was born March 25th, 1856. He died May 27th, 1857. Elizabeth, their fourth daughter, was born March 29th, 1859.

Matthew, the second son of Jonathan and Margaret Archibald, was born in Truro, January 1st, 1818. He was married to Jane Hall, of Sheet Harbour, September, 1839. Sarah Jane, the eldest daughter of Matthew and Jane Archibald, was born March 13th, 1841. She was married to John S. Stewart, February 24th, 1859. They have three sons and two daughters. William, the eldest son of Matthew and Jane Archibald,

5

was born January, 1843. He was married to Lydia Redman, in July, 1863. Sidney, the son of William and Lydia Archibald, was born in the year 1865. Margaret, the second daughter of Matthew and Jane Archibald, was born in January, 1844. Mary, their daughter, was born October 18th, 1846. Jonathan, their second son, was born October 15th, 1848. Susan, their fourth daughter, was born July 16th, 1851. She died July 16th, 1867. Catherine, their fifth daughter, was born May 10th, 1853. Thomas, their third son, was born April 22nd, 1856. He died in January, 1857. Emma, their sixth daughter, was born April 10th, 1859. Neal, their fourth son, was born March 22nd, 1862. David H., their fifth son, was born October 22nd, 1864.

Jane, the eldest daughter of Jonathan and Margaret Archibald, was born in Truro January 18th, 1820. She was married to John Curry, of Sheet Harbor, in the year 1842, and had two sons and four daughters. She died July 25th, 1872, aged 52 years. Margaret, the youngest daughter of Jonathan and Margaret Archibald, was born in Musquodoboit, January 5th, 1827. She was married to David Archibald, Esq., October 31st, 1845. They had five sons and one daughter. Their names appear among the descendants of Robert Archibald, Esq.

Jonathan Archibald, shortly after he was married, removed to Pleasant Valley, and had the Mills at the foot of the Lake. He removed from there to Musquodoboit in the year 1824, where he spent the remainder of his days at farming and milling. He died at Musquodoboit in August, 1861.

Eleanor Wilson, the third daughter of Matthew and Janet Archibald, was born in Truro April 9th, 1781. She was married to George, son of Robert and Nancy Hamilton, November 23rd, 1802. He died September 13th, 1841, aged 68 years, and his wife died August 15th, 1857, aged 76 years.

Jean, the fourth daughter of Matthew and Janet Archibald, was born in Truro, March 15th, 1783. She was married to Edward S., son of Colonel Jotham and Elizabeth Blanchard, February 18th, 1802. They had seven sons and four daughters. She died February 9th, 1873, aged 90 years. Mr. Blanchard died December 24th, 1856, aged 78 years.

Elizabeth, the fifth and youngest daughter of Matthew and Janet Archibald, was born in Truro, January 11th, 1786. She was married to Samuel Archibald, third. Their family appears among the descendants of James Archibald, Esq.

John Archibald second, the second son of Samuel Archibald, Senr., and Eleanor Taylor, was born in the year 1747. He was fifteen years old when they came to Nova Scotia. He was one of the grantees of Truro Township, although he was but 18 years old at the date of the grant. His wife, Margaret, daughter of William Fisher and Eleanor Archibald, was born in the year 1747, and they were married March 4th, 1772. They built their house on their front lot, being the same on which the Episcopalian Church and several other houses now stand. The old cellar is to be seen yet in the field of Mr. Solomon Slack. He owned the front wood lot on the South side of the street. He and his brother built the Mills on the bank of the upland, Southwest of the River Bridge. They dug a race for the water nearly half a mile along the West side of their lots. On this place he reared his numerous family. He died October 15th, 1813, aged 66 years, and his wife, Margaret, died May 12th, 1809, aged 62 years. He was married again to Hannah, daughter of James Archibald, and widow of the late John Cummings.

Rachel, the eldest daughter of John and Margaret Archibald, was born in Truro, December 29th, 1772. She was married to David Morrison Archibald, or David Archibald sixth. Their family appears among the descendants of James Archibald, Senr.

William, the eldest son of John and Margaret Archibald, was born in Truro, September 19th, 1774. He was married to Susan, daughter of William and Dorothy Putnam, January 1st, 1801. He removed; and settled at Upper Musquodoboit, on the farm which was afterwards owned by the Messrs. Annand. He removed from there to the South Branch of Stewiacke, about the year 1826, and settled on the same farm on which his eldest son, John, now resides. He died November 10th, 1850, aged 76 years, and his wife died May 23rd, 1871, aged 89 years.

Sarah, the eldest daughter of William and Susan Archibald, was born December 25th, 1801. She was married to Josiah Stewart, of Musquodoboit, in the month of February, 1823. They had three sons and three daughters. Mr. Stewart was killed, by falling from a barn which he was shingling, August, 1839. She was married again to Samuel Archibald, Esq., of Truro, October, 1847, and died December 28th, 1869.

Eleanor, the second daughter of William and Susan Archibald,

was born December 28th, 1803. She was married to Alexander
Henry in the year 1827. They removed to River John and settled
there, and had four sons and one daughter.

Ruth, their third daughter, was born March 6th, 1806. She was
married to Joseph Thomson. They had five sons and seven daughters.
They removed to Massachusetts, United States.

John, the eldest son of William and Susan Archibald, was born
July 7th, 1808. He was married to Lydia, daughter of James
Rutherford, Senr., and Letitia Putnam, August 15th, 1837. Timothy
Putnam, the eldest son of John and Lydia Archibald, was born
August 27th, 1838. William James, their second son, was born in
Stewiacke, February 1st, 1841. John F., their third son, was born
March 3rd, 1843. Susan, their eldest daughter, was born July 15th,
1845. She died January 29th, 1855. Esther, their second daughter,
was born October 10th, 1847. Sarah, their third daughter, was born
November 3rd, 1849. She was married to Harris Holdman,
December 5th, 1867. They have two daughters. Mary Jane, the
fourth daughter, was born February 3rd, 1852. Ebenezer, their
fourth son, was born April 11th, 1854. Susan Eleanor, their fifth
daughter, was born March 25, 1856. Letitia, their sixth daughter,
was born July 26, 1858. Mrs. Archibald died July 5th, 1870, and
he was married again to Elizabeth Hutchinson, of Musquodoboit,
April 27th, 1871.

William Putnam, the second son of William and Susan Archibald,
was born in Musquodoboit, April 23rd, 1810. He was married to
Mary Jane, daughter of Jesse and Mary Gourley, of the Lower
Village of Truro, January 30th, 1838. Eunice McNutt, the eldest
daughter of William P. and Mary Jane Archibald, was born December
4th, 1838. Margaret, their second daughter, was born in Truro,
October 20th, 1840. She was married to John Dunlap Johnson,
October 16th, 1860. They have three sons and one daughter. Jesse
Gourley Archibald, their eldest son, was born March 26th, 1842. He
was married to widow McNeil, daughter of David Fulton and his
wife, of Debert River, October 16th, 1866. They removed to
California. They have one son. His name is Locretia.

Prescott Lewis, their second son, was born March 10th, 1844.
He has gone to California. He was married to Jane Jeffers, of Nova
Scotia, November 5th, 1872, in California. Mary Ellen, their third
daughter, was born December 9th, 1845. She removed to California,
and was married there to Fred Barson. They have two sons and one

daughter. Sarah, the fourth daughter of William P. and Mary Jane Archibald, was born in Truro March 2nd, 1847. She was married to Thomas McBurney, of Tatamagouche, April 20th, 1866. They have one son and one daughter. Simon H., their third son, was born January 3rd, 1850. William R., their fourth son, was born December 12th, 1853. Arthur, their fifth son, was born July 9th, 1855. Mrs. Archibald died February 27th, 1857. He was married again to widow Gourley, the daughter of Joseph and Eleanor Fulton, of Upper Stewiacke, December 27th, 1860. Elizabeth Gourley, their eldest daughter, was born December 23rd, 1861. Anne M., their second daughter, was born in Truro, March 11th, 1863. Harriet R., their third daughter, was born January 23rd, 1865.

Alexander, the third son of William and Susan Archibald, was born in Musquodoboit, May 23rd, 1812. He was married to Catherine, daughter of James and Jean Laughead, of Clifton, January 10th, 1837. Joseph Howe, the eldest son of Alexander and Catherine Archibald, was born October 20th, 1839. He was married to Maria, daughter of James and Sarah Yuill, of Clifton, in the month of March, 1864. Clarence, their eldest son, was born at Clifton, December 25th, 1865. Sarah Eveline, their daughter, was born August, 1867. They have removed to California. Susan, the eldest daughter of Alexander and Catherine Archibald, was born June 27th, 1841. She was married to Robert Logan, of Musquodoboit, June 10th, 1862. They have three sons and two daughters. They have removed to Minnesota. James Smith, their second son, was born July 20th, 1843. Isaac Noble, their third son, was born March 12th, 1846. Maria, their second daughter, was born April 27th, 1848. She was married to Walter Marshall, of Beaver Brook, January 10th, 1866. They have two sons. Sarah, their third daughter, was born November 20th, 1850. William Prescott, their third son, was born December 20th, 1852. Samuel, their fourth son, was born June 8th, 1854. Jessie, their fourth daughter, was born November 26th, 1857. Mrs. Archibald died August 26th, 1869. He was married again to Mary Jane, daughter of Alexander and Janet McCurdy, widow of the late Henry Archibald, June 23rd, 1870.

George, the fourth son of William and Susan Archibald, was born in Musquodoboit, May 6th, 1814. He removed to the East River of Pictou, and settled there. He was married to Margaret Fraser, January, 1845. Hugh James, their eldest son, was born in January, 1846. He was married to Jessie Thomson in September, 1869.

William Alexander, the fourth son of George and Margaret Archibald, was born in Pictou in the year 1849. John George and Jesse, their twins, were born in 1852. Prescott, their son, was born in 1854. Alfred, their son, was born in 1856. Clarence was born in 1867.

Susan, the fourth daughter of William and Susan Archibald, was born September 11th, 1818. She was married to Robert, son of William and Hannah Creelman, of Stewiacke, January 29th, 1841. They had seven sons and eight daughters ; eight of those are dead.

Prescott Putnam, the fifth son of William and Susan Archibald, was born March 5th, 1822. He was married to Jane, daughter of James Rutherford, Senr., and Letitia Putnam, March 23rd, 1848. They now reside in Halifax, and keep a Country Market and a Hotel.

Margaret Mary, the fifth daughter of William and Susan Archibald, was born August 4th, 1824. She was married to Colin McLennon, of Pictou, February 22nd, 1853. They had three sons and two daughters. They removed to the United States, and Mr. McLennon died there, January 27th, 1868. She returned to Truro, and was married to John Smith, August 11th, 1870.

Samuel Burke, the second son of John Archibald, second, and Margaret Fisher, his wife, was born in Truro, December 12th, 1778. He was married to Margaret Dickman, November 26th, 1801. He removed from Truro, and settled in Upper Musquodoboit, on the farm adjoining his brother William's. On this place he reared his numerous family, and died there November 27th, 1861, aged 83 years. His wife died August 31st, 1861.

Rachel Morrison, the eldest daughter of Samuel B. and Margaret Archibald, was born March 24th, 1804. She was married to Samuel Creelman, of Stewiacke, July 20th, 1827. Mr. Creelman died, and she was married again to George S. Rutherford, March 20th, 1843. She died January 16th, 1865.

Margaret, their second daughter, was born November 19th, 1806. She was married to William Green, January 17th, 1825. They had two sons and three daughters. Mr. Green died, and she was married again to Daniel Tupper, of Upper Stewiacke. They had one daughter. Mrs. Tupper died April 14th, 1850, aged 43 years.

Grizell, their third daughter, was born March 5th, 1812. She was married to Abraham Newcomb, January 15th, 1830. They had eight sons and five daughters. She died July 3rd, 1857.

Daniel, the eldest son of Samuel B. and Margaret Archibald, was born November 15th, 1808 He was married to Rebecca Newcomb,

January 14th, 1830. Abraham, the eldest son of Daniel and Rebecca Archibald, was born November 29th, 1830. He was killed by falling from a load of hay, September 19th, 1835. Margaret, the eldest daughter of Daniel and Rebecca Archibald, was born February 1st, 1832. She was married to James Charles, son of Stephen Johnson and Nancy Miller, his wife, July 4th, 1855. They have two sons and five daughters. Judson, their second son, was born January 27th, 1835. He removed to the United States, and was married there to Agustesly Ayer, in the year 1860. Byron, their eldest son, was born in the year 1863. Mary, their eldest daughter, was born in 1865. Eliakim, the third son of Daniel and Rebecca Archibald, was born April 9th, 1836. He was married to Anne Bradshaw. He is now a Minister of the Gospel in the State of Illinois. Mary Ann, their second daughter, was born March 30th, 1838. David Dimock, their fourth son, was born August 4th, 1842. He is married, and settled in P. E. Island. Charles, their fifth son, was born May 3rd, 1844. Jacob, their sixth son, was born August 4th, 1845. Abraham, their seventh son, was born June 2nd, 1849. Rosannah, their third daughter, was born August 23rd, 1850. Isaac Chipman, their eighth and youngest son, was born January 9th, 1852. Daniel Archibald settled at the South branch of Stewiacke, where he carries on farming and tanning.

James D., the second son of Samuel and Margaret Archibald, was born July 11th, 1811. He was married to Amy Harvey, January, 1832. He settled in Upper Stewiacke. He removed from there to the County of Yarmouth, in April, 1867. Mrs. Archibald died there April 26th, 1871, aged 71 years. James Harvey Archibald, their eldest son, was born January 1st, 1834. He was married to Jane, daughter of David Dean and Margaret Archibald, his wife, of Musquodoboit, December 15th, 1856. David M., their eldest son, was born in Stewiacke, March 20th, 1859. George Isaac, their second son, was born May 7th, 1861. James Rupert, their third son, was born in Halifax February 15th, 1865. Samuel B., their fourth son, was born in Halifax, May 15th, 1867. Edgar S., their fifth son, was born in Stewiacke June 5th, 1869. Margaret, the eldest daughter of James D. and Amy Archibald, was born in Stewiacke May 6th, 1836. She was married to Harvey Spinney, of Yarmouth, November, 1860. They have two sons and two daughters. George, their second son, was born June, 1838. He died April 16th, 1853, aged 15 years. Samuel B. Archibald, their third son, was born April 6th, 1840. He

died May 17th, 1861, aged 21 years. Ebenezer Erskine Archibald
was born February 16th, 1843. He was married to Mary Spinney,
of Yarmouth, May 3rd, 1864. Joanna, their eldest daughter, was
born March 30th, 1865. Amy, their second daughter, was born
March, 1867. Elvira, their third daughter, was born in Yarmouth,
1869. James D. Archibald was born in Yarmouth, September 10th,
1871.

John G. D., the third son of Samuel B. and Margaret Archibald,
was born in Musquodoboit, July 14th, 1814. He was married to
Janet, daughter of George Hamilton and Eleanor Wilson Archibald,
his wife, February 8th, 1838. He settled near his brother Daniel, at
the South Branch of Stewiacke, where he and his family are still
residing. George, the eldest son of John G. D. and Janet Archibald,
was born November 18th, 1838. He died May 25th, 1857. Edwin,
their second son, was born August 16th, 1844. He was married to
Sarah, daughter of Matthew Burris, Esq., and Mary Archibald, of
Musquodoboit, November 10th, 1870. Alfred, their third son, was
born February 11th, 1847. Julia and Harriet, their twin daughters,
were born June 5th, 1849. Louisa, their third daughter, was born
October 18th, 1851. Adams J., their fourth and youngest son, was
born August 28th, 1854.

George W., the fourth son of Samuel B. and Margaret Archibald,
was born May 30th, 1816. He was married to Elizabeth, daughter
of George and E. W. Hamilton, March 30th, 1839. They have
removed to Portland, Me. Margaret, their eldest daughter, was born
in the year 1846. Samuel, their eldest son, was born in the year
1844. Alfred, the second son, was born in the year 1848. Adelaide,
their second daughter, was born in the year 1854. Augustus, their
third son, was born in the year 1857. Frederick, their fourth son,
was born in the year 1860. Henry, their fifth son, was born in the
year 1863.

Wallace, the fifth son of Samuel B. and Margaret Archibald, was
born February 19th, 1818. He was married to Anna Richardson,
October 27th, 1840. He inherited his father's farm in Musquodoboit,
where he reared his family. He died December 25th, 1860, and his
wife died October 3rd, 1868. William, their eldest son, was born
September 19th, 1842. Harriet, their eldest daughter, was born June
3rd, 1844. Jemima, their second daughter, was born June 26th,
1848. George, their second son, was born January 31st, 1850.
Arthur, their third son, was born December 15th, 1853. Sarah, their

third daughter, was born June 2nd, 1856. Anna, their fourth daughter, was born July 5th, 1858.

Burke, the sixth son of Samuel B. and Margaret Archibald, was born April 15th, 1820. Jane, their eldest daughter, was born in the year 1848. Margaret W., their second daughter, was born in the year 1850. Elizabeth, their third daughter, was born in the year 1852. Amy, their fourth daughter, was born in the year 1854. Grace, their fifth daughter. was born in 1857. She died when about nine months old. Alice was born in 1859. Judson W., was born in 1861. Clara was born in 1864. Anna T. was born in 1867.

Samuel, the seventh son of Samuel B. and Margaret Archibald, was born January 7th, 1822. He was married to Alice, daughter of Alexander K. and Janet Archibald. Janet, their eldest daughter, was born January 19th, 1854. Howard, their eldest son, was born October, 1856. Ernest was born May 7th, 1860. Mary was born June 30th, 1862. Bunyan, their third son, was born May 20th, 1864. Alexander was born March 28th, 1866. Maud, their third daughter, was born April 28th, 1868. Samuel Archibald removed from Stewiacke and settled in Yarmouth. In 1872 he and his two eldest sons were crossing to a small Island, where they kept sheep. The boat filled, and he and his eldest son, Howard, were drowned ; the other son was rescued. William A., the eighth and youngest son of Samuel B. and Margaret Archibald, was born in Musquodoboit October 9th, 1824. He studied and became a Doctor of Medicine, and died a bachelor, February 18th, 1857, aged 32 years.

Eleanor, the second daughter of John Archibald, second, and Margaret Fisher, his wife, was born in Truro September 24th, 1776. She was married to Adam, son of James Dunlap and Mary Johnson, his wife. Their names appear among the Dunlaps. Ruth, the third daughter of John and Margaret Archibald, was born Feby. 23rd, 1781. She died unmarried. Susannah, their fourth daughter, was born November 18th, 1783. She was married to Edward Brydon, and had two daughters. She died of consumption at her father's house in Truro, while her husband was confined in Jail for debt. Her corpse was taken into the Jail, that he might have the last sight of the remains of his beloved wife, while they were on their way to the Cemetery for burial. This took place about the year 1806 or 1807.

Daniel, the third son of John and Margaret Archibald, was born in Truro, February 9th, 1786. He died of consumption when a young man. George, their fifth son, was born June 6th, 1790. He also died of consumption when he was a young man.

Matthew James, the fourth son of John and Margaret Archibald, was born in Truro February 9th, 1788. He was married to Rebecca, daughter of John Cummings and Hannah Archibald, July 11th, 1811. He inherited a part of his father's farm, also the mills which had been erected by his father and uncle Matthew. He lived in the house which is now occupied by Mr. George W. Hamlon, who has now a number of houses standing on what was formerly the mill pond. Mr. Archibald died July 7th, 1855, aged 67 years, and his wife died March 5th, 1861. Margaret, the eldest daughter of Matthew James and Rebecca Archibald, was born November 3rd, 1811. She was married to Edward Lynds, of Onslow Mountain, January 19th, 1830. They had four sons and eight daughters. She died December 13th, 1855, and Mr. Lynds died December 15th, 1860. Rachel, the second daughter of M. J. and Rebecca Archibald, was born November 23rd, 1812. She was married to Ephraim, son of John and Catherine Staples, of Chiganoise, July 4th, 1839. They had three sons and four daughters. Their eldest son, Alfred, was married to Susan McLellan July 26th, 1864. He was working on the top of a steep bank about sixty or seventy feet high, from which he fell, and lived but three hours after. Susannah, their eldest daughter, was born May 11th, 1814. She was married to Jacob Miller, of Newport, October 24th, 1847. They had one son. She died at Newport, December, 1851. Hannah, their fourth daughter, was born November 23rd, 1815. She was married to John Miller (a brother of the above named Jacob), February 14th, 1838. They had four sons and one daughter. Mr. Miller died December 10th, 1854, aged 37 years, and she is living a widow. Sarah, their fifth daughter, was born April 22nd, 1817. She was married to William Lockhart Miller (another brother of the above named Miller's), January 29th, 1850. They had one son, and he died when about two years old. Rebecca, their sixth daughter, was born August 10th, 1818. She died November 15th, 1819. Rebecca, their seventh daughter, was born February 27th, 1820. She has removed to New Zealand. Ruth, their eighth daughter, was born August 10th, 1821. She was married to George Cole, recently from England, September, 1856. They had one daughter. Mr. Cole died, and she was married again to John Dickson, and they had one daughter. She is now in the Lunatic Asylum. George Washington, the eldest son of M. J. and Rebecca

Archihald, was born January 2nd 1823. He removed to the United States in the year 1845, and was married their to Amanda ———. He died there October, 1869, aged 47 years. John, their second son, was born August 10th, 1824. He was married to Eliza Chesley, of Wilmot, June 19th, 1844. Belvidera, their eldest daughter, was born in Truro-in 1846. Rupert was born in 1851. Rynold Howard was born in 1853. Eliza was born 1855. Mr. Archibald died August, 1866. Eleanor, their ninth daughter, was born March 20th, 1826. She died August 18th, 1826. Eleanor, their tenth daughter, was born July 3rd, 1827. She was married to George W. Hamlon, in the United States, November 19th, 1856. She returned to Nova Scotia, and died February 10th, 1870, aged 43 years.

William, the third son of Matthew J. and Rebecca Archibald, was born January 9th, 1829. He was married to Sarah Shand, of Halifax, April 14th, 1849. Rebecca, the eldest daughter of William and Sarah Archibald, was born April 14th, 1853. Joseph Allen, their third son, was born April 7th, 1855. Minnie and Laura, their twin daughters, were born January 29th, 1864. Matthew James, the fourth son of Matthew James and Rebecca Archibald, was born May 2nd, 1830. He was married to Eleanor McLaughlan, December 1st, 1852. John James, their eldest son, was born May 7th, 1858. Henry Albert, the second son, was born in Truro, February 11th, 1861. Ella Priscilla, their eldest daughter, was born December 17th, 1866. Mary Ann, their second daughter, was born December 28th, 1863. Jane, the eleventh daughter of Matthew J. and Rebecca Archibald, was born in Truro, December 7th, 1831. She was married to Almon Barry, of the United States, July 4th, 1853. They have one son and two daughters. Mary Ann, the twelfth daughter of Matthew J. and Rebecca Archibald, was born in Truro, July 1st, 1833. She was married to George Nichol. They have two sons and one daughter. They have removed to New Zealand. Samuel, their fifth and youngest son, was born in Truro, June 10th, 1835. He removed to the Southern States, and has not been heard from for a number of years.

Sarah, the fifth and youngest daughter of John and Margaret Archibald, was born in Truro November 20th, 1791. She was married to James Yuill, of Clifton, August 20th, 1809. Their family appears among the Yuills.

Janet, the eldest daughter of Samuel Archibald, Senr., and Eleanor Taylor, his wife, was born in the year 1750, being twelve years before they came to Nova Scotia. She was married to John Hingley and had seven sons and four daughters. She died June 10th, 1811, aged 61 years. John Hingley was one of the grantees of Truro Township, and had his front land on the North side of Salmon River, being the North part of Messrs. Henderson's farm. He sold his front lands to John Oughterson, and removed to Salmon River, now Kemptown, and settled on the farm on which his grandson, Alexander Scott Hingley, now resides, where he died.

David Archibald, second, the third son of Samuel Archibald, Senr., and Eleanor Taylor, was born in the year 1752, ten years before they came to Nova Scotia.· He was married to Jane, the eldest daughter of Alexander Miller and Nancy Anderson, his wife, December 1st, 1778. Mr. Archibald's name is among the grantees of Truro Township, although he was but thirteen years old at the date of the grant. He settled on the farm which is now occupied by William T. Archibald and John Hattie, on the South side of Salmon River, where he resided about eleven years after he was married. He then sold his farm and removed about ten miles further up the River, and settled on the farm which is still known by the name of the old Archibald farm, in Kemptown. He erected mills at the same place which Mr. George Hamilton has his saw-mill now. In the summer of 1790, as Dr. McGregor was returning from a mission at Amherst, he stopped at Mr. Archibald's house, and, finding some of his people working at the mill, he remained the afternoon and night, in order that he might have their company the next day through the woods. During the afternoon the doctor took a plan of the mill, so that some of his people in Pictou, who were engaged in erecting mills, might have the benefit of this plan. In about three years after this Mr. Archibald removed to the Middle River of Pictou, and erected a set of mills near the same place that the mills are now, and in about nine years after this, in 1802, he returned to Kemptown, where he resided to near the close of his life. He was afflicted, for a number of years, with a sore leg. In September, 1818, he went to Pictou Town, to be attended by the doctors. They amputated his leg, and he lived but a few days after. He died September 19th, 1818, aged 66 years. His body was taken to Middle River, and interred near the place where he had built the mills. His wife died at Kemptown, November 28th, 1824, and her body was interred beside her husband's.

Alexander Miller, their eldest son, was born in Truro, August 14th, 1779. He was married to Janet Clark, of the West River of

Pictou, September 24th, 1802. He continued to reside at the mill at Middle River, until the year 1812, when he removed to St. Mary's, and settled on an interval farm near the Forks, being the same on which three of his sons now reside.

William Clarke, the eldest son of Alexander M. and Janet Archibald, was born September 21st, 1803. He was married to Sarah Tate, November 9th, 1826. He settled on the farm on which his son John William now resides, upon the West River of St. Mary's. He left this farm, and purchased a house and small farm from the Rev. John Campbell, at Glenelg. Agnes, the eldest daughter of William C. and Sarah Archibald, was born October 22nd, 1827. Maria Jane, their second daughter, was born June 13th, 1829. She was married to John Crookshank, January 1st, 1855. They have four sons and three daughters. Sarah Esther Clarke, their third daughter, was born April 9th, 1831. She was married to Thomas Smith, July 15th, 1866. They have one daughter. Mary Lewis, their fourth daughter, was born May 17th, 1835. John William, their only son, was born April 30th, 1841. He was married to Mary Ann Whidden, November 23rd, 1867. Isaac William, the eldest son of John William and Mary Ann Archibald, was born April 13th, 1869. Sarah Esther, their daughter, was born August 6th, 1870. Sarah, the wife of William C. Archibald, died August 20th, 1849. He was married again to Hannah E. Kanodell, January 17th, 1866.

David, the second son of Alexander M. and Janet Archibald, was born August 23rd, 1805. He was married to Eliza McIntosh, November 23rd, 1837. Elizabeth, their eldest daughter, was born December 4th, 1838. She was married to James Dickson, December 20th, 1865. They have one daughter. William A., their eldest son, was born September 16th, 1840. John C., their second son, was born January 26th, 1844. He was married to Margaret McIntosh, September 27th, 1868. Charles Howard, their son, was born December 7th, 1869. Jane the second daughter of David and Eliza Archibald, was born October 9th, 1845. She was married to John Chisholm, of Antigonish, July 12th, 1864. She died April 9th, 1873, aged 58 years. Amanda, their third daughter, was born January 23rd, 1848. David Archibald settled at Stillwater, about four miles up the River from Sherbrooke, where he and his two sons still reside. Grizell, the eldest daughter of Alexander M. and Janet Archibald, was born August 9th, 1807. She died unmarried December 2nd, 1867, aged 60 years.

Samuel, their third son, was born October 9th, 1809. He was married to Agnes Tate, July 7th, 1865. He is now residing on the same farm on which David McKeen settled, about the year 1802. John C., their eldest son, was born February 11th, 1868. Janet Sarah, their daughter, was born May 25th, 1869.

John, the fourth son of Alexander M. and Janet Archibald, was born January 4th, 1812. He was married to Caroline McDaniel, January 23rd, 1845. Henry Alexander, their eldest son, was born April 3rd, 1846. He is married to Miss Matheson, in Cape Breton. Lorenzo, the second son of John and Caroline Archibald, was born May 16th, 1848. Janet, their eldest daughter, was born December 27th, 1853. Catharine Eliza, their second daughter, was born August 5th, 1855. John, their third son, was born in the year 1862. Clara, their third daughter, was born in 1866. Margaret M., their fourth daughter, was born in 1868. This Mr. Archibald having learned the trade of tanning with his uncle, Matthew Archibald, of Pictou Town, settled and carried on his trade at Stillwater, near his brother David, and a few years ago removed to Cape Breton.

Isaac, the fifth son of Alexander M. and Janet Archibald, was born January 24th, 1815. He inherited a part of his father's farm, and now lives in the house in which his father lived and died.

Alexander, the sixth son of Alexander M. and Janet Archibald, was born October 17th, 1817. He was married to Catharine McKay, of Fishpool, East River, Pictou, January 7th, 1846. Jane Agnes, their eldest daughter, was born March 28th, 1848. Alexander William, their eldest son, was born October 24th, 1852. Christiana, their second daughter, was born January 27th, 1855. John Campbell, their second son, was born July 13th, 1857. Samuel Johnson, their third son, was born April 17th, 1861. Mr. Archibald is settled a short distance up the West River, where he carries on farming and milling.

Janet, the second daughter of Alexander and Janet Archibald, was born November 19th, 1820. She was married to Alexander Grant, of the East River of Pictou, January 24th, 1845. They have three daughters.

Matthew, the seventh son of Alexander and Janet Archibald, was born December 1st, 1822. He was married to Isabel McNab, of Halifax, December 29th, 1847. Margaret McKenzie, their eldest daughter, was born October 24th, 1848. Alexander David, their eldest son, was born April 2nd, 1852. Ebenezer McNab, their second son, was born December 19th, 1853. Jane, their second daughter, was born November 17th, 1858. Julia Campbell, their third daughter, was born June 20th, 1865. Mr. Archibald inherits a part of his father's farm, and keeps the Post Office at Glenelg.

Alexander M. Archibald died August 8th, 1857, aged 78 years, and his wife died May 3rd, 1855, aged 78 years.

Eleanor, the eldest daughter of David ,Archibald, second, and Jane Miller, his wife, was born in Truro June 23rd, 1781. She was married to William Fraser, of the Middle River of Pictou, January 17th, 1801. They had four sons and ten daughters. Mr. Fraser was born April 15th, 1776. David A. Fraser is their second son. He now resides in Truro. They lived and died on a farm adjoining the one on which Mr. Archibald built his Mills. Mrs. Fraser died May 11th, 1854, aged 73 years. Mr. Fraser died February 14th, 1848, aged 73 years.

Samuel, the second son of David and Janet Archibald, was born in Truro, April 21st, 1783. His wife, Jane Fraser, was born at Middle River, Pictou, December 22nd, 1788. They were married October 15th, 1805. They settled on a farm at the head of the tide, on Middle River. Mrs. Archibald died December 27th, 1842, aged 54 years. He was married again to Catherine Keellor, the widow of the late James Haulkens. Mrs. Archibald died September 1st, 1856, aged 73 years.

Janet, the eldest daughter of Samuel and Janet Archibald, was born July 22nd, 1806. She was married to Andrew Simpson, of Merigomish, in January, 1825. They had six sons and six daughters.

Simon, the eldest son of Samuel and Janet Archibald, was born June 31st, 1808. He was married to Nancy Cameron, of the West River of Pictou, April 10th, 1832. Samuel, their eldest son, was born July 3rd, 1839. He was married to Hannah Ann Campbell, January 20th, 1867. Florence Jane, the eldest daughter of Samuel and Hannah A. Archibald, was born May 1st, 1868. Agnes C. E., their second daughter, was born December 29th, 1869. Grizie Jane, the eldest daughter of Simon and Nancy Archibald, was born July 3rd, 1833. She was married to Alexander Campbell, of Caraboo. They have three sons and three daughters. Duncan Cameron, their second son, was born January 12th, 1842. Janet, their second daughter, was born May 22nd, 1837. She was married to Daniel Fraser, April 11th, 1867. They have two sons. Alexander William, their third son, was born April 30th, 1844. Charles Simon, their fourth son, was born February 28th, 1847. David Matthew, their fifth son, was born May 20th, 1853. Agnes Watson was born March 10th, 1855, and died July 11th, 1867. Catherine, the second daughter of Samuel and Janet Archibald, was born July 2nd, 1810. She was married to Charles Fraser, January 19th, 1830. They had two sons and six daughters. She died February 9th, 1867.

David, the second son of Samuel and Janet Archibald, was born July 8th, 1812. He was married to Nancy Fraser, March 6th, 1835. Sarah, their eldest daughter, was born June 22nd, 1837. Caroline, their second daughter, was born August 3rd, 1839. William, their eldest son, was born in August, 1844. Daniel Fraser, their second son, was born ——. Isaac Smith, their third son, was born ——.

Mr. Archibald died at Middle River, January 30th, 1862. His widow still lives at the homestead.

Eleanor, the third daughter of Samuel and Janet Archibald, was born June 16th, 1814. She was married to Elbridge Kennedy, in Salem, Mass., U. S., in the year 1851. She died at Watervale, Pictou, N. S., in the year 1865. Sarah, their fourth daughter, was born June 12th, 1816. She was married to John Culton, tanner, of the East River of Pictou, January 25th, 1843. They had three sons and one daughter. She died September 15th, 1859. Alexander, their third son, was born August 17th, 1818. He removed to Restigouche, N. B., and was married there to Susan Adams, in the year 1850. He removed again to New London, State of Michigan.

Nancy, their fifth daughter, was born April 17th, 1820. She was married to James McDonald, of the West River of Pictou, January 5th, 1843. They have one son and one daughter.

Robert, the fourth son of Samuel and Janet Archibald, was born July 23rd, 1822. He was married to Ann Fraser, granddaughter of the late Dr. James McGregor, the first Presbyterian Minister of Pictou, October, 1851. Samuel Archibald, their eldest son, was born 1852. Elbridge Archibald, their second son, was born 1856. They reside on Greenhill, Pictou. He follows farming.

William Samuel, their fifth son, was born October 25th, 1824. He removed, when young, to Boston, Mass., where he learned painting, and was married there to Susan Mason. He removed again to California, and lived there four or five years, and, returning home, he died suddenly in Albany, July 8th, 1854. He left a widow and one son. Matthew, their sixth son, was born March 17th, 1828. He was married to Elizabeth Putnam Monteith, in Salem, Mass., U. S.,

July 20th, 1851. They removed to Truro, N. S., and he carries on manufacturing medicine. John Samuel, their eldest son, was born August 31st, 1852. Sarah Ellen, their eldest daughter, was born and died when young. George William, their second son, was born July 11th, 1861. Esther Janet, their second daughter, was born April 21st, 1864. Joseph, the third son, was born December 7th, 1866. Anne Price, their third daughter, was born December 27th, 1868.

Martha, the sixth daughter of Samuel and Janet Archibald, was born May 6th, 1830. She was married to Alexander Douglas in July, 1856. They had one son. Mrs. Douglas died August 27th, 1862. Isaac Smith, their youngest son, was born December 6th, 1834. He died February 12th, 1837.

Isaac, the third son of David Archibald 2nd, and Jane Miller, was born in Truro, July 13th, 1785. He was married to Janet, the second daughter of David Archibald 3rd, December 1st, 1808. They settled at Middle River, Pictou, where they reared their family. Mr. Archibald died February 8th, 1858, aged 73 years, and his wife died January 19th, 1859, aged 67 years. Sarah, their eldest daughter, was born October 1st, 1809. She was married to William Crocket, September 17th, 1843. They had one son and three daughters. Mrs. Crocket died November 3rd, 1849. Jane, the second daughter of Isaac and Janet Archibald, was born January 20th, 1812. She was married to John Fraser November 12th, 1835. They had four sons and five daughters.

David, the eldest son of Isaac and Janet Archibald, was born at the Middle River of Pictou January 8th, 1814. He was married to Sarah, the eldest daughter of William T. and Janet Archibald, of St. Mary's, September 16th, 1840. Silas Anderson, their eldest son, was born August 10th, 1841, he died May 14th, 1866. Melville, their second son, was born March 20th, 1843. Lorenzo, their third son, was born April 14th, 1845. Edmond, their fourth son, was born February 6th, 1847. He was married to Adelaide Fraser April 22nd, 1871. Mrs. Archibald died May 3rd, 1847. He was married again to Lucy Ann the daughter of Frederick and Abigail Wilber, and widow of the late James Archibald, March 15th, 1848. Sarah L., their daughter, was born February 28th, 1852. Wilber L., their son was born June 10th, 1854.

Elizabeth, the third daughter of Isaac and Janet Archibald, was born at Middle River, Pictou, November 16th, 1817. She was

6

married to David Clark of the West River, Pictou, October 6th, 1842. They had five sons and five daughters.

Alexander, the second son of Isaac and Janet Archibald, was born August 1st, 1819. He was married to Elizabeth, the fifth daughter of William T. and Janet Archibald, of Sherbrooke, September 19th, 1843. Isaac, their eldest son, was born July 24th, 1844. Jessie, their eldest daughter, was born February 8th, 1846. James William, their second son, was born January 8th, 1848. He died April 19th, 1871. Raymond F., the third son of Alexander and Elizabeth Archibald, was born June 29th, 1854. He died November 28th, 1863. Clarence, their fourth son, was born November 4th, 1856. Hiram Davis, their fifth son, was born January 27th, 1858. Sarah Elizabeth, their second daughter, was born November 16th, 1860. She died September 9th, 1861. David Anderson, their sixth son, was born January 15th, 1864. Mrs. Archibald died May 21st, 1868, and he was married again to Janet, daughter of James and Eliza Archibald, of Clifton, in the township of Truro, February 23rd, 1870.

William, the third son of Isaac and Janet Archibald, was born April 12th, 1821. He was married to Elizabeth, the eldest daughter of Alexander and Ann Archibald, of Truro, July 1st, 1844. William Henry, their eldest son, was born December 15th, 1845. He was married to Susan, daughter of Duncan Creelman, of Stewiacke, January 18th, 1869. On June 21st, 1870, Wm. Henry Archibald went, with his wife to Stewiacke on a visit, and while they were there, he was kicked by a horse, and lived but an hour and a half. Ann Louisa, their eldest daughter, was born June 27th, 1848. She was married to Noble Cleveland, March 1st, 1864, and has three daughters. Eveline, their second daughter, was born January 20th, 1851. Chester, their second son, was born January 30th, 1859. Edson F., their third son, was born June 18th, 1861.

Nancy, the fourth daughter of Isaac and Janet Archibald, was born April 9th, 1823. She was married to James McDaniel Sept. 17th, 1841. They removed to the United States. They had two sons and two daughters. Mrs. McDaniel died November 1st, 1854.

Matthew, the fourth son of Isaac and Janet Archibald, was born June 19th, 1825. He was married to Sophia Matilda Irish, July 23rd, 1850. Edmond William, their eldest son, was born June 10th, 1851. He died August 6th, 1870. Levi, their son, was born January 20th, 1855. Emma, their daughter, was born April 2nd, 1857. Catherine, their daughter was born February 22nd, 1860. Matthew

Archibald inherited part of his father's farm, and died in the same house in which his father and mother lived and died. He died August 10th, 1863, and his wife died January 4th, 1870.

Hannah B., the fifth and youngest daughter of Isaac and Janet Archibald, was born October 16th, 1827. She was married to John G., son of Samuel McKeen, of Cape Breton, October 16th, 1848. They have four sons and six daughters.

Isaac Waddell, the fifth and youngest son of Isaac and Janet Archibald, was born February 28th, 1834. He was married to Sophia, daughter of David W. and Jane Archibald, of Truro, July 15th, 1857. They had one son and one daughter; both died when young.

James the fourth son of David and Jane Archibald, was born in Truro June 7th, 1787. He married Sarah, the second daughter of James and Agnes McCurdy, of Onslow. James, the eldest son of James and Sarah Archibald, was born in the year 1812. He was married to Lucy Ann, daughter of Frederick Wilber and Abigail Hoar, of Shepody, June 28th, 1838. He died in September, 1839. David, their second son, died while a young man.

David Anderson, the fifth son of David and Jane Archibald, was born at Truro April 20th, 1789. He was married to Nancy, the third daughter of David Archibald, October 31st, 1811. They had one son who died when about two years old. Mr. Archibald settled at Middle River, Pictou, and owned the Mills with his brother Isaac, till about the year 1832, when he removed to Truro and purchased a part of the farm which had been owned by his father, at the time of his birth. He continued on this farm while he was able to work; he then sold it and removed to the village of Truro where he died April 22nd, 1871, aged 82 years, and his wife died May 2nd, 1868, aged 74 years.

Matthew, the sixth son of David and Jane Archibald, was born in what is now called Kempton, October 14th, 1791. He was married to Martha, daughter of Finlay and Jane Murdoch, of Halifax, February 1st, 1820. George William, their son, was born in Pictou town October, 1830. Mrs. Archibald died March 27th, 1861, and he was married again to Jane Lowden, widow of Mr. Haukins, May 9th, 1862. He carrried on tanning in Pictou town for a considerable time. He died March 27th, 1863.

John, the seventh and youngest son of David and Jane Archibald, was born at Middle River of Pictou, February 10th, 1799. He was married to Catherine Murdoch, sister of his brother Matthew's wife

April 5th, 1822. Charles, their eldest son, was born in Kemptown March, 1824. He removed to the United States, and was married there to Frances Hurbert May 1848. He died there April 7th, 1859. Jane, the eldest daughter of John and Catherine Archibald, was born in Kemptown in the month of September, 1828. She removed to the United States and was married there to Alfred S. Morgan, and has two daughters. Lewis, their second son, was born in Kemptown August 27th, 1834. He left home when a young man and followed the sea for a number of years, and is now residing in Manitoba. Maria, their second daughter, was born in Kemptown July 27th, 1836. Martha, their third daughter, was born in Kemptown, May 27th, 1838. She was married to David McDonald, of Sherbrooke, February 24th, 1859. They have two sons and one daughter. John Archibald was in his saw mill at Kemptown, repairing some part of her below, when a man above started the mill. The lower part of the saw-gate struck him on the head and caused his death almost instantly. This took place June 23rd, 1854. His widow is still living at Sherbrooke, St. Mary's. Jane, the youngest daughter of David and Jane Archibald, was born at Middle River, Pictou, February 8th, 1802, and brought by her parents to Kemptown, before she was one year old. She was married to David W. Archibald, of Truro, Sept. 25th, 1827. Their family appears among the descendants of James Archibald, Esq.

James, the fourth son of Samuel Archibald, Senr., and Eleanor Taylor his wife, was born in the year 1754, being eight years before they came to Nova Scotia. He was married to Rebecca, daughter of John Barnhill and Letitia Deyarmond, of Chiganoise, February 25th, 1779. He inherited a part of his father's property, with his dwelling house, and had at one time owned part of the Mills. He was a Justice of the Peace for a length of time. Also an Elder of the Presbyterian Church from the year 1799 until his death June 13th, 1828. His wife died October 8th, 1818, aged 55 years.

John Barnhill Archibald, their eldest son, was born in Truro, August 13th, 1780. He was married to Catherine, daughter of Ebenezer and Catherine Hoar, of Onslow, February 27th, 1806. Rebecca, the eldest daughter of John B. and Catharine Archibald, was born in Truro, November 17th, 1806. She was married to the Rev. James Read, June —, 1840. She died at Portaupique August 1st, 1863, aged 56 years. Her body was buried beside her sister Mary, in the Baptist Cemetery at North River, Onslow.

Mary, the second daughter of John B. and Catherine Archibald, was born October 8th, 1808. She was married to Daniel son of Robert Blair and Mary Hoar his wife, of North River, Onslow, October 12th, 1830. They had two sons and five daughters. She died October 12th, 1861, aged 53 years.

Samuel James, the eldest son of John B. and Catherine Archibald, was born September 17th, 1810. He was married to Anne Waddell, daughter of Ebenezer and Rebecca Archibald, January 21st, 1836. He settled in Harmony on the farm on which John H. Archibald now resides, being among the first who settled there. He remained there nearly 20 years, and then removed to Musquodoboit, where he and his family are still residing. He was elected an Elder in the Presbyterian Church of Truro in the year 1845. Amelia, the eldest daughter of Samael J. and Anne W. Archibald, was born in Truro December 3rd, 1836. She has been teaching school in Halifax for a number of years. Wellington, their only son, was born in Harmony June 8th, 1839. He was married May 6th, 1869, to Esther McKeen, daughter of David McKeen, of Musquodoboit. Mr. McKeen and three other men were drowned in a lake where they were out fishing, about 20 years ago. Richmond L., the son of Wellington and Esther Archibald, was born January 27th, 1870. Agnes, the second daughter of Samuel J. and Anne W. Archibald, was born in Harmony December 22nd, 1841. She was married to James McDonald of Musquodoboit, November 21st, 1866. They have two sons. Georgina, their third daughter was born August 11th, 1846. She is now teaching school in Halifax.

Ebenezer M., the second son of John B. and Catherine Archibald, was born in Truro November 19th, 1812. He was married to Ann, daughter of Archibald Nelson and Jenny Hill, of Clifton, January 24th, 1837. He is settled at Clifton, and carries the mail and passengers from Truro to Shubenacadie. Nancy Archibald, their eldest daughter was born .at Clifton, June 26th, 1838. She was married to Wallace Gray in October 1859. They have two sons. She died April, 1873. Rebecca, their second daughter, was born at Clifton, July 4th, 1840. Nelson, their eldest son, was born September 17th, 1841. He has removed to California. Peter Suther, their second son, was born December 29th, 1843. He died April 7th, 1868. Jane, their third daughter, was born August 19th, 1846. Minerva, their fourth daughter, was born February 16th, 1849. Kate, their fifth daughter, was born February 13th, 1854, and died May

16th, 1858. William W., their third son, was born March 20th, 1856. Adilbert, their sixth and youngest daughter, was born August 6th, 1861.

Robert, the third son of John B. and Catherine Archibald, was born in Truro January 21st, 1815. He inherits what was his father's farm on Prince Street, Truro. He was married to Margery, daughter of Thomas and Elizabeth Lynds, of Truro, in the year 1840. Melissa, their eldest daughter, was born in Truro April 12th, 1841. She was married to Samuel Nelson in April, 1870. They have one son. Ralph, the eldest son of Robert and Margery Archibald, was born October 14th, 1842. He removed to New Brunswick, and was married there to Miss Lucilla Rogers, in the year 1861. Their children's names are George, Oran, Bessie, Longo and James A. Luther, their second son, was born in Truro December 21st, 1844. He removed to California. James Clark, their third son, was born March 3rd, 1847. Marshall, the fourth son of Robert and Margery Archibald, was born in Truro August 19th, 1849. He was married to Miss Dorcas Elvincent of New Brunswick, December 16th, 1870. Peter McGregor, their fifth son, was born October 23rd, 1851. Ross, their sixth son, was born ———. Daniel, their seventh son, was born May 23rd, 1856. Elizabeth, their second daughter, was born May 30th, 1858. Logan, their eighth son, was born September 24th, 1860. Silas, their ninth son, was born June 15th, 1864.

Isaac Logan, the fourth son of John B. and Catherine Archibald, was born in Truro May 28th, 1817. He was married to Margaret, the third daughter of John J. and Mary Archibald, November 28th, 1840. They removed to New Brunswick shortly after they were married. Joseph Howe, their eldest son, was born in Richmond, N. B., August 20th, 1845. He died March 21st, 1849. Samuel Porter, their second son, was born June 12th, 1849. Irvine, their daughter, was born May 4th, 1851. She died May 23rd, 1866. John James, their third son, was born in Monticello, Me., January 6th, 1856. Alfred, their fourth son, was born in the same place July 26th, 1858. He died May 3rd, 1861. Mary O'Brien, their second daughter, was born in Bloomfield, July 30th, 1862.

Catherine, the third daughter of John B. and Catherine Archibald, was born in Truro, September 4th, 1819. She was married to James A. Logan, of Upper Stewiacke, October 1st, 1844. They had three sons and three daughters. Mr. Logan died September 9th, 1869, and she was married again to Daniel Blair, of North River, October 24th, 1871.

John L., the fifth son of John B., and Catherine Archibald, was born February 1st, 1822. He was married to Jane, second daughter of Thomas and Janet C. Miller, November 17th, 1846. Arthur Allen, their eldest son, was born in Harmony, January 8th, 1849. He was married to Janet, daughter of James Hall of Onslow Mountain, November 8th, 1870. Edward Martin, their second son, was born January 27th, 1851. Isaac, their third son, was born in Harmony March 13th, 1854. Eldridge, their fourth son, was born January 27th, 1857. Thomas Robert, their fifth son, was born September 6th, 1859. Mary Allison, their daughter, was born July 14th, 1862. James Gordon, their sixth son was born June 18th, 1870.

Eliza Jane, the fourth and youngest daughter of John B. and Catherine Archibald, was born in Truro August 30th, 1824. She was married to Adam Logan of Stewiacke, October 28th, 1847. They have three sons and three daughters. They removed to Halifax about the year 1866, where he is now engaged in City Mission work. John B. Archibald died June 2nd, 1855, aged 75 years, and his wife Catherine Hoar died June 23rd, 1860.

Nancy, the eldest daughter of James and Rebecca Archibald, was born in Truro March 15th, 1782. She was married to Samuel, eldest son of John and Nancy Blair, of Onslow, January 25th, 1805. They had three sons and six daughters. She died December 29th, 1857, aged 75 years, and Mr. Blair died October 14th, 1862, aged 80 years.

Samuel Archibald, 3rd, the second son of James and Rebecca, was born in Truro October 14th, 1784. He was married to Elizabeth, the youngest daughter of Matthew and Janet Archibald, February 19th, 1807. He was a very active man and forward in every good cause. He held a commission of the Peace for more than forty years, and was an elder in the Presbyterian Church of Truro for about the same length of time. He purchased the farm on which his two sons now reside, shortly after he was married, and about the year 1815 he built a house, being the same in which his son John E. now resides. Here he spent the remainder of his life. His wife died April 3rd, 1846, aged 60 years. He was married again to Sarah, the eldest daughter of William and Susan Archibald, of Stewiacke, widow of the late Josiah Stewart, of Musquodoboit, in the month of October, 1847. He died April 10th, 1864, in the eightieth year of his age, and his widow died December 28th, 1869, aged 68 years.

Jean Isabella, the eldest daughter of Samuel and Elizabeth Archibald, was born in Truro November 17th, 1807. She died young.

Elizabeth, their second daughter, was born February 3rd, 1810. She was married to Matthew McCurdy, of Onslow, January 1st, 1828. They had five sons and five daughters. They are living at Clifton, Truro. Rev. Edward McCurdy, of New Glasgow, Pictou, is their second son.

James, the eldest son of Samuel and Elizabeth Archibald, was born March 7th, 1812. He was married to Eliza, daughter of the late Robert Harris and Hannah Hoar his wife, December 31st, 1833. He resides at Clifton, and carries on farming extensively. Janet, their daughter, was born February 23rd, 1835. She was married to Alexander, second son of Isaac and Janet Archibald, February 23rd, 1870. They now reside in Sherbrooke, and he is engaged in milling. Robert Harris, the eldest son of James and Eliza Archibald, was born November 16th, 1836. He was married to Mary Jane, daughter of David Clark and Elizabeth Archibald his wife, of the West River of Pictou, January 1st, 1867. Augustus Clark their son, was born at Clifton October 12th, 1867. Mrs. Archibald died November 20th, 1870. Edmond, the second son of Jane and Eliza Archibald, was born December 9th, 1844. Samuel, their third and youngest son, was born January 22nd, 1853. He died October 10th, 1858.

Adams George, the second son of Samuel and Elizabeth Archibald, was born in Truro May 3rd, 1814. He was an active and successful Barrister. He filled the different offices of Registrar, Judge of the Court of Probate, of Solicitor and Attorney General, and was a member of the Government of Nova Scotia. He represented Colchester in Parliament from the year 1851 to the year 1865. He again represented Colchester in Parliament until September, 1867, and was a Delegate to the Colonial Office, London, in 1867. The people of Colchester elected him again to represent them in the House of Commons of the Dominion of Canada, in the year 1869, which he did but for one year. In 1870 he was appointed Governor of Manitoba, and removed there. He has since returned. He was married to Elizabeth, the only daughter of the Rev. John Burnyett, and Lavinia Dickson his wife, June 1st, 1843. Joanna, their eldest daughter, was born May 29th, 1844. George Adams, their only son, was born in Truro May 29th, 1847. On the 19th day of October, 1861, he was gaming in the woods on the island south of the Truro

Cemetery, in company with two other boys, when his gun was accidentally discharged and the contents lodged in his body. In about five hours he died. He was 14 years old. Lilly, the second daughter of A. G. and Elizabeth Archibald, was born November 16th, 1851. Mary Lavinia, their third and youngest daughter, was born September 13th, 1862.

John E., the third son of Samuel and Elizabeth Archibald, was born in Truro April 12th, 1816. He inherits a part of his father's farm, and resides in the house that his father built, about the year 1815. He was married to Martha Dickey of Cornwallis, September 18th, 1845. Frederick William, their only son, was born in Truro, August 23rd, 1854. Jane, the third daughter of Samuel and Elizabeth Archibald, was born in Truro April 7th, 1818. She was married to the Rev. James Bayne, of Pictou Town October 6th, 1846. They have four sons and five daughters.

Isaac N., the fourth son of Samuel and Elizabeth Archibald, was born in Truro September 16th, 1820. He inherits a part of what was his father's farm and was surveyor and commissioner of Crown Lands for the County. He was married to Harriet, the sixth daughter of James McCurdy, and Agnes Archibald, of Onslow, January 28th, 1845. Elizabeth S. their eldest daughter, was born February 21st, 1846. Agnes F., the second daughter of Isaac N. and Harriet Archibald, was born in Truro, August 2nd, 1849. James Melville, their only son, was born April 18th, 1851. Mrs. Archibald died February 4th, 1853. He was married again to Sarah Stiles, of Pictou, June 15th, 1854. Harriet N., their eldest daughter, was born in Truro, April 15th, 1855. Emma, their second daughter, was born January 16th, 1857. Mary Stiles, their third daughter, was, born May 25th, 1859. Charles Adams, their son, was born August 4th, 1862. Mr. Archibald died February 3rd, 1872, aged 51 years.

Rebecca, the fourth daughter of Samuel and Elizabeth Archibald, was born in Truro, January 9th, 1823. She was married to Alexander McDonald, of Sherbrook. They had two sons and four daughters. Mrs. McDonald died September 17th, 1870.

Thomas Logan, the fifth and youngest son of Samuel and Elizabeth Archibald, was born in Truro, March 15th, 1825. He was married to Elizabeth, daughter of the late John Blair, of Onslow Mountain, and Isabella McNutt, his wife, July 25th, 1848. Sarah Ann, the fifth and youngest daughter of Samuel and Elizabeth Archibald, was born December 31st, 1829. She was married to Rupert O'Brien, of

Noel, September 12th, 1855. They have six sons and two daughters. They have removed to Kansas, United States.

James, the third son of James and Rebecca Archibald, was born May 6th, 1786. He was married to Rosannah, daughter of David McKeen and Janet Taylor, his wife, of St. Mary's, in the month of October, 1808. Jane, their eldest daughter, was born in the year 1809. She was married to William Wetherby, and had four sons and six daughters. Rebecca, the second daughter of James and Rosannah Archibald, was born in the month of November, 1810. She was married to Joseph Laughead, of Clifton, January 10th, 1833. James, the only son of James and Rosannah Archibald, was born in the month of November, 1812. He was lame, worked at tailoring, and died a bachelor when about 40 years old. Mrs. Archibald died October 30th, 1814, and he was married again to Hannah, widow of the late Robert Harris, and daughter of Ebenezer and Catherine Hoar, of Onslow, April 11th, 1816. Rosannah, their eldest daughter, was born in Truro, February 27th, 1817. She was married to William Bradley about the year 1842. They removed to St. John, N. B., and then to Boston, Mass. William P., the eldest son of James and Hannah Archibald, was born in Truro, August 6th, 1818. He was married to Phœbe Ann Heustis, of Prince Edward Island, September 21st, 1847. Martha Elizabeth, their eldest daughter, was born June 17th, 1849. Rosannah Bradley, their second daughter, was born in P. E. Island, October 1st, 1851. She was married to Werwick Willis, of Boston, Mass., U. S., April 8th, 1869. Emma, their third daughter, was born May 21st, 1853. She was married to Daniel Holmes, moulder at the Iron Foundry, August 24th, 1871. William Bradley, their eldest son, was born April 12th, 1855. He died November 26th, 1859. Walter P., their second son, was born September 21st, 1858. Herbert H., their third son, was born April 27th, 1861. Anna Kate, their fourth daughter, was born January 21st, 1864. She died February 8th, 1866. Freddy Willis, their fourth son, was born in Truro, February 21st, 1867.

John Harris, the second son of James and Hannah Archibald, was born in Truro, August 18th, 1820. He was married to Rebecca, the eldest daughter of Thomas and Janet C. Miller, January 29th, 1844. Emeline, their daughter, was born July 9th, 1846. Hannah, the second daughter of James and Hannah Archibald, was born June 2nd, 1822. Mary, their third daughter, was born October 9th, 1825. She was married to Robert Bennett, of Shepody, N. B., November 22nd,

1848. They have one daughter. Kate, their fourth daughter, was born in the year 1827. She was married to Robert Stinton, third son of Thomas and Letitia Crowe, of Clifton, January 27th, 1857. She died May 20th, 1864, and her husband died May 7th, 1864. Harriet, the fifth and youngest daughter of James and Hannah Archibald, was born in Truro, December 25th, 1829. She was married to James Crowe, Esq., of Clifton, February 12th, 1850. They have four sons and one daughter.

Asher Black, the third and youngest son of James and Hannah Archibald, was born February 10th, 1832. He was married to Harriet McElhenny, of Londonderry, September 1st, 1852. George Washington, their eldest son, was born July 6th, 1853. Albert R., their second son, was born March 30th, 1855. Everett A. was born August 8th, 1857. Charles E. was born June 13th, 1859. Florence E. was born July 12th, 1862. Kate Crowe, their daughter, was born January 2nd, 1866. William Bradley, their son, was born March 11th, 1869.

Matthew, the fourth son of James and Rebecca Archibald, was born in Truro, February 1st, 1788. He was married to Susannah, daughter of John and Nancy Blair, of Onslow, December 30th, 1813. Sarah Lynds, their eldest daughter, was born December 7th, 1814. She was married to John, son of John and Janet Kent, of the Lower Village of Truro, April 7th, 1835. They had four sons and three daughters. George Frederick, the eldest son of Matthew and Susannah Archibald, was born in Truro, May 2nd, 1817. He was married to ————, in Boston, U. S. Mrs. Archibald died, and he was married again to Anne Moses. Olive, the second daughter of Matthew and Susannah Archibald, was born in Truro, August 2nd, 1820. She was married to Alexander, son of John and Janet Kent, of the Lower Village of Truro. They have four sons and two daughters. Charles B., the second son of Matthew and Susannah Archibald, was born in Truro, May 30th, 1823. He was married to Lophema Kedder, daughter of the late Ezra and Margaret Witter, of Truro, July 9th, 1848. Luther B., their eldest son, was born in Truro, April 12th, 1849. Franklin, their second son, was born January 29th, 1854. Cyrus W., their third son, was born April 27th, 1857. Susan A., their daughter, was born April 5th, 1860. Lophema Amelia, their second daughter, was born December 21st, 1869. Charles B. Archibald is the proprietor of the stage coaches which run daily between Truro and Cumberland. Nancy Blair, the third

daughter of Matthew and Susannah Archibald, was born in Truro,
September 2nd, 1825.   She was married to Robert Chambers, Esq.
They have four sons.   Elizabeth, the fourth and youngest daughter of
Matthew and Susannah Archibald, was born in Truro, July 15th,
1828.   She was married to George, son of William and Nancy Hall.
They had one son.   Mr. Hall died September 20th, 1861, and she
was married again to James Crosscup.   Matthew Archibald died July
24th, 1831, aged 44 years, and his widow died July 29th. 1850.

Letitia, the second daughter of James and Rebecca Archibald, was
born in Truro, July 1st, 1791.   She was married to George Wilson,
of Chiganoise, in the year 1812.   They had two sons and eight
daughters.   She died in the year 1839.   Mr. Wilson died March,
1844.

Robert, the fifth son of James and Rebecca Archibald, was born
March 27th, 1793.   He was married to Margaret Young, who came
from Scotland shortly before, in the year 1819.   Mary Ann, their
eldest daughter, was born in Truro, May 6th, 1820.   She was married
to William, son of John Logan and Anne Johnson, of Upper
Stewiacke, October 11th, 1845.   They have seven sons and two
daughters.   Margaret, the second daughter of Robert and Margaret
Archibald, was born in Truro, August 16th, 1822.   Hannah, their
third danghter, was born October 15th, 1824.   She was married to
Robert McElhenny, of Londonderry, in the month of September,
1862.   They have one son.   John Henderson, their eldest son, was
born in Truro, September 6th, 1826.   He died August 20th, 1829.
John Henderson, the second son of Robert and Margaret Archibald,
was born in Truro, February 23rd, 1830.   He was married to Sarah
Ann, daughter of Adam and Sarah Miller, of Upper Stewiacke, April
5th, 1853.

James, the third son of Robert and Margaret Archibald, was born
in Truro in the year 1832.   He removed for a time to the United
States, and was married there to Mary Rogers, of Salem, Mass.
October 3rd, 1854.   He returned and settled on the Mountain of
Truro, and died there June 20th, 1866, aged 34 years.   Zilpha, their
eldest daughter, was born in Truro, September 10th, 1857.   Frank,
their son, was born March 6th, 1862.   He died at Stewiacke,
November 18th, 1869.   Lucenia, their youngest daughter, was born
June 10th, 1864.   Elizabeth, the fourth daughter of Robert and
Margaret Archibald, was born in Truro February 3rd, 1834.   She
was married to James, son of Andrew Creelman and Susan Johnson,

November 22nd, 1853. They have five sons and three daughters. David Waddell, their fourth and youngest son, was born February 9th, 1837. He was married to Sarah, daughter of Jamas D. and Nancy Baird, of Stewiacke, February 28th, 1865. Teressa, their eldest daughter, was born January 4th, 1866. Erdilla, their second daughter, was born April 30th, 1869. Clarissa Jane, the fifth and youngest daughter of Robert and Margaret Archibald, was born May 14th, 1840. She was married to David A. Baird, of Stewiacke, February 4th, 1863. Mrs. Margaret Archibald died November 12th, 1840, aged 42 years. He was married again to Mary Miller, in the month of November, 1841. They had two sons, but they both died when young. Robert Archibald died February, 1857.

Elizabeth, the third daughter of James and Rebecca Archibald, was born in Truro, March 4th, 1795. She was married to Hugh Logan, of Cumberland County. They had four sons and two daughters.

Alexander, the sixth son of James and Rebecca Archibald, was born October 22nd, 1797. He was married to Ann, the third daughter of William Field (who came out from England but a short time before), March 8th, 1821. Elizabeth, their eldest daughter, was born in Truro, May 18th, 1823. She was married to William, third son of Isaac and Janet Archibald, of Pictou, July 1st, 1844. Their family appears among the descendants of David Archibald, second. William Field, the eldest son of Alexander and Ann Archibald, was born December 22nd, 1825. He was married to Amelia, the second daughter of Thomas and Elizabeth Lynds, of Truro, May 22nd, 1850. Bessie Ann, their eldest daughter, was born in Truro, February 22nd, 1851. Olive Blair, their second daughter, was born December 11th, 1852. Henrietta, the third daughter of William F. and Amelia Archibald, was born in Truro, January 9th, 1855. Wilbert C., their son, was born February 7th, 1859. Addie L., their daughter, was born in Truro, April 1st, 1864.

Thomas, the second son of Alexander and Ann Archibald, was born July 23rd, 1829. He removed to the United States, and died there April 17th, 1854. Henry, their third son, was born in Truro, June 1st, 1832. He removed to the United States when young. He died at Kansas, August 2nd, 1872, aged 40 years. Louisa, their second daughter, was born in Truro, December 17th, 1834. She was married to Rev. Stephen F. Heustice in July, 1861. They have three sons and one daughter.

Edward, the fourth son of Alexander and Ann Archibald, was born in Truro, February 9th, 1838. He was married to Addie Moore, of New Brunswick, December 25th, 1857. They have two sons and three daughters. Jessie Ann, the third and youngest daughter of Alexander and Ann Archibald, was born in Truro, September 4th, 1840.

Rebecca, the fourth daughter of James and Rebecca Archibald, was born June 27th, 1799. She died unmarried, December 4th, 1838, aged 39 years.

David Waddell, the seventh and youngest son of James and Rebecca Archibald, was born September 5th, 1801. He inherits a part of his father's farm, and resides near the place on which his father and grandfather resided. He was married to Jane, the youngest daughter of David and Jane Archibald, of Kemptown, September 25th, 1827. Martha Jane, their eldest daughter, was born March 13th, 1829. She was married to John McGrath, a school teacher, July 15th, 1857. She died without children. Sophia, their second daughter, was born March 21st, 1833. She was married to Isaac W., son of Isaac and Janet Archibald, of Pictou, July 25th, 1857. They had one son and one daughter ; both died young. James Anderson, their eldest son, was born August 15th, 1835. He died when young. Rev. John Howard, their second son, was born in Truro, January 26th, 1838. He studied for the ministry, and removed to Australia, and was settled over the congregation at Euroa Duck Pond, Long-wood, in the year 1870. Isaac Adams, their third son, was born March 14th, 1843. He was married to Eleanor, widow of the late James Blair, of North River, and daughter of James Hall and Jane King, of Onslow Mountain, November 5th, 1867. Lilly Hall, their daughter, was born February 26th, 1870.

Anne Maria, the third and youngest daughter of David W. and Jane Archibald, was born in Truro, August 23rd, 1845. She was married to Joseph Chapman, of Upper Musquodoboit, December 29th, 1863. They have one son and two daughters. Henry Melville, the fourth and youngest son of D. W. and Jane Archibald, was born August 3rd, 1851. Eleanor, the fifth and youngest daughter of James and Rebecca Archibald, was born July 30th, 1803. She was married to Asher Black, of Cumberland County. They had five sons and two daughters.

Nancy, the second daughter of Samuel Archibald, Senr., and Eleanor Taylor, was born in the year 1756, being six years before they came to Nova Scotia. She was married to John, the eldest son of

Matthew Taylor, Senr., and Elizabeth Archibald, his wife. They had four sons and six daughters. They removed to St. Mary's about the year 1802, and died there.

Robert, the fifth son of Samuel Archibald, Senr., and Eleanor Taylor, his wife, was born in New England in the year 1758, four years before they came to Nova Scotia. He was deaf and dumb. He lived with his brother David, at the Middle River of Pictou, where he died a bachelor, June 3rd, 1794, aged 36 years. His body was interred at Middle River, and a stone erected to his memory.

Martha, the fourth daughter of Samuel and Eleanor Archibald, was born in New England in 1760. She was married to John Pratt. They removed to Stewiacke, where they settled and died. They had five sons and three daughters. Margaret, the third daughter of Samuel and Eleanor Archibald, was born in New England in the year 1759. She was married to David Nelson, November 28th, 1775. They lived on the interval of Salmon River,-near the place that Samuel J. Blair now resides. They had four sons and two daughters. Mr. Nelson died August 28th, 1788, and she was married again to Jeremiah Murphy in the month of June, 1789. They had two sons.

Samuel, the sixth and youngest son of Samuel and Eleanor Archibald, was born in the year 1762, shortly before they came to Nova Scotia. He was known by the name of Lame Samuel. He was married to Margaret, the second daughter of Thomas and Janet Archibald, January 13th, 1790. They settled on the farm which John James Archibald afterwards owned, and is now owned by James Johnson. His house stood on the hill on the east side of the Salmon River road. Rachel, their eldest daughter, was born in Truro, September 1st, 1793. She was married to Ephraim Taylor, of St. Mary's, in the year 1824. They had four sons and one daughter. She died in the month of October, 1865. Samuel, the eldest son of Samuel and Margaret Archibald, was born in the year 1795. He died a bachelor, June, 1821. Margaret, their second daughter, was born June 15th, 1797. She was married to Peter Grant, November 3rd, 1828. They had four sons and one daughter. She died March 15th, 1866. Martha, their third daughter, was born in the year 1799. She died unmarried, January 15th, 1868. Thomas, their second son, was born May, 1806. He was married to Margaret McKinlay, January 15th, 1828. They are now residing up the Salmon River, about a mile above Alexander S. Hingley's, in Kemptown. Mary

Jane, the eldest daughter of Thomas and Margaret Archibald, was born March, 1831. She was married to Jacob Fenton, February, 1852. They have four sons and four daughters. Samuel, the eldest son of Thomas and Margaret Archibald, was born 1834. Isabell, their second daughter, was born 1836. Charles, their second son, was born April, 1840. He was married to Lucy Campbell, of Westchester Mountain, March, 1870. Eleanor and Margaret, their twin daughters, were born October, 1842. David, the third and youngest son, was born October, 1846.

David Archibald, tenth, the second son of Samuel and Margaret Archibald, was born December 16th, 1808. He was married to Sarah Hammond, February 6th, 1832. Miriam, their eldest daughter, was born April 28th, 1835. She removed to the United States. Charles, the eldest son of David, tenth, and Sarah Archibald, was born January 12th, 1837. He was married to Margaret, daughter of Asa and Margaret Hoar, of Onslow Mountain, January 1st, 1863. Martha, their eldest daughter, was born December 16th, 1863. Alexander, their eldest son, was born in the month of March, 1855. Sarah, their second daughter, was born in the month of October, 1866. Samuel Matthew, the second son of David, tenth, and Sarah Archibald, was born January 29th, 1839. He was married to Rebecca Sarah, daughter of John McDonald and Rebecca Archibald, his wife, April 28th, 1863. John H., their eldest son, was born in the month of March, 1864. Sarah, their eldest daughter, was born in the month of March, 1866. Alexander James, their second son, was born October 16th, 1868. Sarah Jane, the second daughter of David, tenth, and Sarah Archibald, was born June 18th, 1841. She was married to Hopkin McNutt, of North River. They have one son and one daughter. John S., the third son of David, tenth, and Sarah Archibald, was born October 14th, 1843. He was married to Mary Jane, daughter of David T. and Eleanor Archibald, July 25th, 1865. Agnes, their eldest daughter, was born October 28th, 1865. Alexander, their son, was born in the month of May, 1867. Sarah, their second daughter, was born June 15th, 1870. Esther, the third daughter of David, tenth, and Sarah Archibald, was born April 6th, 1846. She was married to Thomas McKenzie, April 24th, 1863. They have two sons and one daughter. Alexander, their fourth and youngest son, was born June 15th, 1848. Margaret, the first wife of Samuel Archibald, second, died January 15th, 1809, and he was married again to Nancy Clayton, April 18th, 1810. About this time he removed to St. Mary's, where he died May 15th, 1833.

Matthew, the eldest son of Samuel and Nancy Archibald, was born March 18th, 1811. He was married to Louisa Miles. They had a daughter, Isabell, and a son, Henry. They removed to the United States, and he died there, February 11th, 1871.

Henry C., the second son of Samuel and Nancy Archibald, was born May 1st, 1813. He was married to Caroline Bradshaw, January 5th, 1833. Samuel Thomas, their eldest son, was born January 15th, 1834. He was married to Margery McBain, August 12th, 1855. William Henry, their eldest son, was born August 3rd, 1857. Alexander Thomas, their second son, was born March 28th, 1859. James George, their third son, was born October 8th, 1862. John Hugh, their fourth son, was born November 2nd, 1864. Annabel, the eldest daughter of Henry C. and Caroline Archibald, was born in the year 1836. She was married to Angus McLain, in the year 1861, and died in the month of August, 1862. Eliza, their second daughter was born 1838. She was married to Alexander Sutherland 1857. They have three sons and two daughters. Elmira, their third daughter, was married to Donald McInnis. They have two sons and three daughters. Alexander, the second son of Henry C. and Caroline Archibald, was born March 16th, 1841. He has removed to the United States. Ephraim Howard, their third son, was married to Anne Flake, August 1st, 1870. Margaret Jane, their fourth daughter, was married to Henry Taylor. They have two daughters. Charlotte, their fifth daughter, was married to Samuel Flake, August 1st, 1870. Robert, their fourth son, was born in the month of June, 1851. Caroline, their sixth daughter, was born ——. Catherine Eleanor, their seventh daughter, was born ——.

Charles, the third son of Samuel, second, and Nancy Archibald, was born June 12th, 1816. He was married to Miriam, daughter of Asa Daniels and Miriam Hoar, his wife, June 3rd, 1836. Asa, their eldest son, was born October 8th, 1837. He was married to Lavinia McLain, of Folly River, October, 1857. George Robert, their eldest son, was born at the Folly River, September 18th, 1858. Mary Elizabeth, their eldest daughter, was born August 8th, 1861. Charles Francis, their second son, was born October, 1863. Samuel McLain, their third son, was born April 16th, 1867. Susan Amelia, was born December 26th, 1869. Eleanor, the eldest daughter of Charles and Miriam Archibald, was born in Truro, February 6th,

7

1840. Miriam, their second daughter, was born February 20th, 1842. Margaret, their third daughter, was born April 25th, 1844. Samuel, their second son, was born April 8th, 1846. Mary, their fourth daughter, was born April 10th, 1848. David, their third son, was born March 25th, 1853. Nancy, their fifth daughter, was born February 3rd, 1855. Julia, their sixth daughter, was born December 30th, 1855. Charles, their youngest son, was born February 25th, 1858. Eleanor, the only daughter of Samuel and Nancy Archibald, was born May 6th, 1819. She was married to Robert Hingley, of Kemptown, June 18th, 1841. They have two sons and five daughters.

Ephraim, the fourth son of Samuel and Nancy Archibald, was born August 14th, 1821. He was married to Margaret McLain, March 17th, 1841. John Henry, their eldest son, was born in the year 1842. He removed to the United States. Eleanor, the eldest daughter of Ephraim and Margaret Archibald, was born in the year 1844. Oscar Wellington, the second son of Ephraim and Margaret Archibald, was born in 1848. He removed to the United States, and was married to S. A. Stevens, May 18th, 1871, and he is now practising as M. D. in Iowa. Mary, their second daughter, was born in the year 1850. She was married to James Duncan in the year 1867. They have two daughters. Matilda, the third daughter of Ephraim and Margaret Archibald, was born in the year 1856. Sabrina, their daughter, was born in the year 1858.

James, a twin son of Samuel, second, and Nancy Archibald, was born August 24th, 1826. He was married to Abigail, daughter of James Whidden and Hannah Johnson, his wife, January 8th, 1847. Henry, their eldest son, was born November 3rd, 1847. He was married to Joanna M., daughter of Benjamin Lynds, of North River, December 30th, 1868. Leonard Read, their son, was born October 20th, 1869. Samuel James, the second son of James and Abigail Archibald, was born September 8th, 1849. He was married to Minerva, daughter of Samuel McLaughland, Esq., of Economy, July 10th, 1871. Eliza, the eldest daughter of James and Abigail Archibald, was born February 10th, 1858. Susan Catherine, the second daughter, was born September 24th, 1862. Hannah, their third daughter, was born April 13th, 1864. James Archibald died at North River, June 4th, 1871. Alexander, the other twin son of Samuel and Nancy Archibald, was married to Nancy, daughter of John McDonald and Rebecca Archibald, his wife, March 3rd, 1852. John, their eldest son, was born November 14th, 1853. Rebecca, their eldest daughter, was born March 7th, 1862. Isabell, their second daughter, was born June 2nd, 1868. Caroline Louisa was born July 30th, 1871.

Samuel Philip, the seventh and youngest son of Samuel and Nancy Archibald, was born August 14th, 1831. He was married to Frances Sarah, daughter of Charles Wallace and Clara Emeline Godfrey, his wife, September 19th, 1853. Elisha Godfrey, their eldest son, was born March 30th, 1856. Alexander Lewis, their second son, was born February 17th, 1858. Samuel Charles, their third son, was born November 16th, 1859. Louisa Eleanor, their daughter, was born March 19th, 1862. Clara Isabell, their second daughter, was born May 15th, 1864.

Elizabeth, the fifth daughter of Samuel Archibald, Senr., and Eleanor Taylor, his wife, was born in Truro, January 14th, 1764. She died unmarried. Eleanor, the youngest daughter of Samuel and Eleanor Archibald, was born in Truro, January 23rd, 1768. She was married to Robert Morrison. They had two sons and three daughters. They removed to the United States.

James Archibald, the third brother of the four Archibald's who came to Nova Scotia together in the year 1762, was a Grantee of Truro Township. His front land was on the North side of Salmon River. He was among the first settlers of Middle Stewiacke, and obtained a grant of 500 acres of land lying on the East side of Simeon Whidden's land. On this land he settled, and lived for a considerable length of time. He sold out to George Scott, of Truro. Scott gave the farm to his two grandsons, George Scott Rutherford and William Rutherford, Esq., and it is now owned by their sons and grandsons. James Archibald was married and had some family before they came to Truro. They had one son and six daughters. Rebecca, their daughter, was born December 23rd, 1761. She was married to Matthew, son of Matthew Taylor and Elizabeth Archibald, February 6th, 1783. They had four sons and one daughter before they left Truro. They removed to Ohio, United States.

Hannah, another daughter of this James Archibald, was married to John Cummings. They had six sons and five daughters. John Cummings, their son, was married to Letitia, the eldest daughter of Alexander Barnhill and Alice Hunter, his wife. They had eight sons and two daughters. James Cummings removed to Manchester. Matthew enlisted and left Truro about the year 1811, and never returned. David Cummings, their fourth son, learned the mason trade with Mr. James Drysdale. He married and settled in London derry, where he died, September, 1870. Daniel Cummings, their fifth son, was married to Margaret McDougall, widow of the late William McElhenney, of Londonderry. They had four sons and one daughter. They are both living yet in Onslow. William Cummings, their youngest son, removed to New Brunswick. Joanna Cummings, their daughter, was married to William Rude, and had a family of children. Eleanor Cummings was married to George Goodwin. He enlisted and left Truro the same time that Matthew Cummings left. Rebecca Cummings, their third daughter, was married to Matthew James Archibald, and had a large family. Rachel Cummings was married to John Kenty, at the Grand Lake, and had a family of children. Hannah Cummings was married to Mr. Jinkens, of Shubenacadie River.

Elizabeth, another daughter of this James Archibald, was married to Mr. McElhenney. Another daughter was married to William Long, and removed to Ohio, United States. Another of their daughters was married to Richard Sudicks. They removed to Ohio, United States. Another of their daughters was married to Adam Boyd. She died May 15th, 1790. Mr. Boyd was married again to Mary, daughter of James and Elizabeth Johnson.

David Archibald, sixth, or David Morris Archibald, was the only son of this James Archibald. He was married to Rachel, the eldest daughter of James Archibald, second, and Margaret Fisher, in the year 1798. Margaret, the eldest daughter of David M. and Rachel Archibald, was born early in the year 1799. She was married to David Dean, of Musquodoboit, April 4th, 1815. They had four sons and seven daughters. She died March 1851, aged 52 years. Ruth, the second daughter of David M. and Rachel Archibald, was born in the year 1801. She was married to Barnabas Lynds, of North River, October, 1818. They had three sons and five daughters. She died November 18th, 1853, aged 52 years. Rebecca, their third daughter, was born in the year 1803. She died unmarried. David M. Archibald and his wife both died while their three daughters were very young.

Thomas Archibald was the youngest of the four brothers who emigrated from the North of Ireland to New England, and thence to Truro, Nova Scotia. He came in company with his brothers and their wives and families, also with his three sisters and their families. Elizabeth, his sister, was married to Matthew Taylor, Senr. Eleanor

Archibald was married to William Fisher, and Martha Archibald was married to Samson Moore. Thomas Archibald was born in Ireland in the year 1733. He was married to Janet Orr, about the year 1757. He settled on the interval North of Salmon River, on the same farm that was owned afterwards by his son, David Archibald, fourth, and by David's son, John. John's son, Richard Archibald, now resides upon the same farm, near the River bridge, by Charles D. Upham's. On this farm he reared his family, and spent the remainder of his life. His first wife, Janet Orr, died March 13th, 1784, aged 51 years. He was married again to Elizabeth Long, widow of the late James Faulkener, of the Lower Village of Truro, July 15th, 1785. He died June 27th, 1796, aged 63 years, and his widow died about the year 1822. Eleanor, the eldest daughter of Thomas and Janet Archibald, was born about the year 1760. She was married to David Taylor about the year 1783. Her family appears among the Taylors.

John, the eldest son of Thomas and Janet Archibald, was born about the year 1758, four years before they came to Nova Scotia. He was married to Mary, daughter of Robert and Agnes Hamilton, about the year 1784. He was known by the name of Long John. He made an attempt to settle at Brookfield, but soon left, and was one of the first settlers in Upper Stewiacke. He was one of the eight who went to Stewiacke to settle in the spring of the year 1784, and their twin sons were the first deaths in Stewiacke. At this early date was the place fixed upon for a public Cemetery, and these were the first who were buried in it. The funeral took place on March 8th, 1786. The farm that Mr. Archibald settled on lies on the South side of the River, opposite the Presbyterian Church. Here he spent the remainder of his life, and died September 1st, 1832. His wife died in Brookfield, August 20th, 1847. They had four sons and four daughters, who lived to grow up. Their sons Robert and John both died bachelors. David, their son, was married to Catherine Munro. They had four sons and two daughters; their names are Robert, David, Thomas, Hector, Catherine and Nancy. This family have all left the country. Mary, the daughter of John and Mary Archibald, was married to John Boomer, of Brookfield, and had five sons and four daughters. Ann, the daughter of John and Mary Archibald, was married to Hantz, son of John and Elizabeth Hamilton, of Brookfield. They settled at Pembroke, Upper Stewiacke. Nancy, the daughter of John and Mary Archibald, died unmarried. Janet, their daughter, was married to John Power, and had two sons and three daughters

William Archibald, their son, was married to Nancy McQuinn, and is settled in New Annan.

David Archibald fourth, the second son of Thomas and Janet, was born on board the vessel in which they came from New England, December 13th, 1762. He was married to Esther, daughter of Charles and Eleanor Cox, February 14th, 1788. He inherited his father's farm. Thomas, their eldest son, was born October 7th, 1788. Nancy, their eldest daughter, was born in Truro, April 23rd, 1795. She was married to Henry, son of John Christie and Nancy Denny, March 12th, 1818. They have two sons and four daughters. Charles, the second son of David and Esther Archibald, was born in Truro, October, 1791. He was married to Martha Stewart, of Halifax, March 12th, 1815, and shortly after this they removed from Truro to Country Harbor, where he carried on a considerable business, was Justice of the Peace, and remained there during the remainder of his life. He died in May, 1852, aged 61 years. They had one son, whose name is John Steel Archibald. He was born December 25th, 1815. He was married to Isabell Liswell. He resides in Halifax, and follows the sea occasionally. Charles Archibald's wife, Martha, died shortly after she had her first son, and he was married again to Margaret Stewart, about the year 1827. David, their eldest son, was born May 5th, 1830. He was killed in Wisconsin, April 30th, 1850, in the twentieth year of his age. The following is from the " Watertown Chronicle," Jefferson County, Wis. :—

" Beaver Dam, March 1, 1850.

"FRIEND HADLEY,—Permit me, through the columns of your paper, to return the warmest thanks of the mourners of a beloved brother, to those who kindly attended the funeral of my brother, David Archibald, who lately met with a sudden death. Yesterday morning he was as strong in health and life as he ever was, but about 9 o'clock, a. m., he was taken from life's circle in a moment of time. They were raising a mill about eight miles from this village, and in the act of raising one of the bents, they had attached to the end of the takle a log chain, so that, if needed, a pair of oxen could be used. However, they had it nearly secured, when it is supposed the deceased took hold of the wrong part of the rope, and unwound it from the stump to which it was made fast, and sooner than thought, it went, carrying him in an instant about five rods—dashing his head and breast against the lower part of the mill. He never moved, but only gave a few faint breathings. It is supposed that the hook on the chain caught his right arm, as it was torn though above the elbow and broken. The Sons of Temperance turned out in procession, numbering about 42, some of them coming ten miles at a moment's warning, to bestow the last kind offices to a young brother of the order. The whole was conducted by our respected W. P., Henry W. Finch, in a solemn and respectable manner. And I can do no other than to say, in the midst of grief we were surrounded by all kindness and love. Our meeting house was crowded, and our devoted pastor, Rev. A. Montgomery, addressed us from xxvii Prov. 1st v. I therefore trust that the deep interest felt on our part by the truly worthy citizens of Beaver Dam, may never be erased from our hearts. And it would have done your heart good to have seen the sons of the division, old men and sires, wearing the badge of respect for a brother. Oh! may they be an ornament to their sex and a beacon to the injured, and so walk worthy of their order below, that finally we may all meet together around the throne of our God, through the precious blood of our Lord and Savior Jesus Christ, is the fervent desire of their brother and ever humble Servant, M. SELLARS."

Isabell, their eldest daughter, was born February, 1828. She was married to Mr. Sellars. They removed to the United States. Charles, their second son, was born August 9th, 1836. Henry, their third son, was born September 12th, 1838. Martha, their youngest daughter, was born in June, 1840. She was married to Robert Murray, of Halifax. Lewis, the youngest son, was born January 30th, 1843.

David Archibald, ninth, the third son of David and Esther Archibald, was born in Truro, February, 1793. He was married to Rebecca, daughter of George Spencer and Rebecca Denny, his wife, November 4th, 1818. Matilda, their eldest daughter, was born in Truro, December 25th, 1819. She was married to Alexander M. Baird, of Onslow, February 29th, 1848. They have one son and one daughter. Jane, the second daughter of David and Rebecca Archibald, was born March 2nd, 1821. She was married to Peter Cameron, of Lochbroom, Pictou, October 30th, 1848. They have three sons and four daughters. Alexander Hanley, the eldest son of David and Rebecca Archibald, was born October 14th, 1822. He was married to Esther, daughter of Jacob Lynds and Eleanor Archibald, his wife, April 13th, 1853. Blanchard, their eldest son, was born in Truro, March 29th, 1854. Rebecca, their eldest daughter, was born May

13th, 1856. Eleanor, their second daughter, was born October 7th, 1857. George, their second son, was born April 9th, 1859. Jacob, their third son, was born December 14th, 1863. Allen, their fourth son, was born December 4th, 1865. He died July 23rd, 1867. Jane, their third daughter, was born August 16th, 1868. Martha, their fourth daughter, was born August 16th, 1870. George, the second son of David and Rebecca Archibald, was born in the year 1825. He died a bachelor, April 4th, 1852, aged 27 years. Nancy, the third daughter of David and Rebecca Archibald, was born in the month of January, 1828. She was married to Alexander Kent, third, August 10th, 1854. They had two sons and five daughters. Mrs. Kent died March 4th, 1866. Mary, the fourth daughter of David and Rebecca Archibald, was born in Truro, September 13th, 1830. She was married to Henry, son of the late William Cotton and Nancy Baird, his wife, October 15th, 1856. They have one son and one daughter. Catherine, their fifth daughter, was born September 21st, 1832. Esther, their sixth daughter, was born September 27th, 1837. She was married to Matthew, son of Matthew and Elizabeth Taylor, March 24th, 1868. They have one daughter. Alice, the second daughter of David and Esther Archibald, was born in Truro in the month of February, 1797. She was married to John Ryan July 2nd, 1820. They had one son and two daughters. John Ryan, their son, has been a Conductor on the cars since they first ran to Truro.

John, the fourth and youngest son of David and Esther Archibald, was born March 8th, 1799. He was married to Nancy, the youngest daughter of John Christie and Nancy Denny, April 16th, 1832. Henry, their eldest son, was born August 19th, 1833. He died October 5th, 1834. Nancy Christie, their eldest daughter, was born November 4th, 1836. She was married to James Pitblado, August 18th, 1863. They have one son and one daughter. Charles Henry, the second son of John and Nancy Archibald, was born August 8th, 1839. He is in California. Esther, their second daughter, was born February 15th, 1842. She was married to Hugh McDormond, November 30th, 1869. Richard the third and youngest son of John and Nancy Archibald, was born in Truro July 15th, 1844. He was married to Eleanor, second daughter of Charles and Jane Christie, December 18th, 1872. Sarah, their youngest daughter, was born September 22nd, 1846. David Archibald, fourth, died July 11th, 1830, aged 68 years, and his wife, Esther Cox, died November 13th, 1837, aged 73 years.

Rebecca, wife of David Archibald, ninth, died July 15th, 1870. John, son of David and Esther Archibald, died August 23rd, 1869, aged 70 years. Martha, the third daughter of David and Esther Archibald, was born October 17th, 1801. She was married to Jonathan Blanchard, November 2nd, 1837. They had one son and one daughter; they both died young. Mr. Blanchard died May 31st, 1843, and his widow was married again to Isaac Logan, December 5th, 1854. Mr. Logan died March 11th, 1872, aged 87 years. Eleanor, the youngest daughter of David and Esther Archibald, was born September 15th, 1804. She was married to Jacob Lynds, March 12th, 1828. They had one son and four daughters.

William, the third son of Thomas and Janet Archibald, was born in Truro, March 4th, 1765. He was married to Martha Denny, of Londonderry, February 17th, 1791. He settled on the farm on which James Johnson now resides. He then removed to the farm that his grandson, John C. Archibald, now lives upon, about the year 1812. Here he spent the remainder of his life, and died in the month of July, 1836, and his wife died December 11th, 1858. Janet, their eldest daughter, was born in Truro, July 27th, 1795. She was married to William McDonald, of Pictou. They had two sons and two daughters. William, the eldest son of William and Martha Archibald, was born in Truro, January 22nd, 1798. He died a bachelor, April 24th, 1859. John D., their second son, was born December 15th, 1799. He died when he was young. Rebecca, their second daughter, was born March 15th, 1801. She died when she was young. David Taylor, the second son of William and Matthew Archibald, was born in Truro, May 19th, 1802. He was married to Eleanor, the only daughter of Thomas Taylor and Lucy Hoar, his wife, August 13th, 1830. They settled on the farm which was owned by her father, Thomas Taylor, where they reared their family and spent the remainder of their lives. He died January 12, 1862, aged 59 years, and his wife died April 1st, 1854, aged 46 years. Nancy, their eldest daughter, was born in Truro, November 18th, 1830. She was married to Alexander L., eldest son of S. G. W. and Susan Archibald, September 27th, 1859. They have two daughters. Martha, the second daughter of David T. and Eleanor Archibald, was born in Truro, February 20th, 1832. Lucy, their third daughter, was born April 18th, 1834. She was married to David, the only son of Jacob and Eleanor Lynds, May 6th, 1857. William F., the only son of David T. and Eleanor Archibald, was born in Truro May 1st,

1836. He was married to Catherine Carlyle, of Onslow Mountain, September 21st, 1865. Lucy Eleanor, their eldest daughter, was born in Truro, June 28th, 1866. Clara, their second daughter, was born December 23rd, 1867. Susan Elmira, their third daughter was born in Truro, August 2nd, 1870. Susan, the fourth daughter of David T. and Eleanor Archibald, was born January 29th, 1840. She died unmarried, November 17th, 1863, aged 23 years. Mary Jane, their fifth daughter, was born July 14th, 1844. She was married to John S., son of David Archibald, tenth, July 25th, 1865. Olivia, their sixth and youngest daughter, was born in Truro, November 22nd, 1849. She was married to William Alexander Miller, December 18th, 1872. Isaac, the youngest son of William and Martha Archibald, was born April 19th, 1805. He was married to Rebecca, daughter of John D. and Margaret Christie, November 17th, 1836. John C. their eldest son was born February 25th, 1837. He was married to Isabell, daughter of John and Susan Creelman, of Stewiacke, in the month of May, 1867. Martha, eldest daughter of Isaac and Rebecca Archibald. was born in Truro, August 6th, 1839. She was married to William Dickson, of Onslow Mountain, December 31st, 1859. They have two daughters and one son. Jessie, the second daughter of Isaac and Rebecca Archibald, was born April 10th, 1841. She died February 10th, 1864, aged 23 years. Margaret, their third daughter, was born February 13th, 1844. She was married to John Yorston, of New Brunswick, 1866. They have three sons. William, the second son of Isaac and Rebecca Archibald, was born November 11th, 1845. Eleanor, their fourth daughter, was born October 10th, 1847. Janet, their fifth daughter, was born January 24th, 1852. Andrew Christie, their third and youngest son, was born July 31st, 1854. Nancy, the third daughter of William and Martha Archibald, was born August 27th, 1808. On September 1st, 1871, she took her dinner in good health, and in about two hours she died. Mary, their fourth and youngest daughter, was born October 12th, 1811.

Margaret, the second daughter of Thomas and Janet Archibald, was born in Truro, August 13th, 1767. She was married to Samuel, the youngest son of Samuel Archibald, Senr., and Eleanor Taylor, his wife, January 13th, 1790. She had three sons and three daughters. She died January 15th, 1809, aged 42 years. Janet, the third daughter of Thomas and Janet Archibald, was born in Truro, March 22nd, 1769. She was married to Alexander Cameron, of Pictou.

They had six sons and one daughter. Elizabeth, their fourth daughter, was born April 21st, 1771. She was married to John Hamilton, October 27th, 1796. They had five sons and three daughters. They settled in Brookfield, where she died, February 8th, 1831, aged 60 years, and Mr. Hamilton died July 1st, 1835, aged 67 years. Their bodies were interred in the Truro Cemetery.

Martha, the fifth daughter of Thomas and Janet Archibald, was born May 15th, 1774. She was married to William Blackie, of the Green Hill of Pictou. She died shortly after they were married.

Rachel, the sixth and youngest daughter of Thomas and Janet Archibald, was born in Truro, June 10th, 1777. She was married to George Dill, of Londonderry, May 3rd, 1804. Mr. Dill removed to Truro, and purchased James Wright's front wood lot, and built his house on the hill where Mr. Richard Upham now resides. Here he spent the remainder of his life. He was the school teacher of the Village for about twenty-five years. Afterwards he was Registrar of Deeds and Prothonotary of the Supreme Court. These offices he held until a short time before his death. Janet, their daughter, was born in Truro, December 4th, 1806. Rachel, their second daughter, was born April 17th, 1811. She died in the month of September, 1811. Mrs. Dill died May 7th, 1811, aged 34 years. He was married again to Rosannah, the eldest daughter of Michael Tucker and Mary Moore, his wife, January 31st, 1815. Robert, their eldest son, was born December 29th, 1815. He died of consumption, December 25th, 1842, aged 27 years. Rachel, their daughter, was born March 29th, 1817. She died of consumption, November, 1847. William Hill, their second son, was born February 12th, 1819. He started to go to Boston for the benefit of his health, and was lost in the ill-fated brigantine " Enterprise." Mary, their second daughter, was born in Truro, July 17th, 1820. She was married to William, son of Thomas McCollum and Janet Logan, his wife, of Musquodoboit, November 22nd, 1838. They had five sons and eight daughters. Catherine, the third daughter of George and Rosannah Dill, was born in Truro, March 14th, 1822. She was married to John Smith, second son of William C. Eaton and Lucy Smith, his wife, December 17th, 1850. They had three sons and three daughters. Mr. Eaton died June 5th, 1865, aged 37 years. His widow died February 22nd, 1872. Margaret, their fourth daughter, was born December 27th, 1823. She was married to Samuel J. Fulton, of Bass River, October, 1860. They have three sons. George Dill, their third son, was born

February 12th, 1828. He died of consumption, December 22nd, 1845. Rosannah, their fifth and youngest daughter, was born October 23rd, 1832. She was married to George Gunn, June 15th, 1853. They had two sons and three daughters. Mrs. Gunn died in March, 1866, aged 34 years, and Mr. Gunn was married again to Emma Clark, October 24th, 1868. Mr. Dill died January 4th, 1854, aged 77 years. Mrs. Dill died January, 1853, aged 66 years.

CHAPTER VI.

Matthew Taylor, Senr., came from New England to Nova Scotia, in company with his brothers-in-law, Messrs. Archibald, and others, who arrived at Fort Belcher December 13th, 1762. He was born in Londonderry, N. H., October 30th, 1727. He was married to Elizabeth Archibald before they came to Nova Scotia. He was one of the Grantees of Truro Township, and had his front land lying between Isaac N. Archibald's and the South line of Onslow. His house stood on the hill west of John E. Archibald's house. Here he reared a numerous family. He died at the house of Mr. David Dickey, on the Halifax road, south side of Stewiacke River, when he was on his way to Halifax. He died January 22nd, 1796, aged 68 years. His widow was taken by her sons to St. Mary's, and died there about the year 1810. She was buried on a small Island in the Lake, a short distance up the East River of St. Mary's, above the forks.

John Taylor, their eldest son, was born in New Hampshire, June 2nd, 1752, and was brought by his parents to Truro, when he was ten years old. His name is among the grantees of the Township, although he was only in his fourteenth year at the time. His front lot was adjoining his father's land, and he inherited his father's farm. About the year 1802 he sold his farm in Truro, and removed to St. Mary's, and settled on an interval farm at the forks, being the same on which the Rev. Mr. Pitblado and the Messrs. Archibald now reside. In the year 1812 he sold his farm there to Alexander M. Archibald, and removed up the East River, and died there. He was married to Nancy, the eldest daughter of Samuel Archibald, Senr., and Eleanor Taylor, his wife. They had three sons and five daughters.

James, the second son of Matthew and Elizabeth Taylor, was born in New Hampshire in the year 1754, and was brought by his parents to Truro when eight years old. He was married to Rebecca Bartlett. They removed to Majorfield, New Brunswick, and carried on farming there very extensively. He had his barn so constructed that he could unload a ton of hay from his cart into the mow in a minute and a half.

Matthew, the third son of Matthew and Elizabeth Taylor, was born in New Hampshire June 28th, 1755, seven years before they came to Truro. He was married to Rebecca, daughter of James Archibald, Senr., February 6th, 1783. John Archibald, their eldest son, was born in Truro February 9th, 1784. James, their second son, was born February 19th, 1786. Matthew, their third son, was born June 16th, 1787. David, their fourth son, was born October 22nd, 1788. Elizabeth, their daughter, was born March 2nd, 1790. Mr. Taylor settled on the farm on which the late John D. Christie lived and died. He had a Saw Mill about half a mile up the brook. He and his family removed to Ohio, United States, about the year 1792.

David, the fifth son of Matthew and Elizabeth Taylor, was born about the year 1760. He was settled on the farm on which William T. Archibald now resides. On January 15th, 1799, when he was chopping in the woods, a large limb fell from the tree and struck him on the head. He was found dead. He was married to Eleanor Archibald in the year, 1783. Janet, their eldest daughter, was born in Truro, August 19th, 1784. She was married to Adam McKeen, of St. Mary's, August 15th, 1805. They had four sons and four daughters. Thomas, the eldest son of David and Eleanor Taylor, was born April 26th, 1786. He inherited his father's farm, and was married to Lucy, daughter of Ebenezer and Catherine Hoar, of Onslow, October 6th, 1807. Their only daughter, Eleanor, was born August 3rd, 1808. She was married to David T. Archibald, and had one son and six daughters. On the 3rd of January, 1809, Thomas Taylor and his brother Matthew were in the woods together. In chopping down a tree it fell upon Thomas and killed him. Matthew ran home with the sad tidings to his wife. She ran, with her child, five months old, in her arms, and was the first on the spot. She removed the hat, in which was the brains of her husband. The scene may be more easily imagined than described. His widow was married again to David, the second son of William and Ann McKeen, and they had two sons and one daughter. Elizabeth, the second daughter of David and Eleanor Taylor, was born in Truro, July 31st, 1788. She was married to William, son of Gavin Johnson. William

Johnson built the house, and lived in it some time, which is now owned by John Hattie, of Salmon River. He removed to Ohio, United States, about the year 1815. Matthew, the youngest son of David and Eleanor Taylor, was born in Truro, May 29th, 1791. He was married to Elizabeth, daughter of Ebenezer and Catherine Hoar, of Onslow, April 1st, 1813. Eleanor, their eldest daughter, was born in Truro, April 18th, 1814. She was married to William McLeod, of Bible Hill, May 21st, 1855. Susan, their second daughter, was born October 27th, 1818. She was married to Charles Blackie, of New Annan, October 22nd, 1844. They had three sons and one daughter. She died March 27th, 1859. Thomas, the eldest son of Matthew and Elizabeth Taylor, was born June 16th, 1821. He was married to Susan, daughter of Benjamin Lynds, of North River, March 27th, 1863. George L., their eldest son, was born in Truro, December 31st, 1863. Thomas B., their second son, was born March 27th, 1865. Catherine, the third daughter of Matthew and Elizabeth Taylor, was born October 10th, 1824. James, their second son, was born April 2nd, 1829. He was married to Elizabeth Watson, November 16th, 1854. They had one son. Mrs. Taylor died January 19th, 1856, and he was married again to Margaret Miller, of New Annan, February 23rd, 1864. Matthew, the youngest son of Matthew and Elizabeth Taylor, was born May 27th, 1831. He was married to Esther, daughter of David Archibald 9th, and Rebecca Spencer, his wife, March 24th, 1868. Bessie, their daughter, was born January 5th, 1869. Eleanor, the youngest daughter of David and Eleanor Taylor, was born in Truro May 2nd, 1796. She was married to Charles Hall of Halifax. They had one son and one daughter. Mr. Hall died some time ago, and she was married again to Martin Murphy of Maitland. Margaret, daughter of Matthew Taylor, Senr., and Elizabeth Archibald, was born in Truro July 12th, 1763, being the next summer after they came to Nova Scotia. She died young.

Samuel, the sixth son of Matthew Taylor, Senr., and Elizabeth Archibald, was born in Truro February 17th, 1765. He was married, and had a family of children. He was one of the eight who settled first in Upper Stewiacke in the spring of the year 1784. Shortly after, he removed to Ohio, United States. Robert, the fourth son of Matthew and Elizabeth Taylor, was born in New Hampshire about the year 1757, and was brought by his parents to Nova Scotia in December, 1762. He was married to Mehetabel Wilson of Chiganoise December 6th, 1781 ; they had two sons and three daughters. He bought the mill which stood then between the North River bridge and James McNutt's shop, from Simeon Howard (who first built it). He afterwards sold out and removed to Ohio, United States.

Archibald, the seventh son of Matthew and Elizabeth Taylor, was born in Truro December 28th, 1766. He was married to Jane, the eldest daughter of William and Mary Blair of North River. She died shortly after they were married. He removed to St. Mary's and was married again to Mary McDonald of Pictou ; they had three sons and two daughters. He died suddenly, at St. Mary's, about the year 1837, aged 70 years. Elizabeth, the second daughter of Matthew and Elizabeth Taylor, was born in Truro February 28th, 1769. She was married to Gain, son of Richard Bartlett ; they had one son and one daughter. Gain Bartlett was born in Truro, June 28th, 1764 ; he was married, and had two children. When driving home a load of wood one day, he fell from the sled in front of the runner. The team stopped, and when he was found the sled was on his body, and he was dead.

William, the eighth and youngest son of Matthew and Elizabeth Taylor, was born in Truro November 7th, 1771. He was married to Margaret, daughter of Alexander McCurdy of Onslow ; they had one son and three daughters. Mrs. Taylor died when her children were all young. Their son's name was Daniel Taylor. He was married to a daughter of William Lynds of North River, and had a family of children. They•removed to Illinois, United States, about the year 1835. Elizabeth, the daughter of William and Margaret Taylor, was married to Robert Blair of North River. Her family appears among the Blair families. William Taylor removed to St. Mary's, was married again, and had a family of children. About the year 1840 he was chopping in the woods at Sherbrooke, and was killed by the falling of a tree. Matthew Taylor, Senr., was the second son of Matthew and Janet Taylor, who came from Londonderry, Ireland, to Londonderry, N. H., in the year 1722.

CHAPTER VII.

James Dunlap was one of the first settlers, and a Grantee of Truro Township. His front land was in the Lower Village, his house stood near the place that his grandson, Isaac Dunlap's house, now stands.

He was married to Mary, daughter of Lieut. John Johnson, of the Lower Village, December 6th, 1763. It is said that this was the first marriage in Truro after its settlement by the English. Sarah, their eldest daughter, was born in Truro January 6th, 1765. She was married to William, son of James and Ann Fulton of the Lower Village, in the year 1783. Their family appears among the Fulton families ; they had seven sons and seven daughters. James, the eldest son of James and Mary Dunlap, was born in Truro January 26th, 1767. He was married to Jane, one of the twin daughters of William and Janet Kennedy, about the year 1794. He removed and settled on the east side of the South Branch of Stewiacke. Some of his grandsons now reside there. They had two sons and one daughter. He died there in the month of October, 1809, aged 42 years. William, their eldest son, was married to Rachel, daughter of Hugh and Elizabeth E. Logan, December 12th, 1816. James, their eldest son, was born July 21st, 1818. John Duncan, the second son, was born August 24, 1820. He was married to Sarah, daughter of George and Elizabeth Mç-Naught, in 1847 ; they have two sons and eight daughters. Thomas, their third son, was born December 7th, 1822. He was married to Sarah, daughter of William McNutt and Mary Johnson, his wife, March 31st, 1845 ; they had five sons and four daughters. Hugh, their fourth son, was born January 4th, 1825. He was married to Nancy, daughter of William K. Gammel March 2nd, 1856 ; they had three sons and two daughters. Mrs. Dunlap died January 3rd, 1866, and he was married again to Clara, daughter of James Hamilton of Middle Stewiacke, February 28th, 1867 ; they have one daughter. Elizabeth, the eldest daughter of William and Rachel Dunlap, was born October 16th, 1827. She was married to Hans Hamilton, and has two sons and four daughters. She died June 30th, 1865. William, their fifth son, was born May 15th, 1830. Charles, their sixth son, was born December 7th, 1832. Mary, their daughter, was born in 1835. She was married to Robert Geddes in 1859. They have two sons and four daughters. William Dunlap died August, 1867, and his wife died November, 1838.

James, the son of James Dunlap and Jane Kennedy, was born in Stewiacke December 4th, 1797. He inherited a part of his father's farm, and resided upon it until the time of his death, which took place very suddenly, November 16th, 1859. He was married to Elizabeth, daughter of Timothy Putnam and Janet Hunter, his wife, February, 1820. James, their son, was born April 14th, 1821, and Mrs. Dunlap died the same day. James Dunlap, Jun., was married to Mary, daughter of John Cox and Margaret Creelman, his wife, February 4th, 1846 ; they have two daughters. James Dunlap, Senr., was married again to Christiann Aikins, March, 1828. William, their eldest son, was born June 11th, 1824. He was married to Eleanor Murray January 18th, 1847, and they have two sons and three daughters. Jane and Elizabeth, twin daughters of James and Christiann Dunlap, were born March 9th, 1826. Jane was married to William Gourley in the month of November, 1847 ; they had three sons and five daughters. Elizabeth was married to John, the eldest son of John and Margaret Cox, and they had one son. Mr. Cox died suddenly, and she was married again to James, son of Robert and Mary Tupper ; they had three sons, and Mr. Tupper died a few years ago. Margaret, the third daughter of James and Christiann Dunlap, was born in the year 1828, and died unmarried. Mary, their fourth daughter, was born October 11th, 1829. She was married to Charles Cox, and had one son and one daughter. Mrs. Cox died July 22nd, 1869. Samuel Tupper Dunlap, their second son, was born November, 19th, 1831. He was married to Hannah Creelman, in the month of November, 1854. They have four daughters. Robert, their third son, was born January 9th, 1834. He was married to Margaret Creelman, March 21st, 1861. They have two sons and four daughters. Rachel, their fifth daughter, was born February 15th, 1836. She was married to Robert Jeffers, and has five sons and two daughters. Susan, their sixth daughter, was born June 28th, 1838. She was married to Jotham B. Cox, and has one son and three daughters. Eleanor, their seventh daughter, was born October 15th, 1841. She was married to George Russel Cox, and has two sons and two daughters. John, their fourth son, was born June 12th, 1843. He was married to Esther Creelman, daughter of Samuel Ashmore Creelman and Eleanor Cox, his wife, February 28th, 1871. She died 1872. Margaret Ann, their eighth daughter, was born October 12th, 1849. Mrs. Christiann Dunlap died July, 1872.

Mary, the only daughter of James Dunlap and Jane Kennedy, was born March 21st, 1799. She was married to Robert Tupper in 1820. Their family appears among the Tuppers. Mary, the second daughter of James and Mary Dunlap, was born in Truro, October 25th, 1768. She was married to Samuel, son of James and Ann Fulton, of the Lower Village of Truro. They removed to Upper

8

Stewiacke. She had one son. She died December, 1790, aged 22 years.

John, the second son of James and Mary Dunlap, was born in Truro, April 22nd, 1770. He was married to Martha, daughter of William and Dorothy Putnam, of Stewiacke, March 11th, 1802. They resided on the farm on which the Messrs. Notting now reside, in the Lower Village of Truro, until about the year 1808, when they removed to the farm on the West side of the South Meadow, in Stewiacke. He died there, February 15th, 1848, aged 78 years. The writer saw and conversed with his widow, then in good health, on July 8th, 1871. Mary, their eldest daughter, was born in Truro, January 14th, 1803. She was married to Benjamin Tupper, Esq., February 19th, 1822, and had three sons. Dorothy, their second daughter, was born in Truro, November 19th, 1804. She was married to Daniel Smith Yuill, of Clifton, February 11th, 1830. They had one son and four daughters. She died at Clifton, November 17th, 1857. Sarah, their third daughter, was born January 24th, 1807. She was married to William, the fifth son of William and Mary Cox, of Stewiacke, February 15th, 1827. They had four sons and four daughters. She died May 10th, 1855, in the 49th year of her age. James, the eldest son of John and Martha Dunlap, was born September 20th, 1809. He was married to Lydia, daughter of John Gourley and Elizabeth Tupper, his wife, January 18, 1832. They had two children, and they both died when they were young. Susannah, the fourth daughter of John and Martha Dunlap, was born June 15th, 1812. She was married to William Gammel, Esq., March 30th, 1844. They had one son and one daughter. Mr. Gammel died August 21st, 1848, and she was married again to Barry Hamilton, January 15th, 1850. They had two daughters. She died December 29th, 1860. William, their second son, was born February 27th, 1815. He was married to Martha, daughter of Robert Fisher and Mary Cox, his wife, February 9th, 1841. He inherits a large part of his father's farm, and lives in the house that his father built about the year 1825. Martha, the fifth daughter of John and Martha Dunlap, was born May 18th, 1819. She was married to William McCulloch, and had one son. She died May 28th, 1847. Lydia, their sixth daughter, was born August 30th, 1821. She was married to Putnam O'Brien, and had two sons and four daughters. They removed to the United States. She died August, 1859, aged 38 years.

Adam Johnson, the third son of James and Mary Dunlap, was

born June 20th, 1771. He was married to Eleanor, daughter of John Archibald, second, and Margaret Fisher. He settled first between Stewiacke and Musquodoboit, the same place on which Alexander Stewart lived and died. After this he removed to the farm on which his son James' widow now resides, which is situated West of the Halifax road, near Johnson's Crossing. He died there May 25th, 1808, aged 37 years. Mary, their eldest daughter, was born about the year 1796. Her father and mother both died when she was young, and she was taken by her uncle Archibald to Musquodoboit. She was married there to William Dean. They had four sons and four daughters. She died April, 1867, aged 71 years. Mr. Dean died about the year 1861. John the eldest son of Adam J. and Eleanor Dunlap, was born March, 1798, and, after the death of his father and mother, he and his brother James and sister Ruth were taken to their grandfather Dunlap's, and taken care of. He was married to Jane, the eldest daughter of Captain William Cock, widow of the late William Ross, December 1st, 1825. They had two sons and four daughters. The sons, Thomas and Henry, are now doing business in Amherst. The daughters' names are Eleanor, Anner, Elizabeth, and Jane. Anner and Elizabeth are both dead. About the year 1830, he purchased the house which was built by Eliakim Tupper, Esq.. and he resided in it the remainder of his life. In the year 1831 he built a store, which is now occupied as a printing office, and carried on business as a merchant until the time of his death. In April, 1842, he went to St. John, N. B., on business, and he there took ill and died, May 1st, 1842, aged 44 years. His body was brought home and interred in the Truro Cemetery.

James, the second son of Adam and Eleanor Dunlap, was born November 19th, 1800. He was married to Hannah, daughter of Thomas and Jane Gourley, March 16th, 1826. He inherited his father's farm, where he died March 5th, 1856, aged 55 years. Eleanor, their daughter, was born January 7th, 1827. She was married to John, son of Benjamin Tupper, Esq., and Mary Dunlap, December 31st, 1850. They have six sons and two daughters. They now reside on the South side of Musquodoboit River, on the farm that was originally John Archibald's. Hugh, the only son of James and Hannah Dunlap, was born November 8th, 1828. He died a bachelor, January 27th, 1869, aged 40 years. Ruth, the second and youngest daughter of Adam J. and Eleanor Dunlap, was born in the year 1802. She was married to Timothy, son of Timothy Putnam and Janet

Hunter, his wife, February 14th, 1828. They had six sons and six daughters. She died August 7th, 1851, aged 49 years. Mr. Dunlap's first wife, Eleanor, died about the year 1803, and he was married again to Elizabeth, daughter of William and Janet Kennedy, widow of the late James Dickey, of Stewiacke, Sept. 28th, 1805.

Hugh, the fourth son of James and Mary Dunlap, was born in Truro, April 28th, 1773. He was married to Susannah, daughter of Thomas and Jane Gourley, of the Lower Village, Jan'y. 24th, 1805. They removed to Stewiacke in 1807 and settled at Otter Brook, where their son Hugh now resides. He died September 6th, 1852, aged 79 years. His wife died November 22nd, 1857, Aged 74 years. Catherine, their eldest daughter, was born May 8th, 1806. She was married to Robert H. Smith, March 4th, 1828. They had five sons and three daughters. Mary, their second daughter, was born November 26th, 1807. She was married to William Chisholm, Esq., of Wallace River. They had six sons and four daughters. Jane, their third daughter, was born August 29th, 1809. She was married to Robert G. Rutherford, Esq., in the month of March, 1838. They had three sons and four daughters. Sarah, their fourth daughter, was born April 13th 1813. She was married to Ebenezer Smith, March 12th, 1845. They have one son and four daughters. Margaret, their fifth daughter, was born January 24th, 1817. She was married to Bradford Black of Cumberland, November 9th, 1843. They have two sons and five daughters. Hugh, their eldest son, was born January 14th, 1819. He inherits his father's farm, holds a commission of the Peace, and is an elder of the Presbyterian Church. He was married to Eliza M., daughter of Captain David Archibald and Elizabeth Kent his wife, November 7th, 1847. They had one son and two daughters. She died April 26th, 1854, aged 32 years. He was married again to Margaret, daughter of John D. Christie and Margaret Johnson, April 14th 1856. They had four sons and two daughters. Mrs. Dunlap died May 11th, 1869. He was married again to Eliza Baxter, June 27th, 1871. Susannah, their sixth daughter, was born May 13th, 1822. She was married to Eddy Tupper November 9th, 1847. They have two sons and four daughters. James Thomas, the second and youngest son of Hugh and Susan Dunlap, was born April 17th, 1824. He was married to Agnes, daughter of Andrew Creelman and Susan Johnson, June 20th, 1848. They have five sons and five daughters.

Rachel, the third daughter of James and Mary Dunlap, was born

January 25th, 1776. She was married to Samuel Tupper, Esq., of Upper Stewiacke in the year 1793. They had seven sons and five daughters. She died June 9th, 1852, aged 67 years. Samuel Tupper, Esq., died August 29th, 1831, aged 67 years.

Thomas, the fifth son of James and Mary Dunlap, was born February, 28th, 1778. He resided near the same place that Thomas Dunlap now resides, in the Lower Village of Truro. He died a bachelor September 7th, 1862, aged 84 years.

Samuel, the sixth and youngest son of James and Mary Dunlap, was born in the year 1782. He was married to Mary, daughter of Isaac Miller and Elizabeth Dickey, February 11th, 1813. He inherited a part of his father's farm, and lived in the same house with his father for some time, and then built the house in which his son Isaac now lives, where he spent the remainder of his life. He died March 2nd, 1850, aged 68 years, and his wife died January 12th 1861, aged 77 years. Adam, their eldest son, was born March 24th, 1814. He was married to Rebecca, daughter of Samuel and Nancy Blair, March, , 1837. They had two sons and one daughter. Mrs. Dunlap died December 21st, 1855, aged 39, and he was married again to Amelia, daughter of James D. and Esther Blair, February, 1857. Elizabeth, the eldest daughter of Samuel and Mary Dunlap, was born November 5th, 1815. She was married to Daniel C., fourth son of William and Esther Smith, December 17th, 1834. They have seven sons and four daughters. She died December 18th, 1871. James, the second son of Samuel and Mary Dunlap, was born October 30th, 1817. He died September 11th, 1819. Sarah, their second daughter, was born April 27th, 1819. She was married to Jacob, son of William Frieze and Janet D. Miller, August, , 1840. Isaac, their third son, was born in Truro, August 10th, 1820. He was married to Susannah, eldest daughter of Robert H. and Catherine Smith, February 10th, 1854. They have two sons and four daughters. He is one of the elders of the Presbyterian Church. Nancy, the third daughter of Samuel and Mary Dunlap, was born June 29th, 1822. She was married to John M., eldest son of David H. Crowe and Mary Smith, May, , 1851. They had one son and three daughters. Mary, the fourth daughter of Samuel and Mary Dunlap, was born in Truro, May 15th, 1824. She was married to James, the only son of Alexander Kent, Esq., and Jean Christie, June , 1858. They have one son and two daughters. James Dunlap, Senr., died December 5th, 1832, aged 92 years, and his wife

died May 22nd, 1823, aged 85 years.   It may here be observed that
their fifth son, Thomas Dunlap, went to the United States, and
travelled as far as Ohio.   He returned home about the year 1814, and
built a large truck waggon, the first that was built in Truro.   It was
first driven to Halifax, with a team of five horses by Barnabas
McQueen, who lived then in the Lower Village of Truro.

There was a Thomas Dunlap among the first settlers of Truro.
He was a Grantee of the Township, we know nothing of his decendants, it is said that he got discouraged in the settlement of a new
country, and returned to the United States.   Sarah, daughter of
Thomas and Elizabeth Dunlap was born in Truro, March 11th,
1763.

CHAPTER VIII.

Janet Logan, her two sons, and three daughters, with their
families, came from Londonderry, Ireland, to Nova Scotia in the year
1760, and were among the first settlers of Truro.   She was one of the
Grantees of the Township.   John, her eldest son, was born in 1727.
He was one of the Grantees of Truro, and had his front lands where his
grandsons William and David now reside.   His house stood quite
near the spot on which David Logan's house now stands.   He was
married before he came to Nova Scotia, or very shortly after.   Their
eldest son, Robert, was born in Truro, May 6th, 1763.   He was
married to Eleanor, daughter of William Fisher and Eleanor Archibald, about the year 1788, and removed to Upper Stewiacke.   John,
their eldest son, was born January 19th, 1789.   They had another
son who died when a few months old.   Mrs Logan died 1792.   He
was married again to Elizabeth, daughter of James and Ann Fulton,
widow of John Johnson, in 1801.   Janet, their only daughter, was
born April   , 1802.   Edward, their only son, was born February
13th, 1804.   Mrs. Robert Logan died February 20th, 1827, and he
died December 31st, 1833, aged 70 years.

John, the eldest son of Robert and Eleanor Logan, was married to
Ann, third daughter of James and Ann Johnson, of Middle Stewiacke,
December 17th, 1813.   He inherited one half of his father's farm, on
which he reared the following family, seven sons and two daughters.

Robert, the eldest son, was born April 23rd, 1815. He was married to Nancy E., daughter of William O'Brien and Anna Putnam, of Noel, February 7th, 1841. They have seven sons and two daughters living, and one son dead. They reside in Halifax. He is an elder in the Presbyterian Church.

Jane, the eldest daughter of John and Ann Logan, was born June 12th 1817. She was married to George, son of James and Elizabeth Guild, of Musquodoboit, February 15th, 1841. They had eight sons and five daughters. They now reside in Pembroke.

James A., the second son, was born July 27th, 1819. He was married to Catherine, third daughter of John B. and Catherine Archibald of Truro, October 1st, 1844. They had three sons and four daughters. He was an elder in the Presbyterian Church. He died Sept 17th, 1869, aged 50 years.

William, their third son, was born April 20th, 1821. He was married to Mary Ann, the eldest daughter of Robert and Margaret Archibald, of Truro, October 11th, 1845. They have seven sons and two daughters. He is an elder in the Presbyterian Church.

Adam, the fourth son, was born December 24th, 1822. He was married to Eliza Jane, youngest daughter of John B. and Catherine Archibald, of Truro, October 26th, 1847. They have three sons and three daughters. They reside in Halifax; he is engaged in City Mission work.

Andrew and Edward, twins, were born June 27th, 1824. Andrew was married to Martha, daughter of William Cox and Sarah Dunlap, October 20th, 1853. They have four sons and three daughters.

Edward was married to Mary Fulton, of Bass River, widow of John Johnson, June , 1861. They have one son. She died December 14th, 1871. He was married again to Margaret, daughter of Robert Archibald, Truro, March 20th, 1873.

Samuel Johnson Logan, the youngest son, was born November 24th, 1826. He was married to Ann, daughter of William and Jerusha Fulton, April 27th, 1858. They have four sons and one daughter. He inherits his father's farm. He is an elder in the Presbyterian Church.

Mary, the youngest daughter, was born February 27th, 1829. Ann, wife of John Logan, died December 18th, 1830, aged 35 years. He died March 23rd, 1863, aged 74 years.

Janet, the only daughter of Robert Logan and Elizabeth his second wife, was born in April , 1802. She was married to John, son of Matthew Johnson and Ruth Fisher, April, 1825. They had five sons and four daughters. Matthew, their eldest son, was married to Miss Bryson, of Musquodoboit. He died and left a widow with six children. Ruth, their eldest daughter, was married to Thomas, son of David Fulton, Esq., of Bass River. They have a family. Edward, the second son of John and Janet Johnson, was married to Alison Miller of Truro. They had four sons. He died in Halifax, March 20th, 1864. George, the third son, was married to Jane, daughter of John and Susan Creelman. They lived in Halifax some time, then removed to Minnesota. John, the fourth son, is married to Sarah, daughter of George and Mary Ann Fulton, of Bass River. They now reside at Great Village Londonderry. Alexander, the youngest son, is married, and lives in Onslow. The other sisters' names are Elizabeth, Margaret Ann, and Sarah Jane.

Edward, only son of Robert and Elizabeth Logan, was born February 13th, 1804. He was married to Janet, eldest daughter of James and Elizabeth Guild, of Musquodoboit. He removed from Stewiacke to Musquodoboit. Elizabeth, their eldest daughter, was married to Robert Bryden. They had a family, and removed to Minnesota. Margaret, the second daughter, was married to Mr. Tregidgion. They have two daughters. They now reside at Montague, Gold diggings. Robert, the only son of Edward and Janet Logan was married to Susan, the daughter of Alexander and Catherine Archibald, June, 1842. They have three daughters. They removed to Minnesota. Mary, their third daughter, was killed in climbing over a log fence. The top log fell across her breast, causing instant death. Mary, their fourth daughter, died February 7th, 1860, aged 18 years. Edward Logan died November 23rd, 1863, aged 59 years. His widow removed to Minnesota, with her son and daughter.

William, the second son of John and Mary Logan, was born in Truro, November 23rd, 1764. He was married to Janet, the second daughter of Robert Archibald and Hannah Blair. He settled at Pembroke, in Upper Stewiacke, for a time, and then removed to Middle Musquodoboit. He died in the month of October, 1796, aged 32 years. His body was buried on his own farm. His widow was married again to Alexander McNutt Fisher. They had two sons and one daughter.

Robert A., the eldest son of William and Janet Logan, was born December 8th, 1794. He was married to Janet McInnis, November 28th, 1815. Miles McInnis, their eldest son, was born September

6th, 1816. He was married to Agnes Cook, November, 1841. They have two sons and one daughter. Mary McInnis, the eldest daughter of Robert A. and Janet Logan, was born January 13th, 1820. She is married to Robert A., son of William Guild and Susan Archibald, his wife. They have three sons and four daughters. Hannah Ann Christie, their second daughter, was born May 26th, 1822. She was married to Edward S. Taylor, November 8th, 1842. They have seven sons and two daughters. William, their second son, was born May 24th, 1824. He was married to Catherine Danbrack in the year 1850. They have three sons and four daughters. Samuel B. Logan, their third son, was born March 26th, 1826. He removed to Boston, U. S., and is married to Jemima Nyman, and has three sons. Margaret Ann, their third daughter, was born October 28th, 1828. She was married to John Dickman, May 20th, 1860. They have four sons and one daughter. Robert Archibald Logan, their fourth son, was born July 13th, 1833. He was married to Esther Higgins, October, 1856. They have two sons. Angus McInnis Logan, their fifth son, was born December 17th, 1830. He was married to Mary Gladwin, in the month of July, 1852. They have one son and four daughters. Malcolm McInnis Logan, their sixth son, was born July 4th, 1836. He was married to Maria McNab, October, 1864. They have one son and one daughter. Robert A. Logan's wife, Janet, died October 17th, 1859, and he was married again to Barbara Shaw, June 14th, 1860. He died August 22nd, 1871, aged 77 years.

Mary, the only daughter of William and Janet Logan, was born after the death of her father. She was married to Samuel Bryden, of Musquodoboit, April, 1815. They have seven sons and three daughters. She died in the year 1857. Esther, the eldest daughter of John and Mary Logan, was born in Truro, May 26th, 1766. She was married to William, fifth son of William Fisher and Eleanor Archibald, his wife, February 14th, 1786. Their family appears among the Fishers.

Janet, the second daughter of John and Mary Logan, was born in Truro, September 7th, 1770. She was married to William Murdoch, They resided for a time in a house which stood near her father's, and afterwards removed to Pictou Town, where they spent the remainder of their days. They had four sons ; their names are William, Rev. John L. Murdoch, of Windsor, James, and Robert.

Edward, the third son of John and Mary Logan, was born April 28, 1772. He inherited one-half of his father's farm. He was married to

Hannah, daughter of John Cutton, of Onslow, January 28th, 1800. Mary, their eldest daughter, was born in Truro, July 23rd, 1801. She was married to John Gordon, son of John and Elizabeth Nelson, January 12th, 1826. They had one son, whose name was Edward Logan Nelson. He was born April 27th, 1827, and was burnt to death, with four other persons, March 31st, 1841. The house that was burnt stood on the same corner on which the house now stands in which Mr. William McCully resides. Mrs. Nelson died of consumption, June 28th, 1829, aged 28 years. Janet Staples, the second daughter of Edward and Hannah Logan, was born October 13th, 1802. She was married to John Wilson, of Chiganoise. She and her husband both died of consumption a few years after they were married, and they left no issue. She died June 24th, 1827. John and William, twin sons of Edward and Hannah Logan, were born January 15th, 1804. John removed to Miramichi, and remained there a few years, until his health failed. His brother William went to assist in getting him home, and he died within a year after of consumption, July 25th, 1834, aged 30 years. William Logan was married to Sarah, daughter of Alexander and Rebecca Miller, January 8th, 1829. They had five sons and two daughters. Alexander M., their eldest son, was born February 11th, 1830. He died in California, July 20th, 1852, aged 22 years. John, their second son, was born May 10th, 1832. He was married to Jane, daughter of James Kent and Sarah Archibald, his wife, October, 1864. He died December, 28th, 1865. Edward, their third son, was born April 16th, 1834. He died September 10th, 1836. William K., their son, was born September 2nd, 1837. He was married to Flora, daughter of John Dickson and Margaret Kent, his wife, January 1st, 1867, and had two daughters. Jane, their daughter, was born December 2nd, 1839. She died November 2nd, 1854. Charles, their fifth son, was born June 1st, 1842. He died August 2nd, 1867. Mary was born December 24th. 1849. She died July 2nd, 1869, in the 20th year of her age. Robert, the third son of Edward and Hannah Logan, was born November 9th, 1805. He was married to Elizabeth, daughter of Alexander and Rebecca Miller, January 22nd, 1828. Their only daughter, Hannah, was born November 19th, 1828. She died October 30th, 1829. Mrs. Elizabeth Logan died February 26th, 1830, aged 23 years, and Robert Logan died February 3rd, 1831, aged 25 years. They all died of consumption. Susannah, the third daughter of Edward and Hannah Logan, was born March 8th, 1807.

She died of consumption, April 7th, 1831, aged 24 years. David, their fourth son, was born April 9th, 1809. He was married to Sarah, daughter of George Conley and Elizabeth Dunn, his wife, widow of the late Joseph Russell, March 24th, 1856. They have six sons. He died December 7th, 1871. Edward, their fifth son, was born February 13th, 1811. He died March 18th, 1829, aged 17 years. Hannah, their fourth daughter, was born October 13th, 1812. She was married to William Conkey. They had one one son, and she died of consumption shortly after he was born, in January, 1836 Elisha, their sixth son, was born May 23rd, 1816. He was married to Nancy, daughter of Samuel and Sarah Whidden, May, 1842. They have five sons and two daughters. He died September 27th, 1870, aged 54 years. His wife died December 27th, 1865, aged 49 years. James Harper Logan, their seventh son, was born May 1st, 1820. Esther, their fifth and youngest daughter, was born July 15th, 1822. She died of consumption, April 19th, 1832, aged 10 years. Hannah, wife of Edward Logan, died July 1st, 1828, and he was married again to Lydia Bishop, widow of the late Samuel Nichols, of Onslow, October 20th, 1833. He died July 15th, 1859, aged 87 years.

Mary, the third daughter of John and Mary Logan, was born in Truro, April 20th, 1774. She was married to Abner Doggett, January 30th, 1800. Mr. Doggett built the South part of the house in which Mr. William Cummings now resides, where he died, January 26th, 1807, aged 32 years. Rebecca, daughter of Abner and Mary Doggett, was born November 3rd, 1800. She was married to David Forbes, February 2nd, 1819. They had five sons and five daughters. She died June 29th, 1848, aged 47 years. John L. Doggett, the only son of Abner and Mary, was born June 8th, 1805. He was married to Esther Smith, widow of the late Robert Pearson, December 4th, 1828. They had five sons and one daughter.

Eleanor, the fourth daughter of John and Mary Logan, was born November 7th, 1775. She was married to John Smith, of Hants County, April 25th, 1799. He settled on what was then called the Townsend farm, the same on which William Eaton, Esq., and others now reside. He died November 12th, 1810, aged 37 years. His widow died May 26th, 1857, aged 81 years. Lucy, their eldest daughter, was born March 26th, 1800. She was married to William C. Eaton, September 27th, 1820. They had seven sons and three daughters. Isaac Smith, their only son, was born 12th April, 1802.

He was married to Mary Waddel, February 23rd, 1823. They had two sons and four daughters. Mrs. Smith died November, 1838. Mary Smith was born July, 1804. She was married to Matthew T. Smith, 1827. They had four sons and four daughters. They settled in Pictou. Nancy Smith was born June 10th, 1808. She was married to James W. Keeler, April 2nd, 1833. They had one son and two daughters.

Nancy the fifth daughter of John and Mary Logan, was born in Truro, October 31st, 1778. She was married to John McKay, of Pictou, and had two sons and one daughter. Mary, wife of the said John Logan, died December, 1778, and he was married again to Ann Full, December, 1781. Susannah, the eldest daughter of John and Ann Logan, was born November 10th, 1783. She was married to David, son of William and Ann McKeen, in 1811. She died in 1813.

Sarah, the second daughter of John and Ann Logan, was born in Truro, June 8th, 1785. She was married to Samuel, son of Captain John McKeen, June 16th, 1803. They had three sons and one daughter. They removed to St Mary's, where they spent the remainder of their days. She died about the year 1866. Hannah, their third daughter, was born April 2nd, 1788. She was married to Donald Fraser, of Pictou, and they had six sons and two daughters. John, the only son of John and Ann Logan, was born April 13th, 1790. He inherited one-half of his father's farm. He sold his farm, and went to sea a number of years. He sailed from St. John, N. B., in June, 1837. Neither the ship nor any of the crew has since been heard of. John Logan, Senr., died August 15th, 1822, aged 95 years, and his second wife, Ann, died in the month of April, 1790.

William Logan, brother of John, was another of the first settler of Truro, and a Grantee of the Township. His front land was the same that Dr. David B. Lynds recently owned. His house stood on the same place that the house now stands which belongs to the estate of the late Dr. Lynds. He was married to Janet Moore (sister of Hugh Moore, Senr.), before they came to Nova Scotia. Mary, their eldest daughter, was born January 17th, 1761. She was married to Daniel McKenzie. Janet, the daughter of Daniel and Mary McKenzie, was born in Truro, March 12th, 1785. Mrs. McKenzie died, and he was married again to Sarah, daughter of Hugh and Janet Moore. They appear among the family of the Moores.

Hugh, the eldest son of William and Janet Logan, was born in Truro, March 28th, 1763. He was married to Elizabeth Elliott, daughter of Samuel Archibald, in 1794. They settled in Upper Stewiacke, on the farm that Benjamin Davison now resides upon, where they spent the remainder of their days. William, their eldest son, was born in 1795. He settled on the South side of Stewiacke River, where Gilbert Rutherford now resides. Here he lived a considerable number of years, and died a bachelor in the year 1856, aged 61 years. John, another son of Hugh and Elizabeth Logan, was born in 1797. He removed to the United States in 1840. He was married to Margaret McDonald. They had two sons and three daughters. He died in 1852, aged 55 years. Rachel, their daughter, was married to William Dunlap, and had six sons and two daughters, who appear among the Dunlaps.

Samuel, the second son of Hugh and Elizabeth Logan, was born about the year 1799. He died a bachelor, in the year 1847. Janet, the second daughter of Hugh and Elizabeth Logan, was born in 1801. She was married to William Gammell, Esq., December 31st, 1821. They had four sons and five daughters. She died February 12th, 1843, aged 42 years. Mary Logan. their fourth daughter, was born about the year 1806. She was married to John McCulloch, of South Branch, in 1832. Margaret, their third daughter, was born in 1804. She was married to George S. Rutherford. They had two sons and two daughters. She died September 22nd, 1839, aged 35 years, and her husband died October 17th, 1871.

Edward, the second son of William and Janet Logan, was born December 16th, 1765. He left home when a young man, and nothing is known about him since. Alice, the second daughter of William and Janet Logan, was born January 2nd, 1770. She was married to Thomas, son of Dr. John Harris, and settled in Pictou. They had four sons and one daughter.

William, the third son of William and Janet Logan, was born August 15th, 1773. He was married to Sarah, daughter of Robert Archibald, Esq., and Hannah Blair, his wife. They had three sons and six daughters. He inherited his father's farm in Truro. He built the house that John Ross now lives in, on the North side of the Common, in the same place that Daniel Eaton, Esq., and his sons now reside. It was removed down to where it now stands by Mr. Jonathan Blanchard, about the year 1813. Mr. Blanchard lived in this house until he removed to the West River of Pictou, in the year 1817. William Logan sold his farm in Truro and removed so Middle Musquodoboit, where he spent the remainder of his life. Robert was their eldest son.   He died a bachelor, February, 1871.   Janet, their eldest daughter, was married to Thomas Kaulback.   They had two sons and five daughters.   William, the second son of William and Sarah Logan, was born about the year 1813.   He died a bachelor, about the year 1847.   David, their third son, was born in the year 1815.   He is still living, a bachelor.   Mary Alice, their second daughter, was born in the year 1817.   She was married to Joseph Bruce.   They have two sons and seven daughters.   They inherit her father's farm in Musquodoboit.   Margaret, their third daughter. was born 1819.   She removed to Porter's Lake, is married there, and has a family of children.   Elizabeth, their fifth and youngest daughter, was born about the year 1823.   She was married to Thomas, son of Frederick Hurley and Janet Archibald, his wife.   They had one son. Mrs. Hurley died, and he was married again to Susan, the fourth daughter of William and Sarah Logan.   They had a numerous family of children.

Janet, the youngest daughter of William and Janet Logan, was born March 19th, 1776.   She was married to Thomas McCollum. They removed to Musquodoboit, where they spent the remainder of their lives.   They had two sons and five daughters.   She died December, 1864, aged 89 years.   Her husband died in the Spring of 1859, aged 81 years.

CHAPTER IX.

Hugh Moor, Senr., was another of the first settlers of Truro.   He came with his brothers, sisters and their husbands, in the year 1760· he was one of the Grantees of the Township, and had his first house on the interval of Salmon River.   After this he built a house on the upland, near the Pictou Rail Road, on the east end of Mr. Andrew Moor's orchard.   He purchased the house from Mr. Robert Cock, where he spent the remainder of his life, being the same house in which his son Hugh lived and died, and his grandson, Andrew Moor, lived in until October, 1871.   Hugh Moor, Senr., died December 10th, 1820, a few days after having his leg amputated.   He was 82 years of age.   His wife Janet died November 28th, 1818, aged 72 years.   He had been married to Janet Logan but a short time before they came to Nova Scotia. Mary, their eldest daughter, was born about the year 1762. She was married to Michael Lovett Tucker, October 13th, 1785. Rosanna, their eldest daughter, was born April 22nd, 1786. She was married to George Dill, January 31st, 1815, and had three sons and four daughters. She died January, 1853, aged 66 years. Janet, their second daughter, was born October 11th, 1787. She was married to Robert McNutt. She died January 20th, 1853, aged 66 years. Charles Tucker, their eldest son, was born September 4th, 1789. He was married to Mercy Parker Polley, August 1st, 1811. They had two sons and seven daughters. Mr. Tucker died at Bermuda, September 18th, 1858, aged 69 years ; his body was brought home and interred in the Truro Cemetery. Mary, the third daughter of Michael L. and Mary Tucker, was married to Alexander McCabe, of Greenhill, Pictou. They had three sons and two daughters. Hugh, their second son, was married to Ruth Lynds, April 6th, 1815. They had six sons and two daughters. He died in the month of June, 1871. Michael John, their third son, was born January 12th, 1796. He was married to Charlotte Brown of Macan, Cumberland, January 7th, 1823. They had two sons and four daughters. He died at Macan in the year 1871. Michael L. Tucker died July 7th, 1798, aged 48 years, and she was married again to Robert McCartney ; they had one son, his name was Robert. He was married to Jane, eldest daughter of Robert and Margaret Moor. They had six sons and two daughters. They removed to the United States. Old Mrs. McCartney died at Truro, May 20th, 1847, Aged 85 years.

Janet, the second daughter of Hugh and Janet Moor, was born in Truro, March 28th, 1765. She was married to John Faulkner. Sarah, their eldest daughter, was married to James Perkins, they had one daughter whose name was Sarah Ann. James Perkins was drowned down the bay, when engaged in fishing, about the year 1818. His widow was married again to Alexander Miller, December 19th, 1822. They had three sons and two daughters. Alexander Miller died May 31st 1855. Elizabeth, the second daughter of John and Janet Faulkner, was married to John Laughead, September 14th, 1846. She died February 29th, 1860. Robert, the eldest son of John and Janet Faulkner, was married to Ann Edds of Halifax. He died suddenly of small pox in Pictou town about the year 1828. His widow was married again to Mr. Robert Barry. They had five sons and one daughter. John, the youngest son of John and Janet

Faulkner, was born in 1800.   He was married to Jane McKim, of Londonderry, April, 1847.   He died February 9th, 1863, aged 63 years.   He was an elder of the Presbyterian Church 18 years before his death.

Sarah, the third daughter of Hugh and Janet Moor, was born March 3rd, 1769.   She was married to Daniel McKenzie.   They removed to the West River of Pictou, where they spent the remainder of their days.   They had three sons and four daughters.   He died April 1815 ; his wife died March 10th, 1853.

Robert, the eldest son of Hugh and Janet Moor, was born in Truro, October 2nd, 1770.   He learned the Wheelwright business with his uncle, William Moor.   He was married to Margaret, daughter of William O'Brien and Lydia Harris, December 28th, 1797.   Janet, their eldest daughter, was born in Truro, January 2nd, 1799.   She was married to Robert McCartney, and had six sons and two daughters. They removed to the United States, Lydia, their second daughter, was born September 20th, 1800.   She was married to James Fisher, of Stewiacke, February, 1833.   They kept an Inn at Brookfield until Mr. Fisher died March, 1850.   They had two sons and two daughters.   Alice, their third daughter, was born August 29th, 1803. She was married to Alexander McLain, August 15th, 1831.   They had six sons and three daughters.   Mr. McLain died April 9th, 1869. Frances, the fourth daughter of Robert and Margaret Moor, was born October 2nd, 1805.   She died unmarried, December 26th, 1837, aged 32 years.   Eliza, their fifth daughter, was born December 15th, 1807. She died unmarried, July 2nd, 1830, aged 23.   John, their eldest son, was born in Truro, March 23rd, 1810.   He died a bachelor, September 17th, 1839, aged 29 years.   Mary, the fifth daughter of Robert and Margaret Moor, was born October 18th 1812.   She was married to Lemuel Lynds, of North River, January 18th, 1835. They had seven sons and four daughters.   William Isaac, their second son, was born in Truro, March 14th, 1816.   He was married to Eleanor Shand of Halifax, October, 1848.   They had two sons and four daughters.   Sarah Ann, their youngest daughter. was born January 6th, 1819.   She was married to Charles, son of Elias Nelson and Elizabeth Forbes his wife, of Hants County, February 11th, 1845.   They have two sons, and now reside on a part of what was her father's farm.   Robert Moor, died February 27th 1852, aged 82 years, and his wife died July 19th, 1862.

John, the second son of Hugh and Janet Moor, was born in Truro,

February 14th, 1772. He was married to Susannah Hunter Harris, daughter of Dr. John Harris, June 7th 1803. They had three sons and five daughters. They removed to the West branch of River John, where they settled, reared their family, and died.

Elizabeth, the fourth daughter of Hugh and Janet Moor, was born November 27th, 1773. She was married to John Dickson of Onslow Mountain, in November, 1804. They had three sons and three daughters. She died May 17th, 1842, aged 68 years, and her husband, John Dickson, died May 25th, 1855, aged 92 years.

Hugh, the third son of Hugh and Janet Moor, was born in Truro, May 20th, 1776. He was married to Margaret, daughter of Andrew O'Brien and Margaret Denny his wife, of Noel, October 20th, 1814. He inherited his father's farm, where he spent his life. He died January 11th 1864, aged 88 years, and his wife died March 4th, 1857, aged 73 years. Andrew, the eldest son of Hugh and Margaret Moor, was born in Truro, January 25th, 1816. He inherits a part of his father's farm, and is still living a bachelor. Janet Logan Moor, their eldest daughter, was born September 18th, 1817. She died April 1st, 1819. Margaret O'Brien Moor, their second daughter was born June 10th, 1819. She was married to William Munro, of Portuguese Cove, Halifax, January 13th, 1849. They had two sons and three daughters. Alice Moor, their third daughter, was born June 3rd, 1821. Rebecca Denny Moor, their youngest daughter, was born November, 15th 1823. She has been confined to bed about six years with the acute rheumatism.

Alice, the fifth and youngest daughter of Hugh and Janet Moor, was born in Truro, August 27th, 1778. She died unmarried, December 26th, 1860, aged 82 years. William Moor, was brother of Hugh, and Daniel, and they had four sisters who came to Nova Scotia. He was but a boy when they came to Truro. He was a Wheelwright by trade, and was called Clean Billey Moor. He removed to Shubenacadie, where he spent the remainder of his life, and died. He was married to Susannah Long, June 30th, 1774. Elizabeth, their eldest daughter, was born in Truro, December 6th, 1774. Janet, their second daughter, was born April 6th, 1776. Robert, their eldest son, was born February 4th, 1778. Sarah, their third daughter, was born January 18th, 1780. She was married to William Forbes. They lived, reared their family and died on the farm that Mr. Elisha James now resides upon, near the mouth of the Shubenacadie River. Hugh, their second son, was born April 25th,

9

1782. He died October 7th, 1783. William, their third son, was born January 14th, 1784. He was married to Rebecca, daughter of Alexander and Margaret Nelson, of Old Barns. They removed to the United States. Daniel, their fourth son, was born March 30th, 1787. Charles, their fifth son, was born March 11th 1789. Susannah, their youngest daughter, was born in the month of August, 1791.

Daniel Moor came to Nova Scotia with his brothers and sisters, when he was a boy 6 years old. He was married to Eleanor, daughter of Charles Cox and Eleanor Stewart, his wife, in 1780. They removed and settled in Brookfield about the year 1786. William Hamilton and they were the first settlers in Brookfield. He reared his family and died there, February, 1826, aged 72 years ; his wife died in 1851, aged 91 years. Hugh, their eldest son, was born about the year 1786. He removed from this Province, and has not been heard from since. Robert, their second son, was born in 1788. He followed the sea when young, returned home and died a bachelor in the year 1854. Charles, their third son, was born February 14th, 1790. He was married to Mary Bonnell, November 3rd, 1814. They had two sons and seven daughters. He died October 23rd, 1861, aged 71 years. Mary, the eldest daughter of Daniel and Eleanor Moor, was born 1791. She was married to Robert Lynton of North River, they had one son and one daughter. Daniel, their fourth son, was born in the year 1794. He was married to Sarah Green, November 17th, 1825. They had three sons and four daughters. William, their fifth son, was born in the year 1796. He was married to Alice Kennedy, March 1820. They had one son and two daughters. He died September 1856, aged 60 years. Margaret, the second daughter was born in 1798. She died unmarried, August 1825.

Esther Moore, sister of Hugh, William and Daniel Moore, shortly before they came to Nova Scotia, was married to Robert Hunter. They had one son and six daughters, who appear among the Hunter family. Janet Moore, another sister, was married to William Logan before they came to Truro. Margaret Moore, another sister, was married to David McCollum, of North River. They had six sons and three daughters. Alice Moore, their fourth sister, was married to John, the third son of David Archibald, Esq., June 2nd, 1768. They had four sons and four daughters. They removed to Musquodoboit, where they spent the remainder of their days.

CHAPTER X.

George Scott was another of the Grantees of Truro Township. His house stood near the place that Mr. Flemming's old house stood. He was married before he came to Truro. They had three daughters. Esther, their eldest daughter, was born before they came to Nova Scotia. She was married to James Rutherford, November 27th, 1777. They had three sons, which appear among the Rutherfords. She died April 5th, 1783.

Ann, the second daughter of George and Elizabeth Scott, was born in Truro, November 27th, 1762. She was married to William, the eldest son of old Mr. James Flemming, who settled in the Folly, Londonderry. The Folly took its name from the old saying that it was folly for Mr. Flemming to settle on so poor a place. They were married July 17th, 1789. Esther Scott Flemming, their eldest daughter, was born November 20th, 1790. She was married to John L. Fisher, August 29th, 1816. They had four sons. Mr. Fisher died December 28th, 1863. Isabell, the second daughter of William and Ann Flemming, was born in Truro, March 22nd, 1793. She was married to Alexander Knight, a saddler (who had come out from Scotland), October 22nd, 1818. They had four sons and five daughters. They removed from Truro to Halifax, in the year 1830. Mrs. Knight died there, March 5th, 1866, aged 73 years. Mr. Knight died February 8th, 1873. Elizabeth, the third daughter of William and Ann Flemming, was born November 29th, 1795. She was married to Robert Putnam of Middle Stewiacke, July, 1821. They had three sons and two daughters. George Scott, the eldest son of William and Ann Flemming, was born April 13th, 1798. He was married to Charlotte, daughter of Dr. Upham and Mary Dickson, his wife, December 26th, 1824. They had four sons and four daughters. He was drowned at Brookfield, December, 1846. He settled on the farm that James McGlench now resides upon. His wife died August 1844. James, the second son of William and Ann Flemming, was born July 27th, 1800. He was married to Lydia, the third daughter of Eliakim Tupper and Lydia Putnam, his wife, July 1st, 1826. They had three sons and five daughters. He settled on the farm that had been owned by John Kennedy and is now owned by John Putnam, Junr., of Middle Stewiacke, where he built a house. He removed from there to Halifax, and kept a house of entertainment. He died in Stewiacke, July, 1851, and his wife died April, 1862. William, the third and youngest son of William and Ann Flemming, was born in Truro, January 23rd, 1803. He was married to Mary, daughter of Alexander Kent, Esq., and Jane Christie, his wife, March 11th, 1828. They had five sons and three daughters. He inherited his father's farm in Truro. He represented Truro in Parliament from the year 1843 to 1847. He died January 24th, 1873, aged 70 years. Ann, the youngest daughter of William and Ann Flemming, was born September 23rd, 1805. She was married to Robert Laughead, of Old Barns, December 29th, 1825. She died September 25th, 1829, aged 24 years. William Flemming, Senr., died in Truro, July 31st, 1829, aged 62 years, and his wife, Ann Scott, died March 6th, 1847, aged 84 years.

Elizabeth, the third and youngest daughter of George and Elizabeth Scott, was born in Truro October 23rd, 1766. She was married to Thomas Dickey, June 22nd, 1788. He built a house, which is owned by the heirs of the late David C. Wilson. In this house they reared their family. Mr. Dickey died October 18th, 1798, aged 33 years, and his widow died March 19th, 1830, aged 63 years. George Scott Dickey, their eldest son, was born January 5th, 1790. He was married to Esther, daughter of John Wright and Sarah Lynds, his wife, December 27th. 1833. They had two sons and three daughters. He inherited his father's farm until about the year 1845, when he sold it and removed to the Lower Village. He died there May 2nd, 1864, aged 74 years. Elizabeth, the only daughter of Thomas and Elizabeth Dickey, was born November 15th, 1791. She was married to Hugh, son of Robert Johnson and Susannah Gourley, his wife, November 22nd, 1811. They had five sons and five daughters. They appear among the Johnsons. Mr. Dickey died November 17th, 1841, aged 55 years. James, the second son of Thomas and Elizabeth Dickey, was born in Truro, February 8th, 1794. He died a bachelor December 25th, 1858, aged 64 years. Thomas, the third and youngest son of Thomas and Elizabeth Dickey, was born June 4th, 1797. He was married to Mary, daughter of William Joyce and Mary Elliott, his wife, December, 1828. They settled in Middle Stewiacke, where they reared their family. Mr. Dickey, died May 12th, 1868, aged 71 years ; and his wife died September 8th, 1859, aged 53 years. George Scott divided his farm between his two daughters, Ann and Elizabeth. He died about 1811, aged 94 years, and his wife died about 1815.

CHAPTER XI.

James Rutherford was among the earlier settlers of Truro, but not a Grantee. He purchased and settled on the farm which is now owned by Mr. George Yuill and son, and Mr. Thomas S. Crowe, at Beaver Brook. He resided on this farm until after his first wife died. He then sold his farm to Thomas Crowe, Senr., and settled near the place on which Wellington Blair now resides. He removed again to Middle Stewiacke about the year 1790, where he spent the remainder of his life. He was rather a peculiar man ; one of his replies to the argument that it was the work of necessity to house grain on Sabbath during the time of brittle weather in harvest, was, " Cannot you trust Him who sends wet to wet it for wind to dry it again." Mr. Rutherford, was married to Esther, the eldest daughter of George and Elizabeth Scott of Truro, Nov. 27th, 1777.

George S. Rutherford, their eldest son, was born in Truro, March 10th, 1779. He was married to Martha Thompson, March 24th, 1801. Esther, their eldest daughter, was born in 1802. She was married to Charles Corbet. Mr. Corbet died May 25th, 1871. Archibald Rutherford, their eldest son was married to Nancy Howard. They are residing in Halifax. They have six sons and four daughters. George S. Rutherford was married to Margaret, daughter of Hugh Logan and Elizabeth E. Archibald. She died September 22nd, 1839, aged 35 years. He was married again to Mary, daughter of Thomas Corbet and Sarah Smith, in the year 1841. She died May 10th, 1842, aged 31 years. He was married again to Rachel, daughter of Samuel Burke Archibald, and widow of the late Samuel Creelman. She died January 16th, 1865, aged 61 years. Mr. Rutherford died October 17th, 1871, aged 66. James, their third son was married to Margaret Taylor. He now owns the mill at Middle Stewiacke.

Robertson, their fourth son was born April 1st, 1809, and was married to Eleanor, daughter of Robert Putnam and Jane Cox, his wife, November, 1842.

William, their fifth son, was married to Susan Fulton. He inherits a large portion of his father's farm.

Nancy, their youngest daughter, was born March 10th, 1813. She was married to Thomas Fulton, December, 1842. They had three sons and two daughters.

George S. Rutherford, Senr., died July 27th, 1859, aged 80 years, and his wife died July 28th, 1854, aged 70 years.

Robert, the second son of James and Esther Rutherford, was born in Truro February 22nd, 1781. He was married to Nancy, eldest daughter of William Johnson and Sarah Miller, his wife. They had four sons and four daughters. They settled in Upper Stewiacke on the same farm that their sons William and James now reside. He died July 26th, 1856, aged 75 years, and his wife died June 2nd, 1849, aged 61 years.

William, the third son of James and Esther Rutherford, was born in Truro, November 10th, 1782. He was married to Eleanor, daughter of William Cox and Mary Smith, his wife, February 5th 1807. They had one son and three daughters. One of these daughters was married to the late Robert King, one to Alexander Fisher, and the other to Henry Campbell. George S., the son, was born December 6th, 1811. He was married to Margaret Howard, December 31st, 1835. They had five sons and three daughters. He inherits what was once his father's farm. Mrs. Eleanor Rutherford died January 15th, 1813. He was married again to Sarah, daughter of William Fulton and Sarah Dunlap, his wife, November 1813. His second wife died November, 1814, and he was married to Eleanor Croker, November, 1814. He was a Justice of the Peace, and went by the name of Squire Rutherford. He died Oct. 19th, 1856. His third wife died December 30th, 1854. Esther Scott, the first wife of James Rutherford, Senr., died at Beaver Brook, April 5th, 1783. He was married again to Elizabeth, daughter of James and Elizabeth Johnson, of the Lower Village of Truro, February 15th, 1785.

James, the eldest son of James and Elizabeth Rutherford, was born February 12th, 1787. He was married to Ruth Lane, November 19th, 1812. They had two sons and seven daughters. He settled on the farm that his son George Scott Rutherford now resides upon. He died August 6th, 1869, aged 82 years.

Gilbert, the second son of James and Elizabeth Rutherford, was born in Truro, October 20th, 1788. He was married to Ruth, the fourth daughter of Archibald Gammel and Sarah Fisher his wife. He had one of his legs amputated and, afterwards, he was engaged selling goods through the country. He died in the prime of life. Robert G. Rutherford, Esq., his only son, was married to Jane, the third daughter of Hugh Dunlap and Susannah Gourley, March, 1838. They had three sons and four daughters.

Esther, the eldest daughter of James and Elizabeth Rutherford, was born in Stewiacke in the year 1790. She died unmarried, December, 1811, aged 21 years.

Margaret, the second daughter of James and Elizabeth Rutherford, was born in the year 1796. She was married to John, third son of Samuel Creelman and Mary Campbell, his wife, December 8th, 1812. They had five sons and six daughters. She died June 3rd, 1830, aged 33 years.

Adam, the third son of James and Elizabeth Rutherford, was born January 12th, 1794. He was married to Lucy Lane, in the year 1815. They had two sons. Mrs. Rutherford died, and he was married again to Hannah, daughter of John Fletcher and Margaret Graham, his wife, December 20th, 1825. They had three sons and three daughters. He died April 1st, 1845, aged 51 years. He settled first on the farm which is now owned by Henry Campbell, near the Stewiacke River. He sold out there and built on the hill north of the road. It is now owned by William Fisher's sons.

John, the fourth son of James and Elizabeth Rutherford, was born in the year 1798. He was married to Margaret, daughter of James Fulton, Esq., and Margaret Campbell, widow of the late Samuel Creelman. Mrs. Rutherford died February 10th, 1824, aged 31 years, and he was married again to the widow Pears. He settled at Smithfield where he died April 22nd, 1843.

Elizabeth Johnson, James Rutherford, Senr.'s second wife died, and he was married again to Letitia, daughter of Timothy Putnam, Senr., and Janet Hunter, 1808. They had one son and six daughters. He died May 28th, 1828, aged 79 years, and his wife died April 27th, 1824, aged 38 years.

CHAPTER XII.

Alexander Nelson, was a native of Ireland. He came out to New England when young, and having formed acquaintance with James Yuill, Esq., they removed together to Nova Scotia in the year 1761. He settled on the same place on which his grandson, William Nelson, now resides, near what was called "Old Barns." He was one of the Grantees of Truro Township. He and James Yuill, Esq., and James

Yuill, Junr., had the whole of their rights of land laid off together in one lot. It was about one mile in breadth, and four miles back from the Bay. The greater part of this land is still owned by their descendants. Alexander Nelson was married to Margaret Robertson shortly before they came to Nova Scotia.

Elizabeth, their eldest daughter, was born in Truro, December 15th, 1763. She was married to Thomas McFadion, and had one son and five daughters.

William Montague, the eldest son of Alexander and Margaret Nelson, was born in Truro, July 15th, 1765. He was married to Jane Ellis in 1790. He settled on the west side of the Shubenacadie River near the Railroad bridge. He died there December 15th, 1842, aged 77 years. His wife died December 1st, 1827, aged 57 years. Sarah Nelson, their eldest daughter, was born September 17th, 1791. She died unmarried, August 18th, 1872, aged 81 years. Alexander Nelson, their eldest son, was born June 7th, 1793. He died a bachelor September 11th 1824, aged 31 years. James Nelson, their second son, was born March 21st, 1795. He was married to Alice, the eighth daughter of James Moore and Susan Teas, his wife, October, 1828. They had two sons and one daughter. Mrs. Nelson died March 21st, 1834. He was married again to Isabell Gilrie from England, July, 1836. They had three sons and one daughter. His second wife died December 24th, 1843. He inherited a part of his father's farm. William, the third son of William M. and Jane Nelson, was born July 14th, 1797. He was married to Rachel Wallace, December 16, 1834. They had six sons and four daughters. (The Rev. J. W. Nelson of New Brunswick is their son). He inherited a part of his father's farm. He died April 4th, 1867, aged 70 years. Archibald Nelson, their fourth son, was born September 7th, 1799. He died May 17th, 1820, aged 21 years. Margaret Nelson, their second daughter, was born March 11th, 1802. She died September 20th 1820, aged 18 years. Jane Nelson, their third daughter, was born November 16th, 1803. She was married to Daniel Moor January, 1829. They had three sons and four daughters. Mr. Moor died April, 1863, aged 73 years. Robinson Nelson, their fifth son, was born July 10th, 1806. He was married to Elizabeth Bradley, widow of the late Alexander Archibald, November 29th, 1838. They had one son and one daughter. Dorothy Nelson, their fourth daughter, was born May 4th, 1809. Isabell Nelson, their fifth daughter, was born April 21st, 1812. She was married to Thomas John Andrews, December 1st, 1830. They had four sons and one daughter. She died January 6th, 1865, aged 53 years. Mr. Andrews died February, 1872, aged 67 years. Thomas Nelson, their sixth son, was born September 7th 1815. He was married to Sarah Casey, January, 1840. They had two sons. Mrs. Nelson died in 1845. He was married again to Mary Archibald in 1846. They had one son and two daughters. Mr. Nelson died May, 1855. Agnes, their second daughter, was born February 14th, 1767. She was married to Stephen Jackson, and had one son and two daughters.

Archibald, the second son of Alexander and Margaret Nelson, was born September 6th, 1768. He was married to Jane Hill, December 9th, 1812. He inherited the homestead part of his father's farm, where they reared their family. He died December 5th, 1861, aged 93 years, and his wife died February 24th, aged 66 years. Margaret Nelson, their eldest daughter, was born October 30th, 1813. She was married to John Rose of the county of Digby in August, 1841. They had two sons and three daughters. ' Elizabeth, their second daughter, was born November 10th, 1814. She was married to Robert, son of Robert and Catherine Corbet, May 12th, 1855, and settled in Hants county. Anne, their daughter, was born May 28th, 1817. She was married to Ebenezer, son of John B. and Catherine Archibald, January 24th, 1837. They had four sons and five daughters. These appear among the Archibalds. Alexander Hill, the eldest son of Archibald and Jane Nelson, was born January 21st, 1819. William, their youngest son, was born April 17th, 1820. He is living a bachelor on the homestead.

Charles, the third son of Alexander and Margaret Nelson, was born April 22nd, 1770. He was married to Renew Fish, of Newport, October 24th, 1794. Sarah B., their eldest daughter, was born in Truro, September 26th, 1795. She was married to Mr. Daniel Campbell, and removed to St. John, N. B. Margaret, the second daughter of Charles and Renew Nelson was born March 9th, 1797. She was married to James Smith, who came from England a short time before, February 18th, 1821. They had three sons and seven daughters. Shortly after they were married, they settled in the woods at Harmony, being the same place on which their sons now reside. Here they reared their family, and he died there June 22nd, 1865, aged 72 years. His wife died April 29th, 1862, aged 65 years. Alexander, the eldest son of Charles and Renew Nelson, was born May

4th, 1799.   He was married to Jane, the fourth daughter of Alexander and Rebecca Miller, April 8th, 1823.   They had six sons and four daughters.   Charles, the second son of Charles and Renew Nelson was born in Truro, June 4th, 1801.   He removed to Boston, Mass., where he married and had a family.   Robinson, their third son, was born June 15th, 1803.   He died a bachelor, March 30th, 1829. Elias and Nancy, their twin son and daughter, were born March 23rd, 1805.   Nancy was married to William Hall, May 4th, 1830.   They had two sons and two daughters.   Renew (Mr. Nelson's first wife) died February 11th, 1807, aged 33 years.   He was married again to Mary, daughter of John and Mary Logan, widow of the late Abner Doggett, April 13th, 1809.   He inherited a part of his father's property, at Old Barns, until he was married the second time ; then he sold his farm to James Laughead, Senr., and removed to the Upper Village of Truro, and built an end to the house in which Mr. William Cummings now resides.   Here they kept an inn during the remainder of their lives.   He died August 20th, 1847, aged 77 years ; and his wife, Mary, died June 23rd, 1850, aged 77 years. Abner Doggett, died January 26th 1807, aged 32 years.   Renew, the eldest daughter of Charles and Mary Nelson, was born February 14th, 1810.   She was married to William Cutten, eldest son of William Smith and Esther Hunter, his wife, January 7th, 1831.   They had four sons and six daughters.   Mary Ann, their second daughter, was born July 24th, 1812.   She was married to Daniel, second son of Captain William Cock and Ann Frost, January 7th 1831.   They had six sons and six daughters.   William, the only son of Charles and Mary Nelson, was born July 22nd 1815.   He was married to Mizey Ann, the eldest daughter of John Yuill and Jane McNutt, his wife, December 25th, 1836.   They had six sons and three daughters.

John, the fourth son of Alexander and Margaret Nelson, was born February 12th, 1772.   He was married to Elizabeth Polley, widow of the late Ebenezer Cock, March 21st, 1799.   He was drowned, December, 1857, aged 85 years.   His wife died at Pitch Brook, December, 1838.   Ebenezer Cock Nelson, their eldest son was born June 17th, 1800.   He was married to Mary Noble in 1839.   They had five sons and three daughters.   He died August 1st 1864.   His wife died March, 1859, aged 38 years.   Alexander Young Nelson, their second son, was born November 26th, 1802.   He was married to Alice, the eldest daughter of Robinson and Isabel Nelson, February, 1833.   They had four sons and two daughters.   Their children are all dead. John Gordon Nelson, their third son, was born October 7th, 1804. He was married to Mary Logan, January 12th, 1826. They had one son. Mrs. Nelson died June 28th, 1829, aged 28 years. He was married again to Sarah Kent, March 12th, 1831. They had five sons and two daughters. Mrs. Nelson died in 1845. He was married again to Eleanor Fraser, January 8th, 1852. They have three daughters. Nathaniel Nelson, their fourth son, was born in 1806. He was married to Jane, third daughter of Robinson and Isabel Nelson, December, 1832. They had three sons and three daughters. He settled in Hants County. Archibald Nelson, their fifth son, was born in 1808. He was married to Nancy Colter, July, 1832. They had five sons and two daughters. He died in 1858. Phoeby Nelson, their eldest daughter, was born December 8th, 1810. She was married to John Gibbens February 5th, 1836. They had one daughter. Mr. Gibbens died away from home in 1837. She was married again to John Lennerton November, 1841. They had four sons and one daughter. Mr. Lennerton died October 10th, 1864. Eleanor Nelson their second daughter, was born August, 1812. She removed to Prince Edward Island, and was married there to James Conway. They had sons and daughters. She died there April, 1869, aged 57 years. Susan Nelson, their third daughter, was born at Stewiacke, in 1814. She removed to Canada and was married there. Margaret Nelson, their fourth daughter, was born August, 1816. She removed to New Hampshire, and was married there.

James, the fifth son of Alexander and Margaret Nelson, was born in Truro, January 21st, 1773. He was married to Abigail, daughter of Solomon Hoar and Mary Lynds, his wife, Nov. 17th, 1803. He was a blacksmith by trade. He removed to Stewiacke in 1809, and settled on the farm, on which his son Robinson now resides, on the west side of the South Meadow. He died there March, 1858, aged 85 years. His wife died December 28th, 1844, aged 63 years. Solomon Nelson, their eldest son, was born August 28th, 1804. He was married to Sarah, daughter of William Dickey, and Eleanor Gammell, his wife, in 1828. He died in 1830. Alexander Nelson, their second son, was born July 28th, 1806. He was married to Margaret Conley March 25th, 1825. They had four sons and four daughters. He settled in Upper Brookfield, where he reclaimed his farm from the forest. Margaret the eldest daughter, of James and Abigail Nelson, was married to Asa Hoar, December 25th, 1835. She died July 25th, 1838. Abigail Nelson, their second daughter, was married to James Mullon.

Elizabeth Nelson, their third daughter, was married to Joseph Moxom. They had six sons and five daughters. She died in 1854. Robinson Nelson, their third son, was married to Rachel Dean of Musquodoboit. They had three sons and two daughters. Mrs. Nelson died, and he was married again to Eleanor, daughter of Stephen Johnson and Nancy Miller, his wife, in 1862. Ruth Nelson, their fourth daughter was married to James Boomer. They had two sons and three daughters. James Nelson, their fourth son, was born May 1st, 1818. He was married to Margaret Archibald of Stewiacke, February, 1841. They had four sons and four daughters. He settled north of Brookfield, where he reclaimed his farm from the forest. William Nelson, their fifth son removed to the United States, was married, and had a family there. Charles Nelson, their sixth son, was married to Nancy Dunn. They had three sons and three daughters. He settled in Pleasant Valley. Mary Nelson, their fifth daughter, was married to John Burris of Pleasant Valley. They had three sons and five daughters.

Robinson, the sixth son of Alexander and Margaret Nelson, was born in Truro, August 23rd, 1774. He was married to Isabell, daughter of William and Alice Philips, Dec. 31st, 1807. He settled on the Bay Shore, where his son William now resides. He died there April, 1850, aged 76 years. His widow removed to the United States to reside with her daughters. She died there June, 1870, aged 81 years. Alice Nelson, their eldest daughter was born December 25th, 1808. She was married to Alexander Y., son of John and Elizabeth Nelson, February, 1833. They had three sons and two daughters. Their children are all dead. Margaret Nelson, their second daughter, was born Oct. 17th, 1810. She was married to Francis Forbes, Nov. 16th, 1828. They had three sons and three daughters. She died March 15th, 1849, aged 38 years. Mr. Forbes died June 28th, 1848, aged 54 years. Jane Nelson, their third daughter, was born November 17th, 1812. She was married to Nathaniel, son of John and Elizabeth Nelson, December, 1832. They had three sons and three daughters. They settled in the County of Hants. Rebecca Nelson, their fourth daughter, was born Oct. 15th, 1814. She was married to Thomas Dart, of Pleasant Valley, December, 1835. They had seven sons and one daughter. Mr. Dart died June 14th, 1864, aged 54 years. William, the only son of Robinson and Isabell Nelson, was born November 17th, 1816. He was married to Mary Sibley, June, 1855. He inherited his father's farm. They had two sons. Mrs. Nelson died May 22nd, 1858. He was married again to Mary Dunbrack of Musquodoboit, March, 1860. Elizabeth Nelson, their fifth daughter, was born February 14th, 1820. She removed to the United States, and was married there to Mr. Danney in 1867. They had one daughter. Mr. Danney died in 1871. Nancy Nelson, the sixth daughter, was born November 19th, 1822. She removed to the United States, and was married there to James Price. They had one son and one daughter. Mary Susan Nelson, their seventh daughter, was born October, 1827. She removed to the United States, and was married there to Henry Allon, September, 1848. Martha Ann, their eighth daughter, was born January, 1831. She removed to the United States, and was married there to John Stork in 1854. They had two sons and one daughter. She died there in 1865. Isabell and Abigail Nelson, their twin daughters. were born in 1836. Isabell was married to James Price in the United States. She died there. Abigail was married to John Graham. She died in 1857.

Jane, the third daughter of Alexander and Margaret Nelson was born September 12th, 1775. She was married to Daniel, son of Samson and Martha Moore. They had one son and two daughters. Mr. Moore was lost at sea, and she was married again to James Gradie, and removed to Halifax.

Margaret, the fourth daughter of Alexander and Margaret Nelson, was born July 10th, 1779. She was married to Edward Faulkner of Economy. They had three sons and four daughters.

Alexander, their seventh son, was born March 1st, 1781. He was married to Margaret T., daughter of Samuel Miller, and Elizabeth Davison, December 23rd, 1812. They settled on the east side of Shubenacadie River, about 12 miles from its mouth, where they reared their family. He died there July, 1839, aged 58 years, and his wife died October 1st, 1865, aged 74 years. Robinson, their eldest son, was born 1814. He removed to Vermont, U. S., and was married there to Lucy Minerva Fitch in 1857. Samuel, their second son, was born 1816. He died a bachelor in August, 1868. Nancy, their eldest daughter, was born in 1818. She was married to William, son of Elias Nelson, January, 1840. They had three sons and three daughters. Archibald, their third son, was born September, 1820. He was married to Jemima, daughter of John Douglass, of Maitland, February 2nd, 1843. They have three sons. They are settled at the Rail Road station at Shubenacadie, where they keep an Inn. Elizabeth, their second daughter, was born 1823. She was married to Joseph Crosby, from England, January, 1858. They have one son and three daughters. They settled in New Brunswick.

Elias, the eighth son of Alexander and Margaret Nelson, was born April 26th, 1783. He was married to Elizabeth Forbes, January 7th, 1806. He settled, reared his family, and spent the remainder of his life at Rockville, in the County of Hants. He died there April 14th, 1871, aged 88 years. Robert, their eldest son, was married to Sarah Hayes. They had two sons and four daughters. He died April 18th, 1854. Alexander, their second son, was married to Lavinia, daughter of Robert Smith, of Maitland. They had two sons and four daughters. Mrs. Nelson died, and he was married again to Laura Perkins. Samuel, their third son, was born June 21st, 1810. He was married to Catherine Dart, January 1st, 1834. They had four sons and one daughter. William, their fourth son, was born 1811. He was married to Nancy, daughter of Alexander and Margaret Nelson, January 1840. They had three sons and three daughters. Charles, their fifth son, was born May 6th, 1812. He was married to Sarah Ann Moor, February 11th, 1845. They have two sons. Mary Ann was born 1814. She was married to Charles Wilson, 1842. They have two sons and two daughters. Renew, their second daughter, was born 1816. She died in 1860. John, their sixth son, was born 1818. He died 1847. Elias, their seventh son, was born 1820. He was married to Mary Ann Lawrence, of Maitland, January, 1848. They had three sons and three daughters. He was drowned September 4th, 1871. Letitia, their third daughter was born 1822. She was married to James Lawrence. They had two daughters. Mr. Lawrence died, and she was married again, to Richard Scalling in 1869. Archibald, their eighth son, was born 1824. He was married to Ruby Faulkner. December, 1858. They had one son and four daughters. He lately removed to the United States.

Alice, the fifth daughter of Alexander and Margaret Nelson, was born April 26th, 1785. She died when she was young. Rebecca, their sixth daughter, was born March 20th, 1787. She was married to William Moore, son of William Moore and Susan Long, his wife. They removed to the United States. Alexander Nelson, Senr., died about the year 1810, and his widow died January 24th, 1823.

CHAPTER XIII.

James Wright was one of the first settlers of Truro and a Grantee of the Township. His house lot was at the east end of the Village, lying between the cross streets east of the old Methodist Chapel and extending north to the River. His first house stood near the place that the old Baptist Chapel now stands. He lived in this house for a length of time, and then sold the south part of his lot to Daniel Cock, and the remaining part to Timothy Prout. Mr. Wright built his next house on his front wood lot, on the hill near the place that Mr. L. J. Walker now resides. He sold this place to George Dill, Esq., about the year 1804, and lived with some of his sons the remainder of his life. He died at the house of his eldest son, John, who lived then in a house which was built by William McKeen, near the place that Mrs. McClure now resides. He died about the year 1820. He was married to Deborah, daughter of Ephraim Howard, Senr., in the year 1765.

John, the eldest son of James and Deborah Wright, was born in Truro, November 7th 1766. He was married to Sarah, daughter of Jacob Lynds, Senr., November 25th, 1788. Deborah, the eldest daughter of John and Sarah Wright, was born in Onslow, October 9th, 1789. She was married to Edward McCollum, October 3rd, 1816. They had five sons and one daughter. Mr. McCollum died April 5th, 1855, aged 65 years. Ruth Wright, their second daughter, was born December 25th, 1790. She was married to Amos Maynord, January 1st, 1815. They had four sons and five daughters. They settled in Lower Stewiacke. She died there November, 1870, aged 80 years. Mr. Maynord died December 9th, 1872, aged 82 years. James Wright, their eldest son, was born July 17th, 1792. He was married to Abigail Ryan, of Hants County, June 10th, 1817. He settled on Onslow Mountain. They had four sons and six daughters. Sarah Wright, their third daughter, was born October 25th, 1793. She died unmarried, August 28th, 1825, aged 31 years. David Wright, their second son, was born August 7th 1796. On August 6th, 1825, he was engaged getting hay at Fort Ellis, on the Marsh. He went into the river to bathe and was drowned. William Wright their third son, was born March 1st, 1798. He was married to Hannah Crowell. He settled at Pleasant Valley. They had five sons and five daughters. Mrs. Wright died September 8th, 1846. He was married again to Mary Fisher, widow of the late John Conley, June, 1849. They had two daughters. Mrs. Wright died. Rebecca Wright, their fourth daughter, was born August 22nd, 1799. She was married to Job Field. They had three sons. Jacob Wright, their fourth son, was born January 14th, 1801. He was married to Mary Fulton, of Stewiacke, December 7th, 1825. They had three sons and three daughters. Mrs. Wright died August 12th, 1854. He was married again to Elizabeth McMullon. They had two sons and five daughters. Lucy Wright, their fifth daughter, was born July 17th, 1802. She was married to Ephraim, son of Moses and Lydia Wright. They had three sons and three daughters. They reside in the Wright settlement of Stewiacke. Esther Wright, their sixth daughter, was born September 1803. She was married to George S. Dickey, December 27th, 1833. They had two sons and three daughters. Mr. Dickey died May 2nd, 1864. Miriam Wright, their seventh daughter, was born in 1805. She was married to Solomon, son of Moses and Lydia Wright of Stewiacke. They had five sons and three daughters. Elizabeth Wright, their eighth daughter, was born in 1806. She was married to William Blair January 24th, 1827. They had six sons and six daughters. They removed to Illinois, U. S., in 1842.

James, son of James and Deborah Wright, was born in Truro, August 9th, 1769. He removed to the United States, and was married there to Miss Bartlet.

Jonas, their third son, was born December 3rd, 1770. He removed to Cape Breton, and died a bachelor.

George, their fourth son, was born October 2nd, 1772. He removed to Cape Breton about the year 1813. He died there a bachelor.

Sarah, the only daughter of James and Deborah Wright, was born in Truro, October 26th, 1773. She was married to Henry Miller, March 22nd, 1796. They settled first in the woods on the old Halifax road, about four miles from the iron foundry in Truro, southeast of the place where William Holstead now resides. The first road from Truro to Halifax passed the place where the iron foundry now stands, and over the high hill, south of this place, passing through Brookfield, east of the present road. Mr. Miller and family removed about the year 1818 to Brandy Brook, being the same place that Peter Serret now resides. They continued there, and kept an inn, until

Mr. Miller died. She then removed to the place that her sons had settled, now called the Miller Settlement, on the Mountain on the south side of Stewiacke River, where she died. They had four sons and seven daughters ; their sons' names were James, Moses, George, and Henry.

Robert, the fifth son of James and Deborah Wright, was born in Truro, November, 1775. He followed the sea when he was a young man, and was on board a ship of war for some time. He returned to Truro about the year 1815, and worked for Mr. Charles Nelson and others, for a few years, and then removed to Shepody. He married and died there.

William Wright, their sixth son, was born in Truro, November 18th, 1777. He removed to Shepody, and was married to Miss Clark. They lived and died there.

Ephraim, their seventh son, was born in Truro, April 8th, 1779. He was married to Mary Blachford in 1805. They settled at St. Andrew's, south of Lower Stewiacke, where they reared their family, and spent the remainder of their days. Mrs. Wright died in 1835, and he was married again to Nancy, widow of the late Samuel Archibald, of St. Mary's, July, 1843.

James, the eldest son of Ephraim and Mary Wright, was born in 1806. He was married in the State of Maine to Miss Stevens. Sarah, their eldest daughter, was born March 12th, 1808. She married John Godfry. They had three sons and seven daughters. They removed to Wisconsin. Elizabeth, the second daughter, was born in 1810. She was married to James Ramsey. They had three sons and three daughters. She died June 12th, 1853, and he died July 21st, 1862. Robert Wright, their second son, was born May 2nd, 1814. He was married to Elizabeth Sibley in 1836. They had six sons and five daughters. Mrs. Wright died August, 1857. He was married again to Phebe Ann Howard, February 1860. Daniel McHaffey Wright, was born March 17th, 1817. He was married to Ann Thomas of New Brunswick. They had seven sons and three daughters. Mary Ann, their third daughter, was born August, 1819. She was married to John Richardson. They had three sons and five daughters. They removed to Cape Breton. She died there in March, 1863. He died in November 1855, aged 76 years.

Moses, the eighth and youngest son of James and Deborah Wright, was born in Truro, December 3rd, 1780. He was married to Lydia, daughter of Solomon Hoar, of Onslow, about the year 1806. They settled on the east side of the South Meadow of Stewiacke, on the same farm on which Hugh Graham Cox now resides. About the year 1826, he sold this farm and removed to Goshen where he spent the remainder of his life.

Ephraim, their eldest son was born in the year 1807. He was married to Lucy, the fifth daughter of John and Sarah Wright, They had three sons and three daughters. Solomon, their second son, was married to Miriam, the seventh daughter of John and Sarah Wright. They had five sons and three daughters. Lydia, their eldest daughter, was married to Moses, second son of Henry Miller and Sarah Wright, his wife. Mr. and Mrs. Miller both died a considerable time ago.

Mary, their second daughter, removed to the United States, and died there. James, their third son, was married to Sarah Dickey. They had eight sons and three daughters. William, their fourth son, is still living a bachelor. Moses their fifth and youngest son, was married to Rebecca, daughter of Amos Maynord and Ruth Wright, his wife. They had five sons and six daughters. Olive, the youngest daughter of Moses and Lydia Wright, was married to Daniel Tupper, and had two daughters. Jane, the youngest daughter of James and Deborah Wright, was born in Truro in the year 1782. She lived until old and died unmarried.

John Ryan was another of the early settlers of Truro, and a Grantee of the Township. He owned lot number six of the front division of wood lots, being the east lot, owned now by Mr. John L. Doggett. He had his house on the north east of Mr. Doggett's house. He sold out to Alexander Miller and removed to the county of Hants, where there are some of his decendants now. His house was burnt shortly after he left it. He had five sons and three daughters.

CHAPTER XIV.

There was one Right of the Township of Truro granted for the first Presbyterian Minister who would settle in Truro, one Right for a glebe, and another Right for the benefit of schools. It may here be observed that all the first settlers, and grantees of Truro were Presbyterians from Scotland, and the north of Ireland. They soon began to feel the loss to themselves and their children, from the want of a

Preached Gospel. They soon began to exert themselves to obtain a minister to labour amongst them. In the year 1763, they petitioned the Presbytery of Glasgow for a minister, but this petition never reached its destination. May 21st, 1764, they sent their application to the Synod of Edinburgh, and in July or August of the year 1765 the Rev. Mr. Kenlock arrived in Truro, and continued to labour in and about Truro for about three years. Then he returned to Scotland, and did not accept the call from the people of Truro to be their settled pastor.

At the earnest request of the people of Truro, the Rev. Daniel Cock came out from Scotland in the fall of the year 1769. He was sent out as a Missionary for the whole Province, and continued to labour in Truro and other parts of the Province for a time.

On the 27th day of February, 1770, David Archibald, George Scott, Robert Hunter, and John Savage (being a committee) directed the inhabitants of Truro to be warned to meet at the house of Robert Archibald on March 13th to hear the report of the Clerk of the Presbytery of Newton Lambavady, in Ireland, read. Also to hear the report of their commissioner, Colonel Alexander McNutt, concerning the prospect of obtaining a Minister to be settled among them. At this meeting held on March 13th, 1770 (John Savage in the chair), It was resolved that David Archibald, John Johnson, William Fisher, James Johnson, and John Savage, be a committee to renew their application to the Presbytery of Lambavady in Ireland for a Minister to labour amongst them. And on July 28th, 1770, David Archibald, Esq., directs the heads of families of Truro to be warned to meet at the Meeting-house, on Thursday next, at 2 o'clock, P. M., to see what their minds are respecting the making application to the Rev. David Cock to be their settled Minister, and to agree upon proposals to be made to him. Also to see if they will desire Mr. Cock to appoint a fast day for the election of elders in this town, so that there may be a session constituted in the congregation. And to see about having the Church put in some kind of order, so that public worship may be held in it, as it will soon be inconvenient to have public worship in barns.

It may here be observed that the frame of this Church was raised in the spring of the year 1768. As it was made of very large and heavy timber, it took all the men that could be got in Truro and Onslow to raise it, with the assistance of a number of the women. It is said that when they came to fix the site for the Church there was a difference of opinion about where it should be. Some were for having it placed on the site of William Nelson's house, and others were for having it where it was erected, in the Truro Cemetery. There was a majority of the congregation residing in the Lower Village and Old Barns, consequently the lower place was chosen as the place for the Church. It may be easily understood that a house of its size could not be put up and finished as soon as it could be done now-a-days. At a meeting held July 6th, 1772, it was resolved that nails, glass, &c., for the outside of the Meeting House be got immediately.

A few years after this, Eliakim Tupper, Esq., took a contract to complete the inside of the Church, and the workmen who finished it were John Christie, who came out from Scotland in the same ship with Mr. Cock and his family in the summer of the year 1772, and Daniel McKenzie, who was afterwards married to Sarah, daughter of Hugh Moor, Senr. This was the only Church in Truro until about the year 1821, when the Episcopalians erected their Church in the east end of the Village. In the year 1832 the Baptists of Truro and Onslow with the assistance of the Presbyterians, built the small Church at the east end of the Village which is now being made into a private dwelling by Mr. Samuel Nelson. This house, when built, was for the use of all denominations. In the year 1844 the Methodists built their small Church in the east end of the Village which they have now abandoned. Their new one was opened for Divine Service on December 24th, 1871. The established Church of Scotland erected their Church in Truro in the year 1861. The Baptists erected their new splendid Church in the year 1869. The Roman Catholics opened their small brick Chapel for Service in November, 1871.

The Presbyterians built their Church in the Village in the year 1853. In the year 1859 it was found to be too small for the accommodation of the congregation, and 19 feet were added to its length. In the month of May, 1855 the old Church which was raised in 1768, was taken down and removed, some time after all those who had assisted in erecting it had passed away. It was used for a place of worship for 85 years.

September 13th, 1770, is the date of the call that was made out and presented to the Rev. Daniel Cock, from the Truro congregation, which he accepted. This call was signed by seven elders who had been chosen but a few weeks before, and 42 adherents. The names of the elders were, David Archibald, John Johnson, William Fisher,

James Johnson, Robert Hunter, John Savage, and Samuel Archibald. The names of the adherents are, James Yuill, Senr., Thomas Gourley, Samuel Archibald, James Archibald, Matthew Taylor, Thomas Archibald, Matthew Archibald, John Archibald, John Archibald, Junr., James Faulkner, John Fisher, James Dunlap, Robert Archibald, Alexander Nelson, William McKeen, John McKeen, John Oughterson, William White, Samuel Wetherby, Adam Dickey, James Wright, John Fulton, George Scott, David Nelson, Adam Boyd, Adam Johnson, James Archibald, Junr., James Fisher, David Archibald, Junr., James Johnson, Junr., David McKeen, James Yuill, Junr., Alexander Miller, John Gourley, John Logan, William Logan, Thomas Skeed, John Taylor, Joseph Moore, Henry Gluen, James Whidden, David Whidden, and Alexander McNutt. This call was signed in the presence of Ephraim Howard and William Blair, of Onslow. It was accompanied by a bond signed by thirty of the foregoing named persons, binding themselves, their heirs, executors, administrators and assigns, to pay the full sum of sixty pounds for each year for the first two years, commencing on April 1st, 1770. Seventy pounds a year for the next two years, and eighty pounds a year for the time to come, the one half to be paid in cash, and the other half in neat stock or produce, at cash price. Also the one Right of land that was granted for the first Minister who would settle in Truro, to himself, his heirs, and assigns forever. Also the use of the glebe Right. And they bind themselves to keep both of these Rights of land fenced and dyked ; and to pay the sum of thirty pounds towards the expense of removing his family from Scotland.

The subscribers to the foregoing call were all inhabitants of Truro. The people of Onslow must have come in and joined this congregation some time after the date of the call. They continued to be one congregation until about the year 1816, when Onslow was set off as a separate congregation, and the people of Onslow obtained the services of the Rev. Robert Douglass as their first Minister.

The 13th day of September, 1870, one hundred years after the date of the call before mentioned, was observed in Truro as a day of thankfulness. A large number of people assembled in the Church in the morning, and engaged in Devotional exercises, and then marched in orderly procession to the drill shed, where about fifteen hundred persons sat down to a well prepared dinner, and after dinner addresses were given by a number of the aged Ministers who were listened to attentively by about two thousand persons.

Mr. Cock returned home to Scotland, and brought out his wife and family in the summer of the year 1772. Although the grant of the Township was obtained in the year 1765, it was not sub-divided until after Mr. Cock was settled, and his Right, as the first Minister, was set off to him, and his name marked on the general plan of the Township, on the several lots set off to him. He had his house built on his front wood lot where the house now stands which was afterwards owned by the Rev. John Waddell. A part of this lot is now used as the Railway Station.

On May 8th, 1796, being Sabbath, he was preaching in the old Church before mentioned. The people being nearly all at Church, his house took fire on the roof by a spark from the chimney, and before assistance could be had the house was in flames. George Wright ran to the Church for assistance (a distance of about two miles). He went to the door and cried out fire! fire! and returned with haste. Few persons heard him, and those who did hear began to go out, which created quite a confusion in the house. It was some time before the cause of the stir was generally known. At length his youngest daughter, who had been married to John Smith about two months before, went up to the Pulpit and told her father that his house was burning. He closed the Bible and stepped down from the Pulpit, quite composed, and recommended the people to try and save the Village. It being a very dry time, and the wind blowing very strong from the southeast, the fire soon caught on Major John Archibald's three barns. The burning shingles were flying, and the smoke so thick it was with difficulty that the people got up through the Village. John Logan's barns next took fire, and then William Logan's barns. The fire continued to sweep the buildings of the Village to the lower end of it. The number of buildings destroyed that day was eighteen. The dwelling houses were saved, with the exception of Mr. Cock's and William Flemming's. This house stood near the place that William Flemming's old house stood, which he recently took down. Thomas Dickey's house, being the same one that is still standing west of Mrs. Wilson's, was in great danger, the chips catching fire at the door; and, as there were neither men nor water at hand to save the house, Mrs. Dickey took her churn full of cream and applied it to quench the fire, and by doing so made out to save her house. There was a valuable horse tied in William Logan's barn, which stood in the flames until the rope burnt off, and then the horse bolted into the street and fell dead. Mr. Cock's house, with the most of its contents being burnt, is sufficient to show the reason that so few of his writings are now to be had, as he would be nearly eighty years old at the time of the fire. He had another house erected for him on the same place. He lived but a few years in it.

About two and a half years after this, an assistant, and a successor, was obtained in the person of Rev. John Waddell, and Mr. Cock was soon laid aside from active and public labors, as the infirmities of old age were fast coming upon him. He made over his property to his youngest son, Daniel, and about the year 1802, he sold it to Mr. Waddell. He removed, with his son Daniel, to the place where George Cock now resides, and continued to reside with his son Daniel the short remainder of his earthly existence. He died March 17th, 1805, aged 88 years, and his wife died at the house of John Smith, June 7th, 1814, aged 80 years.

CHAPTER XV.

Mr. Cock was born in Clydesdale, Scotland, in the year 1717. He was married to Alison Jamison about the year 1754. He was settled in Greenock for a length of time before he came to Nova Scotia.

William, their eldest son, was born in Scotland about the year 1755. He followed the sea when young, and went by the name of Captain Cock during the remainder of his life. He was married to Ann Frost, of Boston, U. S., in the year 1792, and shortly after this he purchased the house that Eliakim Tupper, Esq., built in the Village, being the same house that Mr. John Dunlap owned and resided in for a considerable length of time.

Jane, the eldest daughter of William and Ann Cock, was born in Truro, November 25th, 1793. She was married to William Ross. December 31st, 1818. They had two sons ; their names were John and William. Mr. Ross died April 28th, 1824, aged 44 years, and she was married again to John Dunlap, December 1st, 1825. They had two sons and four daughters which appear among the Dunlap families. She died March 1st 1867, aged 73 years, and her husband died May 1st, 1842, aged 44 years.

Mary Ann, the second daughter of Captain William Cock and Ann Frost, was born May 15th, 1797. She was married to Robert C.

Blair, March 18th, 1818.   They had seven daughters who appear among the Blair family.   Mr. Blair died May 6th, 1869, aged 77 years.

Anna, their third daughter, was born in Truro, October 3rd, 1799. She was married to Robert, the youngest son of James Kent, Esq., and Margaret Williams, December 31st, 1818. They had six sons and five daughters.   Mr. Kent died January 3rd, 1867, aged 76 years.

William Jamison, the eldest son of Captain William and Ann Cock was born in Truro, April 29th, 1803.   He inherited his father's property ; he died a bachelor, June 17th, 1870, aged 67.

Daniel, their second son, was born June 18th, 1805.   He was married to Mary Ann, the youngest daughter of Charles and Mary Nelson, January 6th, 1831.   They settled on the interval of Salmon River where they still reside.   Harriet, the eldest daughter of Daniel and Mary Ann Cock, was born in 1831.   She was married to Robert Christie, March 7th 1850.   They had four sons and three daughters. William Cock, their eldest son, was born November 28th, 1832.   He was married to Janet Kent, December 27th, 1865.   They have one son and one daughter.   Mary Cock, their second daughter was born February 9th, 1835.   She was married to Walter Christie, May 15th, 1862.   They had one son and three daughters.   Anna Cock, their third daughter, was born April 3rd, 1837.   She was married to Frederick Freize of Hants county, February, 1864.   Charles N. Cock, their second son, was born September 3rd, 1839, He was married to Elizabeth Stearns, October, 1865.   They have one son and two daughters.   Henry Cock, their third son, was born January 28th, 1842.   He was married to Hannah Margaret McLeod, of the West River of Pictou, January 11th, 1871.   Jane Cock, their fourth daughter, was born July 18th, 1845.   Herbert Cock, their fourth son, was born October 26th, 1847.   He removed to the Southern States. Emily Cock, their fifth daughter, was born March 11th, 1850. Daniel Cock, their fifth son, was born November 1852.   Agnes Cock, their sixth daughter, was born June 19th, 1855.   Albert Cock, their sixth son, was born May 15th, 1858.

Alison Jamison, the fourth daughter of Captain William and Ann Cock, was born September 29th, 1808.   She was married to Samuel James, the eldest son of Samuel and Nancy Blair, December 24th, 1833.   They had two sons and five daughters, and a number of grand-children which appear among the Blairs.

Elizabeth Johnson, the youngest daughter of Captain William and Ann Cock, was born November 1st, 1815.   Captain William

Cock died, May 1st, 1832, aged 77 years, and his wife died April, 1854.

Patrick, the second son of the Rev. Daniel Cock and Alison Jamison, was born in Scotland in the year 1757, and was brought by his parents to Nova Scotia when he was about 15 years old. He remained with them while they lived, and after their death he continued to live with his youngest brother, Daniel Cock. He was deaf and dumb and died a bachelor, June 7th, 1822, Aged 65 years.

Mary Ann, the eldest daughter of the Rev. Daniel and Alison Cock, was born in Scotland about the year 1759. She was married to Richard Upham. They settled in Stewiacke in the year 1785. They were married in the year 1784. Mrs. Upham died March, 1842, and Mr. Upham died October, 1825.

Daniel, the eldest son of Richard and Mary Ann Upham, was born in Truro, September 22nd, 1786. He settled at Otter Brook, Stewiacke. He was very successful in trapping and shooting bears. He was married to Charlotte, the fourth daughter of Samuel Fisher and Mary Tupper, his wife, in the month of October, 1826. They had two sons and three daughters. He died at Middle Stewiacke, May 15th, 1871, aged 85 years, and his wife died June 11th, 1865, aged 65 years. Richard, the second son of Richard Upham and Mary Ann Cock, was born in May 1788. He was married to Elizabeth McCann of Wallace River, about the year 1838. He inherited a part of his father's property on the north side of the North Meadow of Stewiacke for a time, and then sold out and removed to Wallace, and died there May 2nd, 1871. Elizabeth, the eldest daughter of Richard and Mary Ann Upham, was born in the year 1791. She lived and died unmarried. She died April 29th, 1855. Alison Jamison, their second daughter, was born in the year 1793. She was married to John Jeffers. She died February 26th, 1861. Mary Ann, their third daughter, was born in the year 1795. She died unmarried, August 1st, 1855, aged 60 years. Ebenezer, their third son, was born in March 1797. He was married to Sarah, daughter of Eddy Whidden and Sarah Fisher his wife, about the year 1828. They had two sons and four daughters. He removed and settled in New Annan, where his wife died May, 1857. William, their fourth son, was born May 3rd, 1800. He is living a bachelor. Robert, their fifth son, was born April 28th, 1803. He married Jane Davison, January 18th, 1843. They had four sons and six daughters. They reside near the Albion Mines.

Christiann, the second daughter of the Rev. Daniel and Alison Cock, was born in Scotland about the year 1762, and was brought by her parents to Truro when about 10 years old. She was married to Mayhew, the eldest son of Eliakim Tupper, Esq., and Elizabeth Newcomb his wife, April 22nd, 1784. They had three sons and three daughters ; they appear among the Tuppers. Mr. Tupper died in 1803. She was married again to John, son of James and Ann Fulton, of the Lower Village of Truro. John Fulton had been married before and had two sons and five daughters. They are all dead. They removed to Ohio, U. S.

Robert, the third son of Rev. Daniel and Alison Cock, was born in Scotland about the year 1765. He followed the sea when young. He quit the sea and was married to Mary, daughter of Dr. John Harris in the year 1795. They built a part of the house that Andrew Moore recently sold. He sold this place to Hugh Moore, and removed to the Parade, and built the house in which William Bowden now resides, and kept an Inn there until about the year 1818, when they removed to Tatamagouche Mountain, where they spent the remainder of their lives. He died there about the year 1843, aged 78 years, and his widow died in the month of November, 1864. Aged 96 years.

William, the eldest son of Robert and Mary Cock, was born in Truro, in the year 1796. He was married to Catherine, daughter of John Hingley of Tatamagouche, in the year 1823. Mary, the eldest daughter of William and Catherine Cock, was born in the year 1824. She was married to Robert Akenhead in the year 1845. They had six daughters. She died October, 1869, Aged 45 years. Jane, their eldest daughter, was born at Tatamagouche Mountain in the year 1826. She was married to Samuel Gray of New Annan in the year 1850, and has a family of children. John and Charlotte, twin son and daughter of William and Catherine Cock, were born in the year 1828. John was married to Jane, daughter of David Wilson and Mary Arbuckle his wife, of New Annan, in the year 1855. She died in the month of February; 1867, and he was married again to Mary, daughter of Alexander Conkey and Mary McCurdy his wife, September 1869. They have one child. Charlotte was married to Henry Porter, of Earltown, in the year 1854, and has sons and daughters.

Elizabeth, the fourth daughter of William and Catherine Cock, was born in the year 1830. She was married to George, son of Hugh Tucker and Ruth Lynds, his wife, in the year 1859. They have sons and daughters. Robert, the second son of William and Catherine Cock, was born in the year 1832. He has removed to the United States. William, their third son, was born in the year 1834. He has removed to the United States. Alison Jamison, the fifth daughter of William and Catherine Cock, was born in the year 1836. She was married to John, son of David Wilson of New Annan. Annie their sixth daughter, was born in the year 1838. She has removed to the United States. William Cock died February, 1862, aged 66 years.

Ebenezer, the second son of Robert and Mary Cock, was born in Truro in the year 1799. He went to Tatamagouche Mountain to chop and clear the farm to which the family afterwards removed. He was alone in camp one night, when a large bear came and looked in at the door. He soon left, but Mr. Cock said, " He sat all night with his gun in his hand to give him a ' salute ' in case he returned." Probably Bruin smelt powder. He was married to Christiann, the sixth daughter of Aaron Crowe and Abigail Murray, his wife, January 25th, 1825. Shortly after this he obtained the farm that he still lives upon in Onslow, from her brother Aaron Crowe, and they removed to it, where they reared their family. Mrs. Cock died there August 8th, 1858, aged 56 years. Abigail, the eldest daughter of Ebenezer and Christiann Cock, was born January, 1826. She was married to Charles, son of William Soley, and Isabell Hill, his wife, March 17th, 1855. She died December 6th, 1856, aged 30 years. John, the only son of Ebenezer and Christiann Cock, was born 1828. He removed to the United States, settled there and was married to Phydora Hays, March 8th, 1855. They had four sons and four daughters. Maria, their second daughter, was born in Onslow, January 4th, 1831. Lucy, their third daughter was born July 8th, 1844. Charlotte, their fourth daughter was born June 20th, 1848.

Eliza, the eldest daughter of Robert and Mary Cock, was born March 18th, 1801. She was married to James Clark Stevens, March 1st, 1827. Mary Ann, the eldest daughter of James C. and Eliza Stevens, was born June 4th, 1829. She was married to Alexander Pears of Wallace Bay, Nov. 16th, 1858. They had two sons and four daughters. Thomas, the eldest son of James C. and Eliza Stevens, was born June 26th, 1831. He removed to the United States, and was married there to Mary Ellen Wilson, in the year 1863. They have two daughters. Maria, their second daughter, was born May 5th, 1833. David Cutton, their second son was born May 25th,

1835. He removed to the United States, lost his health there, and returned home, and died a few days after, February 12th, 1859, aged 23 years. Charlotte, their third daughter, was born February 5th, 1839. She was married to James Berrell, Esq., February 17th, 1863. They have two sons and one daughter. Elizabeth, their fourth daughter, was born May 21st 1841. She died February 20th, 1863. Harriet, the fifth and youngest daughter of James C. and Eliza Stevens, was born June 10th, 1844. Mr. Stevens died November 20th, 1863.

Robert, the third son of Robert and Mary Cock, was born 1803. He was married to Lavinia, the second daughter of James Drysdale and Nancy Brown, his wife, in the year 1836. He inherits his father's farm on Tatamagouche Mountain. Amelia, their eldest daughter, was born in the year 1838. She was married to Robert, son of David and Mary Wilson, of New Annan, in the month of July, 1859. They have two sons and four daughters. George, the eldest son of Robert and Lavinia Cock, was born in the year 1841. He was married to Kate, daughter of Alexander Conkey and Mary McCann, his wife. in the month of December 1867. They have one son and one daughter. James, their second son, was born in the year 1845. He was married to Janet King, May 8th, 1872. Mary, their second daughter, was born in the year 1847. Nancy, their third daughter, was born in the year 1851. Lavinia, their youngest daughter, was born in the year 1853. The above Mary Cock was married to William Kennedy, February 20th, 1872, and Nancy was married to George Nelson, February 20th, 1872.

Charlotte, the second daughter of Robert and Mary Cock, was born in Truro, in the year 1809. She was married to Daniel Field in the year 1848. Luther, their only son, was born in the year 1849. They reside in New Annan.

Maria, the youngest daughter of Robert and Mary Cock, was born in the year 1812. She was married to Robert, the youngest son of Robert and Hannah Harris, of Truro, about the year 1839. They now reside at New Annan. Walter, their eldest son, was born in the year 1842. He removed to the United States. George, their second son, was born in the year 1844. He also removed to the United States. Mary, their only daughter, was born in the year 1847. Robert, their third son, was born 1849. Isaac, their third son, was born 1852. Robert, their youngest son, was born ———.

Ebenezer, the fourth son of Rev. Daniel and Alison Cock, was born in Scotland about the year 1769. He was married to Elizabeth

Polley in 1795. Alison Jamison, their only daughter, was born in Truro, February 16th, 1796. He and Charles Dickson, Esq., of Onslow, were in Halifax at the same time. Mr. Dickson took the yellow fever, and died there, September 30th, 1796. Mr. Cock waited upon him during his illness, and he also took the fever and died there, leaving a young widow and her infant child to bemoan their sad bereavement. His widow was married again to John, the fourth son of Alexander and Margaret Nelson, of the old Barns, March 21st, 1799. Their family appears among the Nelsons. Alison Jamison Cock, was married to James Rose, of Hants County, and had six sons and three daughters. Mr. Rose died a number of years ago.

Jane, the third and youngest daughter of Rev. Daniel and Alison Cock, was born in Truro in the year 1774. She was married to John, the second son of John and Mary Smith, May 10th, 1796. Their family appears among the Smiths. She died July 16th, 1845, aged 71 years, and Mr. Smith died June 2nd, 1848.

Daniel, the fifth and youngest son of Rev. Daniel and Alison Cock, was born in Truro in the year 1776. He inherited his father's property for a time, but about the year 1803 he sold his house and lot to the Rev. John Waddell, and removed to the North side of the River. He purchased land from John Taylor, and built the house that his youngest son, George W. Cock, now resides in, where he spent the remainder of his life. He was married to Elizabeth, daughter of John Carter, Senr., of Onslow, in the year 1802. He died October 1st, 1849, aged 73 years, and his wife, Elizabeth, died December 6th, 1824, aged 46 years. Christiann Nicholson Cock, their eldest daughter, was born in Truro, June 7th, 1803. She was married to Major Alexander L. Archibald, March 29th, 1831, and had two sons. They appear among the Archibalds.

Daniel, the eldest son of Daniel and Elizabeth Cock, was born October 3rd, 1805. He was married to Nancy, the second daughter of Samuel Blair and Nancy Archibald, his wife, January 2nd, 1837. He inherited a part of his father's farm. He died May 19th, 1849, aged 44 years. Henry, their eldest son, was born September 29th, 1837. He was married to Minerva, youngest daughter of Samuel J. and Alison J. Blair, August 18th, 1868. They have one daughter. Amelia, the eldest daughter of Daniel and Nancy Cock, was born March 20th, 1841. Mary Anne, their second daughter, was born April 14th, 1843. Susan, their third daughter was born March 14th,

1845. Edmond A., their second son, was born October 25th, 1847. Norman, their third son, was born January 6th, 1849.

Jane Smith, the second daughter of Daniel and Elizabeth Cock, was born October 3rd, 1808. She was married to John, the second son of Samuel Blair and Nancy Archibald, his wife, Dec. 31st, 1832. They have three sons and three daughters that appear among the Blairs. Sarah Lawson, the third daughter of Daniel and Elizabeth Cock, was born May 8th, 1811. She was married to John D. McNutt and they have one daughter. Alison Jamison, the fourth daughter of Daniel and Elizabeth Cock, was born in Truro, April 11th, 1814. She died December, 1838, aged 24 years. Ann Frost, their fifth and youngest daughter, was born April 8th, 1817. She was married to James Farnham, and has two daughters. Alexander Dick, the second son of Daniel and Elizabeth Cock, was born in Truro, September 23rd, 1820. He removed to California, where he has been practising as Doctor for a number of years. George W., the third son of Daniel and Elizabeth Cock, was born June 20th, 1824. He inherits what was his father's house and farm. He was married to Maria, daughter of John Blair and Elizabeth McNutt, his wife, October 20th, 1846. Bessie Allison, their eldest daughter, was born February 2nd, 1848. Georgie, their second daughter, was born April 23rd, 1849. Emily Teresa, their third daughter, was born April 2nd, 1851. She was married to Burpie Skinner, August 22nd, 1871. Maria Louisa, their fourth daughter, was born February 12th, 1853. Cassie, their fifth daughter, was born March 31st, 1855. Alice Maud, their sixth daughter, was born August 11th, 1857. Annie Gordon, their seventh daughter, was born August 22nd, 1859. Arthur Ellsworth Cock was born Oct. 31st, 1861. Harry Eugine Cock was born May 13th, 1864.

In the biography of Miss Marion Blough, which was written and brought to Wallace, Nova Scotia, by Mr. James Henderson, it is stated that this "Miss Blough told others that the first impression which was made upon her mind relative to her eternal welfare was made by the preaching of the Rev. Daniel Cock, in Scotland. She went to him after hearing him preach, and conversed with him freely, which seemed to her the means, in the hands of God, of bringing her to Jesus Christ, to seek the salvation of her soul through His mediation.

CHAPTER XVI.

The first elders who were chosen in Truro, in the year 1770, by the Presbyterian congregation were David Archibald, Esq., John Johnson, William Fisher, James Johnson, Robert Hunter, John Savage, and Samuel Archibald, as before named ; and before 1790 Alexander McCurdy and Solomon Hoar were chosen. They resided in Onslow. About the same time Hugh Moore, Senr., Matthew Archibald, and James Fulton, of the Lower Village, where added to the Session of the congregation of Truro and Onslow. In the year 1799 (being the next year after Mr. Waddell was settled over this congregation) Ebenezer Hoar, James McCurdy, of Onslow, James Archibald, Esq., of the Upper Village, and Robert Johnson, of the Lower Village, where chosen elders. In the year 1803, John Christie, Alexander Miller, and Alexander Kent were chosen elders. In the year 1818, John D. Christie, Ebenezer Archibald, Edward Logan, and Stephen Johnson were elected elders ; and, about the year 1828, John J. Archibald, Hugh Moore, Junr., Samuel Archibald, Esq., William McCully, John Smith, and James Laughead were elected to the Session. In the year 1845, John Faulkner, Samuel J. Archibald, David W. Archibald, Dr. John Waddell, William C. Smith, and Robert O. Christie, were chosen as elders ; and in the year 1863, Isaac Dunlap, Robert Smith, John F. Crowe, James F. Blanchard, Robert H. Smith, James K. Blair, Andrew Johnson, Edward Blanchard, John L. Archibald, and Thomas Miller were elected and added to the Session of the Presbyterian Congregation of Truro.

At a meeting held in the Meeting House, April 3rd, 1783, it was agreed that Charles Dickson, Joseph Scott, Ephraim Howard, Samuel Nichols, and Capt. Blackemore be a committee to set a value on the pews in the Meeting House, and that the minister's salary be assessed on the pews according to their value. It was also agreed that David Archibald, Esq., Matthew Archibald, Rev. Daniel Cock, and Eliakim Tupper, Esq., be a committee to give instructions to their representative to have an act passed agreeable to the foregoing resolution.

CHAPTER XVII.

Rev. John Waddell was born in Scotland, April 10th, 1771, and obtained his education in Glasgow. He was licensed to preach the everlasting Gospel in the month of May, 1797, and in June following he was ordained and set apart for Nova Scotia. He left Scotland never again to see his native land, on August 12th, 1797, and on November 6th of the same year arrived in Truro, having been a short time in New York. Shortly after he arrived he accepted a call from the congregation of Truro, to be an assistant and a successor to Mr. Cock, and was inducted on November 16th, 1798. Mr. Cock being then about 82 years of age, of course the ministerial labors would be mostly performed by Mr. Waddell. He commenced and carried on his work with vigor and perseverence. He preached the first sermon that was ever preached in Brookfield, in the year 1800. His congregation extended over the whole of Onslow, Truro, and Brookfield, and continued so for about 18 years, when Onslow was set off as a separate congregation. In the year 1832, Brookfield was set off from Truro. At this time they commenced to erect a Church there. It was raised July 17th, 1833.

Mr. Waddell boarded with Alexander Barnhill, until he was married to Nancy, daughter of Colonel Jotham and Elizabeth Blanchard, September 2nd, 1802. Soon after this Mr. Waddell purchased Mr. Cock's house and wood lot, and removed into the house, where he and his partner spent the remainder of their days.

Mary, their eldest daughter, was born September 17th, 1803. She was married to Isaac Smith, February 23rd, 1823. They had two sons and four daughters. She died in the month of November, 1838.

James, the eldest son of Rev. John and Nancy Waddell, was born May 4th, 1805. He was also a minister of the Gospel. He was married to Elizabeth, the third daughter of Edward S. Blanchard, Esq., and Jane Archibald, September 28th, 1837. William Henry, their eldest son, was born June 29th, 1838. He was married to Eliza T., the third daughter of Hiram Blanchard, November 15th, 1866. They have one son. Jane Walker, the eldest daughter of James and Elizabeth Waddell, was born December 19th, 1840. She was married to the Rev. Edward A. McCurdy, November 6th, 1866. They have one son. They are settled in New Glasgow, Pictou County. Eliza B., the second daughter of Rev. James and Elizabeth Waddell, was born August 8th, 1844. She was married to John, son of James Tupper and Isabell Graham, his wife, February 28th, 1869. They have two sons. Edward Sherburne, their second son, was born August 18th, 1847. Mary, their third daughter, was born June 20th, 1849. Sarah, their fourth daughter, was born March 9th, 1855. John, their youngest son, was born September 19th, 1858. Rev. James Waddell died in Halifax, March 14th, 1870, aged 65 years. His body was interred in the family lot in Truro Cemetery.

Jotham Blanchard, the second son of the Rev. John and Nancy Waddell, was born May 1st, 1808. He was married to Nancy, the second daughter of Alexander Kent, Esq., and Jane Christie, April 6th, 1830. John, their eldest son, was born April 5th, 1831. He left home about the year 1847, and was engaged in business at Pictou, until about the year 1860, when he removed to Hearts Content, Newfoundland, and is managing the business of the Submarine Telegraph. J. B. Waddell's wife, Nancy, died August 14th, 1852, aged 45 years. Nancy, the eldest daughter of Jotham B. and Nancy Waddell, was born January 5th, 1833. Richard Christie, the second son of Jotham B. Waddell and Nancy Kent, his wife, was born in Truro, May 3rd, 1835. He removed to Upper Stewiacke, and carried on his business there as blacksmith. He was married there to Margaret, daughter of William Fulton, Esq., and Isabell Rutherford, June, 1864. They had two sons and one daughter. On May 24th, 1871, as he was leading a horse from a neighbor's stable to his shop, the horse took fright, sprang and kicked him, and injured him so badly that he lived but about thirty-six hours after. He died on the 26th day of May, aged 36 years. He left a widow and three young children to mourn their loss. Alexander Kent, the third son of Jotham B. and Nancy Waddell, was born December 23rd, 1837. He removed to the United States about the year 1858. He carries on the business of carriage building there. He was married there to Lucinda Woodberry, about the year 1860. They have two daughters. Jane, the second daughter of Jotham B. and Nancy Waddell, was born July 23rd, 1840. Susan Lynds, their third daughter, was born July 13th, 1842. William McCulley, their fourth son, was born January 2, 1845. He removed to the United States in the year 1860. Samuel James, their fifth and youngest son, was born August 8th, 1847.

John, the third son of Rev. John and Nancy Waddell, was born in Truro March 10th, 1810. He was engaged in business as a mer-

II

chant when young, and built the house that George Reading, Esq.,
now resides in, for a store. He was married to Susan, the only
daughter of Dr. David B. Lynds and Sarah Blair, October 3rd, 1833.
Shortly after this he commenced to study, and about the year 1837
he went home to Scotland to complete his education. He returned in
about two years, and commenced to practise as a Doctor of Medicine,
and continued to practice in Truro until the Fall of the year 1849.
He then removed to St. John, N. B., took charge of the Lunatic Asylum, and still has charge of it at this date, May, 1873. Susan, his first
wife (and her twin babes), died December 28th, 1834, aged 23 years.
He was married again to Jane, the second daughter of Edward S.
Blanchard, Esq., and Jane Archibald, his wife, June 25th, 1844.
Susan, their eldest daughter, was born September 8th, 1846. Sarah,
their second daughter, was born March 29th, 1848. Charles Melville
Waddell, their only son, was born December 30th, 1849. He died at
St. John, N. B., March 15th, 1859, being in the tenth year of his
age. His body was interred in the Truro Cemetery.

Elizabeth, the second daughter of Rev. John Waddell and Nancy
Blanchard, was born March 29th, 1812. She died at St. John, N. B.,
where she had been stopping with her brother, November 13th, 1870,
aged 58 years. Her remains were brought to Truro, and interred in
the family lot in Truro Cemetery.

Jane Walker, the third daughter of the Rev. John and Nancy
Waddell, was born in Truro, April 27th, 1814. She was married to
John Albro, son of Colonel William Dickson and Rebecca Pearson,
August 16th, 1836. Their only son, Robert Douglas Dickson, was
born in Truro, June 16th, 1837. Mrs. Dickson died June 1st, 1840.
Her husband, a few years after, perished at sea on board of a wrecked
ship.

Sarah, the fourth and youngest daughter of Rev. John and Nancy
Waddell, was born in Truro, January 5th, 1817. She died January
14th, 1824, aged 7 years. Mrs. Waddell died August 18th, 1818.
By this sad bereavement he was left with seven young children, but
with the assistance of his Master, he was enabled to persevere in his
Master's work. In the month of October, 1828, he went to Upper
Stewiacke to assist the Rev. Hugh Graham at a sacrament. He
preached on Saturday, and on Sabbath morning when the people
assembled Mr. Waddell was absent, having been struck during the
night with paralysis. He was laid aside from active labor for a few
months by this stroke, and after this he was not able to stand to

preach, but had to sit in a chair, which was fixed up in the pupit for that purpose. When he was assisted into the pulpit. and took his seat in the chair to resume his public labours, he gave out the 116th Psalm. The words of the Psalm being so very appropriate, his feelings .were overcome, so that it was with difficulty he could proceed. He continued to persevere in his Master's work, until the summer of the year 1836, when he started to go to Pictou to attend Synod. The waggon was driven by his niece, Sarah Archibald. At that time there were very steep hills to pass over, and while going down what is called the Halfmoon Hill, about a half mile from Mr- Christie's, by some means he and his niece, together with the horse and waggon, were all thrown over the embankment. By this fall he was so much injured that he was laid aside again from his public labors, and in November of this year he demitted his charge of the Truro congregation.

His zeal for doing good may be judged from one fact. In the summer of 1837, the widow of one of his elders was sinking under consumption, and he was assisted into his waggon and driven to the door of her house. As he was not able to be got out of the waggon, she was drawn to the door in her chair, where he conversed and prayed with her for the last time in this world. About his last public address was at the funeral of the five persons who were burnt to death in the house that was burned March 31st, 1841. Mr. Waddell closed his earthly existence Nov. 13th, 1842, in the 72nd year of his age.

It may here be observed that there was no other denomination of Christians in Truro, or its neighborhood, but Presbyterians from its first settlement, in 1760, until the year 1782. This year Mr. Henry Alline, who belonged to the Congregationalists, was travelling through Nova Scotia, exhorting the people· to break off from their sins and come to Jesus Christ that their souls might be saved. He started from Pictou, in company with another man, August 5th, 1782, to travel through the woods to Truro on foot. The journey being too great for one day, they lodged in the woods all night, having no other shelter than the trees that overhung them. The second day, when they came to the upper part of Truro, it was with the utmost difficulty that they obtained food or lodging. The people, having heard of him before, gazed on him as he passed their doors, as if he had been one of the Antediluvians ; and when he came down to the Village of Truro he went to the only Inn that was kept in the Village. The Innkeeper refused him lodgings for any amount of money ; and while he was strolling about the road he met with Alexander Miller, who consented to lodge him, on condition that he would not speak to any of the family. He put him and the man who was with him into a room by themselves. They soon began to sing, and some of the family knocked at the door and asked if they might come in and hear them singing. He replied that they might, if they were not afraid of being caught with the spirit that went about with him. More freedom was then shown between Mr. Miller and him, and he was asked to pray in the family. The next day he was allowed to preach in Mr. Miller's barn. After this he continued to preach in the Village. He was summoned to appear before the Session of the Truro congregation, to give an account of himself for coming into another man's congregation and preaching *what they believed to be* false doctrine; but they could not stop him. He continued his preaching in Truro for three or four days, and then crossed over to Onslow, and labored there for some time, and went to Horton in September of the same year. In the year 1809, Henry Hail and Amos Alline visited Truro and commenced to preach, and again there was an attempt made to stop them. The Justices of the Peace threatened to have them arrested if they did not cease from preaching what they believed to be false doctrine; but they preached on, and they applied to the Government for permission to preach, and received a free license to preach to all who were willing to hear them.

CHAPTER XVIII.

Capt. John Morrison was another of the first settlers of Truro, and was a Grantee of the Township. His front land was adjoining the Parade, on the North side, and extending North to the interval. Also the interval adjoining it, which is owned by Mr. John McClure and Robert Chambers, Esq. He built on his house lot, and resided there about seven years. He exchanged farms with Robert Archibald, and removed to Little Dyke, Londonderry, where he spent the remainder of his life. On June 6th, 1770, he took his seat in the General Assembly of this Province, and was the representative of Londonderry until 1778. He having left the Province for a few years to look after his business in New Hampshire, James, son of the Rev. David Smith, took his seat in the House of Assembly, December 5th, 1785, as representative of Londonderry. Mr. Morrison was born in New Hampshire, in the year 1725. He was married to Martha Anderson, daughter of Mr. Anderson who was shot by the Indians, while engaged thrashing grain in his barn. Martha, having gone to the barn with a drink for her father, and seeing the Indians behind the barn, ran for the house, but before she reached the house the Indians fired after her, and when she got into the house she found that her dress had nine ball holes in it and she was unhurt. They were married about the year 1757. Eleanor, their eldest daughter, was born in New Hampshire, September 21st, 1758. She was married to Edward Faulkner. They had nine sons. They settled in Economy where they spent their lives, and reared their nine sons, and died.

Mr. Morrison came with the first company that came to Truro in the Spring of the year 1760. His wife remained in New Hampshire until the Spring of the year 1761, and then came on with a number more who came that Spring. Daniel, their eldest son, was born in New Hampshire, November 24th, 1760. He was married to Rachel McLellan about the year 1790. He inherited a part of his father's farm, and was a Justice of the Peace for the District of Colchester for a number of years before he died. They had five sons and five daughters. His house stood near the place on which his son, Alexander D. Morrison, Esq., lived and his grandson, Joseph Howe Morrison now resides. Daniel Morrison died at Little Dyke, November 26th, 1832, aged 72 years, and his wife died December 21st, 1843.

Hannah, the second daughter of Capt. John and Martha Morrison, was born in Truro, December 25th, 1762. She died unmarried, at Londonderry, December 25th, 1792. John, their second son, was born in Truro, October 25th, 1764. He perished, in the month of December, 1799, on board of a vessel that foundered in the Bay, near Londonderry. He died a bachelor.

Jonathan, the third son of Capt. John and Martha Morrison, was born in Truro, October 24th, 1766. He was married to Martha Faulkner in the year 1794. They had six sons and three daughters. They settled at Five Islands, where they reared their family and spent the remainder of their lives. He died there in the year 1843.

Joseph A. Morrison, their fourth son, was born in Londonderry, July 13th, 1769. He was married to Isabella, the third daughter of

Thomas Fletcher and Jane Vance, his wife, of Masstown, in the year
1802. They have four sons and four daughters. (Their third son,
Thomas F. Morrison, Esq., now represents the County of Colchester
in the Local Parliament of Nova Scotia.) He inherited a part of his
father's farm at Little Dyke, and had his house near the place that his
son, Samuel, now resides, where they reared their family, spent the
remainder of their lives, and he died there in the year 1846, aged 77
years, and his wife died October, 1821, aged 43 years.

Samuel, the fifth son of Capt. John and Martha Morrison, was
born at Londonderry, August 19th, 1771. He was married to
Frances Hays in the year 1801. They had two sons and four
daughters. He died February 12th, 1820, aged 48 years, and his
wife died February 11th, 1828, aged 47 years.

Martha, the third daughter of Capt. John and Martha Morrison,
was born March 13th, 1774. She was married to John Williamson.
They removed, and settled in the County of Pictou. They had two
sons and six daughters. Margaret, their fourth daughter, was born in
Londonderry, March 3rd, 1776. She was married to Edward
Faulkner, second. They settled in Economy, and had three sons and
five daughters. She died there in the year 1860, aged 84 years.
Ezekiel, the sixth son of Capt. John and Martha Morrison, was born
in New Hampshire, October 10th, 1780. He was married to Elizabeth
McLellan. They settled in Londonderry for a time. They had five
sons and two daughters. They removed to the County of Hants, and
he died in St. John, N. B.

As before mentioned, Capt. John Morrison having left property
unsold in New Hampshire, returned there at the time of the rebellion.
He sold his property, but could not get his pay for a length of time.
He worked at his trade as a blacksmith, and had to remain there so
long that his seat in the Assembly was declared vacant, June 25th,
1778, and his family went to him and remained there until peace was
restored. He obtained payment for his property, and he and his family
returned to Londonderry, where he spent the remainder of his life.
He died there December 27th, 1816, aged 91 years, and his wife died
March 31st, 1811, aged 72 years.

CHAPTER XIX.

A large, splendid, and expensive monument was erected about the year 1825 in the city of Londonderry, in the North of Ireland, to the memory of the brave men and apprentice boys who defended that city so manfully during the siege, in the years 1688 and 1689. On this monument is engraved the name of Colonel Robert Blair, with a large number of others of the most brave. This Robert Blair belonged to the family of Blairs of Blairathol, in Scotland. His son, of the same name, Colonel Robert Blair, came to North America with his regiment, and brought with him his wife and family, and afterwards settled in Worcester, Mass., where they spent the remainder of their lives. Mr. Blair died there in the year 1774, aged 91 years, and his wife, Isabella, died in the year 1765, aged 82 years. They had seven sons. Their names were Matthew, James, Joseph, John, David, William, and Francis. Joseph remained on the homestead at Worcester. He had one son, whose name was Charles, and five daughters. John and David settled at Warren, and had families. Capt. Alfred Blair, of Warren, is greatgrandson of this Colonel Blair. Dr. Blair, of Rome, is grandson of Colonel Blair.

Capt. William Blair came first to Nova Scotia on military duty in the year 1758, to assist in subduing the French and taking Louisburg. He returned to New England and was relieved from military duty, and came again to Nova Scotia, and brought with him his wife and family, in company with the other first settlers who came to Truro in the Spring of the year 1760. They settled on the farm on the interval of North River that was afterwards owned by his son, John, and he had his house near the place that his greatgrandson, William Blair, now resides. A few years after they obtained a grant of the Township of Onslow.

Francis Blair, brother of William, came with the first settlers of Onslow, and was a Grantee of the Township, and it is said that he, being discouraged with the hardships of settling in a new country, sold out his Right of land in Onslow for the small sum of eight dollars, and returned again to New England.

The grant of the Township of Onslow was made to Richard Upham and sixteen others for a certain number of shares or rights; to Francis Blair and thirty others for certain other rights or shares, in all forty-eight persons. This grant was for 50,000 acres, being the whole of the Township of Onslow. It is dated February 21st, 1769, and is signed by Lord William Campbell, who was then Governor of Nova Scotia. In laying off the land of this Township, so much surplus measurement was given that it now contains about 80,000 acres.

Capt. William Blair was born in the year 1716. He was married to Jane Barns, in New England, about the year 1740. He died August 4th, 1791. Susan, their eldest daughter, was born in the year 1741. She was married to Mr. Isaac Farrell, June 10th, 1763. They returned to New England. He was an officer on military duty, and he fell at the battle of Bunker Hill.

Sarah, the second daughter of Capt. William Blair, was born in New England in the year 1743. She was married to Ephraim Howard, December 8th, 1763. Mr. Howard settled near the North River bridge, and built the first mill that was built in Onslow. This mill stood near Mr. James McNutt's shop. A mill was kept there until about the year 1812, when the heavy freshets filled the race and pond with gravel, and the mill was allowed to go down. Mr. Howard had sold this mill a considerable time before this date, and removed to St. Andrew's River, and built some mills, where he carried on milling during the remainder of his life. They had one son and six daughters.

William, the eldest son of Capt. William Blair, was born in New England in the year 1750, and was brought by his parents to Nova Scotia when he was ten years old. He was married to Mary, daughter of James Downing and Janet Montgomery, November 26th, 1772. They settled on the farm that was afterwards owned by his two sons, Alexander and Oliver, up the North River, where they reared there numerous family, and spent the remainder of their lives. He died in March, 1841, aged 91 years, and his wife, Mary Downing, died in the month of November, 1817, aged 67 years.

Jane, their eldest daughter, was born in Onslow, March 30th, 1773. She was married to Archibald, son of Matthew Taylor and Elizabeth Archibald, May 4th, 1797. She had one child, which died young. She died October 19th, 1799. Mr. Taylor removed to St. Mary's, and was married again to Mary McDonald, of Pictou. They had three sons and two daughters. Robert, the eldest son of William Blair and Mary Downing, his wife, was born in Onslow, November 1st, 1774. He was married to Mary, daughter of Ebenezer and

Catherine Hoar, of Onslow, January 20th, 1801. They settled on the farm on which Turner Blair now resides. In the year 1819 he exchanged places with his brother William, and removed to the mills where his son David now resides. About this time the first carding mill was set agoing in the lower part of the saw mill which stood where Robert Blair's mill now stands. This was the first carding machine that was set agoing in the County of Colchester, and I think in the Province of Nova Scotia. It was considered a great curiosity, and attracted numerous visitors.

William, the eldest son of Robert and Mary Blair, was born in Onslow, November 23rd, 1801. He learned the shoemaking business with his uncle, Ephraim Blair, who then carried on the business where Mr. William Gregor now resides. He was married to Elizabeth, the youngest daughter of John Wright and Sarah Lynds, January 24th, 1827. In the Spring of the year 1828 they removed to River John, and remained there until about the year 1842, when they removed to Illinois, U. S., where they are still living. They had six sons and six daughters.

Ebenezer, the second son of Robert Blair and Mary Hoar, his wife, was born in Onslow, June 6th, 1802. He died in the year 1810, aged eight years.

Daniel, their third son was born February 2nd, 1806. He was married to Mary, the second daughter of John B. Archibald and Catherine Hoar, his wife, October 12th, 1830. He inherited a part of his father's farm at North River. They had two sons and five daughters. Mrs. Blair died October, 12th, 1861, and he was married again to Catherine, widow of the late James Logan of Upper Stewiacke, October 24th, 1871. Mary Hoar, first wife of Robert Blair, died November, 1810. He was married again to Elizabeth, daughter of William Taylor, and Margaret McCurdy, May 1st, 1814. James, their eldest son, was born December 1st, 1814. He was married to Phœbe Ann, daughter of William Lynds and Margaret McCollum, his wife, July 7th, 1835. They had five sons and three daughters. They removed to Tatamagouche about the year 1853. He and his sons have been engaged ever since running stage coaches from Truro to Tatamagouche, and from Pictou to River Philip, County of Cumberland.

David, the second son of Robert Blair and Elizabeth Taylor, was born in Onslow, June 10th, 1816. He was married to Mary, daughter of John Miers and Elizabeth Lynds, of Wallace River, June 3rd,

1857. They have three sons. He inherits the homestead part of his father's farm.

Mary, the eldest daughter of Robert and Elizabeth Blair, was born January 13th, 1820. She was married to William, son of William and Margaret Lynds, November 1st, 1839. They are settled on the south branch of North River, and have four sons and three daughters.

Margaret, the second daughter of Robert and Elizabeth Blair was born December 30th, 1821. She removed to the United States, and was married there to George Glaison in the year 1858.

Robert, the third son of Robert and Elizabeth Blair, was born March 3rd, 1823. He was married to Jane, daughter of William and Margaret Lynds, January 15th, 1844. They have two sons and four daughters. He inherited a part of his father's farm and the sawmill, and now resides on part of the farm that was owned by Mr. Alexander Blair.

John, the fourth son of Robert and Elizabeth Blair, was born September 12th, 1825. He was married to Mary Ann Welsh, of the State of Maine. They had one son who died when seventeen years old and one daughter.

Charles, their fifth son was born March 4th, 1828. He removed to the United States and married there and has three sons.

Henry, their sixth son, was born November 12th, 1831. He is now in the Lunatic Asylum.

Elizabeth, their third daughter, was born January 13th, 1835. She was married to John, son of David Murray and Mary Dickson, Feby. 8th, 1855. They have two sons and five daughters. Robert Blair, Senr., died December 21st, 1843, aged 69 years, and his wife died November 4th, 1855, aged 62.

John, the second son of William Blair and Mary Downing, his wife, was born February 8th, 1778. He was married to Isabella McNutt, the only daughter of Samuel McNutt, September 22nd, 1807. They settled on Onslow Mountain, on the same farm on which their son Jotham Blair, Esq., now resides, where they reared their family, and spent the remainder of their days. He died January 31st, 1831. His wife died September 11th, 1846, aged 57 years. On one occasion Mr. Blair tackled his horse, and went to work ploughing potatoes Sabbath morning; one of his neighbours went to him, and with some difficulty convinced him that it was Sabbath. When he was convinced, he soon untackled his horse, and was very much grieved at the thought of his sad mistake.

Samuel, the eldest son of John and Isabella Blair, was born in Onslow September 20th, 1808. He was married to Elizabeth, daughter of Samuel McNutt and Ann McMullon, his wife, March, 1852. They have three sons.

Mary, the eldest daughter, of John and Isabella Blair, was born April 22nd, 1810. She removed to the United States, and was married there to Mr. Brody.

William, their second son was born April 22nd, 1812. He removed to the United States, and was married there, and has not been heard from for a length of time.

Myzeann, their second daughter, was born January, 31st, 1815. She was married to David Carlyle, June, 1844. They have one son and six daughters.

Elizabeth, their third daughter, was born August 4th, 1817. She was married to Thomas, youngest son of Samuel Archibald, Esq., and Elizabeth, his wife, July 25th, 1848.

Jotham M., their third son, was born July 27th, 1819. He inherits his father's farm. He is a Justice of the Peace, and is still living a bachelor.

Margaret Jane, their fourth daughter, was born August 4th, 1821. She is still living, unmarried, with her brother Jotham M., at the homestead.

John N., their fourth son, was born April 4th, 1824. He removed to New Zealand.

James H., their fifth son, was born November 8th, 1826. He removed to Boston, Mass., and is married there.

Alexander, their sixth and youngest son, was born May 19th, 1828. He removed to the United States, and was married there to Annie Hughes. They have two sons and one daughter. They now reside in Halifax.

William, the third son of William Blair and Mary Downing, his wife, was born in Onslow, August 1st, 1779. He was married to Sarah Campbell, of Queen's County, New Brunswick, March 6th, 1815. They settled first where David Blair now resides at North River; and in the year 1819 removed to the place on which his son, R. Turner Blair now resides, where he spent the remainder of his life. He died June 10th, 1852, aged 73 years. Abiathar, their eldest son, was born August 3rd, 1817. He was married to Eleanor, the fifth daughter of Samuel Whidden and Sarah Stevens, December 27th, 1842. They had eight sons and two daughters. Mary Jane, their eldest daughter, was born November 16th, 1819. She died August 2nd, 1851, aged 32 years. Robert Turner Blair, their second son, was born July 15th, 1824. He was married to Hannah, daughter of Ralph Johnson and Phœbe Whidden, his wife, October 8th, 1852. He now inherits his father's house and farm. Rachel H., the second daughter of William and Sarah Blair, was born January 29th, 1830. She was married to Isaac Smith, (being his second wife) November 29th, 1857. They had one son and one daughter. She died March 26th, 1864, aged 34 years. Matilda, their third daughter was born July 16th, 1833. She was married to James, the youngest son of John Staples and Catherine Blair, his wife, August, 17th, 1851. They have one son and five daughters.

Catherine, the second daughter of William Blair and Mary Downing, was born April 22nd, 1782. She was married to John Staples, May 30th, 1803, being Mr. Staples' second wife. Their family appears among the Staples.

Daniel, the fourth son of William and Mary Blair, was born October 20th, 1784. He was married to Rebecca Freeman, of Cumberland County in the year 1807. (This Mrs. Blair was born September 11th, 1790.) They settled near the Onslow Cemetery, where he died January 10th, 1862, aged 77 years.

William, the eldest son of Daniel and Rebecca Blair. was born January 5th, 1808. He removed to Horton, and was married there to Rebecca Payzant, in the year 1837. They had three sons and two daughters. He died May 1845.

Hannah, the eldest daughter of Daniel and Rebecca Blair, was born June 1st, 1812. She was married to Joseph Hamilton, of Lower Onslow, March 1838, being Mr. Hamilton's second wife. They had one son and one daughter.

Samuel Freeman, their second son was born May 27th 1814. He was marrred to Eliza, daughter of James Blair and Mary Breggs, of New Brunswick, December, 1837. They had three daughters. He lost his eyesight, and died in the year 1847.

Oliver, their third son, was born September 10th, 1816. He was married to Ruth Atkinson, of Cumberland County, in the year 1842. She died, and he was married again to Margery, daughter of James Hamilton and Jane Carter, his wife, August 10th, 1851. They removed to Wallace River, where they now keep an Inn. They had three sons and two daughters.

John M., the fourth son of Daniel and Rebecca Blair, was born October 3rd, 1827. He was married to Margaret McNutt, November 28th, 1850. They had one son and two daughters. He was a blacksmith. He died January 12th, 1869, aged 42 years.

Isaac, the fifth son of Daniel and Rebecca Blair, was born June 1st, 1830. He was married to Rebecca, daughter of Rufus McNutt and Margaret Crowe, February 17th, 1852. He inherits a part of his father's farm.

Almira, their youngest daughter, was born April 22nd, 1833. She was married to William, son of Daniel Cummings and Margaret McDougall. They have three sons and one daughter. They now reside in Truro Village, and he is carrying on business as a merchant.

Alexander, the fifth son of William and Mary Blair, was born March 6th, 1787. He was married to Sarah Bebee, of Wallace River, in the County of Cumberland, December 28th, 1815. He inherited the homestead half of his father's farm. He was Captain of a company of Militia for a length of time. In the month of September, 1816, he was assisting to raise the house in which Mr. Charles H. Blair now resides, when a joist of the upper floor gave way, and he fell to the bottom of the cellar, on a heap of small stones, which injured him so badly that he could not be taken home for about two weeks. He still shows the effects of this fall by the way that his head stands forward.

Secor McDonald, the eldest son of Alexander and Sarah Blair, was born August 3rd, 1818. He removed to California some time ago. Amelia, their eldest daughter, was born March 13th, 1822. She died December 24th, 1860, aged 38 years. Susannah, their second daughter, was born August 3rd, 1824. She was married to Lockhart Dimock, of Newport. They had two sons and one daughter. Lemuel S. Blair, their second son, was born December 18th, 1826. He was married to Jane Irish, of Antigonish, January, 1858. They have one son and three daughters. They have removed to Boston, Mass. Nancy M., their third daughter, was born June 26th, 1829. She was married to Rev. George Wethers. They have one son and one daughter. She died at Newport, 1871. Amanda M., their fourth daughter, was born May 2nd, 1831. She was married to the Rev. George Wethers, October, 1872.

Harriet N. Blair, their fifth daughter, was born December 19th,

1835. She was married to Rev. Hiram Wallace, in the month of January, 1862. They removed to Ohio, U. S. Henrietta F. Blair, the sixth daughter of Alexander and Sarah Blair, was born April 28th, 1838. She was married to Oliver. son of Mr. David Hurd and Deborah Bebee, of Wallace River, May 27th, 1868. They have one daughter. Mrs. Sarah Blair, mother of the foregoing family, died December 4th, 1864.

Ephraim, the sixth son of William and Mary Blair, was born February 17th, 1789. He was married to Abigail Hall, of Onslow Mountain, January 20th, 1814. He carried on the shoemaking business at the place where Mr. William Gregor now resides. He sold this place to Mr. Gregor about the year 1830, and removed up the North River, and settled on the farm on which his two sons now reside. Here he spent the remainder of his life, and died January 22nd, 1864, aged 75 years. Jane, the eldest daughter of Ephraim and Abigail Blair, was born December 28th, 1814. She was married to Adam McNutt, November 2nd, 1836, and had four sons and two daughters. William, their eldest son was born May 3rd, 1817. He removed to P. E. Island, and was married there to Sarah Baker. They had four sons and two daughters. They removed to Illinois, U. S., and he died there in August, 1862, aged 45 years. Mary, their second daughter, was born March 11th, 1820. She was married to William McCulley, of Debert River. They have two sons. Margaret, their third daughter, was born November 21st, 1822. She was married to Charles McCully, 1849. They had four sons and five daughters. Alexander, their second son, was born August 6th, 1825. He was married to Isabell Beggs. She died December 22nd, 1868, and he was married again to Barbary Wilson, of Chiganois, July 11th, 1870. He died March 3rd, 1871. John, the third son of Ephraim and Abigail Blair, was born May 10th, 1828. He was married to Rebecca, daughter of Daniel Blair and Mary Archibald, 1853. They have one daughter. George, their fourth son, was born May, 1830. He removed to Wisconsin, and was married there and had one daughter. They removed again to California. Charles, their fifth son, was born May 31st, 1832. He removed to Wisconsin, and is married there and has two daughters. Ephraim Howard, their sixth son, was born August 6th, 1838. He was married to Sarah Ann, daughter of Robert McCollum and Mary Moore, 1866. They have one son and one daughter. Renew, the fourth and youngest daughter, was born July 6th, 1841. She was married to David, son of Thomas McCollum and Jane Irvin. They have one son and three daughters.

James, the seventh son of William Blair and Mary Downing, was born May 28th, 1792. He removed to New Brunswick and was married there, to Mary Breggs, of Queen's County, in the year 1815. They had three daughters. Their eldest daughter, Eliza, was married to Samuel, son of Daniel Blair, of Onslow, 1837. They had three daughters. Mr. Blair died in 1847. James Blair was drowned from a fishing boat 1830, in the Bay of Fundy, below St. John's. His body was found and brought to the City of St. John's and buried there.

Oliver, the eighth and youngest son of William Blair and Mary Downing, was born October 7th, 1794. He was married to Mary, the eldest daughter of John Smith and Jane Cock, December 20th, 1817. He inherited one-half of his father's farm, where they reared their family. He died there November 23rd, 1871, aged 77 years, and his wife died July 1869, in the seventieth year of her age.

Ebenezer Smith, their eldest son, was born December 15th, 1820. He was married to Mary King, January 15th, 1843. Tryphena, their eldest daughter, was born November 22nd, 1844. She died August 22nd, 1862, aged 18 years. Mary Jane was born October 29th, 1847. Caroline was born December 15th, 1850. Sarah was born March 22nd, 1853. Jessie Ellen was born May 22nd, 1855. Nancy was born September 1st, 1857. She died March 18th, 1859. Emma was born Sept. 4th, 1859. McDonald was born Jany. 29th, 1863.

Mary Ann, the eldest daughter of Oliver and Mary Blair, was born October 28th, 1823. She was married to John Harris Blackemore in the year 1844. They had one son and two daughters. They removed to the United States, where he, his son, and one daughter died some time ago, and Mrs. Blackemore is now living, with her daughter, in Addison, State of Indiana.

John Smith, the second son of Oliver and Mary Blair, was born February, 1826. He was married to Louisa, daughter of John and Elizabeth Blair. She died August 21st, 1853, aged 20 years. He was married to Eliza Kendrick, of Boston, where they now reside. They have two sons, named Howard and John Blair, and one daughter, Carnice Blair.

Jane Smith, the second daughter of Oliver and Mary Blair, was born September 10th, 1829. She was married to George C. Phillips, September 12th, 1851. Margaretta, their eldest daughter, was born

February 5th, 1854. Charles Noble, their eldest son, was born March 31st, 1856. John Amos was born March 20th, 1858. Caroline S. was born August 12th, 1860. Eva was born March 27th, 1863. Lewis G. was born April 1st, 1865. Emma Louisa was born July 23rd, 1867. Mary Black was born November 21st, 1869.

James, the third son of Oliver and Mary Blair, was born May, 1832. He was married to Eleanor, daughter of James Hall, of Onslow Mountain. They had two sons, who both died while young. James Blair died March 16th, 1861, aged 29 years.

Charles Hill, the fourth son of Oliver and Mary Blair, was born January 12th, 1835. He was married to Jane, daughter of David V. Crowe, Esq., and Esther Barnhill, September 9th, 1862. Lizzie, their eldest daughter, was born April 9th, 1864. Mary Alice, their second daughter, was born February 23rd, 1866. Alison, the third and youngest daughter of Oliver and Mary Blair, was born March 27th, 1839. She was married to Augustus, son of Isaac Mc-Curdy, Esq., and Nancy Blanchard, October 1st, 1860. Isabell, their eldest daughter, was born September 9th, 1862. Mary Blanch, their second daughter, was born September 29th, 1864. Lilly Thomson was born September 18th, 1837.

Hannah, the third daughter of Capt. William Blair and Jane Barns, his wife, was born in New England about the year 1747. She came to Nova Scotia with her parents, in the year 1760. She was married to Robert Archibald, Esq., April 2nd, 1767. They had two sons and six daughters. They appear among the Archibalds. She died at Musquodoboit, November 4th, 1834, when she was about 87 years old, and her husband died in October, 1812, aged 67 years.

Dorothy, the fourth daughter of Capt. William Blair and Jane Barns, was born in New England about the year 1753. She was married to Simeon Whidden, of Truro, about the year 1775. They had six sons and five daughters.

Rebecca, the fifth daughter of Captain William and Jane Blair. was born in New England in the year 1757. She was married to Thomas Lynds about the year 1774. They had five sons and six daughters who appear among the Lynds families. She died January 9th, 1838, aged 80. Her husband died January 6th, 1839, aged 92 years.

John, the second son of Captain William Blair and Jane Barns, was born in New England in the year 1758, and was brought by his parents to Nova Scotia in the spring of the year 1760, when he was about two years old. Agnes Downing, who was afterwards his wife, was born in Truro, January 23rd, 1762. (She was daughter of James Downing and Janet Montgomery). They were married September 20th, 1781. He inherited his father's farm in Onslow, where they reared their family, and spent the remainder of their days. He died there October 5th, 1847, aged 89 years, and his wife died January 9th, 1829, aged 67 years.

Samuel Barnes, the eldest son of John Blair and Agnes Downing, was born March 10th, 1782. He was married to Nancy, the eldest daughter of James Archibald, Esq., and Rebecca Barnhill, January 25th, 1805. He inherited a part of his father's farm and built his house, which is still standing, on the hill south-east of his son David's house. In this house they reared their family, and spent the remainder of their lives. He died October 14th, 1862, aged 80 years, and his wife Nancy died December 29th, 1857, aged 75 years.

Samuel James, the eldest son of Samuel and Nancy Blair, was born October 27th, 1805. He was married to Alison Jamison, fourth daughter of Captain William Cock and Anne Frost, December 24th, 1832. He built his first house, which is still standing, on the west side of the lane, west of the Episcopalian Church. He sold this place to the late John Bass, Esq., and then built the house in which William Faulkner, Esq., now resides. About the year 1853 he sold out again. and built the house in which he now resides, on the interval of Salmon River.

Thomas, their eldest son, was born January 20th, 1834. He removed to Canada, and was married there to Margaret Campbell. They returned to Truro, and now inherit a part of his father's farm. They have four sons and two daughters. Joanna, the eldest daughter of Samuel J. and Alison J. Blair, was born January 2nd, 1836. She was married to Robert Dickson, September 17th, 1862. They have four sons and one daughter. Richard, the second son of Samuel J. and Alison J. Blair, was born in Truro, June 18th, 1838. He removed to Canada in the year 1859, and continued there a few years, and removed again to the Southern States. He was there engaged in the war for nearly four years, and endured many hardships, but escaped with a few slight wounds. He was married to Nancy Lafray, of Canada. They had two daughters. Mrs. Blair and one of their daughters are dead. Harriet, their second daughter, was born January 25th, 1841. She was married to William Blair, son of Simeon H. and Janet Blair, January 26th, 1864. They have two

12

sons and two daughters.   Frances, their third daughter, was born
April 26th, 1843.   Maria Augusta, their fourth daughter, was born
November 18th, 1846.   Minerva, their fifth and youngest daughter,
was born September 26th, 1850.   She was married to Henry, son of
Daniel Cock, third, and Nancy Blair, August 18th, 1868.   They
have one daughter.

John Blair, fourth, second son of Samuel and Nancy Blair, was
born June 20th, 1807.   He was married to Jane S., second daughter
of Daniel Cock and Elizabeth Carter, his wife, December
31st, 1832.   Charles, their eldest son, was born June 2nd,
1834.   He left home in 1856, and is now settled on the
Island of Tanna, in the South Seas.   George, their second son,
was born July 4th, 1836.   He removed to New Zealand, and
was married there in the year 1868.   He is now settled on the Island
of Tanna, with his brother Charles.   Elizabeth, their eldest daughter,
was born September 15th, 1838.   She was married to Capt. Henry
B. Park, in the United States, in January, 1862.   They have one son
and one daughter.   Jessie, their second daughter, was born February
15th, 1841.   She was married to Thomas, eldest son of William
McKay and Nancy McLeod, his wife, October 28th, 1868.   They
have one daughter.   He is now carrying on business as merchant in
Truro.   Clara, their third daughter, was born November 7th, 1846.
She was married to Edmond O. Fitch, January 9th, 1868, and on
November 19th, 1869, as she was riding in a waggon with her
husband, and had a horse leading behind the waggon, in passing the
house of Mr. William Nelson, a dog ran out and frightened the horses.
They started suddenly and upset the waggon.   When she was taken
up life had departed.   Edgar, their third son, was born February 4th,
1853.   He removed to the United States.

Sarah, the eldest daughter of Samuel and Nancy Blair, was born
March 20th, 1809.   She was married to John Bishop, of Onslow, July
4th, 1844.   They had one son and two daughters.   Mr. Bishop died
November 11th, 1865.   Nancy, their second daughter, was born
March 20th, 1812.   She was married to Daniel Cock, third, January
2nd, 1837.   They had two sons and three daughters, who appear
among the Cock families.   Mrs. Cock died May 19th, 1849, aged 44
years.

David the third son of Samuel and Nancy Blair, was born May
20th, 1814.   He was married to Esther, daughter of William
Fletcher and Margery Wilson, February 15th, 1848.   He inherits a

part of what was his father's farm, and is an elder of the Baptist Church. Adelaide, their eldest daughter, was born December 22nd, 1848. Luther, their eldest son, was born February 27th, 1850. Herbert, their second son, was born May 28th, 1851. He died May May 14th, 1853. Frances Amelia, their second daughter, was born September 16th, 1858. Elida Anna, their third daughter, was born March 3rd, 1861.

Rebecca, the third daughter of Samuel and Nancy Blair, was born April 17th, 1816. She was married to Adam Dunlap, March, 1837. They had two sons and one daughter. Mrs. Dunlap died December 21st, 1855, aged 39 years.

Esther, the fourth daughter of Samuel and Nancy Blair, was born April 21st, 1818. She was married to James Linton, of Onslow, April 8th, 1834. They had three sons and three daughters.

Elizabeth, the fifth daughter of Samuel and Nancy Blair, was born May 25th, 1820. She was married to William, son of Major A. L. Archibald and Mary Fulton, November 4th, 1845. They had two sons and five daughters.

Susan, the sixth and youngest daughter of Samuel and Nancy Blair, was born June 3rd, 1822. In September, 1827, in her play, she climbed up a cart body that was leaning against a fence. The cart body upset and fell upon her, and she was taken from under it a lifeless corpse.

James Downing, the second son of John Blair and Agnes Downing, his wife, was born December 28th, 1783. He was married to Esther, daughter of Joseph McLain and Esther Hamilton, October 26th, 1809. Mr. Blair died November 4th, 1867, aged 84 years. Nancy, their eldest daughter, was born August 16th, 1810. She was married to Hugh L. Dickie, Esq., May 24th, 1849. They have two sons. Mr. Dickie has filled the office of Custodes Rotulorum of King's County for some time past. Lavinia, their second daughter, was born November 6th, 1811. She was married to Joseph M. Dickson, Esq., March 3rd, 1835. They had one son and four daughters. Mr. Dickson died February 21st, 1865, aged 58 years. Amelia, their third daughter, was born December 19th, 1813. She was married to Adam Dunlap, February, 1857. Wellington Blair, their only son, was born April 13th, 1817. He was married to Lavinia Roach, of Cumberland, March 3rd, 1848. They have three sons and six daughters. He inherits a part of his father's farm. Margaret, the fourth daughter of James D. and Esther Blair, was born May 28th, 1820. She was married to Alexander D. Whidden, of Maitland, February 24th, 1841. They settled in Portland, Me. They had two sons and four daughters. Rachel, their fifth daughter, was born October 29th, 1823. Olivia, their sixth daughter, was born September 2nd, 1826. She was married to George W. Marsters, of New Brunswick, June 16th, 1866. Sarah, their seventh daughter, was born December 13th, 1829. Susan, their eighth daughter, was born April 13th, 1834. She was married to Dr. Alexander Crofford Page, September 20th, 1860.

Susannah, the eldest daughter of John and Nancy Blair, was born March 8th, 1786. She was married to Matthew, fourth son of James and Rebecca Archibald, December 30th, 1813. They had two sons and six daughters, that appear among the Archibalds. She died July 29th, 1850, aged 63 years, and her husband died July 24th, 1831, aged 44 years.

Sarah, the second daughter of John and Nancy Blair, was born November 15th, 1788. She married Dr. David B. Lynds, October, 1811. They had one daughter. Dr. Lynds died June 9th, 1871, aged 89 years.

John, the third son of John and Nancy Blair, was born February 3rd, 1793. He was married to Elizabeth McNutt, February 3rd, 1814. Margaret, their eldest daughter, was born November 1st, 1815. She was married to Thomas H. Gibbs, of Shubenacadie, in the year 1843. They had one son and four daughters. Nancy, their second daughter, was born March 11th, 1817. She was married to Charles Blanchard, Sheriff of the County of Colchester, January 30th, 1845. They had two sons and three daughters. John, their eldest son, was born January 5th, 1821. He was married to Olive, eldest daughter of Thomas Lynds and Elizabeth Clark, his wife, May 1st, 1845. They had one daughter. Mrs. Blair died November 26th, 1848, aged 34 years. He removed to New Brunswick, and was married there to Caroline M. Forsyth, November 5th, 1851. They had three sons and three daughters. Maria, their third daughter, was born September 24th, 1823. She was married to George W. Cock, October 20th, 1846. They had two sons and seven daughters. Charles Dickson Blair, their second son, was born May 24th, 1827. He was married to Elizabeth, daughter of James Blair and Phœbe Ann Lynds, September, 1852. They had two sons and five daughters. He has kept an Inn on the Mountain between Onslow and Tatamagouche for some time. Henry, their third son, was born February

15th, 1829, he was married to Mary Ann, second daughter of John Dickson, Esq., and Margaret Kent, December 30th, 1852. They had three sons and five daughters. Ann, their fourth daughter, was born August 2nd, 1832. She was married to Albert Lock, in 1860. They have one daughter. Louisa, their fifth and youngest daughter, was born February 1st, 1834. She was married to John S., second son of Oliver Blair and Mary Smith. They had one child. She and her child died. She died in Boston, August 21st, 1853, in the 20th year of her age. Her body was removed and interred in Onslow Cemetery.

William, the fourth son of John and Nancy Blair, was born in Onslow, September 27th, 1795. He was married to Susan, youngest daughter of James Kent, Esq., November 19th, 1819. He learned the trade of tanning and shoemaking with Major A. L. Archibald. He purchased the tannery which Samuel Fulton put up in 1816. His son Charles now resides on the same place. He died there, August 9th, 1834, aged 39 years, and his widow died February 7th, 1864, aged 68 years. Charles H. Blair, their eldest son, was born November 29th, 1822. He was married to Nancy, daughter of Thomas Smith and Mary Young of Londonderry, October 28th, 1869. They have one daughter. James Kent, their second son, was born August 28th, 1826. He was married to Nancy McCully, 1850. They had one son and two daughters. Mrs. Blair died suddenly October 11th, 1854, aged 30 years. He was married again to Caroline, daughter of Thomas M. and Letitia Crowe, September 11th, 1857. They have three sons and one daughter. He has held the office of Registrar of Deeds for the County of Colchester, since February, 1854. Silas, the third son, was born March 15th, 1829. He left home in the year 1847 to go to Canada, but changed his mind and went to Michigan. He remained there a few years, and was married to Sarah Fellows, in 1850. They had one daughter. Shortly after this, he removed to California, where he engaged in gold digging. On the 16th of May, 1854, while he was down in the pit it caved in, and he was taken out dead. He was 25 years of age.

Simeon H., the youngest son of John and Nancy Blair, was born in July, 1789. He was married to Janet G., second daughter of Daniel and Eunice McCurdy, December 14th 1820. He inherited the homestead part of his father's property. Here he spent his life, and died October 19th, 1866, aged 68 years. Eunice Wright, their eldest daughter, was born October 2nd, 1821 ; she died January 25th, 1848. Mary McCurdy, their second daughter, was born February

8th, 1824. She was married to A. M. Wells, July 14th, 1847 ; they had one son and two daughters. Daniel McCurdy Blair, was born January 9th, 1827 ; he died January 30th, 1827. George Blair, their second son, was born January 9th, 1828. He was married to Matilda Harrison, in June, 1856. They had two sons ; one is dead. Bessie, their third daughter was born March 7th, 1830. She was married to the Rev. Henry Charlton, in May, 1855. They had eight children ; five of these are dead. Israel Blair, their third son, was born January 29th, 1834. He was married to Alida DeWolf, in the month of November, 1868. They have one daughter. William, the fourth son of Simeon H. and Janet Blair, was born May 25th, 1836. He was married to Harriet, daughter of Samuel J. and Alison J. Blair. He inherits the homestead part of his father's farm. (This property was owned by his grandfather, John Blair, and his greatgrandfather, Wm. Blair.) William Blair is now Major of the Militia of Onslow ; he has taken an active part in the agricultural society and in getting a cheese factory started ; the first cheese factory that was started in Colchester was built on his farm in the year 1871. Nancy Harriet, the youngest daughter of Simeon H. and Janet Blair, was born in Onslow, October 9th, 1838. She was married to Edmond W. Hamilton Sept. 21st, 1858. They have one son and three daughters besides three children who died when they were young.

Olive, the youngest daughter of John and Nancy Blair, was born February 14th, 1805. She was married to Charles, eldest son of Daniel and Eunice McCurdy, December 14th, 1829. They had one son and three daughters. They removed to Pugwash, where she died September 28th, 1860, aged 55 years.

Elizabeth, the sixth and youngest daughter of Capt. William Blair and Jane Barns, his wife, was born in Onslow, July 2nd, 1768. She was married to Shelomith Woodworth, September 19th, 1793. Hannah, their eldest daughter, was born November 28th, 1796. She was married to Elijah Bill. They had one son. Jane, their second daughter, was born November 4th, 1798. She was married to Joseph Sibley. They had six sons and four daughters. Mr. Sibley died February 1st, 1862, aged 71 years. Benjamin, their eldest son, was born February 9th, 1801. He was married to Fanny Jane O'Brien, 1827. They had three sons and six daughters. He inherits a part of his father's property at Lower Stewiacke. Lydia Barns, their third daughter, was born January 11th, 1803. She was married to Barnabas Knowles, 1833. They had three sons and three daughters.

Sarah, their fourth daughter, was born November 25th, 1804. She was married to Absalom Pickings, September 21st, 1845. They had one son. Ingram William, their second son, was born February 9th, 1807. He was married to Hannah McDonald, June, 1844. He died in Halifax, January 16th, 1873, aged 66 years. Asel, their third son, was born May 22nd, 1809. He was married to Louisa Williams, February 19, 1836. They had six sons and five daughters. He died May 1st, 1857. His widow died May 31st, 1859. Nancy Barns, their youngest daughter, was born May 2nd, 1811. She was married to William Faulkner, Esq., of Truro, June 3rd, 1839. They had two sons and two daughters. Mr. S. Woodworth died May 19th, 1850, aged 84 years, and his wife died October 5th, 1848, aged 80 years.

James, the third and youngest son of Capt. William Blair, was born July 19th, 1766. He was married to Isabella Catherwood, July 20th, 1792. They lived and reared their family where Augustus McCurdy now resides. Robert Catherwood Blair, their only son, was born March 25th, 1793. He was married to Mary Ann Silkring, second daughter of Captain William and Anne Cock, March 18th, 1818. He built a part of the house which stands on the corner, on the Southeast of the Parade, where Mr. Atkins now resides. He resided in this house until 1834. He then purchased a farm from Robert Kent, in the Lower Village of Truro, where he spent the remainder of his life. He died May 6th, 1869, aged 77 years. Ann Frost, their eldest daughter, was born February 14th, 1819. Isabella, their second daughter, was born September 3rd, 1820. She was married to William Cutton, December, 1848. They had three sons and two daughters. Jane, their third daughter, was born November 21st, 1822. She was married to Charles McNutt, and has four sons and one daughter. Sarah Lynds, their fourth daughter, was born December 6th, 1829. She was married to Alexander U. Cutton, April 20th, 1857, and has four sons. They now inherit her father's farm in the Lower Village of Truro. Mary Ann, their fifth daughter, was born January 10th, 1833. She was married to J. C. Black, 1861. They have one son. Henrietta Blair, their sixth daughter, was born June 8th, 1840. She died June 8th, 1866.

Isabell, the only daughter of James and Isabell Blair, was born in 1795. She was married to John Browning. They had two sons and six daughters. She died in 1868. Mr. Browning died some time before. Mr. Blair's first wife died April 16th, 1795. He was married again to Sarah Cutton, February 4th, 1800. He died November 1st,

1858, aged 91 years. His widòw died October 27th, 1872. Eliza Blair, their eldest daughter, was born February 9th, 1805. She was married to George Herron, and had a family. Jane, the second daughter, was born February 8th, 1807. She was married to William Elliott, 1835. They had five sons and two daughters. She died in 1848. Lydia, their third daughter, was born February 3rd, 1810. She was married to Emmerson Herron, April 2nd, 1828. They had four sons and five daughters. She died about 1850. Eleanor, their fourth daughter, was married to Robert Redpath, September 19th, 1839. They had one son. Mr. Redpath was drowned in McCurdy's Creek, in Onslow, July 19th, 1841. Mrs. Redpath was married again to Thomas Johnson. They removed to the United States. Rebecca, their fifth daughter, was married to Samuel Perry. They removed to the United States. They had one son and two daughters. She died in 1870.

CHAPTER XX.

Robert Barnhill emigrated from Donegal, in the north of Ireland, to Halifax, Nova Scotia, with his wife, one son, and three daughters, with their husbands and families, with a large number of other persons, being in all about three hundred. This emigration was under the direction of Colonel Alexander McNutt, the British Government agent. They came in the ship called the "Hopewell." She arrived in Halifax Harbor, October 9th, 1761, and the passengers were landed on what is now called McNab's Island. They had to remain about Halifax during the winter, and in the spring of the year 1762 some of these people went to Windsor, some to Horton, some to Londonderry, some to Onslow, and some to Truro. They were sent out and supplied by the British Government. Mr. Barnhill and a number of his family settled in Chiganois, and were Grantees of the Township of Londonderry. His wife is said to be the first person that was buried on the Burying Island, in the Chiganois Marsh; the place is not now known. Rebecca, their eldest daughter, was married to Joseph Foster, and remained in Ireland.

John, their only son, was born in Ireland in the year 1730, and Letitia Deyarmond, his wife, was born in the year 1734. They were married before they left Ireland. John the eldest son of John and

Letitia Barnhill, was born in the year 1762. He' was married to Sarah, the eldest daughter of Joseph Crowe, Senr., and Esther Barnhill, his wife, about the year 1786. Esther, their eldest daughter, was born March 19th, 1787. She was married to Isaac Logan, of Cumberland County, March 22nd, 1810. They settled in Onslow, where she spent the remainder of her life. She died February 10th, 1853, aged 65 years. She left no children. Mr. Logan was married again to Martha, daughter of David Archibald, fourth, and Esther Cox, his wife, and widow of the late Jonathan Blanchard, December 5th, 1854. Mr. Logan died March 11th, 1872, aged 72 years.

Joseph, the eldest son of John and Sarah Barnhill, was born January 27th, 1794. He was married to Rebecca, the second daughter of Alexander and Rebecca Miller, of Truro, February 29th, 1816. They had five sons and two daughters. They settled on the farm on which their three sons, Alexander, Robert, and Charles, now reside, on the East side of the Chiganois River, where they reared their family and spent the remainder of their lives. He died March 15th, 1869, aged 75 years, and his wife died June 1st, 1843, aged 44 years.

James, the second son of John and Sarah Barnhill, was born June 24th, 1796. He was married to Esther, daughter of Timothy Putnam and Janet Hunter, his wife, March 17th, 1818. They had three sons and five daughters. Their son John was driving a team of oxen drawing marsh mud, on the 28th of April, 1848. He was riding in the cart, returning for a load, and fell, and the wheel ran over his body. He was taken up dead. He was fourteen years old at the the time. Mrs. Barnhill died May 3rd, 1868, aged 73 years, and he was married again to Jane McKay, widow of the late John Sutherland, September 7th, 1871.

Alexander, the third son of John and Sarah Barnhill, was born February 28th, 1801. He was married to Elizabeth, daughter of Samuel Davison and Sarah Crowe, his wife, of Portaupique, November 27th, 1823. They had two sons and five daughters. He inherited a part of his father's farm. He died December 31st, 1857, aged 56 years.

Rebecca, the second daughter of John and Sarah Barnhill, was born August 10th, 1803. She was married to Isaac Dickie, of Cornwallis, February 19th, 1826. They had three sons. They resided for a time in Onslow, where their eldest son, John B. Dickie, Esq., now resides. Mrs. Dickie died there suddenly, June 15th, 1847. Mr. Dickie was married again and removed to Cornwallis, where he died February 28th, 1858. John B. Dickie is now Custodes

Rotulorum for the County of Colchester. Alexander, the second son of John Barnhill, Senr., and Letitia Deyarmond, was born in 1765. He was married to Alice, fourth daughter of Robert and Esther Hunter, in 1787. In 1786, John Barnhill purchased Robert Archibald's farm in Truro, also a part of David Whidden's farm. Both Mr. Barnhill and his son settled on these farms and spent their days there. The father died November 12th, 1813, aged 83 years. His wife died July 22nd, 1791, aged 57 years. Their son Alexander died September 22, 1813, aged 47 years ; his widow died December 22nd, 1831, aged 65 years. Letitia, the eldest daughter of Alexander and Alice Barnhill, was born in 1788. She was married to John Cumming in 1808. They had eight sons and two daughters. She died February 17th, 1854. Mr. Cummings died October 30th, 1862, aged 78 years. Thomas, the fourth son of John and Sarah Barnhill, was born August 8th, 1808. He was married to Maria Davison, November 6th, 1832. They had five sons and three daughters. He died suddenly, April 26th, 1870. John Barnhill's first wife died June 30th, 1825. He was married again to Letitia Crowe, June 1st, 1832. Isaac Logan, their son, was born May 23rd, 1836. He was married to Hannah Lockhart, eldest daughter of Jacob and Eleanor Lynds, May 5th, 1858. They had two sons and two daughters. John Barnhill died Oct. 23rd, 1847. His second wife died April 8th, 1839.

John, the son of Alexander and Alice Barnhill, was born August 5th, 1791. He was married to Nancy, second daughter of William Joyce and Mary Elliott, his wife, in the year 1817. He inherited his father's farm, and in the year 1816 he sold his house, and the interval lying on both sides of the Marsh road, and built his house up the Halifax road, where they spent the remainder of their days. They had four sons and three daughters. Mrs. Barnhill died March 11th, 1829, the same day their son Robert was born. He was married again to Sophia, the youngest daughter of dumb John Johnson, May 4th, 1835. They had two sons and four daughters. Mr. Barnhill died May 2nd, 1871, aged 79 years.

Esther, the second daughter of Alexander and Alice Barnhill, was born in Truro, September 25th, 1798. She was married to David V., eldest son of Joseph Crowe and Mary Vance, in the month of January, 1817. They had four sons and three daughters. They settled at Debert River. He died June 15th, 1868, and his widow died October 22nd, 1872, aged 74 years. Alice, the youngest daughter of Alexander and Alice Barnhill, was born July 18th, 1801. She was married to

Joseph Wilson, of Masstown. They had two sons and three daughters. Mr. Wilson died June 6th, 1866, aged 77 years, and his first wife, Susannah Fletcher, of Debert, died July 30th, 1830.

CHAPTER XXI.

Alexander Deyarmond was married to Mary, the third daughter of the foregoing named Robert Barnhill. They remained in Ireland for about six years after the rest of the family removed to Nova Scotia, when her father wrote for them to come to Nova Scotia and take his property in Chiganois, and maintain him the remainder of his life. They removed to Nova Scotia, with their family, about the year 1767, and settled on Mr. Barnhill's property, at Chiganois, where they spent the remainder of their days. They had three sons and three daughters. Rebecca, the daughter of the above named Alexander and Mary Deyarmond, was married to John Spencer, of Londonderry. They had three sons and one daughter. Elizabeth, the second daughter of Alexander Deyarmond and Mary Barnhill, was married to Thomas Ellis, of Musquodoboit, October, 1795, being the first pair that the Rev. Mr. Brown married in Londonderry. They had two daughters. Letitia, their third daughter, was married to Charles Blackie, of Pictou, in 1804. They settled at Upper Stewiacke. They had five daughters. She died May 26th, 1835, aged 63 years, and her husband died October 11th, 1869, aged 86 years.

Robert, the eldest son of Alexander Deyarmond and Mary Barnhill, was born in Ireland in 1761. He was married to Nancy, daughter of the late Thomas Wilson, of Masstown, about the year 1790. They removed and settled at Pembroke, in Upper Stewiacke, where they reared their numerous family. He died there February 11th, 1814, aged 53 years, and his widow died January 26th, 1860, aged 89 years. Alexander and Thomas, their twin sons, were born February 10th, 1792. Alexander was married to Mary Cottom, of Debert River, March 15th, 1815. They had three sons and three daughters. They settled on what was a part of his father's farm, where he carried on the blacksmith work, and reared his family. He died June 19th, 1846, aged 54 years, and his widow died August 13th, 1857, aged 67 years. Thomas was married to Nancy Cottom,

January 1st, 1813. They had four sons and three daughters. He settled on what was a part of his father's farm, being the same on which the Messrs. Bairds now reside. Some time after he exchanged farms with James Hamiltom, and removed to what was a part of the farm of Archibald Gammell, where he spent the remainder of his life. He died April 1st, 1870, aged 78 years. Robert Deyarmond, their third son, was born August 1793. He went into the woods and was lost ; search was made for him, and his body was found dead, March 16th, 1850, aged 56 years. Mary Deyarmond, their eldest daughter, was born March 18th, 1795. She was married to Edward Hughes, January, 1816. They removed to Halifax. They had three sons and four daughters. She died in Halifax, October, 1860, aged 65 years, and her husband died about the year 1856. Joseph Deyarmond, their fourth son, was born March 8th, 1798. He was married to Jane Stark, February 28th, 1822. They had five sons and three daughters. He settled on a part of his father's farm. His wife died September 28th, 1865, aged 68 years. John Deyarmond, their fifth son, was born January 1st, 1800. He was married to Rebecca, daughter of John and Elizabeth Deyarmond, February 5th, 1823. They had five sons and two daughters. He inherited a large part of his father's farm. He died December 11th, 1861. His widow died April 14th, 1866. Samuel, their sixth son, was born November 6th, 1801. He was married to Susan, third daughter of John and Isabell Baird, February 17th, 1829. They had four sons and three daughters. He settled on what was a part of his father's farm, in Pembroke. Sarah, their second daughter, was born March 11th, 1804. She was married to George Proven, June 12th, 1829. They had four sons and three daughters. James Deyarmond, their seventh son, was born in December, 1805. He left home in 1827, and nothing has been heard from him since. Charles, the eighth son, was born in 1807. He removed to P. E. Island. He was married there to the widow Simpson, in 1840. They had one daughter. They removed to New Brunswick. He died there January, 1870. His wife died January, 1869. Rebecca, their third daughter, was born in 1809. She was married to John Graham, December, 1831.

John, the second son of Alexander and Mary Deyarmond, was born in Ireland in 1764, and was brought by his parents to Nova Scotia when he was about three years old. He was married to Elizabeth Wilson, of Masstown, about 1793. He inherited his father's farm in Chiganois, where he reared his three sons and nine daughters.

He died November 17th, 1850, aged 86 years. His widow died August 23rd, 1866, aged 91 years.

Mary, the eldest daughter of John and Elizabeth Deyarmond, was born March 10th, 1794. She was married to William McDormond, of Debert River, October 23rd, 1818. They had two sons and two daughters who are living, besides several that died young. He died April 5th, 1871, aged 78 years.

Alexander, the eldest son of John and Elizabeth Deyarmond, was born December 18th, 1795. He was married to Isabell, daughter of John and Mary Dickson, of Onslow Mountain, February 1st, 1825. They had one son and two daughters. Mrs. Deyarmond died November 30th, 1843. He was married again to Ruth Morrison, of Debert, January 30th, 1846. She died November 1st, 1845. He was married again to Rachel, daughter of James Cottom, October 14th, 1861.

Rebecca, the second daughter of John and Elizabeth Deyarmond, was born March 13th, 1798. She was married to John, son of Robert and Nancy Deyarmond, February 3rd, 1823. They had five sons and two daughters. She died at Stewiacke, April 14th, 1866, and her husband died December 11th, 1861. Jane, their third daughter, was born in November, 1800. She was married to Jasper Crowe, February 15th, 1825. They had two sons and four daughters. Letitia, their fourth daughter, was born 1802. She was married to Charles Graham, of Pembroke, November, 1836. They had three sons and three daughters. Thomas, the second son of John and Elizabeth Deyarmond, was born May 13th, 1806. He was married to Mary Ann, daughter of William H. Wilson and Jane McElhenny, January 27th, 1835. They had one son and three daughters. Mrs. Deyarmond died October 15th, 1864.

Elizabeth, the fifth daughter of John and Elizabeth Deyarmond, was born May 14th, 1809. She was married to Thomas Baird, of Onslow Mountain, November 12th, 1849. They have two daughters.

Sarah, their sixth daughter was born 1811. She was married to James Graham of Pictou, October 14th, 1841. They had three sons and three daughters.

John, their third and youngest son, was born September 2nd, 1816. He was married to Isabel Flemming, daughter of Alexander and Jane Fletcher, of Folly Mountain, November 2nd, 1843. He inherits the homestead part of his father's farm, being the same that was owned by his grandfather Deyarmond, and his great grandfather Robert Barnhill. They have one son.

Nancy, their seventh daughter, was born October, 1814. She was married to William Ray, of Pictou, August 2nd, 1847. They have three daughters. Margaret, their eighth daughter, was born February 28th, 1819. She was married to Wilson Staples, January 7th, 1864.

Susan, their ninth daughter, was born May, 1821. She was married to Robert Young, of Pictou, March, 1845. They have one son and three daughters.

Alexander, the third son of Alexander Deyarmond and Mary Barnhill, was born about the year 1766. He was married to Mary, daughter of the late Thomas Fletcher, of Masstown. They had four sons and five daughters. They lived for some time on the farm that the late Daniel Chisholm recently lived upon at Debert, Londonderry. They removed to Michigan, United States, about 1820.

CHAPTER XXII.

Margaret, the second daughter of Robert Barnhill, was born in Ireland about the year 1736. She was married to Thomas Baird about the year 1754. They had four children before they left Ireland. Three of these died on the passage out. They came out in the ship "Hopewell," that arrived in Halifax, October, 1761. Dorcas, their only child that lived to see Nova Scotia, was married to Alexander, son of John Vance and Mary Kelly his wife, in the year 1777. They settled on the farm that Vinton Faulkner now resides upon at Red Head, Londonderry, where they reared their family, and spent nearly all their lifetime. Mr. Vance died about the year 1828, aged about 74 years, and his wife Dorcas died about the year 1832, aged 75 years. She was four years old when they came to Nova Scotia.

Mary, the eldest daughter of Alexander and Dorcas Vance, was born in the year 1778. She was married to John Morrison, of Debert in the year 1797. They had five sons and three daughters. She died July 14th, 1850, aged 72 years, and her husband died October 11th, 1857, aged 86 years.

John, the eldest son of Alexander and Dorcas Vance, was born in the year 1779. He was married to Catherine McGregor in the year 1800. They had four sons and five daughters. Mr. Vance died in May, 1869, aged 89 years, and his wife died December, 1869. Thomas, their second son, was born in the year 1783, and was married to Rebecca Carr, in the year 1806. They had four children before they removed to Michigan, U. S., and had a number afterwards. He died there in the year 1860, aged 77 years.

Jane, their second daughter, was born in the year 1785. She was married to Richard Upham, of North River, December 31st, 1805. They had three sons and two daughters. Mr. Upham died in the year 1815, before his son Richard was born. Richard was born October, 1815, and she was married again to William Miller, 1819. She died in Truro in the year 1860, aged 75 years. David, their third son, was born in the year 1786. He left home when about twenty years old, to follow the sea, and never was heard from. Margaret, their third daughter was born in the year 1791. She was married to Andrew Fulmore, of Five Islands, in the year 1810. They had five sons and four daughters. She died in May, 1836, aged 45 years ; her husband was married again. He died May 17th, 1872. Isabel, their fourth daughter, was born in the year 1793. She was married to Robert Simpson, of Economy, in the year 1815. They had five sons and three daughters. They removed to Portland, Me. about the year 1845, and died there. Alexander, the fourth son of Alexander and Dorcas Vance, was born February 15th, 1795. He was married to Elizabeth Miller, of Debert, March 17th, 1820. He settled, and built the house that Frederick Pearson, Esq., recently lived in, where they resided until about the year 1834, when they removed to Canada. They had four sons and three daughters. Mrs. Vance died there, and he was married again, and had three sons and four daughters. Mr. Vance died there in the year 1857, aged 62 years. Rebecca, their fifth daughter, was born in the year 1798. She was married to Hugh McInnis in the month of November, 1818. They had four sons and four daughters. They settled on the Wallace Road, near the Folly Lake, and continued there until about 1834, when they removed to Canada. She died there in the year 1858, aged 60 years, and her husband died in the year 1869. James, the fifth and youngest son of Alexander and Dorcas Vance, was born December 1st, 1800. He was married to Margaret daughter of Edward Faulkner and Jane Savage, of Hants County, August 19th, 1820. They had four sons and two daughters. Mrs. Vance died June 18th, 1845, aged 45 years, and he was married again to Elizabeth, daughter of Henry McLaughlan of Economy and Jane Wilson, widow of the late James Campbell, of the Folly. Mrs. Vance died, and he is living with his son at the Folly.

CHAPTER XXIII.

Thomas, the eldest son of Thomas Baird and Margaret Barnhill his wife, was born in Chigonois, April 30th, 1762. As these first settlers who were sent out by the British Government were supplied by provision, served out on the first day of May, so much for every man, woman and child; Thomas being but one day old, the parents received as much provision for him as any other of their family. Thomas Baird, Junr., was married to Magdalen, daughter of John Dickson of North River, October 9th, 1793. James D., their eldest son, was born August 6th, 1796. He was married to Nancy, the third daughter of Alexander and Rebecca Miller, of Truro, July 13th, 1820. They had six sons and two daughters. They resided in Onslow until the year 1861, when they removed to Pembroke in Stewiacke, where he spent the remainder of his days. He died there June 2nd, 1871, aged 75 years. Margaret, the eldest daughter of Thomas and Magdalen Baird, was born July 16th, 1798. She was married to James Fulmore, of Five Islands, in January, 1822. They had three sons and five daughters. Mr. Fulmore died, and she was married again to George Spencer, and resided at Richibucto until he died about the year 1867; she is now living a widow. Jane, their second daughter, was born in Onslow, March 30th, 1800. On November 25th, 1825, in crossing the Bay returning from a visit to the Old Barns on horseback, she got into deep water and fell from the horse. She held by the bridle until she and the horse were both drowned. Mr. Perry was watching her at the time, but could render her no assistance. Darkness set in, by the aid of torches her body was recovered a few hours afterwards, and taken to her father's house.

John, the second son of Thomas and Magdalen Baird, was born October 11th, 1803. He was married to Sarah, daughter of John Fulton and Esther Crowe of Bass River, June 28th, 1827. He inherited a part of his father's farm at Lower Onslow. Rebecca, their third daughter, was born January 7th, 1806. She was married to

John, son of Thomas Crowe and Esther Fulton, of Debert River, March, 1827. They had one son and two daughters. Mrs. Crowe died February 16th, 1845. Mr. Crowe was married again to Susan, daughter of David Blackmore and Janet Hoar, his wife, of North River, March 3rd, 1846.

Thomas, the third son of Thomas and Magdalen Baird, was born July 11th, 1808. He inherited a part of his father's farm, and was married to Eliza Jane, daughter of Joseph Hamilton and Rachel Carter, October, 1842. They had four sons and one daughter. Mrs. Baird died December 12th, 1866, aged 50 years, and he died July 12th, 1872, aged 64 years. Nancy, the fourth and youngest daughter of Thomas and Magdalen Baird, was born November 30th, 1810. She was married to Thomas McLellan, of Great Village, March 9th, 1839. She had two children, and they both died young. She died January 7th, 1852, aged 41 years, and her husband died December 22nd, 1865, aged 66 years. Thomas Baird inherited his father's farm in Chiganois. He sold out there and settled at Lower Onslow, where his two sons, John and Thomas, now reside. He died January 7th, 1837, aged 75 years, and his wife died January 29th, 1849, in the 76th year of her age.

Jane, the daughter of Thomas Baird and Margaret Barnhill, was born in the year 1764. She was married to Joseph McDormond, of Masstown, in the year 1785. They remained in Masstown about ten years, then removed across the Bay, and settled on the farm that John Barber now resides upon, near the mouth of the Shubenacadie River. They continued there until about the year 1830, when they removed across the Bay again and settled on the West side of the Folly River, where they spent the remainder of their lives. He died in the year 1839, and his wife died in the year 1849, aged 83 years. Jane, the eldest daughter, was born in the year 1787. She was married to Samuel Henderson, October 22nd, 1817. They had two sons and two daughters. She died June 22nd, 1817, and her husband died September, 1867. Rebecca, their second daughter, was born in the year 1789. She died unmarried in the year, 1839, aged 50 years.

William, the eldest son of Joseph and Jane McDormond, was born in the year 1793. He was married to Mary, the eldest daughter of John Deyarmond and Elizabeth Wilson, October 23rd, 1818. They have two sons and two daughters, besides several children that died young. They settled at Debert River, where he died, April 5th, 1871, aged 78 years. Mary, their third daughter, was born March 1st,

13

1803. She was married to Robert Burns, November, 1830. They had three daughters. She died July 23rd, 1841, aged 38 years. James, their fourth son, was born March 12th, 1801. He died December 23rd, 1802. John, their son, died December 24th, 1802. Thomas, their son, died December 25th, 1802. Joseph, their fifth son, was born January 3rd, 1805. He was married to Dorcas West, July 15th, 1836. They had three sons and one daughter. He died April 13th, 1866, aged 61 years. Margaret, the fourth and youngest daughter of Joseph McDormond and Jane Baird, was born in Truro, January 12th, 1807. She was married to William West, October, 1836. They had three sons and two daughters, They inherited her father's farm until her death, which took place October 15th, 1849, aged 42 years.

Mary, the third daughter of Thomas Baird and Margaret Barnhill, was born in the year 1767. She was married to John Dickson, of North River, November 4th, 1790. They settled on Onslow Mountain, where they spent the remainder of their lives. Thomas Baird, the eldest son of John and Mary Dickson, was born March 16th, 1792. He was married to Elizabeth, daughter of Nathan Upham and Eleanor Knowlton, his wife, Feby. 25th, 1820. They had one son and one daughter. Mrs. Dickson died May 2nd, 1862, aged 76 years, and Mr. Dickson died May 7th, 1872, aged 80 years, William, the second son of John and Mary Dickson, was born August 2nd, 1793. On July 5th, 1814, in company with a number of men, he went to assist William McKeen to frame a saw-mill. After dinner he, Samuel McKeen, and John Barnhill went out on the pond in a canoe. They upset the canoe, when Barnhill and McKeen swam for the shore. Looking back, they saw Dickson in danger. McKeen swam back and caught him, when Dickson seized him by the shoulder and drew him under the water, and it was with difficulty that McKeen threw Dickson off, which he was obliged to do, in order to save his own life. About three hours after, the body was recovered and taken to his father's house in Onslow. In one month more he would have been 21 years of age.

Rebecca, the eldest daughter of John and Mary Dickson, was born April 9th, 1795. She was married to John, the only son of John Baird and Jane Dickson, January 24th, 1822. They had two sons and one daughter. Mrs. Baird died May 1st, 1864, aged 69 years.

John, the third son of John and Mary Dickson, was born July 25th, 1798. He was married to Margaret, eldest daughter of

Alexander Kent, Esq., and Janet Christie, December 21st, 1826. They had two sons and three daughters. He inherits a part of his father's farm at Onslow Mountain. He is Justice of the Peace, and an elder in the Presbyterian Church. Isabell, their second daughter, was born July 5th, 1800. She was married to Alexander Deyarmond, of Debert River, February 1st, 1825. They had one son and two daughters. She died November 30th, 1843, aged 43 years. James, their fourth son, was born January 16th, 1802. He died June 3rd, 1821. Mary, John Dickson's first wife, died suddenly, November 23rd, 1803, and he was married again to Elizabeth, the fourth daughter of Hugh Moore and Janet Logan, November 6th, 1804. They had three sons and three daughters. Mr. Dickson died May 25th, 1855, aged 92 years, and his second wife died May 17th, 1842, aged 68 years.

John, the second son of Thomas Baird and Margaret Barnhill, was born in Chiganois, June 2nd, 1769. He was married to Janet, daughter of John Dickson and Margaret Burns, in the year 1793, John, their only son, was born November 25th, 1794. He was married to Rebecca, the eldest daughter of John Dickson and Mary Baird, January 24th, 1822. They had two sons and one daughter. Mrs. Baird died May 1st, 1864, aged 69 years. John Baird, Junr., settled first on the farm on which William Little now resides, on Onslow Mountain, where he continued for about twelve years after they were married. He then removed to the place where he now resides, with his son John, about two miles below the Folly. Janet, the first wife of John Baird, Senr., died December 4th, 1794, aged 26 years, and he was married again to Isabell, daughter of Thomas Wilson and Mary McDormond, of Masstown, in the year 1796. (Isabell Wilson, his wife, was born December 18th, 1777.) They removed from Chiganois and settled in the woods on Onslow Mountain, where he reclaimed a farm from the forest, reared the family, and spent the remainder of his life. He died January 21st, 1830, aged 61 years, and his wife died July 10th, 1852, aged 75 years.

Rebecca, their eldest daughter, was born January 1st, 1797. She was married to Thomas Mitchell, of Truro, January 25th, 1821. They had four sons and three daughters. Mr. Mitchell died January 21st, 1839, and she was married again to Andrew Thomson, of Folly Mountain, February 14th, 1845. Mr. Thomson died May, 1853, and she is living a widow. Jenny, their second daughter, was born May 13th, 1801. She was married to Thomas Cottom, February 3rd,

1825. They had three sons and six daughters. She died June, 1869, aged 68 years. Thomas, the eldest son of John and Isabell Baird, was born February 13th, 1803. He was married to Elizabeth Deyarmond, of Chiganois, November 12th, 1840. They have two daughters. They are settled on the Mountain, near the place which his father settled. Susan W., their third daughter, was born February 8th, 1805. She was married to Samuel Deyarmond, of Stewiacke, February 17th, 1829. They had four sons and two daughters. Nancy, their fourth daughter, was born March 26th, 1807. She was married to William Cottom, January, 1830. They had two sons. She died November, 1852. Her husband died September, 1836. Margaret, their fifth daughter, was born March 11th, 1809. She was married to Charles Blackie, April 10th, 1842. They had three sons and three daughters. She died April, 1859, and her husband died July 3rd, 1861. Sarah, their sixth daughter, was born December 4th, 1811. She was married to James Staples, of Chiganois, December 28th, 1841. They had four sons and three daughters. James Dickson, their second son, was born December 28th, 1813. He was married to Sarah, the youngest daughter of James Crowe and Sarah Wilson, November 18th, 1843. They inherited his father's farm. They have three sons. Elizabeth, the seventh daughter of John and Isabell Baird, was born August 22nd, 1817. She died unmarried, July 8th, 1852, aged 35 years. Alexander Miller, their third son, was born November 14th, 1819. He was married to Matilda Archibald, February 29th, 1848. They have one son and one daughter. He is settled at Chiganois, working at tanning and shoemaking. William, their fourth and youngest son, was born August 31st, 1822. He died a bachelor, February 22nd, 1845, in the 23rd year of his age.

Rebecca, the youngest daughter of Thomas Baird and Margaret Barnhill, was born at Chiganois, March 20th, 1771. She was married to Alexander Miller, of Truro, June 29th, 1795. She had two sons and eight daughters, who appear among the Millers. She died October 15th, 1837. Her husband died November 20th, 1834, aged 65 years. (These are the writer's parents.)

Thomas Baird, Senr., settled at Chiganois, near the place that his father-in-law, Robert Barnhill, his brother-in-law, Alexander Deyarmond, and Joseph Crowe, Senr., also John Barnhill, settled, in what is now called Chiganois Village. These were all Grantees of Londonderry Township, and had their land lying together. Mr. Baird had his house on what is now Mr. Graham's field, and he had 1000 acres lying between that and the Debert River. There they reared their family. Mr. Baird died at the house of Alexander Miller, of Truro, March 11th, 1809, aged about 78 years. As the snow was very deep at the time, his body was buried in the Truro Cemetery, as it could not be taken to Chiganois without great inconvenience. His wife, Margaret, died at her son John's house, on Onslow Mountain, July, 1818, aged about 84 years. She was interred in the family burying ground, on the Island in Chiganois Marsh.

Rebecca, the eldest daughter of John Barnhill, Senr., and Letitia Deyarmond, was born in 1763. She was married to James Archibald, Esq., February 25th, 1779. Their family appears among the Archibalds. Elizabeth, daughter of John and Letitia Barnhill, was born 1770. She was married to Capt. Thomas Fletcher, of Debert, 1786. They had three sons and two daughters. She died August, 1821, aged 51 years, and her husband died January 17th, 1844, aged 85 years. Letitia Fletcher, their eldest daughter, was born September 19th, 1787. She died when young.

Eleanor, the second daughter of Thomas and Elizabeth Fletcher, was born December 2nd, 1790. She was married to Jacob Lynds, of North River, November 1st, 1810. They had five sons and five daughters. She died January 17th, 1867, and Mr. Lynds died May 22nd, 1858. Susan Fletcher, their third daughter, was born September, 1792. She was married to Joseph Wilson, of Masstown. They had four sons and three daughters. She died July 30th, 1830, and Mr. Wilson died June 6th, 1866, aged 77 years. John Fletcher, their eldest son, was born October 2nd, 1794. He was married to Rebecca Crowe, February 27th, 1820. They had three sons and four daughters. He died January 27th, 1839. William Fletcher, their second son, was born February 5th, 1797. He was married to Margery Wilson, January 11th, 1820. They had four sons and two daughters. Mrs. Fletcher died March 3rd, 1847. He was married again to Mary Cutton, widow of the late Alexander Wilson, October 26th, 1848. Mrs. Fletcher died May 17th, 1870. David Fletcher, their third son, was born September, 1800. He was married to Jane Davison. They had four sons and six daughters. On October 23rd, 1852, he was engaged attending a mill, and was caught by a circular saw, which took both arms off. He lived about two hours after. Letitia, the third daughter of John Barnhill, Senr., and Letitia Deyarmond, was born about the year 1771. She was married to

David Archibald, fifth, of Musquodoboit, August 9th, 1792. They had three sons and five daughters. These appear among the Archibalds.

Margaret, the youngest daughter of John and Letitia Barnhill, was born in 1773. She was married to Richard, son of Charles and Janet Blackie, of Pictou, November 13th, 1800. They settled in Truro, and he had his blacksmith's shop near the place that Mr. Edmond Hamilton's house now stands, and Mr. Blackie had his house on the opposite side of the street. Here they reared their family and spent the remainder of their days. Mrs. Blackie died April 26th, 1812, aged 39 years. Mr. Blackie was married again to Martha Ryan, and she lived but a short time after they were married. Mr. Blackie was married again to Sarah Wallace, of the old Halifax road. He died November 18th, 1816, aged 40 years. His widow was married to Peter Blair. They had one son and one daughter; the son's name was John. He was drowned attempting to cross the Salmon River, at the head of the tide, June 8th, 1830, aged seven years, and his mother, Sarah Blair, died September 13th, 1839, aged 49 years. Their daughter, Fanny, is now the wife of William Berrell, of Truro Village.

Letitia, the eldest daughter of Richard Blackie and Margaret Barnhill, was born in Truro, September 12th, 1801. She was married to John Downing, April 10th, 1833. They had one son and one daughter. She died February, 1844. Janet, the second daughter of Richard and Margaret Blackie, was born February 9th, 1805. She was married to James Wilson, of Chiganois, February 25th, 1823. They had four sons and one daughter. Mr. Wilson died July 9th, 1867. John Blackie, their eldest son, was born in Truro, August 25th, 1806. He served with George Cook, of Truro, and learned the carpenter trade. He was married to Sarah Ann, fourth daughter of James and Sarah Yuill, of Clifton, January 14th, 1836. They had four sons and two daughters. Their second son, James Yuill Blackie, while residing in the City of Cambridge, Mass., attending to his business as harness maker, on September 15th, 1869, was found by the night watch lying on the sidewalk, at about midnight, in his night clothes. When taken up and examined by the doctor, it was found that his neck was dislocated, and life departed in a few minutes. It was supposed that he rose from his bed while asleep, as he had done before, and fell from the window of the third story of the house in which he had been lodging. He was 26 years old at the time. Charles Harris, the youngest son of Richard and

Margaret Blackie, was born August 8th, 1808. He was married to Margaret, the fifth daughter of John and Isabell Baird, April 10th, 1842. They had three sons and three daughters. He died July 3rd, 1861, aged 53 years, and his wife died April, 1859, aged 50 years.

Esther, the fourth daughter of Robert Barnhill and his wife, was born in Ireland in the year 1740. She was married to Joseph Crowe, about the year 1759, about two years before they left Ireland. They came to Nova Scotia, with her parents, in the ship " Hopewell," October 9th, 1761, and settled in Chiganois. They had three sons and four daughters. These appear among the Crowe family. She died January 6th, 1818, aged 78 years, and her husband died April 15th, 1810, aged 72 years.

Sarah, the fifth and youngest daughter of Robert Barnhill and his wife, was born in Ireland about the year 1746, and came with her parents to Nova Scotia. She was married to Thomas Crowe, about the year 1773. They had three sons and five daughters, who appear among the Crowe families.

CHAPTER XXIV.

James Crow, with his six sons and one daughter, emigrated from Londonderry, in the North of Ireland, to Nova Scotia in the ship " Hopewell." We cannot ascertain whether his wife came to this country or not. He, with four of his sons and one daughter, settled first at Windsor. His daughter's name was Margaret. She was married there to Daniel Frizzell, and had two daughters. One of these daughters was married to Mr. Snide, who removed and settted on the West side of Shubenacadie River, nearly opposite Fort Ellis, where they died.

Joseph, the eldest son of this James Crow, was born in Ireland in the year 1738. He was married to Esther Barnhill, about the year 1759. Margaret, their eldest daughter, was born in Ireland in the year 1760. She was married to Joseph Mahon, of Londonderry. They had three sons and four daughters. Esther, the second daughter of Joseph and Esther Crow, was born in Chiganois in the year 1762. She was married to John, son of James Fulton, Esq., and Margaret Campbell, of Bass River. They had six sons and six daughters. James, the eldest son of Joseph Crow, Senr., and Esther Barnhill,

was born in Chiganois in the year 1764.   He was married to Letitia,
daughter of Jasper McKinlay and Letitia Green, in the year 1785.
They had four sons and six daughters.   He settled on the same place
that was afterwards inherited by his four sons, and had his house near
the place which his son Jasper now resides.   He built mills at the
same place that his son James now has mills.   They reared their
family and died at this place.   Mr. Crow died in the month of
October, 1823, aged 59 years, and his wife, Letitia, died in the month
of January, 1844, aged 78 years.

Esther, their eldest daughter was born in the year 1786.   She was
married to David, the third son of Nicholas Crow, of Bass River.
They settled on the Folly Mountain and had three sons and three
daughters.

Letitia, the second daughter of James and Letitia Crow, was born
May 29th, 1790.   She was married to Thomas, youngest son of
Thomas Crow and Sarah Barnhill, of Beaver Brook, Clifton, October
11th, 1814.   They had five sons and two daughters.   They appear
among the descendants of Thomas Crow, Senr.

Joseph, the eldest son of James and Letitia Crow, was born January 1st, 1792.   He was married to Jane, daughter of John Staples
and Catherine Blair, December 28th, 1828.   He inherited a part of
his father's farm, and the half of the Mills.   He built the house that
is still standing on the north side of the Mill Pond, where they reared
their family and spent the remainder of their lives.   He died January
3rd, 1868, aged 76 years, and his wife died April 29th, 1853.   They
had six sons and six daughters.

Sarah, the third daughter of James and Letitia Crow, was born in
1794.   She was married to Ezra Stevens, of Onslow Mountain, March
8th, 1825.   They had two sons and four daughters.

Jasper their second son was born December 25th, 1796.   He was
married to Jane, the third daughter of John and Elizabeth Deyarmond,
February 15th, 1825.   He inherited the homestead part of his father's
property.   They had two sons and four daughters.   Mr. Jasper Crow
has filled the office of Elder in the Presbyterian Congregation of Onslow, and Superintendent of Sabbath schools since about the year
1835.

Margaret, the fourth daughter of James and Letitia Crow, was
born April 5th, 1799.   She was married to John Carter, of Lower
Onslow, March 12th, 1824.   They had four sons and four daughters.
She died April fifth, 1852.   Her husband died in December, 1870.

James, the third son of James and Letitia Crow, was born February, 1802. He was married to Mary, daughter of Thomas and Esther
Wilson of Shubenacadie, March 9th, 1839. They have two sons and
one daughter. He inherited a part of his father's property, and is
now owner of the Mills.

Rebecca, the fifth and youngest daughter of James and Letitia
Crow, was born August, 1803. She was married to James Crow,
Esq. They had one son and four daughters.

Samuel, the fourth and youngest son of James and Letitia Crow,
was born June 20th, 1805. He was married to Sarah, the eldest
daughter of Joseph and Mary Crow, November 30th, 1829. They
had three sons and one daughter. He inherited a part of his father's
property, where he spent the remainder of his days. He died July
19th, 1871, aged 66 years.

Sarah, the third daughter of Joseph Crow, Senr., and Esther
Barnhill, was born in the year 1766. She was married to John Barnhill, of Chiganois, about the year 1786. They had four sons and two
daughters. These appear among the Barnhill families. She died
June 30th, 1825, aged 59 years, and her husband died October 23rd,
1847, aged 85 years.

Rebecca, the fourth and youngest daughter of Joseph and Esther
Crow, was born in the year 1769. She was married to Alexander
Miller of Truro, December 6th, 1792. She died October 19th, 1793,
aged 24 years.

Joseph, the second son of Joseph Crow, Senr., and Esther Barnhill, was born in the year 1771. He was married to Mary, daughter
of David Vance and Jane Hill, in the year 1794. He inherited his
father's property in Chiganois Village, where they reared their family.
He died December 28th, 1855, aged 84 years, and his wife died
January 3rd, 1832, aged 60 years.

David Vance Crow, their eldest son, was born July 9th, 1795.
He was married to Esther, second daughter of Alexander and Alice
Barnhill, of Truro, January 1817. They settled at Debert
River, where he reclaimed his farm from the forest. He was appointed
Justice of the Peace when a young man, and he filled the office of
Custodes Rotulorum, for the County of Colchester for a number of
years before he died. They had four sons and three daughters. He
died June 14th, 1868, aged 73 years, and his widow died October
22nd, 1872, aged 74 years.

Joseph, the second son of Joseph and Mary Crow, was born in

1799. He was married to Margaret, daughter of Charles Hill, of Economy, February, .1831. They had two sons and one daughter. He carried on business as a Merchant at the Folly for a number of years, and his first wife died there October 15th 1841, aged 32 years. He then removed to Truro, built the store that George Gunn now occupies, where he carried on business until the time of his death. His second wife was Maria Dimock, widow of the late Arnold Shaw of Newport. He purchased the house in which his son Leander J. Crow now resides, where he spent the remainder of his days. He died October 17th, 1860, aged 61 years.

Charles, the third son of Joseph and Mary Crow, was born March 8th, 1801. He inherits a part of his father's farm, where he is living a bachelor.

James Crow, Esq., their fourth son was born June, 1803. He was married to Rebecca, the youngest daughter of James and Letitia Crow, March, 1828. They had one son and four daughters.

Sarah, the eldest daughter of Joseph and Mary Crow, was born August 15th, 1805. She was married to Samuel Crow, January 8th, 1828. They had three sons and one daughter.

Rebecca, their second daughter, was born in 1808. She was married to George Cook, of Truro, February 17th, 1828. They had one son and four daughters.

Jane, the third daughter of Joseph and Mary Crow, was born August, 1810. She was married to George Yuill, of Clifton, July 9th, 1839. They had one son and one daughter.

Mary Ann, their fourth daughter, was born December 27th, 1812. She was married to Francis Layton, Esq., of Truro, February 23rd, 1837. They had two sons and three daughters. Mr. Layton died November 21st, 1871.

Thomas, the fifth and youngest son of Joseph and Mary Crow, was born January 1st, 1817. He was married to Sarah, daughter of Alexander and Elizabeth Barnhill, January 14th, 1844. They have four sons and three daughters. He inherits a part of his father's farm in Chiganois Village.

Thomas, the third and youngest son of Joseph Crow, Senr., and Esther Barnhill, was born in Chiganois in the year 1773. He was married to Esther, daughter of James Fulton, Esq., and Margaret Campbell, of Bass River, in the year 1796. He was the first who settled at Debert River. His house stood on the west side of the road, opposite James McCulloch's store. He reclaimed his farm from the forest, and continued to live there until several of his sons became men, and he divided his farm between several of them, and removed to Bass River, where he settled for the remainder of his life. He died there in the month of November, 1854, aged 81 years, and his wife died October, 1867, aged 88 years. They had eight sons and six daughters.

Rebecca, their eldest daughter, was born 1797. She was married to John the eldest son of Captain Thomes Fletcher and Elizabeth Barnhill, February 27th, 1820. They had three sons and four daughters.

James, the eldest son of Thomas and Esther Crow, was born March 31st, 1799. He was married to Jane, daughter of William Fletcher and Agnes Davison, his wife, of Portaupique, February, 1823. They had four sons and four daughters. Mrs. Crow died May 15th, 1849.

Joseph, their second son, was born January, 1801, He was married to Rossann, daughter of the Rev. John Brown, November 2nd, 1823. They had three sons and three daughters. They inherited the homestead part of his father's farm at Debert River. He died March, 1870, and his wife died May 15th, 1856.

John, their third son, was born February 9th, 1802. He was married to Rebecca, daughter of Thomas and Magdalen Baird, March, 1827. They had one son and two daughters. Mrs. Crow died February 16th, 1845. He was married again to Susan, daughter of David Blackemore and Janet Hoar, of North River, March 3rd, 1846. They had three sons and four daughters.

William, the fourth son of Thomas and Esther Crowe, was born September, 1803. He was married to Isabell Fulton, of Bass River, 1825. They had four sons and four daughters.

Margaret, the second daughter of Thomas and Esther Crow, was born September, 1804. She was married to Thomas Fulton, of Bass River, in 1829. They had four sons and two daughters.

Dr. Robert F. Crow, their fourth son, was born 1805. He was married to Rebecca, fourth daughter of Mark P. and Margaret Martin, 1830. They had one daughter, (who is now the wife of Thomas McCulloch, of Halifax.) He died October, 1844, and his wife died July 6th, 1843, aged 33 years.

Sarah, their third daughter, was married to Archibald Davison. They had five sons and four daughters. He was chopping in the woods, and a tree fell on his leg, and smashed it so badly that it had to be taken off. This took place about the year 1840. He is still living.

Esther, the fourth daughter of Thomas and Esther Crow, was married to William Davison. They had five sons and four daughters. George, their sixth son, was married to Jane Fulton. They had three sons and three daughters. Thomas, their seventh son, was married to Lucy Davison. They had one son. David, their eighth and youngest son, was married to Sarah Ann McCully. They had three sons and four daughters. Hannah Jane, their fifth daughter, was married to George Creelman. She died and left no family. Rachel Ann, their sixth and youngest daughter, was born July 12th, 1826. She was married to John F. Crow, of Economy, January 15th, 1845. They had three sons and four daughters. They removed to Halifax. and she died there May 1st, 1863.

James, the second son of James Crow, Senr., was born in Ireland about the year 1740. He came, with his father and the rest of the family, to Nova Scotia in the year 1761. He would be about 21 years old at the time. He did not remain in Nova Scotia long ; he went to Philadelphia and settled there. He carried on business and became wealthy. He married, and died there without children.

Aaron, the third son of James Crow, Senr., was born in Ireland in the year 1743, and came with his father and family to Nova Scotia when he was 18 years old. He went with his father to Windsor, and was married there to Abigail Murray, from Sutherlandshire, Scotland, April 15th, 1776. He removed to Onslow some time after the Township was granted. He purchased the farm on which his grandson, Daniel Hyslip now resides, where he settled, spent the remainder of his life, and died October 20th 1818, aged 75 years, and his wife died September, 1825, aged 66 years, Sarah, their eldest daughter, was born April 26th, 1777. She was married to William Murray. They had eight sons and one daughter. James, their eldest son, was born March 6th, 1779. He was drowned at Chester when he was about twenty-one years old. Daniel, their second son, was born March 3rd, 1781. He inherited his father's farm, where he lived, and died a bachelor, June 9th, 1871, aged 89 years. Margaret, their second daughter, was born December 28th, 1782. She was married to Rufus McNutt, of North River, July 26th, 1802. They had ten sons and three daughters. She died in the month of April, 1869, aged 85 years.

Abigail, the third daughter of Aaron and Abigail Crow, was born

February 20th, 1785. She was married to Samuel Gray, of Pictou Co. They had two sons and four daughters. She died Nov., 1868.

George, the third son of Aaron and Abigail Crow, was born July 26th, 1787. He was married to Sarah, the eldest daughter of John and Jane Staples, of Chiganois, January 16th, 1816. Mr. Crow followed the sea when he was a young man. He removed to Tatamagouche Mountain, where he settled, cleared a farm, and spent the remainder of his life. They had four sons and four daughters. He died January 15th, 1857.

Elizabeth, their fourth daughter, was born November 15th, 1797. She was married to Richard Hyslip (who had recently come out from Scotland), November, 1818. They had six sons and four daughters.

Aaron, their fourth son, was born April 16th, 1790. He was married to Rachel, daughter of John and Jane Staples, February 3rd, 1819. They had eight sons and four daughters. They removed to Tatamagouche Mountain, where they reared their family. He died there December 23rd, 1852, and his wife died April 2nd, 1872.

John, their fifth son, was born June 4th, 1792. He died about the year 1826, a bachelor. Rebecca, their fifth daughter, was born February 21st, 1800. She died in the year 1866, aged 66 years. David, their sixth and youngest son, was born January 16th, 1796. Christie, their sixth and youngest daughter, was born October 7th, 1802. She was married to Ebenezer Cock, January 25th, 1825. They had one son and four daughters. They appear among the Cock families. She died August 8th, 1858, aged 56 years.

John, the fifth son of James Crow, Senr., was born in Ireland in the year 1748, and came to Nova Scotia with the rest of the family in the year 1761, when he was 13 years old. He went to Windsor with his father, and remained there until after the Township of Onslow was granted, when he and his brother Aaron removed to Onslow, and he purchased the farm on which his two grandsons, John and Charles Crow, now reside. He had his house near the place on which John Crow's house now stands. Here they reared their family and spent the remainder of their lives. He died October 6th, 1825, aged 77 years, and his wife died May 11th, 1838, aged 86 years. He was married to Elizabeth, the eldest daughter of David Marshall and Sidney Holmes, his wife. (This Elizabeth Marshall was born in England in the year 1752.) They were married April 4th, 1776. George Feash, their eldest son, was born April 22nd, 1777. He followed the sea when young, and went by the name of Capt. George

Feash. He was married to Mary Johnson, of New York, a few years before he died. He and his brother John carried on business together, and did something in shipbuilding on the Creek in front of the house that John Crow now lives in. He died October 9th, 1820, aged 43 years, and his widow died in New York, October, 1868, and left no family. Sarah, the eldest daughter of John and Elizabeth Crow, was born April 28th, 1778. She was married to Samuel Davison, of Portaupique, January 22nd, 1801. They had one son and eight daughters. She died July 5th, 1871, aged 92 years, and her husband died February, 1869.

James, the second son of John and Elizabeth Crow was born December 4th 1781. He was a sea captain, and followed the sea until his health began to fail. He died a bachelor, December 5th, 1819, aged 38 years.

John Crow, their third son, was born August 7th, 1784. He was married to Agnes, daughter of William McNutt and Isabella Dickson, April 7th, 1818. They had five sons and two daughters. He followed the sea some time when young. He represented the Township of Onslow in the House of Assembly, from the year 1826, until the year 1851, being elected four different times. He and his wife are both living at date, February 13th, 1872, he being in the 88th year of his age.

Thomas Marshall Crow, their fourth son, was born November 1st, 1790. He was married to Letitia, the eldest daughter of William Smith and Esther Hunter, December 24th, 1816. They had eight sons and one daughter. He filled the office of Collector of Excise for the County of Colchester for a considerable number of years. Also of County Treasurer until he became too old and hard of hearing; and his son John F. now fills the two offices.

Rachel, the second and youngest daughter of John and Elizabeth Crow, was born June 22nd, 1787. She was married to Thomas Lowden, of Pictou. They had five sons and one daughter. She died May 30th, 1861, aged 74 years.

David Holmes, the fifth and youngest son of John and Elizabeth Crow, was born September 24th, 1793. He was married to Mary, second daughter of William Smith and Esther Hunter, January, 1819. They had seven sons and two daughters. He inherited his father's farm, and built the house that his son Charles now resides in, where they reared their family, and spent the remainder of their days. He died August 10th, 1843, aged 49 years, and his wife died May 24th 1861, aged 64 years.

Thomas the fourth son of James Crow, Senr., was born in Ireland in the year 1746. He came with the rest of the family to Nova Scotia, in the year 1761; when he was about 16 years old, and went with his father to Windsor, and remained until about the year 1786, when he removed to Beaver Brook, Clifton, and purchased what is now the farms of his grandsons, Thomas S. Crow and Isaac Yuill. He purchased this farm from James Rutherford, the progenitor of all the Rutherfords of Stewiacke. His house stood in Mr. Yuill's field, on the south side of the road that leads to the mouth of Shubenacadie River. At this place he and his wife spent the remainder of their lives. He died there February 25th, 1801, aged 55 years, and his wife died March 16th, 1813, aged 67 years, and their bodies were interred in the old cemetery of Truro. He was married to Sarah, the fifth and youngest daughter of Robert Barnhill of Chiganois, about the year 1773.

James, their eldest son was born in the year 1774. He was married to Sarah, daughter of Thomas and Mary Wilson of Masstown, December 2nd, 1813. He inherited a part of his father's farm at Beaver Brook, and built his house on it, being the same on which his son, Thomas S. Crowe, now resides. Here he and his wife spent the remainder of their lives.

Mary, their eldest daughter, was born August 21st, 1814. She was married to Thomas Yuill, of Clifton, July 11th, 1854.

Thomas Stinson, the only son of James Crow and Sarah Wilson, was born January 24th, 1816. He was married to Sarah, daughter of James Smith and Margaret Crow of the Folly Mountain, March 14th, 1843. They had seven sons and four daughters. He inherits his father's farm at Beaver Brook. Sarah, the second daughter of James and Sarah Crow, was born January 11th, 1818. She was married to James Dickson Baird, of Onslow Mountain, November 18th, 1843. They have three sons. Sarah, wife of the aforesaid James Crow, departed this life July 30th, 1818. He was married again to Agnes, daughter of Thomas and Jane Brown, of Clifton, February 25th, 1823. Jane, their only daughter, was born November 17th, 1823. She died March 1st 1824, and Mr. Crow's second wife died August 15th, 1824. He died July 11th, 1852, aged 77 years.

Joseph, the second son of Thomas Crow, Senr, and Sarah Barnhill, was born in September, 1776. He was married to Agnes

Williams, November 27th, 1806. He settled on the-road between Beaver Brook and Black Rock, where they reared their numerous family. He died November 10th, 1852, aged 76 years, and his wife died April, 1831, aged 45 years.

Rebecca, the eldest daughter of Joseph and Agnes Crow, was born October 7th, 1807. She was married to John Park, October 13th, 1825. They had three sons and six daughters.

Sarah, their second daughter, was born October, 1809. She was married to John Oderkirk, January 14th, 1836. They had four sons and three daughters. Mrs. Oderkirk died September 13th, 1851. Letitia, their third daughter, was born September 16th, 1811. She removed to the United States, and was married there to Moses H. Sawyer. They have one daughter. Samuel, the eldest son of Joseph and Agnes Crow, was born October, 1813. He was married to Eleanor Miller of Dartmouth, September, 1839. They had four sons and three daughters. Mary, their fourth daughter, was born August 10th, 1815. She was married to Thomas Newhall, November, 1850. They have one daughter. Thomas, the second son of Joseph and Agnes Crow, was born December 3rd, 1817. He was married to Thankful Gray, of Pictou, (being a grand-daughter of Aaron Crow, of Onslow,) April 20th, 1847. They had four sons and three daughters. He inherits his father's farm. William, their third son, was born March 2nd, 1820. He was married to Jane Dill, of Londonderry, December 20th, 1842. They had three sons and four daughters. James, the fourth son of Joseph and Agnes Crow, was born April 16th, 1822. He was married to Patience Dill, of Londonderry, September, 1853. He died at Londonderry, June 26th, 1854, aged 32 years. Susan, their fifth daughter, was born October 20th, 1824. She removed to the United States, and was married there to William Loving, 1856. Ann, their sixth daughter, was born December 6th, 1826. She removed to the United States, and was married there to Ebenezer Rolling, 1856. They have five sons. Joseph, their youngest son, was born January 3rd, 1830. He removed to the United States, and is married there. They have two sons.

Rebecca, the eldest daughter of Thomas Crow Senr., and Sarah Barnhill, was born in the year 1778. She lived with her brother after the death of her parents, and died unmarried, December 9th 1853, aged 75 years. Sarah, their second daughter, was born in the year 1780. She was married to John, son of the Rev. David Smith, of Londonderry, in the year 1801. They had seven sons and two daughters. She died October, 1847, and her husband died November 1st, 1831. Thomas, the third and youngest son of Thomas and Sarah Crow, was born March 16th, 1785. He was married to Letitia, second daughter of James and Letitia Crow, of Onslow, October 11th, 1814. He settled about one mile further up Beaver Brook than his father, where he cleared his farm, built his house, and spent the remainder of his life. His widow and some of his family now reside there. He died there January, 1855, aged 70 years.

James, the eldest son of Thomas and Letitia Crow, was born August 27th, 1815. He was married to Harriet, the youngest daughter of James and Hannah Archibald, February 12th, 1850. They had five sons and two daughters. He settled near the Bay shore, at Clifton, where he carries on a large business at shipbuilding, and is a Justice of the Peace. Joseph, their second son, was born February 26th, 1817. He was married to Margaret Hughes, of Shubenacadie, October 29th, 1844. They had two sons and three daughters. Martha, their eldest daughter, was born December 22nd, 1813. Robert Stinson, the third son of Thomas and Letitia Crow, was born December 22nd, 1820. He was married to Kate, fourth daughter of James and Hannah Archibald, January 27th, 1858. He built the house in which the Rev. James Byers now resides. They lived in it a short time, and carried on shipbuilding. He died suddenly, May 7th, 1864, aged 44 years, and his wife died May 20th, 1864, aged 37 years. They left no family. Sarah Jane, their second daughter, was born November 15th, 1822. Jasper, their fourth son, was born October 25th, 1824. He is deprived of his reason, and has been in the Lunatic Asylum the most of the time these twelve years past. John Smith, the fifth son of Thomas and Letitia Crow, was born July 8th, 1827. He was married to Harriet, daughter of John Sanderson, February 15th, 1855. Mrs. Crow died March 5th, 1860, aged 26 years, and left no family. He was married again to Jane Cox, of Lower Salma, November 29th, 1863. They had two sons and one daughter. He follows shipbuilding. Rebecca, the third and youngest daughter of Thomas Watson and Letitia Crow, was born April 1st, 1829. She was married to William Murray, Oct. 4th, 1864.

Margaret, the third daughter of Thomas Crow, Senr., and Sarah Barnhill, was born in Truro, May 18th, 1787. She was married to James, son of David Smith and Rebecca Cook, his wife, of the Folly Mountain, February 18th, 1818. (This David Smith was son of the

14

Rev. David Smith.) They had five sons and one daughter. She died March 4th, 1861, aged 74 years.

Esther, the fourth daughter of Thomas and Sarah Crow, was born June 19th, 1789. She died young. Letitia, one of their twin daughters, was born in April 1792. She was married to John Barnhill, of Chiganois. They had one son, who appears among the Barnhills. She died April 8th, 1837, aged 45 years. Her husband died October 23rd, 1847, aged 85 years. Mary, the other twin daughter of Thomas Crow, was married to a Mr. Barry. They had one son and one daughter. Mr. Barry died. She was married again to Robert McNeal, of Masstown, 1821. They had four sons and two daughters. She died February 14th, 1867, and Mr. McNeal died January 6th, 1872.

Nicholas, the sixth and youngest son of James Crow, Senr., was born in Ireland about the year 1750. He came to Nova Scotia in the year 1761, when he was 11 years old, and went, with his father and three other brothers, Aaron, Thomas, and John, to Windsor. Shortly after, he and his father settled at Portaupique, where he continued the rest of his life. He was married to Miss Harrison. James Crow, their eldest son, was married to Mary, third daughter of James Fulton, Esq., in 1801. They had five sons and five daughters. They settled in Economy. He died May 1st, 1850 ; his widow died January, 1857. Thomas Crow, their second son, was married to Eleanor Reid in 1803. They had four sons and three daughters. They settled in Portaupique, where he died in 1840. David Crow, their third son, was married to Esther Crow, of Onslow. They had three sons and three daughters. Jane Crow was married to David Totton. They had six sons and three daughters. They settled on the Folly Mountain. In January, 1870, Mr. Totton was drowned in a small brook while watering his cattle. Sarah, another daughter, was married to William McCully, of Masstown, in 1808. They had one son and eight daughters. Mr. McCully was supposed to be lost in the Bay in March, 1826. His widow died in December, 1859.

CHAPTER XXV.

William Corbett was another of the first settlers of Truro, and a Grantee of the Township. He was a Scotchman by birth, and a gunsmith by trade, and was with General Wolfe at the taking of Quebec. He came to Truro with the company that came from New England in the Spring of the year 1760, and he remained in Truro about eight years. He then exchanged farms with Samuel Archibald, second, and removed to Little Dyke, in Londonderry, where he settled for the remainder of his life. In the month of October, 1784, Mr. Corbett, with a number of his neighbors, was going up the Shuben-acadie River in a boat, on their way to Halifax, and by some means the boat was upset, and Mr. Corbett, Elizabeth Fletcher (daughter of William Fletcher) and Jane McLellan (daughter of Michael McLellan) were drowned. William Corbett was married to Elizabeth Robinson, of Plymouth, Mass., in the year 1748. They had five sons and five daughters. Elizabeth, their eldest daughter, was born April 14th, 1749. She was married to David Orr, and they had a family of children. She died in the United States. Agnes, the second daughter of William and Elizabeth Corbett, was born July 6th, 1750. She was married to another Orr, brother of David Orr above mentioned. They lived and died in the United States, and left a family there. Margaret, their third daughter, was born January 28th, 1752. She was married to Joshua Marsh. They had six sons and four daughters. They settled in Economy, where they reared their family and spent the remainder of their days. She died there in the year 1854, aged 102 years.

William Corbett, their eldest son, was born June 13th, 1754. His name is among the Grantees of Truro Township, although he was but 11 years old at the date of the Grant. He was married to Jane Reid, of Londonderry, and settled in Five Islands, where they reared their family and died. They had two sons and three daughters. Robert, the second son of William and Elizabeth Corbett, was born September 15th, 1856. He was married to Susannah Fletcher. They had eight sons and four daughters. He inherited his father's farm at Little Dyke, where they reared their numerous family. He died April 9th, 1808, aged 54 years; his wife, Susannah

Fletcher, was born February 6th, 1763.   She died June 23rd, 1822, aged 59 years.   They were married about the year 1781.

Thomas Corbett, their eldest son, was born September 21st, 1782. He was married to Sarah, daughter of John and Mary Smith, of Truro, January 23rd, 1807.   He inherited his father's farm at Little Dyke, where they reared their numerous family.   He died August 3rd, 1867, aged 85 years, and his wife died April 11th, 1837, aged 49 years.   Daniel, the eldest son of Thomas and Sarah Corbett, was born December, 1807.   He was married to Harriett, daughter of Capt. John Stewart and Rebecca McNutt, his wife.   They had two sons and four daughters.   Susannah, their eldest daughter, was born 1809. She was married to John C. Morrison, a sea Captain, who had come out from Scotland but a short time before.   They had one son and one daughter.   She died January 9th, 1829, aged 20 years, and her husband, Capt. John C. Morrison, died April 15th, 1837.   Mary, their second daughter, was born 1811.   She was married to George S. Rutherford, Esq., in the year 1841.   They had one son.   She died May 10th, 1842, aged 31 years, and her husband died October 17th, 1871, aged 66 years.   John, the second son of Thomas and Sarah Corbett, was born 1813.   He was married to Margaret, daughter of Alexander Urquhart and Nancy McLaughlan, December 24th, 1850. They had five sons and three daughters.   He inherited one-half of his father's house at Little Dyke.   He died there May 3rd, 1867, aged 54 years.   William, their third son, was born October 17th, 1815. He was married to Mary Spencer, August 14th, 1839.   They had five sons and two daughters.   He settled on what was his father's land, where he and his wife are living at date, February 15th, 1872. Their house stands beside the main road, about one mile below the Folly.

Peter Suther Corbett, their fourth son, was born December 5th, 1817.   He followed the sea for a number of years, and is now settled in Liverpool, England.   He was married, and has three sons and one daughter.   Mark Paten Corbett, their fifth son, was born January 31st, 1820.   He was married to Jane C., daughter of Capt. William Pamerton and Mary Vance, October, 1847.   Mrs. Corbett died May, 1850, and he was married again to Sarah McLain, of Folly River, March, 1853.   They had two sons and five daughters.   He inherited a part of his father's farm at Little Dyke, where he spent the whole of his life.   On March 23rd, 1868, he was drawing marsh mud on a sled, and as he was returning home to dinner, the sled ran over

a pole and pitched him forward. He fell with his neck under the
runner of the sled, which broke his windpipe. The team stopped
while his neck remained under the runner. His daughter, who had
seen him start from the field some time before, became anxious and
went to see if all was right. She found him as already described—
quite dead. He was 48 years of age, and left a widow and family of
children to mourn their loss. " Be ye also ready."

Jane C., the third daughter of Thomas and Sarah Corbett, was
born May 24th, 1822. She died unmarried, April 17th, 1840, aged
18 years.

Elizabeth, their fourth daughter, was born in the year 1827. She
was married to Duncan Urquhart, and had one daughter. She died
April 18th, 1853, aged 26 years. Louisa, their fifth daughter, was
born January 13th, 1831. She was married to James Urquhart,
December 24th, 1850. They have six sons and four daughters.
Susannah, their sixth daughter, was born March 14th, 1833. She
was married to Capt. George McBurney, of Five Islands, in the year
1861. They had three sons and one daughter. Capt. McBurney
sailed from Philadelphia on September 17th, 1871, in the ship
" Angedique," of 1600 tons, loaded with wheat, and bound for
Antwerp. Neither crew nor ship has been heard from since.

William, the second son of Robert Corbett and Susannah Fletcher,
was born November, 1783. He was married to Isabell Davison,
about the year 1810. They had three sons and four daughters. Mrs.
Corbett died at Pictou, and he was married again to Elizabeth,
daughter of David Patterson, and widow of Robert Patterson. She
died shortly after they were married, and he was married again to
Lavinia, daughter of Thomas T. Brown, Esq., and Rachel Pearson,
in the year 1837. They had nine children. They removed to Cape
Breton about the year 1850, where he died in the year 1866, aged 83
years, and his third wife died there about the year 1862.

Robert, the third son of Robert Corbett and Susannah Fletcher
was born at Little Dyke, November 10th 1784. He was married to
Catherine daughter of Jacob O'Brien and Mary Spencer, October 16th,
1806. They had five sons and five daughters. Mrs. Corbett died
May 6th 1869.

James, their fourth son, was born 1786. He died when he was
two years old.

Elizabeth, their eldest daughter, was born in 1787. She was married to Robert Vance January, 1807. The had three sons and three

daughters. She died April, 1870, aged 83 years, and her husband died in Londonderry.

George Corbett, their fifth son, was born in 1789. He learned the shoemaking trade with John McKay in Truro. He was married to Eleanor Woodworth January, 1815. He kept an Inn at Gay's River for a number of years. They had four sons and one daughter. Mrs. Corbett died about the year 1832, and he was married again to Margaret McHeffey. They had two sons and two daughters. He died December 1846. His wife is dead.

Sarah Corbett, their second daughter was born 1791. She was married to John J. Fulton in 1808. She died about the year 1838, and left no family.

Eleanor Corbett, their third daughter was born 1793. She was married to Joseph Fulton, of Stewiacke about the year 1812. They had four sons and five daughters. Mr. Fulton died December 6th, 1842, and she was married again to John Graham, of Hants County, in the year 1849.

Susannah Corbett, their fourth daughter, was born in 1794. She died when about two years old.

David Corbett, their sixth son, was born 1796. He was married to Isabell Keys about the year 1820. They had six sons and four daughters. He settled near Gay's River, where he died in the year 1866.

James Corbett, their seventh son was born in 1798. He was a shoemaker by trade. He was married to Sarah Ann Hughes in 1827. They had six sons and six daughters. They removed to Pictou in the year 1835, and settled near the Mines on the East River, where he spent the remainder of his life. In November, 1871, he was out in the woods on a moose hunt. As he was returning home, in climbing over a windfall, he fell. The gun on striking the ground was immediately discharged, and the contents lodged in his knee. Having a long distance to go, he was very much exhausted when he arrived at home. Medical aid was at hand, his leg was amputated, but he lived only three days. He was 73 years of age.

John Corbett, their eighth son was born in 1799. He was a blacksmith, and worked for a time in the Lower Village of Truro. He was married to Rebecca Hughes in 1826. They had five sons and six daughters. He died December, 1848, aged 49 years.

Eleanor, the fourth daughter of William Corbett Senr., and Elizabeth Robinson, was born August 6th, 1759. She was married to John Marsh. They had six sons and seven daughters. They settled in Economy, where they reared their family and died.

James Corbett, their third son was born in Truro, June 14th, 1763. He was married to Elizabeth Marsh. They had five sons and six daughters. They settled at Five Islands, where many of their offspring are still living.

John, their fourth son was born in Truro, August 3rd, 1765. He was married to Mary, daughter of James Flemming, Senr., and Isabel Vance, about the year 1794. They had four sons and two daughters. They settled in the Lower Village of Truro, and continued there until about the year 1810. His house in the Lower Village stood near the place that Alexander Kent second now resides. He removed to Middle Stewiacke, to the farm on which Mr. Ebenezer Fulton now resides, where he lived until about the time that his wife died, July 7th, 1822. He died May, 1849, aged 84 years.

Joseph Corbett, their fifth son, was born May 8th 1767. He was married to Deborah Davenport. They had four sons and one daughter. Mrs. Corbett died and he was married again. He settled in Economy where he died in the year 1862, aged 95.

Martha Corbett, their fifth and youngest daughter, was born February 19th, 1771. She was married to Joseph Marsh. They had seven sons and three daughters. They settled in Economy where they reared their family and died. She died in the year 1864, aged 93 years.

CHAPTER XXVI.

John Smith was among the early settlers of Truro. He was born in Colvin, Scotland, in 1742. He was married to Mary McVicar in 1764. He was a whitesmith by trade. They emigrated to Prince Edward Island, where they arrived about the first of July, 1774. He commenced clearing a farm out of the woods, which is hard, discouraging work to the inexperienced. He said afterwards, "He haggled the tree all round about, and could not get it down." Still he toiled away and did smithwork for the few settlers around him, encouraging Mary his wife, though he was discouraged himself. Being destitute of *public* gospel ordinances, they started for Truro in the summer of

1776, in order that they might hear the Gospel, and have their son John baptized, who was now two years old. They came by Pictou, and travelled on foot from Pictou to Truro, lodging one night in the woods, and carrying their son in their arms. They arrived in Truro and called upon the Rev. Mr. Cock, who had lately come from Scotland. Mr. Cock had a little girl about two years old, and it would appear that little Johnny and she struck up a match which was happily consummated more than twenty years after.

They returned to the Island again and that fall the mice destroyed all their crops, (that year is still known among old men as the year of the mice), and they resolved to move to Truro. Mr. Smith came over to Pictou with a part of their movables and hired Mr. Paterson's horse to assist in bringing them to Truro. One article was an anvil of about two cwt. This he brought on the horse's back. His grandson, Daniel Smith, is still using this anvil at Wallace River. He returned again to the Island for his family, and came back to Truro by Tatamagouche, the distance through the woods being much shorter this way than by Pictou. On account of Mr. Smith's being a blacksmith, the people in the Village were anxious to have him settle near them, so they proposed to *give* him their Right to Birch Island and the adjoining swamp lands. Each Grantee of Truro Township held a lot of this Island and swamp, containing two acres. Mr. Smith having obtained a deed of these lots, built a house which is still standing and owned by his grandson Robert Smith. Here he carried on the blacksmith business until about the year 1799, when he removed to Upper Stewiacke, and built a house and shop near Mr. Abraham Newcomb, and carried on the blacksmith business ten or twelve years. He then sold out and returned to Truro again. He lived in a house which stood between his old house and the house in which Robert Smith now resides. He died June 26th, 1818, aged 76. His widow died April 11th, 1823, aged 76.

Mary, their eldest daughter, was born in Scotland, 1765. She was married to William, son of Charles and Eleanor Cox, January 26th, 1786. They had six sons and three daughters, who appear among the descendants of Charles Cox. They removed to Stewiacke in 1792.

William, the eldest son of John and Mary Smith, was born in 1767. He came with his parents to Nova Scotia. He commenced clearing a farm in Upper Stewiacke about 1790, and very soon raised wheat in abundance. To get this wheat ground they had to carry it on their backs through the woods to Truro, or take it down the Stewiacke River to the Shubenacadie, thence down to the Bay, and up the Bay to Truro. Shortly after, Mr. Smith built a boat, loaded it with wheat, and, in company with another man, started for Truro. They met the flood tide off Salter's Head, when the boat was upset, the wheat lost and the man drowned. Mr. Smith clung to the boat, and was drifted up the Bay still crying out for help. William Cutten, Esq., was coming up the Bay from Noel at the time, and came within hearing of his voice. He pulled for him and succeeded in getting him into his boat very much exhausted having drifted from Salter's Head to Savage's Island. He was married to Esther, daughter of Robert Hunter and Esther Moor, his wife, February 28th, 1793, and in grateful remembrance of his deliverer, he called his first son William Cutten. They settled in Upper Stewiacke on the farm which Jacob Layton recently sold. A few years after, he exchanged farms with James Kennedy and moved to Middle Stewiacke to the farm on which Wm. F. Putnam now resides, when in the year 1806 he exchanged farms with his brother-in-law, John Hunter, and returned to Truro. He lived in the old Hunter House, and maintained Mr. and Mrs. Hunter while they lived. In 1814 he sold out in the Village and built the house on the Island in which his grandson, Richard Smith now resides. Here he died November 3rd, 1853, aged 86 years. His wife died May 10th, 1835, aged 62 years.

Letitia, their eldest daughter, was born December 23rd, 1793. She was married to Thomas M. Crowe, December 24th, 1816. They had eight sons and one daughter. She died December 11th, 1872, aged 79 years.

Mary, the second daughter of William and Esther Smith, was born in Stewiacke, August 1796. She was married to David H. Crow, of Onslow, January, 1819. They had six sons and two daughters. She died May 24th, 1861, aged 64 years, and her husband died August 10th 1843, aged 49 years.

Esther, their third daughter, was born in Stewiacke, February 13th, 1799. She was married to Robert, the youngest son of Colonel Thomas and Martha Pearson, May 25th, 1820. They had three sons. Mr. Pearson died suddenly December 17th 1825, aged 27 years. She was married again to John L. Dogget, December 4th, 1828. They had five sons and one daughter.

William Cutten Smith, their eldest son was born in Stewiacke, July 15th 1801. He was married to Renew, the eldest daughter of

Charles and Mary Nelson, January 7th, 1831. He inherited the half
of his father's farm and built the house in which his widow, and some
of their family now reside. They had four sons and six daughters.
He was an elder in the Presbyterian Church from the year 1845, until
he died, May 7th, 1870, aged 69 years.

Mary, the eldest daughter of William C. Smith and Renew Nelson,
was born January 9th, 1832. She was married to Anthony McKean,
of Pictou Town, November 18th, 1854. She died May 6th, 1856,
aged 24 years. John Smith, their eldest son was born April 15th,
1834. He inherits a part of his father's farm. Esther Hunter, their
second daughter was born February 4th, 1836. She died February
6th, 1838, aged two years. Esther Hunter, their third daughter was
born December 23rd, 1838. She was married to Charles A., son of
John Kent and Sarah Archibald, December 16th, 1869. They have
one daughter. William McCulloch their second son was born January
17th, 1840. He died February 21st, 1853. Charles Nelson Smith,
their third son was born January 30th, 1842. He removed to the
United States, and was married there to Margaret Moran, October
10th, 1870. They had one son. Agnes Kellor Smith, their fourth
daughter, was born November 1 0th, 1844. She was married to Gavin
Walker, youngest son of Isaac Smith and Mary Waddell, June 12th,
1865. They have one son and two daughters. Elizabeth Smith,
their fifth daughter was born April 16th 1846. She was married to
James Richard Smith, from Pictou, June 10th, 1869. They had one
son. She died June 27th, 1871, aged 25 years. Henry Kellor
Smith, their fourth son was born July 27th, 1848. He is settled at
Maitland, carrying on the business of harness making. Caroline
Crow Smith, their sixth daughter, was born July 19th, 1850.

John, the second son of William and Esther Smith, was born in
Middle Stewiacke, August 21st, 1803. His wife being the only
daughter of Samuel and Mary Creelman. She was born September
17th 1810. They were married February 17th, 1829. They now
reside on the farm that James Campbell Creelman owned. Samuel
Creelman Smith, their eldest son, was born June 4th, 1830. He
was married to Eleanor, daughter of Abraham Bentley and Margaret
Fletcher, January 28th, 1850. They have two sons and three daughters. William, their second son was born August 21st, 1832. He
was married to Mary, daughter of George Steel and Rebecca Fulton,
February 15th, 1859. They have two sons and one daughter. Mary
Jane, their eldest daughter, was born November 30th, 1834. She died

unmarried November 24th, 1858. Esther, their second daughter, was born April 18th, 1837. She was married to Alexander Steel, in the year 1856. They had one daughter. Mrs. Steel died March 17th, 1857, aged 20 years. Sidney, their third son, was born January 9th, 1840. Rachel, their third daughter was born February 11th, 1841. John their fourth son was born July 28th, 1843. David Holmes, their fifth son was born March 25th, 1846. Letitia, their fourth and youngest daughter, was born July 28th, 1851.

Robert Hunter, the third son of William Smith and Esther Hunter, was born in Stewiacke, December 23rd, 1805. He was married to Catherine, the eldest daughter of Hugh Dunlap and Susan Gourley, of Stewiacke, March 4th, 1828. They settled on the Halifax road, about three miles from Truro. Susannah, their eldest daughter, was born in Truro, August 4th, 1829. She was married to Isaac Dunlap, of the Lower Village of Truro, February 10th, 1854. They have two sons and four daughters.

William, the eldest son of Robert H. and Catherine Smith, was born November 7th, 1831. In the Spring of 1834, Mr. Smith was driving his team with a heavy load. His little boy was following him and fell, when the cart wheel passed over his body. He was considerably injured, but soon recovered again. Some years afterwards he went to Canada, where he remained about six years. He returned to Truro, and followed pump making. On the 14th of October, 1859, in putting a pump in a well, he had occasion to go down into the well. The stones fell in and buried him. About four hours after he was taken out dead. He was in the 28th year of his age. "Man's life is a vapor." Esther, the second daughter of Robert H. and Catherine Smith, was born August 21st, 1833. She was married to Amos Fowler, of the County of Cumberland, February 13th, 1862. She died April 27th, 1872, in the 39th year of her age. Jesse Gourley Smith, their second son, was born October 19th, 1836. He removed to California and was married there. Robert Hunter Smith, their third son, was born August 27th, 1838. He removed to California a number of years ago, and continues to reside there. Hugh Dunlap Smith, their fourth son, was born January 24th, 1842. He removed to California, and is engaged there in the dairy business. Thomas Bush Smith, their fifth son, was born January 12th, 1847. Kate Smith, their third and youngest daughter, was born November 24th, 1848. Robert H. Smith, Senr., died April 1st, 1872, aged 66 years.

Daniel Cock, the fourth son of William and Esther Smith, was born in Truro, July 15th, 1808. He was married to Elizabeth, the eldest daughter of Samuel Dunlap and Mary Miller, December 17th, 1834. He inherited the half of his father's farm, where they reared their family. Mrs. Smith died December 18th, 1871, aged 56. Letitia, their eldest daughter, was born November 2nd, 1835. James, their eldest son, was born November 17th, 1836. He was married to Elizabeth Hawley, of Mabou, C. B., June 11th, 1867. They have one son and one daughter. Richard, their second son, was born November 13th, 1838. He was married to Jane Letitia Wilson, daughter of Joseph Wilson and Alice Barnhill, July 28th, 1863. They have one son and two daughters. Samuel, their third son, was born November 15th, 1840. David H., their fourth son, was born November 25th, 1848. He was licensed to preach the Gospel, but his voice failing him, he was obliged to give up the good work and is now keeping a book store in Truro Village. Edwin, their fifth son, was born March 12th, 1845. He is settled in Brookfield and Middle Stewiacke as their Minister. He was married to Elizabeth, daughter of Timothy Putnam, Oct. 22nd, 1872. William Vicker, their sixth son, was born Feb. 21st, 1848. He is settled in Dartmouth, where he carries on the business of harness making. Annie, their second daughter, was born February 28th, 1851. She follows school teaching. Maria, their third daughter, was born June 12th, 1853. Frank, their seventh son, was born December 15th, 1855. He is a school teacher. Renew, their fourth and youngest daughter, was born February 21st, 1858.

John, the second son of John and Mary Smith, was born in P. E. Island, July 16th, 1774, and was brought by his parents to Truro in 1776. He was married to Jane, the youngest daughter of the Rev. Daniel Cock, March 10th, 1796. He inherited his father's property in Truro, where he and his wife spent the remainder of their lives. He died June 29th, 1848, aged 74, and his wife died July 16th, 1845, aged 71 years. Ebenezer, their eldest son, was born May 8th, 1797. He was married to Mary, daughter of Eliakim Tupper and Lydia Putnam, his wife, of Stewiacke, December 10th, 1818. She died July 25th, 1820.

He was married again to Nancy, the eldest daughter of Mark Paten Martin and Margaret McElhenney, December 27th, 1824. Margaret Jane, their eldest daughter, was born May 28th, 1828. She died May 6th, 1843, aged 15 years. Mark Paten Martin, their eldest son, was born November 26th, 1831. He was married to Clara, daughter of James Flemming, Esq., and Hannah McElhenney, his wife, December 4th, 1861. He inherits his grandfather Martin's property at Debert. They have four sons and two daughters. Mary Ann, the second daughter of Ebenezer and Nancy Smith, was born May 15th, 1833. She was married to Charles, the youngest son of Robert McElhenney and Elizabeth Stewart, his wife, December 30th, 1858. They have three sons and five daughters. John, the second son of Ebenezer and Nancy Smith, was born December 26th, 1835. He died May 27th, 1862, aged 27 years. Lavinia, their third daughter, was born July 1st, 1839. Maria, their fourth daughter, was born 1841. She died June 29th, 1842. Nancy Martin, Mr. Smith's second wife, died July 14th, 1842, aged 39 years.

He was married again to Sarah, daughter of Hugh Dunlap and Susannah Gourley, March 12th, 1845. Susannah, their eldest daughter, was born May 1st, 1846. Nancy Jane, their second daughter, was born February 16th, 1848. Catherine Margaret, their third daughter, was born March 6th, 1850. Sarah Elizabeth, their fourth daughter, was born May 1st, 1852. Ebenezer Erskine Smith, their only son, was born August 14th, 1854.

Mary, the eldest daughter of John and Jane Smith, was born February 20th, 1800. She was married to Oliver, the youngest son of William Blair and Mary Downing, December 20th, 1817. They had four sons and three daughters. She died July 18th, 1869, aged 69 years, and her husband died November 23rd, 1871, aged 77 years.

Daniel Cock, the second son of John and Jane Smith, was born July 13th, 1802. He was married to Susan Beebe, of Wallace River, July 16th, 1826. He afterwards settled there. Charles, their eldest son, was born in Truro, July 16th, 1827. He was married to Hannah, daughter of John Higgins and Hannah Stevens, widow of the late Miner Embree, of Amherst, June 13th, 1853. They have four sons and one daughter. Nancy, the eldest daughter of Daniel and Susan Smith, was born December 25th, 1829. She was married to David Davison, May, 1851. They had two sons and five daughters. John, their second son, was born February, 1833. He removed to the United States. Harriet, their second daughter, was born February, 1836.

Janet Colven, the second daughter of John and Jane Smith, was born May 15th, 1805. She was married to Thomas Miller, and had six sons and five daughters, who appear among the Miller families. She died January 23rd, 1873, aged 67 years.

John, the third son of John and Jane Smith, was born May 17th, 1808. He was married to Mercy P., eldest daughter of Charles Tucker, Esq., and Mercy Parker Polley, December 13th, 1831.

Rebecca Hughes, the only daughter of John and Mercy P. Smith, was born January 14th, 1833. She was married to William Smith, the third son of David H. Crow and Mary Smith, of Onslow, January, 1856. They had four daughters. Charles Tucker, the eldest son of John and Mercy P. Smith, was born August 19th, 1835. John William, their second son, was born December 25th, 1837. He was married to Sarah Smith, of Cape Breton, February 26th, 1868. They have two daughters. Melville, their third son, was born May 9th, 1842. He removed to the United States. George, their fourth son, was born January 16th, 1845. He was married to Margaret Mary, daughter of the Rev. William Summerville and Sarah Dickey, December 8th, 1868. They have one daughter. He died November 24th, 1872. Henry, their fifth son, was born November 3rd, 1849. He removed to the United States, where he is carrying on the harness making business. Eldridge, their sixth son, was born October 3rd, 1854. Mrs. Smith died October 23rd, 1868, aged 54. He was married again to Margaret Mary, the youngest daughter of William Archibald and Susan Putnam, widow of the late Colin McLennon, of Pictou, August 11th, 1870.

William, the fourth son of John and Jane Smith, was born April 3rd, 1810. He was married to Louisa, daughter of John Higgins and Hannah Stevens, of Onslow, July 17th, 1835. Mary Jane, their eldest daughter, was born September 19th, 1843. She was married to George Embree, of Amherst, February 17th, 1862. They have two sons and three daughters. Amos Burton, the only son of Wm. and Louisa Smith, was born August 9th, 1846. On Dec. 10th, 1862, he was engaged with his gun in his father's house at Wallace River. In setting the gun down on the floor carelessly, it went off and the contents lodged in his brain, causing instant death. Lavinia, their second and youngest daughter, was born January 6th, 1850. She was married to Roderick McLain, of Pictou, February 23rd, 1871. They have one son.

Alison Jamison, the third daughter of John and Jane Smith, was born March 4th, 1813. She was married to James Whidden, the youngest son of John Corbett and Mary Flemming, April 3rd, 1833. They removed to Pictou, near New Glasgow, where she died February 24th, 1834, aged 21 years. Her body was brought to Truro and interred in Truro Cemetery. Her husband went whale fishing, and afterwards settled, married, and died in Sydney, New South Wales.

Robert, the fifth son of John and Jane Smith, was was born April 2nd, 1816. He was married to Margaret, the second daughter of Charles Tucker, Esq., and Mercy P. Polley, January 27th, 1842. He went into a store as clerk when he was a boy. He has been engaged in commercial business ever since, and is in possession of a large amount of property. He owns and resides upon what was his father's property. He is still engaged in business in Truro, and in Cumberland County. Julia, their eldest daughter was born in Truro, December 29th, 1842. She was married to Captain William A. Fraser, of Pictou, November 2nd, 1863. They left in a few days after, in the " Dayspring," for the South Sea Islands. He sailed the mission ship as Captain about eight years. They returned home with one son and three daughters, July 30th, 1872. Charles, the only son of Robert and Margaret Smith, was born November 15th, 1844. He went a few trips to sea and died suddenly in St. Thomas, West Indies, January 21st, 1866, aged 21 years. His body was brought home for interment. Mercy Jane, their second daughter, was born August 15th, 1846. In the summer of 1862, she and Miss Hyde went to Pictou on a visit. While there, in company with several young ladies they took passage in the coal train to the Loading Ground. The passenger car was in front of the engine. Through some mismanagement two trains met on full speed. The passenger car was smashed. Miss Smith was so badly injured that she died in a few hours, July 28th, 1862, aged 16 years. Her body was brought home and interred in the Truro Cemetery. Miss Hyde was considerably injured, but she recovered. Margaret Emma, the third daughter of Robert and Margaret Smith, was born Sept. 13th, 1848. Mary Alice, their fourth daughter, was born April 24th, 1851. Eva, their fifth daughter was born February 18th, 1853. Fanny Hunt their sixth daughter, was born April 5th, 1855.

Peter Suther, the sixth and youngest son of John and Jane Smith, was born September 18th, 1820. He was married to Elizabeth, the youngest daughter of James Campbell Creelman and Alison Jamison Tupper, in the month of March, 1842. He inherited the homestead part of his father's property. He was engaged a few years in business as a merchant. He was driving his horse one day, and standing in his sleigh, turning the corner by John B. Dickie's store, he was thrown from his sleigh, and his head struck the ice, which fractured his skull. He still kept about his business for a few days, until the blood began to press on the brain, when he lost his reason and died January 15th. 1859, about two weeks after he was hurt. He was in the 39th year of his age. His widow died February 17th, 1861, aged 39 years. Maria, their eldest daughter was born in the month of January, 1843. She died at the house of Ebenezer Smith, May 15th, 1866, aged 23 years. Isabell, their second daughter, was born November, 1844. She died July 10th, 1858, in the 14th year of her age. Melissa, their third daughter was born December, 1847. She removed to Lynn, Mass., and was married there to Melen Stokes. She died October 16th, 1872, aged 25 years. Mercy Parker, their fourth daughter was born September 8th, 1850. She removed to the United States, and was married there to Charles A. Stickney, January 6th, 1872. Robert their only son was born September 6th, 1853.

Daniel, the third son, of John and Mary Smith, was born in Truro, June 29th 1777. He died when about 16 years old.

Janet Colven Smith, their second daughter was born August 17th, 1779. She was married to John Vance, April 16th, 1801. He settled at Debert River. They had four sons and two daughters. Mrs. Vance died August 1st, 1816, aged 37 years. He was married again to Charlotte Porter in 1828. She died about 1838. He was married again to Mary Durning, July. 1840. Mr. Vance died January, 1846. Mary, the eldest daughter of John and Janet C. Vance, was born in 1802. She was married to Captain William Palmerton in 1826. They had one son and one daughter. She died July 1841, aged 39 years. David Vance, their eldest son, was born in 1804. He was married to Catherine Stinson of New Brunswick, December, 1827. They had one son. Mr. Vance died April, 1830, aged 26 years. His widow was married again to Robert Smith of Londonderry, February 7th, 1833. She died November 30th, 1871. John Smith Vance, their second son was born March 9th, 1806. He was married to Hannah Yuill, July 13th, 1836. They had two sons and two daughters. Their son David was carried overboard from the deck of a vessel in St. John Harbour, and drowned January 7th, 1872. Mrs. Vance died July 6th, 1846, aged 29 years. He was married again to Jane McCully, July 30th, 1827. They had one son and three daughters.

William Vance, their third son, was born in 1809. He was married to Sarah Stewart, February, 1830. He died and left no children, December, 1834. His widow was married again to Alexander D.

Morrison, Esq. Sarah Vance, their second daughter, was born March 13th, 1813. She was married to John Noble McElhenney, Sept. 5th, 1833. They had five sons and one daughter. They inherited what was her father's farm. Matthew Vance, their youngest son, was born July, 1816. He was married to Margaret McElhenney, June, 1841. They had one son. He died September 15th, 1842. His widow was married again to Henry Urquhart, May 9th, 1843. She died December 14th, 1871.

Hannah, the third daughter of John and Mary Smith, was born January 30th, 1782. She was married to John Yuill, February 3rd, 1803, They had two sons and four daughters. She died September 4th, 1817. Mr. Yuill died October 4th, 1849.

Sarah Smith, their youngest daughter, was born February 4th, 1788. She was married to Thomas Corbett, January 23rd 1807. They had five sons and six daughters. She died April 11th, 1837, aged 49 years. Mr. Corbett died August 3rd, 1867, aged 85 years.

CHAPTER XXVII.

Eliakim Tupper was one of the early settlers of Truro. He removed from New England to the western part of the Province about the year 1760, and about the year 1773 he removed to Truro, and built a two story house, being the same in which Captain William Cock afterwards resided, and Mr. John Dunlap and his heirs afterwards owned and occupied. Here he kept an Inn, which at that time was the only Inn in Truro. On September 16th, 1780, he was appointed Justice of the Peace for what is now the whole of the Counties of Colchester and Pictou. He carried on business as a merchant while in Truro. He was contractor for finishing the inside of the first church that was built in Truro. His business, while in Truro not being very profitable, and having a large family of sons, he was induced to leave Truro, and remove to Stewiacke about the year 1792, and settle on the farm on which Mr. Matthew Johnson had settled about nine years before. This farm is now owned by his grandson, Eliakim Tupper, Esq., and his sons. He was married to Elizabeth Newcomb about the time they first come to Nova Scotia. He died in Stewiacke August 22nd, 1810, and his wife died Feby. 10th, 1824, aged 81 years.

15

Mahew, their eldest son was born in the year 1762. He was married to Christian, daughter of Rev. Daniel Cock, April 22nd, 1784. Alison Jamison, their eldest daughter was born July 15th, 1785. She was married to James Campbell, second son of Francis Creelman and Esther Campbell, February 4th, 1808. They had three sons and six daughters. She died April 22nd, 1860, aged 75 years, and her husband died in Halifax, (where he had been residing with his son John) June 30th, 1869, aged 84 years.

Eliakim, the eldest son of Mahew and Christie Tupper, was born May 4th, 1787. He was married to Ruth Stevens. They had one daughter. Mrs. Tupper died, and he was married again to Jane Benvie of Musquodoboit. They had four sons and two daughters. His second wife died February, 1830. He was married again to Margaret Godfrey, widow of the late John Waddell Fisher. They had three sons and two daughters. He died at New Glasgow, 1865. He was a tinsmith by trade.

Patrick, their second son, was born in the year 1789. He was married to Rachel, daughter of Samuel Fisher and Mary Tupper. They had a family of children. He was a shoemaker by trade. He removed with his wife and family to Ohio, U. S., about the year 1821.

Daniel, their third son, was born in the year 1791. He was married to Nancy, another daughter of Samuel and Mary Fisher, 1814. They had three sons and three daughters. Mrs. Tupper died August 10th, 1846. He was married again to Margaret, second daughter of Samuel B. and Margaret Archibald, widow of William Green, April, 1848. They had one daughter. Mrs. Tupper died April 14th, 1850, aged 43 years. He was married again to Olive, the youngest daughter of Moses Wright and Lydia Hoar, 1853. They had two daughters. He settled on the south side of Stewiacke River, on the interval where he spent the remainder of his life. He died there 1859.

Jane, the second daughter of Mahew and Christie Tupper, removed with her mother to Ohio, U. S., and was married there to Mr. Smith. Christian, their youngest daughter, removed also to Ohio, U. S., and was married there to Mr. Sudicks.

Samuel, the second son of Eliakim Tupper, Esq., and Elizabeth Newcomb, was born November 26th, 1764. He was married to Elizabeth, the eldest daughter of Robert Archibald, Esq., and Hannah Blair, in the year 1786. Hannah, their eldest daughter, was born January 18th, 1787. She was married to William Creelman, January

20th, 1808. They had four sons and four daughters. She died September 27th, 1865, aged 78 years. Her husband died September 9th, 1857. Elizabeth, their second daughter was born in the month ·of January, 1789. She was married to John Gourley, 1807. They had two sons and four daughters. Mr. Tupper's first wife died the same month that Elizabeth was born, January, 1789. He was married again to Rachel, the third daughter of James Dunlap and Mary John- son, of the Lower Village of Truro, in the year 1793. James, their ·eldest son was born April 28th, 1794. He was married to Isabell, the only daughter of the Rev. Hugh Graham, and Elizabeth Whidden February 29th, 1820. They had two sons and five daughters. Mrs. Tupper died December 18th, 1864, aged 65 years. Mary, the eldest daughter of Samuel and Rachel Tupper, was born November 20th, 1795. She was married to John Kelley. They had one son. She died March 17th, 1824. Eliakim Tupper, their second son, was born January 25th, 1798. He was married to Elizabeth Newcomb, March 13th, 1821. He inherited a part of his father's farm, where he re- mained until about the year 1860. He then sold out and purchased the farm on which his grandfather settled at the South Branch of Stewiacke River, where he and his wife and sons are still residing. He filled the office of Justice of the Peace since the year 1842, and his eldest son, A. N. Tupper, was appointed to the same office in the year 1868. They had three sons and six daughters. Robert, the third son of Samuel and Rachel Tupper, was born March 18th, 1800. He was married to Mary, the only daughter of James Dunlap and Jane Kennedy, 1820. They had two sons and two daughters. One son and one daughter were deaf and dumb. He inherited the home- stead part of his father's farm on the south side of Stewiacke River, where he spent his life. He died there December 1st, 1858, in the 59th year of his age, and his wife died May 12th, 1854, aged 55 years. Jerusha, their second daughter, was born September 24th, 1802. She was married to John Kaulback of Musquodoboit. They had two sons and four daughters. John, their fourth son, was born September 15th, 1804. He was married to Janet, second daughter of Adams Archibald, Esq., of Musquodoboit, March 2nd, 1830. They had three sons and one daughter. He died July 26th, 1844, aged 40 years, and his wife died February 8th, 1843, aged 38 years. Sarah, the third daughter of Samuel and Rachel Tupper, was born July 1st, 1806. She was married to John Gammell, 1826. They had three sons and seven daughters. She died October 11th, 1846, aged 40 years, and her husband died in July, 1861, aged 61 years. Samuel, the fifth son of Samuel and Rachel Tupper, was born April 19th, 1808. He was married to Martha Howard. They had six sons and three daughters. (Three of their sons were deaf and dumb.) They removed from Stewiacke about the year 1855, and lived in Halifax some time. They now live on McNab's Island. Rachel their fourth daughter, was born April 25th, 1810. She was married to John McCurdy in 1854. She died December 21st, 1868, aged 58 years. Margaret, their fifth daughter, was born June 16th, 1812. She was married to the Rev. James Smith, D.D., April, 1831. They had one daughter. Mrs. Smith died August 20th, 1832, aged 20 years. Mr. Smith was married again to Jessie, daughter of the Revd. Robert Blackwood, November, 1839. They had three sons and four daughters. Dr. Smith was settled in the year 1830 over the congregation of Upper and Middle Stewiacke, which is now two and a half congregations. He labored faithfully in his congregation, and out of it, for more than forty years. He died May 17th, 1871. Lydia, the sixth daughter of Samuel and Rachel Tupper, was born September 15th, 1814. She was married to Angus McLeod, October, 1831. They removed to the United States. They had six sons and six daughters. Eddy, their sixth son, was born October 13th, 1816. He was married to Susannah West of Halifax. They had three sons and two daughters. He carried on business with Duffus & Co., in Halifax. He died April 3rd, 1857, aged 41 years. Harriet, their seventh and youngest daughter, was born October 24th, 1819. She was married to Alexander Kent of Musquodoboit. They had six sons and three daughters. Samuel Tupper, Esq., settled on the farm on the south side of Stewiacke River, on which his son Robert, and his grandson, James, lived and died. He was a leading man in society. He was a Justice of the Peace, and was the only one in Upper Stewiacke for a number of years. He died at Stewiacke, August 29th, 1831, aged 67 years, and his wife died June 9th, 1852, aged 76 years.

Mary, the eldest daughter of Eliakim Tupper, Esq., and Elizabeth Newcomb, was born in the year 1766. She was married to Samuel Fisher in 1786. They had three sons and six daughters. She died April 23rd, 1812, and her husband died May 10th, 1812.

Jerusha, their second daughter was born about the year 1768. She was married to Dr. Benjamin Prince. They resided for a time on the interval of Salmon River, near the place that Mr. James K.

Eaton now resides. They afterwards removed to Canada, and we know nothing of them or any of their descendants.

Abigail, another daughter of Eliakim and Elizabeth Tupper, was married to Captain Alexander Robb. They removed to the United States for a time, and then returned to Stewiacke about the year 1818. He started one night to cross the interval of Upper Stewiacke, and was lost; his body was never found.

Alice, another daughter of Eliakim and Elizabeth Tupper, was married to Samuel Fulton son of James and Ann Fulton, of the Lower Village of Truro. They removed to Ohio, U. S. This is said to be the first marriage in Upper Stewiacke, and it was in the house of Samuel Fisher.

Elizabeth, another daughter of Eliakim Tupper, Esq., was married to Mr. Smith, from England. They removed to London. They had one son and one daughter. The son's name is Mahew Tupper Smith, who was school inspector for the County of Pictou.

Eliakim the third son of Eliakim and Elizabeth Tupper, was born in the year 1773. He was married to Lydia, daughter of William and Dorothy Putnam, 1798. He inherited his father's farm at the South Branch of Stewiacke, where they spent the remainder of their lives. He died January 4th, 1852, aged 79 years; and his wife died November 13th, 1851, aged 79 years. Mary, their eldest daughter, was born in the year 1799. She was married to Ebenezer Smith of Truro, December 10th, 1818. She died July 25th, 1820, aged 21 years. Elizabeth, the second daughter of Eliakim and Lydia Tupper, was born March 22nd, 1802. She was married to William Tupper of Annapolis. They had one daughter. Mr. Tupper died and she was married again to Elias Tupper. They had three sons and two daughters. She died December 22nd, 1870. Lydia, their third daughter, was born December 22nd, 1803. She was married to James Flemming of Truro, July 1st, 1826. They had three sons and five daughters. She died April, 1862. Mr. Flemming died July, 1851. Sarah their fourth daughter, was born September 1st, 1806. She was married to Charles Dickie of Cornwallis, June 21st, 1826. They had three sons and three daughters. Abigail, their fifth daughter, was born October 20th, 1809. She was married to William Creelman, January 27th, 1831. They had six sons and three daughters. Rachel, their sixth daughter, was born July 26th 1812. She was married to Job Harvey of Newport, October 1835. They had one son. She died April, 1837. Martha, their seventh and youngest daughter, was

born March 22nd, 1815. She was married to Hon. William Annand,
December, 1834. They had three sons and five daughters. Eliakim,
the only son of Eliakim and Lydia Tupper, was born May 11th,
1817. He was married to Janet McLeod, of Musquodoboit, March,
1844. They had three sons and four daughters. He inherited his
father's farm until about the year 1854. He then removed to Halifax,
and from thence to the United States.

Elias, the fourth son of Eliakim and Elizabeth Tupper, was born
in the year 1777. He was married to Miss Elizabeth Bowls. They
had one son, born 1809. Elias Tupper died 1809.

Eddy, their fifth son, was born in Truro in the year 1779. He
was married to Ann, daughter of John Fulton and Mary Simpson, October 12th 1798. He inherited a part of his father's farm. He died
March 17th, 1816, aged 37 years, and his widow was married again to
George Fulton in 1822. Benjamin, the eldest son of Eddy and Ann
Tupper, was born May 14th, 1799, He was married to Mary, daughter of John and Martha Dunlap, February 19th, 1822. They had
three sons. Mary S., their eldest daughter, was born June 17th,
1801. She was married to Ephraim son of William Dickey and
Hannah Howard, January 19th, 1822. They had five sons and three
daughters. Elizabeth their second daughter, was born January 30th,
1804. She was married to Hugh G. Cox, February 5th, 1824. They
had one daughter. Samuel, their second son was born May 8th,
1807. He was married to Elizabeth, daughter of William and Hannah Dickey, December, 1825. They had two sons and seven daughters. He died in Halifax, June, 1862. His wife died in 1860. Jerusha, their third daughter, was born November 5th, 1809. She was
married to William, son of George Fulton and Esther Creelman.
They had four sons and four daughters. She died November, 1867,
and her husband died January, 1868. Alice, their fourth daughter,
was born February 8th, 1813. She was married to James Creelman,
Esq., December 5th, 1833. They had eight sons and one daughter.
Mr. Creelman died May 22nd, 1857. She was married again to Barry
Hamilton, January 2nd, 1860. Sarah, their fifth daughter, was born
October 8th, 1815. She was married to Samuel, son of Samuel and
Margaret Creelman, November 8th, 1834. They had three sons and
four daughters. Mr. Creelman died January 3rd, 1868. She was
married again to Jonathan R. Campbell, April, 1868.

David, the sixth and youngest son of Eliakim and Elizabeth Tupper, was born in August, 1780. He was married to Joanna, daughter

of David Dickey and Martha Howard, of Lower Stewiacke. They had four sons and seven daughters. Mrs. Tupper died September 11th, 1840, aged 53 years. He was married again to Charlotte Green, widow of the late Walter Power, August, 1841. They had three daughters. He died May 19th, 1863, in the 83rd year of his age.

CHAPTER XXVIII.

Colonel Thomas Pearson was among the early settlers in Truro. He was an English officer, and came out to Florida, U. S., and was married there, and from thence to Truro, Nova Scotia, about the year 1784, at the time that the United States gained their independence. He resided in the house in which Mr. Hiram Hyde now resides, from the time he came to Truro until he moved into his own house in the year 1809, being the same house in which Mr. McKenzie now keeps an Inn. S. B. Robie represented Truro Township in the House of Assembly from the year 1799, until the year 1806. This year Mr. Robie obtained a seat for the County of Halifax, and Mr. Pearson represented Truro until the year 1811. This year James Kent, Esq., of the Lower Village, offered as a candidate for Truro. There was a pretty warm contest, and Kent was returned with a majority of two or three votes ; a scrutiny was demanded by Pearson, and when the Assembly met on February 6th, 1812, a committee was drawn to try the matter, when it was proved that one or two of the votes for Kent were so bad that they were struck off. A very strong attempt was made to destroy the vote of Dumb John Johnson, but the committee decided in favor of his vote being good, and Kent retained his seat with a majority of one vote. He died July 24th, 1818, and his wife died February, 1826. He (Mr. Pearson) was married before he came to Truro.

Sarah, the eldest daughter of Thomas and Martha Pearson, was born before they came to Truro. She was married to John Crane. They had six sons and four daughters. Mr. Crane died in Economy, about 1850.

Rebecca, their second daughter was born 1784. She was married to Colonel William Dickson, of Onslow, January 29th, 1801. They had six sons and six daughters. He removed to Truro and purchased the place on which Mr. Hyde now resides, where he carried on a very extensive business selling goods and farming. He held the offices of Registrar of Deeds, Prothonotary of the Supreme Court, and Clerk of the Peace, all at one time for a number of years. He was a very active man for business of almost every kind. He died February 5th, 1834, aged 55 years. His wife died June, 1833.

Rachel, daughter of Thomas and Martha Pearson, was born 1785. She was married to Thomas T. Brown, July 9th, 1801. They had seven sons and two daughters. They lived and reared their family on the farm which the Messrs. Putnam now own, at Fort Belcher. He was a Justice of the Peace, and Judge of the Court of Common Pleas. He died at Pictou. and his body was brought to Truro for interment, October 15th, 1855, aged 77 years, and his wife died Dec. 11th, 1854, aged 69 years.

William, the eldest son of Thomas and Martha Pearson, was born about the year 1788. He was married to Nancy Dempsey, of Aylesford, in the year 1811. They had one son and two daughters. He kept an Inn where William Bowland now resides. In this house his wife died in the year 1818. He was lost overboard from a schooner in the Bay of Fundy, December 3rd, 1834, near Spencer's Island. Thomas, his only son, was born May 10th, 1814. He was married to Sarah, daughter of John and Hannah Yuill, June 23rd, 1836. They had three sons and two daughters. He died on his way to California, February 23rd, 1852, and his wife died April 9th, 1868, aged 55 years. Martha, the eldest daughter of William and Nancy Pearson, was born April 17th, 1812. She was married to Ferguson McNutt, of Masstown, March 10th, 1835. They had four sons and six daughters. Susan, their second daughter, was born May 30th, 1816. She was married to Thomas D., eldest son of Hugh Johnson and Elizabeth Dickey, June 23rd, 1836.

Elizabeth, the fourth and youngest daughter of Thomas and Martha Pearson, was born in the year 1790. She was married to Captain James Pearson. They had one daughter, whose name was Martha; she was married and removed to Cumberland. Captain Pearson died February 12th, 1816, aged 33 years, and his wife died July 7th, 1817, aged 27 years.

John, the second son of Thomas and Martha Pearson, was born in the year 1792. He was married to Esther, the youngest daughter of Robert McElhenny of Londonderry, in the year 1813. Thomas, their son, was married to Esther, the youngest daughter of M. P. Martin.

He was a sea captain, and perished at sea on a wrecked ship a few years after they were married, and his wife died soon after, November 11th, 1842. Robert, another son of John and Esther Pearson, was married to Elizabeth, daughter of James and Esther Barnhill. They had one son and two daughters. He removed to California and died there about the year 1852. William Dickson, another son of John Pearson left home to follow the sea more than 30 years ago, and has not been heard from since. Hannah, their only daughter, removed to the United States. She was married to James, the eldest son of James and Margaret Fulton, of Stewiacke. She died in Boston, 1863. Frederick M., the fourth and youngest son of John and Esther Pearson was born in Pictou, February 13th, 1827. He was married to Eliza Crowe, daughter of James Crow and James Fletcher, 4th April, 1850. They have four sons and three daughters. For a number of years he carried on a large business shipbuilding at Masstown, and importing and selling goods. He is now carrying on a large business in Truro, importing and selling flour and other goods. He is a Justice of the Peace, and in the year 1870, he was elected to represent Colchester in the House of Commons of the Dominion of Canada. On August 15th, 1872, he was re-elected.

John Pearson died at Truro in July, 1844. His widow died at her son's, at Masstown, July 13th 1871, aged 76 years.

Thomas, the third son of Thomas and Martha Pearson, was born in the year 1794. He died a bachelor August 25th, 1822, aged 28 years.

Charles, their fourth son was born in the year 1796. He died a bachelor about 1842.

Robert, the fifth and youngest son of Thomas and Martha Pearson, was born in the year 1798. He was married to Esther, the youngest daughter of William and Esther Smith, May 25th, 1820. They had three sons. Charles R., was their second son. The other two died when they were young. Charles R. Pearson was married to Mary, the only daughter of James and Mary Brining, April, 1850. They had two sons and three daughters. They inherited her father's property. Mrs. Pearson died May 12th, 1870, and Robert Pearson died December 17th, 1825, aged 27 years. His widow was married again to John L. Doggett, December 4th, 1828.

CHAPTER XXIX.

Dr. John Harris was among the early settlers of Truro, although he did not come until a few years after the Township was granted. He and his family were one of the six families that sailed from Philadelphia in the month of May, 1767, sent by a company to settle in Pictou. The people of Truro having heard of this vessel being in Halifax, sent seventeen men through the woods to Pictou to welcome their arrival. When they came in sight of the harbor, June 11th, they saw the ship coming up the harbor at a distance, and they kindled fires on the shore to attract the attention of those on board. When they saw the fires, they concluded that they were set by the savages; they held a consultation what to do—whether they would submit to them or resist. They resolved upon resistance. The next morning, when the people from Truro were walking down the shore, they on board the vessel saw with their glasses that they were white folks, and it was not long until they came ashore, and were welcomed by the men from Truro. These people commenced clearing away the trees and putting up small houses. They sowed some seed in the ground, but it was so late in the season they grew very little crop that year; but the fish were very plenty in the harbor and rivers, so they made out to live with much difficulty. Two of the six families became so much discouraged that they left for Truro. Those that remained had a very hard winter, and the next spring they had to go to Truro, a distance of forty miles, and carry their seed potatoes on their backs through the woods, having no other guide than the blaze upon the trees. The next spring they had to go again to Truro for seed potatoes, but this time they took another plan. They cut the eyes out of the potatoes and only carried the eyes.

The names of the families that remained in Pictou were Robert Paterson, Dr. John Harris, John Rogers and James McCabe. The next year they were joined by two families from Truro. Mr. William Kennedy's family was one of these.

Dr. John Harris removed to Truro about the year 1776, and settled on the interval of Salmon River, and built his house on the same place that Mr. Robert Bennett's house now stands. He was a Justice of the Peace, and was in the habit of celebrating the marriage contract. He was Town Clerk from a short time after he came to

Truro until the year 1790.   April 9th, 1802, he went from home on horseback, and rode to the Village, and as he was turning into Mr. Jonathan Blanchard's yard from the street, he fell from his horse and was killed instantly.   He was married to Elizabeth Scott before they left New England.   She died in the month of July, 1815.   He represented Truro in Parliament from the year 1781 until the year 1784.

Thomas, their eldest son, was born June 10th, 1767, on board of the ship in which they came to Pictou.   He was married to Alice, daughter of William Logan and Janet Moor, of Truro.   They had four sons and one daughter.   They settled near the "Town Gut," so called, near Pictou Town, where they reared there family, and they both died there some time ago.

Mary, the eldest daughter of Dr. John and Elizabeth Harris, was born in 1769, being the first female child that was born in Pictou after it was settled by the English.   She was married to Robert, third son of Rev. Daniel Cock in the year 1795.   They had three sons and three daughters.   They appear among the Cock families.   She died November, 1864, aged 96 years, and her husband died about the year 1843, aged 78 years.   William, their second son, was born in the year 1771.   He studied for a doctor, removed to the United States, and was married there to Susan Hunt.   They had one daughter.   He died there when he was but a young man.

Margaret, their second daughter, was born in Pictou in the year 1773.   She was married to Joseph Notting, June, 1793.   John Harris Notting, their only son, was born in Truro April 5th, 1794. He was married to Martha, the eldest daughter of John Kent and Janet McCurdy, September 29th, 1825.   They had one son and two daughters.   They settled in the Lower Village, where they are still living together.   Joseph Notting was a tanner by trade, and settled and built his house and tan-yard at the same place that James and Ralph Watson now reside.   He died there January 23rd, 1795.   His widow was married again to Robert, son of Thomas Watson, Esq., of Cumberland, February 9th, 1796.   They had seven sons and one daughter.   They continued on this same place, where they reared their family.   He died there March 22nd, 1851, aged 82 years, and his wife died June 6th, 1853, aged 80 years.

Elizabeth, the third daughter of Dr. John and Elizabeth Harris, was born in the year 1775.   She was married to John, son of Capt. John McKeen and Rachel Johnson, December, 1798, being the first that Mr. Waddell married after he came to Truro.   They had three sons and seven daughters. They first settled on the farm that Mr. Hugh Clark now resides upon, about five miles from Truro. They removed thence to St. Mary's. They removed again and settled in the woods on Tatamagouche Mountain, where they spent the remainder of their days. She died January 6th, 1820, aged 45 years, and her husband died October 17th, 1854, aged 84 years.

John Washington Harris, their third son, was born in the year 1777. He was married to Mary Hadley. They had eight sons and four daughters. He settled near Pictou Town, and was Sheriff of Pictou for a long time. He died there October. 1860, aged 92 years. Susanna Hunter Harris, was born in Truro, April 2nd, 1779. She was married to John, son of Hugh Moore, Senr., and Janet Logan, his wife. They had three sons and five daughters. They settled on the West Branch of River John, where they reared their family and died.

Robert, the fourth and youngest son of Dr. John and Elizabeth Harris, was born in Truro, November 21st, 1783. He was married to Hannah, daughter of Ebenezer Hoar and Catherine Downing, January 30th, 1805. He inherited his father's property in Truro, where he spent the whole of his life. He died December 26th, 1812, aged 29 years. Ebenezer Hoar Harris, their eldest son, was born May 13th, 1806. He was married to Lavinia Lynds, June, 1829. They had one son and two daughters. They settled on Onslow Mountain. Mrs. Harris died there March 18th, 1869, aged 62 years. Eliza, daughter of Robert and Hannah Harris, was born October 21st, 1811. She was married to James, the eldest son of Samuel and Elizabeth Archibald, December 31st, 1833. They had three sons and one daughter. They reside at Clifton now. Robert, the second son of Robert and Hannah Harris, was born July 14th, 1813. He was married to Maria, the youngest daughter of Robert Cock and Mary Harris, 1839. They had four sons and one daughter, who appear among the Cock families.

Dr. John Harris, being one of the first settlers of Pictou, was interested in what was called the Philadelphia Grant. This grant being escheated after the death of Dr. Harris, there were grants given of five hundred acres each to John W. and Robert Harris, and their four sisters. This 3000 acres of land was laid out and granted about the year 1813, on each side of the road leading from Truro to Tatamagouche, and soon after, the sons of Robert Cock and John McKeen commenced to clear and make themselves farms at the same place that some of their descendants now reside, on Tatamagouche Mountain. These were the first settlers between Onslow and Tatamagouche.

About the years 1817 and 1818 there were others who had arrived from Scotland and commenced making a settlement West of the place that the heirs of Harris were settled. This has become a considerable settlement, and is called New Annan. It was one unbroken forest between North River and River John until the year 1817, when Alexander Miller made the first survey in what is now called Earltown. He continued to survey a large part of the Crown Land of Colchester and Pictou, which was not included in the Townships of Truro, Onslow and Londonderry. Afterwards he fixed boundary lines for Townships and gave them their names ; that part lying between the East line of Truro, and the County line between Pictou and Colchester he called Greenfield ; that part lying between Pictou County line and Onslow he called Kemptown, in honor of Sir James Kempt, who arrived in Halifax June 1st, 1820. That part which lies North of Kemptown, and North of the East end of Onslow, he called Earltown, for the Earl of Dalhousie.

CHAPTER XXX.

In the spring of the year 1784, seven men, with their families, removed from Truro to Upper Musquodoboit, and commenced a settlement there. Their names were John, James and Samuel Fisher, sons of William Fisher, Stewtly Horton, who was married to Hannah Fisher, Thomas Reynolds, John Holman and Robert Geddes.

In the same spring (1784), eight men, with their families removed from Truro to Upper Stewiacke, to make a settlement there ; their names were Thomas Croker, Samuel Fisher, William and Samuel Fulton, of the Lower Village, Samuel Taylor, John Archibald, and Charles Cox, Matthew Johnson having removed and settled there in the fall of 1783. In 1785 Richard Upham settled at Otter Brook, and after this time there were others removed and settled in Upper Stewiacke. Samuel Creelman was the next settler there. Archibald and Robert Gammell, Robert and Hugh Logan, John and William Johnson, David Fulton, William Cox, and William Smith were among the early settlers.

The Rev. Daniel Cock was the first who preached to these people in Stewiacke. He first preached in Mr. Samuel Fisher's house, about the year 1787. After this, Mr. Cock, Mr. McGregor, Mr. Munro, Mr. Ross and Mr. Waddell, continued to visit them and preach to them. Mr. Munro remained with them about two years, from about the year 1793 to 1795. In the year 1799, they began to make efforts to obtain a settled Minister to labor among them. A number of others had removed from Truro and elsewhere, and had settled in Middle and Upper Stewiacke, and in Middle and Upper Musquodoboit; these all joined together to obtain the services of a minister, and they resolved to give the Rev. Hugh Graham a call. (Mr. Graham came from Scotland in the year 1786, and was settled in Cornwallis until 1799. The call to Mr. Graham is dated August 26th, 1799, and is signed by the following persons, in presence of the Rev. John Waddell, Moderator, and John Simmons, 3rd, Witness. Robert Archibald, Eliakim Tupper, Alexander Stewart, Matthew Johnson, Samuel Tupper, William Kennedy, Robert Geddes, William Putnam, Samuel Fisher, Adam Dunlap, Samuel Fisher Archibald, Matthew T. Archibald, William Archibald, Elizabeth Dickey, Thomas Croker, Simeon Whidden, John Pratt, Robert Morris, Eddy Tupper, Mahew Tupper, William Smith, William Cox, James Dunlap, John Fisher, Thomas Brenton, Eliakim Tupper, Jr., Robert Hamilton, James Johnson, John Archibald, 3rd, Alexander Henry, Alexander Stewart, 2nd, Margaret Ferrell, Thomas Reynolds, John Holman, John Dean, James Kennedy, John Kennedy, John Bonnell, David Dickey, Robert Kennedy, David Archibald, 8th, Samuel B. Archibald, Edward Brydon, Samuel Fisher, Samuel Nelson, John Scott, Peter Hynds, John Archibald, Adams Archibald, John Nelson, James Guild, George McLeod, John Moore, John Higgins, David Archibald, 5th, Hugh Archibald, Johnson Kaulback, Robert Nelson, John Geddes, Richard Upham, John Smith, Alexander McN. Fisher, James Whidden, Wm. Skeed, Hugh Logan, Michael Geddes, and Robert Geddes. There is a seal affixed to this call by each of the signers, and it is certified on the call by William Dickson, Deputy Registrar of Deeds for the Distrsct of Colchester, that it was duly Registered on August 2nd, 1805, at 10 o'clock in the forenoon, persuant to the Laws of this Province, on the oath of John Simmons, recorded in Lib. 4, folio 444. This call was accepted by Mr. Graham, and he was removed and settled over the Congregation of Stewiacke and Musquodoboit.

He continued to have the charge of this large and scattered Congregation for about ten or twelve years. Then Musquodoboit was set off as a separate congregation, and obtained the services of the Rev. Mr. Laidlaw as their first Minister. Mr. Graham continued the remainder of his life, labouring faithfully and zealously, in the Congregation of Stewiacke. As soon as the people of Middle Stewiacke got a settled Minister, they commenced building a Meeting House. But about the time they got the inside finished, it caught fire and was burnt down, They built another about the year 1804. In it they worshipped until about the year 1848, when the present one was built.

The Rev. Hugh Graham was born in Scotland in the year 1754, and removed to Nova Scotia in the spring of the year 1785, when he was 32 years old. He was soon settled in Cornwallis. (And on August 2nd, 1786, the first Presbytery of Nova Scotia was formed by the Rev. Daniel Cock, of Truro, Rev. David Smith, of Londonderry, Rev. Hugh Graham of Cornwallis, Rev. James McGregor, of Pictou, and Rev. Mr. Gilmore, of Hants County, and John Johnson of Truro, and John Barnhill, of Londonderry, Ruling Elders.) He was married to Elizabeth, daughter of John Whidden, Esq., of Cornwallis, in 1792.

Hugh, their eldest son, was born March, 1793. He was married to Janet, daughter of James Kennedy and Janet Dickey, November, 1819. He settled on the farm that Mr. Wm. Logan now resides upon. He removed and settled on the mountain, on the south side of Stewiacke River, where they reared their family and spent the remainder of their lives. He died there January 18th 1857, aged 64 years, and his wife died July 26th, 1832, aged 37 years. Elizabeth, the eldest daughter of Hugh and Janet Graham, was born March 17th, 1818. She was married to George, the third son of Henry Miller and Sarah Wright, December 2nd, 1839. They had three sons and three daughters. She died March 23rd, 1859, aged 41 years. Hannah Prescott, their second daughter, was born October 13th, 1820. She was married to David, the third son of David Fulton and Martha Ellis, his wife, February 9th, 1843. They had nine sons and three daughters. Eleanor, their third daughter, was born April 9th, 1823. She was married to James, son of Murdock Frame and Isabel Wilson, March 12th, 1846. They had two sons and two daughters. They reside on what was his father's farm at Middle Stewiacke. Hugh, the only son of Hugh and Janet Graham, was born March 12th, 1826. He removed to New Brunswick, and was married there to Susan Maynord in 1852. They had two sons and four daughters. They returned and settled on the Mountain South of Stewiacke River.

John Whidden, the second son of Rev. Hugh Graham and Elizabeth Whidden, was born February 22nd, 1795. Rebecca Croker, his wife, was born February 15th, 1800. They were married in the year 1821. Hugh, their eldest son, was born November 25th, 1822. He was married to Hannah Thomson, of Musquodoboit, in the year 1848. They had three sons and three daughters. David, their second son, was born in Stewiacke July 14th, 1824. He removed to the United States and was married there. John W., their third son, was born January 28th, 1826. He was married to Mary E. Albee, of New Brunswick. Thomas, their fourth son, was born May 25th, 1827. He was married to Jessie McKenzie, of Pictou. They had three sons and four daughters. Peter, their fifth son, was born February 21st, 1829. He was married to Margaret Samson, of New Brunswick. They had one son and two daughters. Robert Blackwood, their sixth son, was born July 11th, 1831. He removed to New Brunswick, and died there a bachelor in the year 1855, aged 24 years. William Wilberforce, their seventh son, was born November 25th, 1832. He removed to New Brunswick, and was married there to Sarah Caswell. They had three sons and four daughters. Eliza, their only daughter, was born December 17th, 1835. She died when she was quite young. James, their eighth son, was born February 3rd, 1837. He was married to Lois Allen, January 9th, 1868. They have one son and one daughter. He and his brother Joseph A. are now carrying on business as merchants at Brookfield. Joseph Alison, their ninth son, was born January 20th, 1843. He was married to Emily Allen, February 4th, 1871. The above named John W. Graham died at Stewiacke, June 22nd, 1867, aged 72 years, and his widow, Rebecca, died June 15th, 1869, aged 69 years.

Isabell, daughter of Rev. Hugh Graham and Elizabeth Whidden, was born December 25th, 1799. She was married to James, the eldest son of Samuel Tupper, Esq., and Rachel Dunlap, February 29th, 1820. They had two sons and five daughters. She died December 18th, 1864. Elizabeth Graham was born in 1797. She died about the year 1813, aged 16 years.

William, the third son of Rev. Hugh and Elizabeth Graham, was born August 1st, 1804. He died a bachelor, June 15th, 1849, aged 45 years.

James, the fourth and youngest son of Rev. Hugh and Elizabeth Graham, was born April 30th, 1808. He was married to Rachel, the third daughter of William Creelman and Hannah Tupper, March 4th, 1845. Allen, their eldest son, was born June 19th, 1846. Samuel, their second son, was born May 1st, 1848. William, their third son, was born May 28th, 1850. Bessie, their eldest daughter, was born August 19th, 1852. David, their fourth son, was born June 14th, 1854. Frank, their fifth son, was born April 28th, 1856. Isabell, their second and youngest daughter, was born May 4th, 1863. The Rev. Hugh Graham died at Stewiacke, April 5th, 1829, aged 75 years. His wife died June 12th, 1816, aged 42 years.

The first settlers of Stewiacke had many difficulties to contend against. On September 8th, 1792, there was the great freshet, which carried away a large part of their wheat, which was standing in stook in the field. Many of their houses stood on the interval, and were in danger of being carried away. Many made rafts of boards from the floors of their houses and pushed off for higher land, while those who had canoes were busy saving the people first and afterwards the cattle and sheep. After this they very prudently built more of their houses on the upland.

The people in Brookfield also sustained great loss by this freshet, both in wheat and other crops.

At the same time all the interval and marsh between Truro and Onslow was flooded, so that they could go to Onslow from Truro and back in boats. By looking at the date of this freshet, it will be seen that it would be most disastrous to the farmers of those places.

Then, on the evening of the 12th of November, 1813, was the great hurricane, known by the old men as the " big wind," which devastated the woods, levelled the fences, and very many of the buildings were either blown down or unroofed. Many of the settlers suffered severely.

But long before any of these disasters, the crops of the first settlers of these places were destroyed by mice. This year was called by the old settlers as the year of the mice, and a year or two either before or after this, they had a summer so cold that none of their crops came to perfection. Here are four epochs which the old men of the present day often heard their fathers talk about, viz : The year of the mice, the cold summer, the big wind, and the great freshet, and I believe there has been nothing like any one of them since.

Then, on the 7th October, 1825, there was the great fire in Miramichi, in which 160 persons perished, 595 buildings burned, and 875 horses and cattle lost. The total loss of property was estimated at $994,092, and 8000 square miles of country laid waste. In Great Britain, United States, and the British Colonies about $174,428 were subscribed for the relief of the sufferers.

CHAPTER XXXI.

The first settlers removed to Brookfield about the year 1786. The first who settled there were William Hamilton and Daniel Moore, and shortly after William Downing, William Carter, and James Boomer settled there. William Downing soon left, and John Hamilton settled on what was his farm, in 1793. The first sermon was preached there by the Rev. John Waddell, in January, 1800, and he continued to be their minister until 1832. The people of Brookfield, before this date, attended public worship in Truro quite regularly. At this date it was set off from Truro congregation, and the Rev. John I. Baxter had it as a part of his charge. As mentioned before, the frame of the first Church was raised at Brookfield on July 17th, 1833, and this was the only Church in Brookfield until the year 1857, when the Baptists built their small Church. In the year 1869 the Presbyterians built their new Church and removed the old one. From the settlement of the place up to the year 1832, they came to Truro to bury their dead, but from this time they commenced to bury their dead in a Cemetery west of the Brookfield station. The body of Mr. William Carter was the first that was buried there, in January, 1832. What was called the new level road, from Truro to Halifax, was made through Brookfield in the year 1835, and in December, 1858, the railroad was opened for carrying freight and passengers.

The Lieutenant Governor, Sir George Provost, arrived at Halifax April 15th, 1809, and in July of this year he visited Truro and Pictou, where he received addresses from the inhabitants. He was accompanied by Michael Wallace and S. H. George, Esqs., and his Aid-de-camp, Capt. Provost. The writer believes that this was the first four wheeled carriage that ever passed through Truro. About this time they were getting the roads made so that wheels could be run on them from Halifax to Pictou, and in a few years after this some of the people began to get carriages to ride in, but they were few in number for many years after this. It may here be observed that all the travelling that was done by men, women, or children was done on foot or horseback for more than fifty years after the settlement of Colchester; and it was quite customary in those days for people to ride on horseback ten or twelve miles to attend public worship, or to walk five or six miles for the same purpose, and carry the bodies of their dead on biers, by four men at a time, a distance of three miles to the place of burial. Spirituous liquors were always used at funerals in those days.

CHAPTER XXXII.

John Christie was among the early settlers of Truro, but he did not come until twelve years after the first settlers. He was born in Roxburgshire, Scotland, in the year 1739. He removed to Nova Scotia in the summer of the year 1772. He came out from Scotland with the Rev. Daniel Cock and his family. He was married to Nancy, daughter of John Denny and Rebecca Mitchell, his wife, of Londonderry, about the year 1780. He purchased a farm from Matthew Taylor, second, where they settled, reared their family, and died. Mr. Christie died May 28th, 1830, aged 91 years, and his widow died June 14th, 1844, aged 85 years. Janet, their eldest daughter, was born January 27th, 1782. She was married to Alexander Kent, Esq., January 27th, 1803. They had one son and seven daughters, who appear among the Kent families. She died June 1st, 1872, aged 90 years.

John Denny, the eldest son of John Christie and Nancy Denny, was born April 14th, 1784. He was married to Margaret, daughter of Isaac O'Brien and Mary Denny, of Noel, November 1st, 1808. He inherited a part of his father's farm, where they reared their family and spent the remainder of their days. Isaac, their eldest son, was born August 28th, 1809. He was married to Susannah, the third daughter of James and Sarah Yuill, December 25th, 1834. They had one son and nine daughters. Mrs. Christie died September 17th, 1863, aged 49 years. Oliphant, their second son, was born June 12th, 1811. He learned the blacksmith trade, and removed to New York, U. S. He was married to Ann Godfrey. They had four sons and three daughters. Rebecca, their only daughter, was born May 28th, 1813. She was married to Isaac Archibald, November 27th, 1836. They had three sons and five daughters. George, their third son, was born April 4th, 1815. He is a minister of the Gospel, and settled over a congregation at Yarmouth. He was married to Elizabeth, daughter of John Paterson, of Pictou Town, August, 1840. They had six sons. William, their fourth son, was born November 11th, 1817. He was married to Jane McLain, of Pictou, November 16th, 1846. They have two sons and two daughters. He inherits a part of his father's property. Richard, their fifth son, was born November 5th, 1819. He was married to Eliza Jane, fifth daughter of James and Sarah Yuill, December 31st, 1842. They had six sons and four daughters. Mrs. Christie died June 20th, 1872. John, their sixth and youngest son, was born November 14th, 1821. He removed to California.

Mr. Christie's first wife died January 31st, 1822, aged 35 years. He was married again to Margaret, daughter of James and Ann Johnson, of Middle Stewiacke, February 8th, 1827. Margaret, their only daughter, was born January 3rd, 1829. She was married to Hugh Dunlap, Esq., April 4th, 1856. They had four sons and two daughters. She died May 11th, 1869, aged 40 years. James, their only son, was born July 31st, 1830. He died October 22nd, 1846, aged 16 years. John D. Christie died May 11th, 1866, aged 82 years, and his second wife died November 29th, 1856, aged 64 years.

Rebecca, the second daughter of John Christie and Nancy Denny, was born April 6th, 1786. She was married to Ebenezer, the fourth son of Matthew and Janet Archibald, April 12th, 1804. They had six sons and two daughters, who appear among the Archibalds. She died June 25th, 1854, aged 68 years, and her husband died August 8th, 1829, aged 50 years.

Henry, the second son of John and Nancy Christie, was born October 29th, 1788. He was married to Nancy, the eldest daughter of David Archibald, fourth, and Esther Cox, March 12th, 1818. Esther, their eldest daughter, was born in Truro, March 2nd, 1819. She was married to John Hattie, April 13th, 1852. They had one son and four daughters. Robert, the eldest son of Henry and Nancy

Christie, was born November 4th, 1820. He was married to Harriet, the eldest daughter of Daniel and Mary Ann Cock, March 7th, 1850. They had four sons and three daughters. Charles, their second son, was born March 23rd, 1822. He was married to Jane, the third daughter of the late James Laughead, Junr., and Elizabeth McLellan, January 30th, 1849. They had nine sons and four daughters. He inherits what was his father's farm. Nancy, the second daughter of Henry and Nancy Christie, was born December 20th, 1823. She was married to James Gass, of Shubenacadie, October, 1850. They had four sons and one daughter. Elizabeth, their third daughter, was born June 17th, 1829. Martha, their fourth daughter, was born December 29th, 1835. Henry Christie inherited a part of what was his father's land, where he cleared his farm and put up buildings, in which they reared their family. He died November 27th, 1856, aged 68 years.

Andrew, the fourth son of John and Nancy Christie, was born April, 1792. He was married to Rachel, daughter of Isaac O'Brien and Mary Denny, of Noel, November 11th, 1823. He inherited the homestead part of what was his father's farm. He died May 18th, 1872, aged 80 years. John, their eldest son, was born October 18th, 1829. He died September 5th, 1845, aged 16 years. Isaac, their second son, was born December 5th, 1831. He was married to Adela O'Brien, of Noel, January 18th, 1859. They had two sons. He died May 13th, 1862, aged 30 years. Mary, the only daughter of Andrew and Rachel Christie, was born June 18th, 1834.

Martha, the third daughter of John and Nancy Christie, was born October, 1794. She was married to Capt. Richard Christie, in August, 1824. They had one son and one daughter. Mr. Christie was a sea Captain, and a brother's son of John Christie. He died at sea, March 28th, 1830, and his body was buried in the sea. She died October 17th, 1872, aged 78 years.

Robert Oliphant, the fifth son of John and Nancy Christie, was born April, 1798. He was married to Margaret, the second daughter of James and Sarah Yuill, December 30th, 1831. They settled in the Lower Village of Truro, where they reared their family, and he died there March 22nd, 1867, aged 69 years. Isabell, their eldest daughter, was born March 7th, 1834. She was married to Edward, the fourth son of Ebenezer Archibald and Rebecca Christie, November 27th, 1844. They had two sons and four daughters. They appear among the Archibalds. Henry, the eldest son of Robert O. and

Margaret Christie, was born December 4th, 1835. He was married to Anne Pitblado (sister of the Rev. Charles), January 2nd, 1861. They have four sons and one daughter. He inherits the first farm that his father settled on at Old Barns. Sarah, their second daughter, was born July 25th, 1837. She was married to Henry L. Atkins, druggist, of Truro, April 19th, 1864. Walter, their second son, was born May 23rd, 1839. He was married to Mary, the second daughter of Daniel and Mary Ann Cock, May 15th, 1862. They have one son and three daughters. Oliphant, their third son, was born April 2nd, 1841. He was a minister of the Gospel. He died January 10th, 1868, aged 27 years. James, their fourth son, was born December 4th, 1844. He is now a lawyer, practising in the State of New Jersey. George, their fifth and youngest son, was born June 4th, 1847. He was married to Elizabeth, daughter of Robert Johnson and Janet Notting, July 19th, 1866. They had two daughters, and they inherited his father's property in the Lower Village of Truro. On August 16th, 1870, he was engaged, with three other men, fishing Salmon, and in attempting to sweep a hole in the River, under the Lower Salmon River Bridge, he got entangled with a rope of the net, and was drowned. He left a young widow with her two babes to mourn their sad bereavement.

Alexander, the sixth and youngest son of John and Nancy Christie, was born May 9th, 1802. He was married to Margaret Laidlaw, who came from Scotland but a short time before, June 13th, 1837. They settled on Onslow Mountain, where they are living together at date (May 9th, 1872.)

Joseph Laidlaw, their eldest son, was born April 8th, 1838. He was married to Sarah, daughter of Charles McKenzie, of the West River, of Pictou, and Nancy Dickson, December 14th, 1865. They have two sons and one daughter. He settled on a part of what was his father's farm on Onslow Mountain.

Arthur, the second son of Alexander and Margaret Christie, was born November 5th, 1840. Agnes, their eldest daughter, was born November 22nd, 1842. She died March 13th, 1872, aged 29 years. John Alexander, their third son, was born July 8th, 1845. Herbert, their fourth son, was born June 1st, 1849. Jane Kent, their second and youngest daughter, was born January 22nd, 1853.

Nancy, the fourth and youngest daughter of John and Nancy Christie, was born April 18th, 1805. She was married to John, the youngest son of David Archibald, 4th, and Esther Cox, April 16th,

1832. They had three sons and three daughters. They appear among the Archibald's. Mr. Archibald died August 23rd, 1869, aged 70 years.

George Denny, the third son of John Christie and Nancy Denny, was born November 13th, 1790. He died when he was young.

CHAPTER XXXIII.

David McCollum, Senr., was among the early settlers of Onslow. He was married to Margaret Moore, of Truro, in the year 1775. They settled on the farm on which their grand son, David Lynds, now resides, at North River, where they reared their family and spent the remainder of their lives. He died about 1824. His wife died 1830.

Phebe Ann, their eldest daughter, was born October 14th, 1776. She was married to Robert Hamilton. They settled on the interval of Upper Stewiacke, on the same farm on which Mr. Charles Cox recently lived. At this place Mr. Hamilton died, and she was married again to Robert Gammell, June 20th, 1816. She died April 8th, 1859, aged 82 years. She left no children.

Thomas, their eldest son, was born April 20th, 1778. He was married to Janet, the youngest daughter of William Logan and Janet Moore. They had two sons and five daughters. They removed and settled in Middle Musquodoboit, where they reared their family. He died there April 1859, aged 81 years, and his widow died December, 1864, aged 89 years.

David, their second son, was born July 16th, 1781. He was married to Mary, the third daughter of John Archibald and Alice Moore, of Musquodoboit, 1803. They had six sons and six daughters. He settled on the farm that David Murray has owned for forty years past. He removed into the woods in 1827, and cleared another farm, being the same that his son Johnson now resides upon. Here he and his wife spent the remainder of their days. He died January, 1858. His widow died March, 1866.

Margaret, the second daughter of David and Margaret McCollum, was born July 26th, 1783. She was married to William Lynds, November, 1801. They had five sons and four daughters. They spent the latter part of their lives on the same farm on which their son David now resides. She died November 13th, 1847. Her husband died December 13th, 1843.

Hugh, the third son of David and Margaret McCollum, was born July 16th, 1785. He was a carpenter, and settled at Maitland, and spent the remainder of his life there. He was married to Lucy, daughter of Caleb Smith, Esq., January, 1818. They had two sons and three daughters. He died January, 1870, aged 84 years. His wife died July 4th, 1871.

Janet, their third daughter, was born March 5th, 1787. She was married to Simeon Howard, of St. Andrew's River. They had three sons and six daughters. She died at Wallace.

Edward, their fourth son, was born July 16th, 1790. He was married to Deborah, the eldest daughter of John Wright and Sarah Lynds, October 3rd, 1816. They had five sons and one daughter. He died April 5th, 1855, aged 65 years.

James, the fifth son of David and Margaret McCollum, was born December 18th, 1793. He was married to Mary, daughter of Daniel and Eleanor Moore, of Brookfield, widow of the late Robert Lynton. They removed to Pictou County. He died 1867.

Robert, their sixth and youngest son, was born January 28th, 1795. He inherited his father's farm for a time, and then removed to the South Branch of North River, where he spent the remainder of his life. He was married to Mary, daughter of Charles Moore, of Hants County, 1827. They had two sons and four daughters. He died 1814.

CHAPTER XXXIV

John Dickson, was an early settler of Onslow. He was born in Scotland. He was married before he left Scotland to Margaret Burn, February 1st, 1757. They came out from Scotland about the year 1773, and settled on the farm that his grand son, John Dickson, and his great grand son, George Philips, now reside upon, at North River, where he and his wife spent the remainder of their earthly existence. He died 1801, and his widow died 1822.

Jane, their eldest daughter, was born in Scotland, December 7th, 1757. She lived to be pretty old, and died unmarried, about 1832, aged 75 years. Margaret, their second daughter, was born January 8th, 1760. She was married to James Downing, November 22nd, 1787. They had two children, and they died when young. She died February 15th, 1790, aged 30 years. Her husband died February 21st, 1788.

John, their eldest son, was born in Scotland January 10th, 1763. He was brought by his parents to Nova Scotia, and was married to Mary, the third daughter of Thomas Baird and Margaret Barnhill, November 4th, 1790. They had four sons and two daughters, who appear among the Bairds. Mrs. Dickson died suddenly, November 23rd, 1803. He was married again to Elizabeth, fourth daughter of Hugh Moore and Janet Logan, November 6th, 1804.

Mary, their eldest daughter, was born August 27th, 1805. She was married to Simon McKenzie, March 1st, 1832. They had two sons and three daughters. Robert, their eldest son, was born July 9th, 1807. He removed to the United States when he was a young man, and joined the Mormons, and removed to Salt Lake, and was married there to Lydia Virginia Schnider, 1863. They had one son and one daughter. Hugh, their second son, was born July 1st, 1809. He was married to Rachel, the sixth daughter of James McCurdy and Agnes Archibald, November 4th, 1834. They had six sons and four daughters. He inherited his father's farm on Onslow Mountain, the same that his son William now resides upon. Their son, Henry C., was drowned at the board-landing bridge, June 20th, 1862, aged 26. Nancy, the second daughter of John and Elizabeth Dickson, was born June 17th, 1811. She was married to Charles, son of Daniel McKenzie and Sarah Moore, of the West River of Pictou, March 17th, 1831. They had three sons and seven daughters. Mr. McKenzie died October 25th, 1856, aged 54 years, leaving a widow and nine children to bemoan their sad bereavement. She is still living a widow. Alexander, the third son of John and Elizabeth Dickson, was born November 12th, 1813. He learned the blacksmith trade, and removed to Boston, Mass,, and settled there, where he carried on his business extensively. He was married there to Susan May, September, 1842. They have two sons and four daughters. Elizabeth, their third and youngest daughter, was born September 18th, 1816. She was married to David King, October, 1844. They removed and settled at Wallace Harbor, where he carries on his business as a tanner and shoemaker. They have one son and two daughters. John Dickson died May 25th, 1855, aged 92 years, and his second wife died May 17th, 1842, aged 68 years.

Elizabeth, the third daughter of John Dickson, Senr., and Margaret Burn, his wife, was born April 6th, 1765. She died unmarried. Janet, their fourth daughter, was born March 21st, 1768. She was married to John Baird in the year 1793. They had one son. She died December 4th, 1794, aged 26 years. Myze Ann, their fifth daughter, was born March 6th, 1771. She was married to Samuel McNutt, May 13th, 1790. They settled in the Lower Village of Truro, and had one daughter, She died November 24th, 1790, aged 20 years. Mr. McNutt was married again to Margaret Savage, of Great Village, Londonderry, March 8th, 1792. They had six sons and four daughters. Magdalen, their sixth daughter, was born August 22nd, 1773. She was married to Thomas, the eldest son of Thomas Baird and Margaret Barnhill, in the year 1793. They had three sons and four daughters, who appear among the Bairds. She died January 29th, 1849, aged 76 years, and her husband died January 7th, 1837, aged 75 years. Isabell, their seventh daughter, was born July 5th, 1776. She was married to William McNutt in 1798. They had three sons and three daughters. They lived, reared their family, and died in a house that stood about thirty rods east of the house in which their son James now lives. Mr. McNutt died April 3rd, 1841, aged 73 years. His wife died October 9th, 1844, aged 68 years. Nancy, their eighth and youngest daughter, was born April 4th, 1778. She died at the house of her brother John, unmarried, in the year 1840, aged 62 years.

James, their second and youngest son, was born April 30th, 1780. He was married to Sarah, daughter of Luke Upham and Grace Locker, his wife. They inherited his father's property, where they reared their family and spent their lives. He died there February 6th, 1856, aged 75 years, and his wife died February 24th, 1859, aged 80 years. Margaret, their eldest daughter, was born February 16th, 1799. She was married to David Philips, who came from Scotland but a short time before, February 25th, 1820. They had five sons and three daughters. She died October 20th, 1851, aged 52 years, and her husband died January 22nd, 1862, aged 65 years. John, the only son of James and Sarah Dickson, was born December 10th, 1801. He was married to Hannah Jerusha Faulkner, of Economy, November 1st, 1832. They had three sons and three daughters. He inherits a part of what was his father's farm, which belonged to his grandfather. Elmira, their second daughter, was born January 2nd, 1803. She is living unmarried. Mary Baird, their third daughter, was born August 24th, 1804. She was .married to David Murray, January 26th, 1824. They had four sons and five daughters. She died December 20th, 1854, aged 50 years. Olive, their fourth daughter, was born April 28th, 1808. She was married to S. S. Nelson, merchant, of Truro, February 9th, 1837. They had three sons and three daughters. She died November 10th, 1872. aged 64 years, Grace, their fifth daughter, was born March 10th, 1810. She was married to John Philips, 1830. They had three sons and seven daughters. They now reside at River Philip, County of Cumberland. Elizabeth, their sixth daughter, was born December 17th, 1812. She was married to Richard Upham, of Truro, February 11th, 1841. She died July 17th, 1862, aged 48 years. Sarah, their seventh and youngest daughter, was born July 18th, 1815. She was married to Edward Faulkner, January 25th, 1844. They had two sons and three daughters.

CHAPTER XXXV.

John Oughterson was amongst the early settlers of Truro. He was married to Margaret, daughter of James and Elizabeth Johnson, of the Lower Village of Truro, in the the year 1774. Ann Glover, their eldest daughter, was born in Truro, September 3rd, 1775. She was married to Robert McNutt, of Masstown, March 25th, 1799. They had four sons and two daughters. She died December 18th, 1857, aged 82 years, and her husband died April 3rd, 1851, aged 86 years, George Washington, their eldest son, was born in Truro, May 25th, 1777. He removed to the United States, and was married there to Eliza Coats. He returned to Nova Scotia, and settled beside the old road leading from Truro to Halifax, at the Lake eleven miles from Truro. They had three sons and three daughters. He died May 30th, 1839, aged 62 years, and his wife died December 22nd, 1827. James, their second son, was born March 11th, 1779. He was married to Elizabeth Lord, of Kings County, about the year 1806. He settled for a short time in the woods, beside the old Halifax road, three miles from Truro. This place was afterwards owned by Charles

Morris, Surveyor General, and was sold by his son, John Spry Morris, to the late Robert H. Smith. James Oughterson removed to Canada, with his wife and family, about the year 1812, and died there some time ago. We know nothing of any of his descendants. Elizabeth Johnson, their second daughter, was born January 4th, 1782. She was mrrried to William McNutt of Masstown, 1804. They had three sons and seven daughters. She died July 1st, 1862, aged 80 years, and her husband died November 25th, 1857, aged 75 years. Robert Johnson, their third son, was born December 22nd, 1783. He carried on the business of brick making. He removed to Canada about the year 1828, and was married there to Miss Stubs. About 15 years after this they returned to Onslow, where he died July, 1862, aged 73 years. Nancy Oughterson, their third and youngest daughter, was born in Truro, May 2nd, 1787. She was married to John Hall, of Onslow Mountain, November 7th, 1809. They had five sons and four daughters. He settled and cleared a farm on Onslow Mountain, which is now owned by his son James. He died June 20th, 1861, aged 72 years, and his wife Nancy, died April 23rd, 1853, aged 66 years. John Oughterson died January 1st, 1831, aged 88 years, and his wife died March 27th, 1791, aged 39 years.

CHAPTER XXXVI.

The Township of Londonderry, or the largest part of it, was granted to James Fulton, Esq., and nineteen others, five shares, or rights each, and to Robert Barnhill and forty-eight others, certain other rights or shares, in all sixty-nine persons. This Grant was for 53,000 acres, and is dated March 6th, 1775, and signed by Francis Legge, who was then Governor of Nova Scotia. Colonel Alexander McNutt obtained a grant of 1000 acres of marsh and upland in the upper part of Londonderry, adjoining the Chiganoise River. Anthony Caverly had a grant of 1000 acres at Debert. These grants were dated before the grant of the Township. The ten rights at Debert were divided into eleven, to make one for the Rev. David Smith, being the first settled minister of Londonderry. These first grants caused considerable trouble when they came to subdivide the Township, under the writ of partition, in 1794.

James Fulton, Esq., filled the offices of Justice of the Peace and Judge of the Court of Common Pleas for a long time. He and Edward Mortimer, Esq., of Pictou, were the first from the country to offer themselves as candidates to represent the County of Halifax. A poll was opened at Halifax, Monday, November 18th, 1799, and was closed there Saturday the 23rd. At the close in Halifax Morris had 756 votes, Stewart 621, Wallace 596, Hartshorne 578, Tonge 392, Mortimer 109, and Fulton 86. The poll was adjourned, and opened again at Onslow, the 1st and 2nd days of December. At the close Morris had 782 votes, Stewart 626, Wallace 636, Hartshorne 597, Tonge 889, Mortimer 621, and Fulton 603. It was again adjourned, and held in Pictou from the 5th to the 13th of December. When finally closed, Tonge had 1257 votes, Mortimer 1077, Fulton 1001, Morris 1000, Wallace 888, Stewart 637, and Hartshorne 505. The four first named were returned, but Wallace protested against Tonge's return, and had it tried at the next sitting of the Assembly, when Tonge was unseated. There was a writ issued for another election. A poll was opened at Halifax on Saturday, March 22nd, 1800. The candidates were Michael Wallace and James Kent. On Tuesday following Kent withdrew, having received seven votes. Mr. Fulton represented the County of Halifax from the year 1799 until 1806, and Mr. Mortimer represented it from the year 1798 until the time of his death, which took place October 10th, 1819.

Mr. Fulton was born in Belfast, Ireland, in the year 1740, and came out to New England in the year 1760, when he was 20 years old. He continued there ten years, being engaged the most of the time at surveying land. He removed to Nova Scotia in the year 1770, and was married to Margaret Campbell, of the Folly, in 1771. She was born in Londonderry, Ireland, in the year 1754, and removed with her parents to Nova Scotia about the year 1762. They settled at Bass River, where they reared their numerous family and spent the remainder of their days, being the same place on which their son David lived and died, and their grandson, Thomas Fulton, now resides. They had seven sons and eight daughters. He surveyed and subdivided the whole of the Township of Londonderry under the writ of Partition, and made a plan of the same. This plan is still in use.

CHAPTER XXXVII.

Col. Jotham Blanchard was born in New Hampshire in 1745. He was married to Elizabeth Tredwell, about the year 1766, and in the year 1785 he removed to Truro, and purchased a part of what was Capt. John Morrison's house lot in the Upper Village of Truro, lying on the north side of the Parade. He built a two story house on the corner of the lot, where Mr. William McCully now resides. Here he spent his days, and died March 18th, 1807, aged 62 years, and his wife, Elizabeth, died January 5th, 1811, aged 72 years. His loyalty to the British Crown was the cause of his leaving the United States when they gained their independence.

John, the eldest son of Jotham and Elizabeth Blanchard, was born about the year 1767. He removed to the Southern States, and never came to Nova Scotia. Sarah, their eldest daughter, was born about the year 1769. She was married to Jacob Lipencutt. They had seven sons and two daughters. Mr. Lipencutt was a tanner by trade. He worked in the yard of Matthew Archibald, Esq., on Bible Hill for a number of years. Elizabeth, their second daughter, was born in the year 1770. She was married to Nathaniel Symonds. They had two sons and one daughter. They settled at Antigonish, where Colonel Blanchard had obtained a grant of a large tract of land on account of his loyalty. Mrs. Symonds died there September 25th, 1808, aged 38 years, and it is said that she was the first grown person who was interred in the cemetery of Antigonish Village. Rebecca, the third daughter of Col. Jotham and Elizabeth Blanchard, was born about the year 1772. She remained in New Hampshire and never came to Nova Scotia. She was married there to Mr. Shipard, and had a family of children. Hannah, their fourth daughter, was born about the year 1774. She was married to David Archibald, 3rd, in the year 1799. They had three sons and five daughters; they appear among the Archibalds.

Jonathan, the second son of Jotham and Elizabeth Blanchard, was born in New Hampshire, April 21st, 1776. He was left by his parents in New Hampshire when they removed to Nova Scotia, and he continued there and learned his trade, (which was a saddler and harness maker). He was married to Sarah Goggins, of the township of Dearing, County of Hillsborough, in the State of New Hampshire,

December 2nd, 1798. Sarah Goggins was born March 12th, 1780.
Jotham, their eldest son, was born in this same place, March 15th,
1800.

Jotham Blanchard was brought by his parents to Nova Scotia when
about one year old, and while at school in Truro and at play he fell
on the ice and hurt his knee ; he was quite lame the remainder of
his life. He remained in Truro until he was seventeen years old, and
after he was able to go about until he left Truro, his father
kept a poney for him to ride to school and wherever he went. He
went with his parents to Pictou in the year 1817, where he continued
to go to school, and afterwards he studied the law, and practiced in
the Courts of law pretty successfully. And in the election that was
held in the year 1830, for four persons to represent the County of
Halifax in Parliament, S. G. W. Archibald, William Lawson, George
Smith, and this Jotham Blanchard were the four successful candidates.
Lawrence Hartshorne, John A. Barry, Starr, and Blackadar were the
unsuccessful ones. This was the last election that was held for the
County of Halifax while it was so extensive. It then contained what
is now the whole of the Counties of Halifax, Colchester, and Pictou,
and this election took three weeks to get through with. There was a
great amount of excitement at this election, on account of the old
Council, which was then composed of twelve members, refusing to
pass the revenue act, that the House of Assembly had passed and
sent to them for their approval. In this act there was fourpence
added to the duty to be paid on every gallon of brandy imported into
the Province. And neither the Council nor Assembly would yield,
so there was not any revenue collected during that year. The
Assembly was dissolved, and the people were appealed to to decide
this important question. Either shortly before or after this election
Jotham Blanchard was traveling through Scotland, and he took ill,
and lodged at the house of Mrs. Margaret Spears, a widow, and she
was particularly attentive to him during the time of his sickness. In
a short time after he returned to Pictou ; his father went to Scotland
and accompanied her to Nova Scotia to be his wife, they were married
December, 1832, and shortly after this his health began to fail, and
the last time that he attended in the House of Assembly a covered
sleigh with a small stove in it was provided for his accommodation in
travelling from Pictou to Halifax. He died in Pictou Town, August
1839.

Elizabeth, the eldest daughter of Jonathan and Sarah Blanchard, was born in Truro, September 11th, 1802. She was married to John Gass, 1819. They settled near the West River of Pictou, where they are still living. They had fourteen sons and three daughters. Mrs. Gass died January, 1873.

Sophia, their second daughter, was born in Truro, December 25th, 1803. She was married to the Rev. John McLean, of the West River of Pictou, July 3rd, 1826. They had four sons and two daughters. He commenced his labors in Richibucto, 1826, and demitted his charge in 1833. He died 20th January, 1837, aged 36 years.

John, the second son of Jonathan and Sarah Blanchard, was born in Truro, December 1st, 1805. He learned the tinsmith trade at the West River of Pictou. He removed to Antigonish and settled there, where he spent the remainder of his life. He was married there to Frances Symonds. They had one son and three daughters. He died there November 26th, 1840, aged 35 years. William Earl Blanchard, their third son, was born July 19th, 1807. He settled at Miramichi, and was married to Eleanor Curry. They removed again to Australia. Jas. Blanchard, their fourth son, was born in Truro, March 27th, 1809. He followed the sea as a sea Captain. He died in the West Indies of yellow fever, February 26th, 1830. Stephen Smith Blanchard, their fifth son, was born in Truro, March 6th, 1811. He died February 18th, 1813. Edward Sherburne Blanchard, their sixth son, was born in Truro, December 11th, 1812. He was married to Margaret Pride, July 1st, 1834. They had three sons and eight daughters. They are now residing in Truro Village, and he is in business connected with the railroad and cars. Stephen Smith Blanchard, their seventh son, was born in Truro, April 28th, 1815, Hiram Blanchard, their eighth son was born in Pictou, April 18th, 1818. He died July 21st, 1819. Hiram Blanchard, their ninth son, was born in Pictou, January 17th, 1820. He was married to Eliza Cantrell. Nancy Blanchard, their third and youngest daughter, was born September 13th, 1822. She was married to the Rev. Samuel McCully, of Truro, in 1845. They had one son and six daughters. He is settled over a congregation in Prince William, in New Brunswick.

Sarah Goggins, Jonathan Blanchard's first wife, died in Pictou Town, September 25th, 1836, aged 56 years. He was married again to Martha, the third daughter of David Archibald, fourth, and Esther Cox, of Truro, November 2nd, 1837. They had one son and one daughter, who both died when they were young. Mr. Blanchard died

May 31st, 1843, aged 67 years. He removed to Truro from New Hampshire about the year 1801. He inherited his father's house and lot of land until about the year 1813, when he sold the house, with about half the land, to John Pearson. He purchased the largest part of the house in which Mr. John Ross now resides, on the north side of the Parade, from William Logan, who had built it and afterwards removed to Musquodoboit. This house then stood on the same place that the house now stands in which Daniel Eaton, Esq., and his two sons reside. He lived in it until the spring of the year 1817, when he purchased Mr. George McConnell's farm at the West River of Pictou, and built a house on it, which has ever been known by the name of the Ten Mile House. About seven or eight years after this he removed to Pictou Town, and built a large house there, where he continued the most of the time for the remainder of his life.

Edward Sherburne Blanchard, the third son of Jotham and Elizabeth Blanchard, was born in New Hampshire, February, 1778. He was brought by his parents to Nova Scotia in the year 1785, when he was seven years old. He was married to Jane, the fourth daughter of Matthew Archibald, Esq., and Janet Fisher, February 18th, 1802. He resided for a time in a house that was owned by John Smith, which stood between the house that Mr. Smith then resided in and the place which Mr. Robert Smith now resides. After this he built the house, which is still standing, on the north side of Salmon River, at the mouth of the old road leading to Pictou, where he spent the remainder of his days. At this place, he kept an inn until the year 1832. He then gave it up, and subscribed his name to the rules of a temperance society ; and, after this, he was an active advocate for the cause of temperance. He filled the offices of Justice of the Peace and Commissioner of Schools for a long time, and took a deep interest in the education of the young. He died Dec. 24th, 1856, aged 78 years and 10 months. His widow died February 9th, 1873, aged 90 years.

Nancy Blanchard, their eldest daughter, was born in Truro, Feb'y 5th, 1803. She was married to Isaac McCurdy, Esq., of Onslow, January 21st, 1828. They had five sons and two daughters. Jane Blanchard, their second daughter, was born July 1st, 1807. She was married to Dr. John Waddell, June 25th, 1844. They had one son and two daughters. Charles Blanchard, their eldest son, was born December 22nd, 1809. He was married to Nancy, the second daughter of John Blair, 3rd, and Elizabeth McNutt, January 30th,

17

1845. They had two sons and three daughters. He has been Sheriff of the County of Colchester since 1841. George Augustus Blanchard, their second son, was born Sept. 6th, 1811. He was married to Jane Robson, daughter of the Rev. Mr. Robson, of Halifax, October, 1840. They had two sons and three daughters. He has filled the office of Judge of the Court of Probate of King's County for a number of years. Jonathan Blanchard, their third son, was born July 26th, 1813. He was married to Sarah Story, of Halifax, May 21st, 1849. They had one son and two daughters. Mrs. Blanchard died in Halifax June 21st, 1857. James Flemming Blanchard, their fourth son, was born November 8th, 1815. He settled for a few years in Miramichi, and was married there to Jessie Johnstone Sept. 3rd, 1838. They had five sons and five daughters. He is now doing business as a merchant in Truro. He has filled the offices of Justice of the Peace and Prothonotary of the Supreme Court, for a number of years, in the County of Colchester. Elizabeth Blanchard, their third daughter, was born October 3rd, 1819. She was married to the Rev. James Waddell, September 23rd, 1837. They had three sons and four daughters. They appear among the Waddells. Mr. Waddell died in Halifax, March 14th, 1870, aged 65 years. John Blanchard, their sixth son, was born March 24th, 1822. He was married to Gertrude Woollenhoft, of Windsor, 1845. They had four sons and three daughters. He is settled in Kentville. Edward Blanchard, their fifth son, was born October 10th, 1817. He was married to Margaret Metzler, June 4th, 1864. They had two sons and one daughter. He inherited a large part of his father's farm. Sarah Blanchard, their fourth daughter, was born December 23rd, 1823. William Henry Blanchard, their seventh and youngest son, was born June 16th, 1827. He studied law, and settled in Windsor. He was married there to Maria Timlen July, 1847. They had two sons and one daughter. Mrs. Blanchard died, and he was married again to Hannah, daughter of David McCurdy, of Onslow, and Mary Archibald, widow of the late Angus Tupper, October, 1867. They have one son.

Nancy Blanchard, the fifth and youngest daughter of Jotham and Elizabeth Blanchard, was born in New Hampshire, about the year 1780. She was brought, by her parents, to Nova Scotia when she was about five years old. She was married to the Rev. John Waddell Sept. 2nd, 1802. They had three sons and four daughters, who appear among the Waddells. She died August 18th, 1818, aged 38 years, and her husband died November 13th, 1842, aged 72 years.

CHAPTER XXXVIII.

Deacon Samuel Fisher was born in the North of Ireland, in the year 1722, and was of Scottish descent. His father was a weaver. He came to America in 1740, in the 19th year of his age. The ship in which he came was usually spoken of as "The starved ship." The vessel was so scantily supplied with provisions, that, long before the voyage was completed, one pint of oatmeal for each individual on board, and a proportionate allowance of water, was all that remained. Mr. Fisher once went to the mate with a tablespoon to obtain some water, which was refused him, there being but two-thirds of a bottle-full on board. Mr. Fisher's custom was to take a spoonfull of meal and having moistened it with salt water, to eat it raw. The passengers and crew, having subsisted in this manner for fourteen days, were at length reduced to the necessity of eating the bodies of those who died. Even this resource failed them; and, at length, Mr. Fisher was selected to give up his life to preserve the lives of the rest. Providentially, however, a vessel hove in sight; and their signals of distress being observed, they obtained relief, and he was saved. So deep an impression did the horrors of that passage make upon the mind of Mr. Fisher, that, in after life, he could never see, without pain, the least morsel of food wasted, or a pail of water thrown on the ground carelessly. On his arrival in this country, he was bound by the Captain to a man in Roxbury for the payment of his passage. He came to Londonderry, N. H., about one or two years after, and became a member of the family of Mr. Matthew Taylor, whose daughter, Sarah, he married, when he was twenty-five years of age. He was made ruling elder in the church in this place during the ministry of the Rev. David McGregor, and remained in this office until he was no longer able to perform its duties on account of his age. He was well instructed in the great principles of the gospel. He had a most happy faculty of improving the occurrences which took place about him for the religious instruction of his family. Mr. Fisher was married three times, and had twelve children, eleven of whom arrived at adult age, and ten of whom survived him. Ten of his children were married, and most of them lived to an advanced age. The average age of four of them was ninety-one years. His descendants, in the year 1850, were nine hundred and fifteen, and are scattered through nearly all the States of the Union, through Nova Scotia and Canada. Some of them are ministers and some elders in the church. It is estimated that three-fourths of those over twenty years of age are professors of religion. Mr. Fisher died in Londonderry, New Hampshire, April 10th, 1806, aged 84 years.

Janet, his daughter, was born in New Hampshire, in the year 1750. She was married to Matthew, the eldest son of Samuel and Eleanor Archibald, in 1767. She came to Nova Scotia with her husband, who had returned from Truro to New Hampshire, and they were married there. They had seven sons and five daughters

Samuel, son of Deacon Samuel Fisher, was born in Londonderry, New Hampshire. He removed to Nova Scotia in 1767. He was married to Mary, daughter of Eliakim Tupper, Esq., and Elizabeth Newcomb. He settled on the interval farm that is now owned by Mr. Samuel Butler and Mr. Patterson, on the south side of the Stewiacke River, in 1784. He was a worthy man; *he* went by the name of Deacon Fisher also. He died in Stewiacke, May 12th 1812. His wife died April 23rd, 1812. Elizabeth Fisher, their eldest daughter, was born in 1787. She was married to Adam Johnson Sept., 1806. They had two sons and five daughters. She died February 14th, 1843. Mr. Johnson died August 8th, 1823. Sarah Fisher, their second daughter, was born in 1789. She was married to Eddy Whidden in 1807. They had five sons and five daughters. She died December, 1835. Mr. Whidden died in 1858. Rachel Fisher,, their third daughter, was born in 1791. She was married to Patrick Tupper. They had a family. They removed to Ohio in 1821. Ebenezer Fisher, their eldest son, was born in 1793. He was married to Olivia Carter, of Onslow. They had seven sons and one daughter. He died at Wallace in June, 1867. Nancy Fisher, their fourth daughter, was born in 1795. She was married to Daniel Tupper in 1814. They had three sons and three daughters. She died August 10th, 1846. John Waddell Fisher, their second son, was born in 1798. He was married to Margaret Godfrey. They had one daughter. He died in 1827. Charlotte Fisher, their fifth daughter, was born in 1800. She was married to Daniel C. Upham, of Otterbrook, Oct., 1826. They had two sons and three daughters. James Fisher, their third son, was born in 1802. He learned the saddler trade with Mr. Knight in Truro. He removed to Ohio, U. S., and he died there in 1870. Mary Fisher, their sixth daughter, was born in 1804. She was married to Richard Best. They removed to New Brunswick.

Margaret Fisher, their seventh daughter, was born in 1806. She was married to Samuel Fulton, They had four sons and one daughter. Mr. Fulton died. She was married to James Wilson, of New Annan. They had two sons. She died at Bass River in 1868.

CHAPTER XXXIX.

The Rev. David Smith was born in Scotland in the year 1732. He studied there for the ministry, and in August, 1769, he was appointed by the Synod of Edinburgh as a missionary for Nova Scotia. He came out from Scotland in the year 1770, and received a call from the people of Londonderry to be their pastor, which he accepted. He was settled there and labored among them about twenty-five years, and shared the hardships of a newly settled country with his small congregation. To him his people looked for consolation in the hour of tribulation, and the fruit of his labors may be traced to the generation of the present day. Although he was settled in Londonderry, his labors were not altogether confined to this place. He visited the people of Cumberland and Pictou and preached to them, before the arrival of the Rev. James McGregor in Pictou, which was in the year 1786. He was married to Agnes Spear about the year 1756, about fourteen years before he left Scotland.

James, their eldest son, was born about the year 1757, and was brought by his father to Nova Scotia when about thirteen years old. In the year 1785 he was returned to represent Londonderry in the House of Assembly, and on December 5th of this year he took his seat in the Assembly, and continued to represent the Township of Londonderry until April 6th, 1789, when his seat was declared vacant. He obtained a grant of 500 acres of land in Middle Stewiacke. It was laid out in rear of the front lots, being part of Smithfield, from which the place took its name. James Smith was married to Elizabeth, daughter of William and Dorothy Putnam. They had one son; his name was William Putnam Smith. He married Miss Campbell, and they have a family and are settled at Antigonish. Mr. Robert Hennesy's wife, of the Lower Village of Truro, is a daughter of theirs. James Smith removed to Stewiacke with his father-in-law.

and died there.   His widow was married again to Capt. James Miller about the year 1797.   They removed and settled in Antigonish.

David, the second son of the Rev. David Smith and Agnes Spear, was born in Scotland about the year 1759, and was brought by his father to Nova Scotia.   He was married to Rebecca, the only daughter of William Cock and Sidney Holmes, 1786.   They had four sons.   He was a cabinetmaker, and carried on his business at Halifax, where he died in 1800.   John, the third son of the Rev. David Smith and Agnes Spear, was born in Scotland in the year 1761, and shortly after this Mrs. Smith died, and Mr. Smith came to Nova Scotia a widower, with his two eldest sons, and left his youngest son, John, with his friends in Scotland, until the year 1774.   He then sent for him, and he came to Nova Scotia when he was thirteen years old. He was married to Sarah Crowe, the second daughter of Thomas Crowe and Sarah Barnhill, of Beaver Brook, in the year 1801.   They had seven sons and two daughters.   He inherited his father's property at Debert, which was granted to him (his father) as the first minister of Londonderry, where he and his wife spent the remainder of their days.   He died November 1st, 1831, aged 70 years, and his widow died October, 1847, aged 67 years.

Rev. David Smith was married the second time to Miss Margaret Rogers, of Chiganoise, about the year 1778.   But this was not to be his abiding place.   On March 25th, 1795, he changed his earthly habitation for a mansion prepared for him by his Celestial Father. This melancholy bereavement of so venerable a man at once struck a damp on the cheering prospects of his congregation.

CHAPTER XL.

Rev. John Brown was born in Tossaway, County of Kinross, Scotland, in 1766.   While he was attending to his duties at College, at times he attended the meetings of Synod.   At one of those meetings an urgent appeal was read from Dr. McGregor, of Pictou, stating the destitution of some parts of Nova Scotia for want of a preached Gospel, and calling on the Synod for assistance by sending more ministers to Nova Scotia.   One of those appeals made a powerful impression on his mind.   In connection with his fellow student, the late Rev. Duncan Ross, they drew up and signed a paper, by which they both devoted themselves to the mission work, should their services be accepted. This paper fell into the hands of the Professor of Divinity, having been left unintentionally inside of one of the volumes of the Divinity Library. When their intentions were known by the Presbytery, they were hurried on with their preparations for an early departure. He was ordained in February, 1795. In the same month he was married to Margaret Beveridge, of Paisley. Before he left home he purchased the Bible in two volumes, and wrote the name of Margaret Brown in each of them on March 6th, 1795. They were pocket Bibles, and have been used constantly since that date. The writer had the satisfaction of seeing them on June 8th, 1872, and copying the dates of the births of their children from them. They were in good condition, with scarcely a leaf started from the binding. When they were about to leave their native land, never to see it again, and bid adieu to friends and relations ; the morning they were to leave his father's house to proceed to America, in March, 1795, the 121st Psalm was selected for their song of praise ; no doubt but it was sung in a solemn manner.

> "I to the hills will lift mine eyes, from whence doth come mine aid,
> My safety cometh from the Lord, who Heaven and Earth hath made.
> Thy foot He'll not let slide, nor will He slumber that thee keeps—
> Behold He that keeps Israel, He slumbers not nor sleeps.
> The Lord thee keeps, the Lord thy shade on thy right hand doth stay,
> The moon by night thee shall not smite, nor yet the sun by day.
> The Lord shall keep thy soul, He shall preserve thee from all ill,
> Henceforth thy going out and in, God keep forever will."

After they left home they were detained at the seaport for the sailing of the ship. During their delay Mr. Brown preached on Sabbath. His mother having heard that he was to preach, went to hear him, but she did not enter the Church, where she might be seen by her son ; she remained outside where she could hear him. Having bid him farewell once, she did not wish to have it to do the second time. The ship sailed about the middle of March, with Mr. and Mrs. Brown and the Rev. Duncan Ross on board. They arrived at New York, May 27th, 1795. They stopped there and preached one Sabbath, and then proceeded to Halifax. Mr. Ross went by land, or boat, to Londonderry, and preached there one Sabbath (Mr. Smith having died March 25th, while they were on their passage). He proceeded thence to Truro, and on his way called at Chiganoise and married Alexander Miller to Rebecca Baird, on June 29th, 1795. Dr. McGregor met Mr. Ross at the house of the Rev. Daniel Cock, in

Truro, with a suitable horse for him to ride to Pictou. The next day they proceeded on to Pictou. About the same time Mr. and Mrs. Brown arrived there also, and received a hearty welcome from Dr. McGregor, who had been nine years in the wilderness almost alone. During the time they remained in Pictou, the Sacrament of the Lord's Supper was dispensed on a small piece of interval beside the water of the Middle River, a short distance below the Bridge. They continued their mission work until the summer of 1796. When the Presbytery met this year there were two calls for each of them. One from Prince Edward Island and another from Pictou for Mr. Ross; one from Amherst and another from Londonderry for Mr. Brown. The first sermon Mr. Brown preached in Londonderry produced the most happy results. He preached from Numbers 23rd, and 10th verse, "Let me die the death of the righteous, and let my last end be like His." Although there were divisions in the congregation, they soon laid aside their differences and gave him a unanimous call. He accepted their call, and was inducted to the charge of the congregation about Sept., 1796.

The first whom he married there were Thomas Ellis and Elizabeth Deyarmond, of Chiganoise, about the first of October, 1796. The second pair that he married were Thomas Morrison, of Debert, and Mary O'Brien, of Noel, October 25th, 1796. The last that he married were Matthew Peppard and Miss Sutherland, from Westchester Mountain. He continued to labor faithfully and zealously for nearly fifty-three years in his congregation. In July, 1845, on the same day that he had preached his first sermon in Londonderry fifty years before, a Jubilee was held, at which there was a large gathering of ministers and people of his own congregation, and from neighboring ones also. At the time that the Presbyterian Church of Nova Scotia was about to send a missionary to the Islands of the South Seas, the Rev. John Geddie offered to go forth as her missionary. His offer was accepted, and preparations were made for him and his family to leave Nova Scotia to carry the glad tidings and good news of the Gospel to the heathens. Shortly before they left, there was a large meeting of the ministers and people, held in the old meeting house at Onslow, on November 8th, 1846, to bid them farewell and to encourage them in their work by the prayers and advice of the Church. At this meeting the Rev. Mr. Brown was the person who gave the parting address. This address was given by him in a very solemn manner. He was at the time about eighty years old, and had experienced leaving his native land and removing into the wilds of

America, and knew what it was to leave home with its endearments. It is believed that he never regretted undertaking the work of the ministry, or of settling in Londonderry. When he drew near the close of his life he said that, " If he had his life to live over again he would be a minister. Were I to choose a field of labor, of all the world I would choose America, and of what I know of it, there is no place in it that I would prefer to Londonderry." His attachment to his congregation was strong ; his labor of love and earnest desire for the welfare of souls made that impression on his people which will not soon be forgotten. His desire was that, if it was agreeable to the Divine Will, he might not outlive his usefulness. He died Friday, April 7th, 1848, aged 82 years. After his death his remains were followed by a large concourse of sorrowing friends to the grave. After the burial they repaired to the house of God where their pastor's voice had been so long heard, but was now silent in death, and were addressed by the Rev. Messrs. Baxter and McCulloch, and to call to mind that text which constituted the theme of their departed pastor's first sermon to them : " Let me die the death of the righteous, and let my last end be like his." Mrs. Brown died December 13th, 1848, aged 77 years. They lived together as man and wife more than fifty-two years. When they were first settled in Londonderry they boarded a few years with Robert McElhenney, who then resided on the farm lying on the point between the Folly and Debert Rivers, being the same on which his two grandsons now reside. A few years after, he purchased land, had some of it improved and buildings put up on it, being the same that is now inherited by his daughter, Janet, and her husband, Isaac West.

Agnes Brown, their eldest daughter, was born at the house of Mr. McElhenney, Nov. 26th, 1795. She was married to Thomas Fletcher, of Masstown, July 5th, 1816. They had four sons and five daughters. She died January 3rd, 1866, aged 70 years. Her husband died Oct. 11th, 1872, aged 82 years. John, the eldest son of Rev. John and Margaret Brown, was born August 8th, 1797. He was married to Susannah, daughter of William Davidson, and Sarah Ann Denny his wife, Nov. 25th, 1823. He settled on a part of his father's land. Janet Brown, their second daughter, was born February 27th, 1799. She was married to Isaac West February 15th, 1827. They had three sons and two daughters. They inherit what was her father's property. Sarah Brown, their third daughter, was born Feby. 5th, 1800. She was married to David, the youngest son of James Fulton, Esq., and Margaret Campbell, March 15th, 1825. They had three sons and four daughters. They inherited what was the homestead part of his father's property at Bass River. She died there Sept. 9th, 1858. Mr. Fulton died March 26th, 1862. Thomas and Ross-ann Brown, their twin son and daughter, were born May 1st, 1805. Thomas Brown died a bachelor February 23rd, 1830, in the 25th year ot his age. Rossann Brown, their fourth daughter, was married to Joseph, the second son of Thomas and Esther Crow, of Debert River, November 2nd, 1823. They had three sons and three daughters. She died May 15th, 1856, aged 51 years. Mr. Crow died in March, 1870, aged 69 years.

CHAPTER XLI.

James Johnson was born in the North of Ireland, in the month of June, 1719. He was married to Elizabeth Patterson, about the year 1744. They had six sons and four daughters before they left Ireland. They removed to Nova Scotia in the year 1761, and settled in the Lower Village of Truro. He was one of the Grantees of the Township of Truro. His house stood near the same place that his great-grandson, Robert Johnson, now resides. He was one of the seven elders of the Presbyterian congregation of Truro, who were elected in the summer of the year 1770. His wife, Elizabeth, died December 2nd, 1776, and he was married again to Margaret McRoberts, February 27th, 1777. He died in the year 1798, aged 79 years, and his second wife, Margaret, died March 27th, 1782.

Adam Johnson, their eldest son, was born in Ireland, in the year 1745. He was one of the Grantees of the Township of Truro. It is said that he removed to the United States, and we know nothing of him or his descendants.

Robert Johnson, their second son, was born in the year 1747. He was married to Susannah, daughter of James and Catherine Gourley, of the Lower Village of Truro, December 2nd, 1778. He inherited his father's farm in the Lower Village of Truro. He carried on farming and shipbuilding. He was Major of the Militia of Colchester. He was chosen an elder in the Presbyterian Church in the year 1799, being the next year after the settlement of the Rev. John

Waddell in Truro. He died April 4th, 1815, aged 68 years; and his wife, Susannah, died in July, 1844, aged 86 years.

Adam, the eldest son of Robert and Susan Johnson, was born in Truro October 3rd, 1779. He was married to Elizabeth, daughter of Samuel Fisher and Mary Tupper his wife, of Stewiacke, September, 1806. He removed and settled at the South Branch of Stewiacke, in the year 1809. He removed again, and settled on a part of the farm that was owned by his father-in-law, being the same that is now owned by Mr. Patterson. He died at this place August 8th, 1823, aged 44 years, and his widow died at Brookfield, February 14th, 1843, aged 56 years.

Catherine Johnson, their eldest daughter, was born in Truro, Oct. 26th, 1807. She was married to James McMullon, Oct. 4th, 1825. They had seven sons and four daughters. Mr. McMullon died Aug. 8th, 1869, aged 66 years.

Elizabeth, the second daughter of Adam and Elizabeth Johnson, was born in Stewiacke, February 16th, 1810. She was married to Adam, the fifth son of Matthew Johnson and Ruth Fisher his wife, October, 1830. They had four sons and six daughters. She died November 14th, 1858, aged 48 years, and her husband died August, 1866, aged 70 years. Susan Johnson, their third daughter, was born May 16th, 1812. She was married to William Jeffers December, 1842. They had five sons and one daughter. She died in 1859, aged 47 years. Mary, the fourth daughter of Adam Johnson and Elizabeth Fisher his wife. was born May 16th, 1814. She was married to Daniel Fisher October, 1842. They had four sons and two daughters. She died June 25th, 1865, aged 51 years, and her husband died August 1st, 1864, aged 65 years. Robert, the eldest son of Adam and Elizabeth Johnson, was born April 1st, 1818. He was married to Mary, daughter of William Holstead and Jane Brownrig his wife, July 8th, 1846. They had two sons and three daughters. He died March 7th, 1866. Adam their second son, was born May, 1820. He was married to Sarah Jane, daughter of Captain Samuel Soley and Nancy Hamilton his wife, February 8th, 1842. They had six sons and five daughters. Janet Johnson, their fifth daughter, was born April, 1822. She was married to Charles Carter, of Debert River, in the year 1851.

Thomas, the second son of Robert and Susan Johnson, was born in Truro, February 26th, 1781. He was married to Rachel J., daughter of Captain John McKeen, and Rachel Johnson his wife,

September 20th, 1804. He built a house near the place that Mr. William McNutt now resides, in the Lower Village of Truro, where he kept an inn for a few years. He died there, of consumption, in the year 1809, and his widow was married again to Andrew Yuill October 22nd, 1811. They had one son. She died April 18th, 1813. Robert, the eldest son of Thomas and Rachel Johnson, was born December 25th, 1805. He was married to Margaret, daughter of Daniel Carter and Jane Kennedy his wife, February 28th, 1851. They had three sons and three daughters. John, the second son of Thomas and Rachel Johnson, was born January, 1808. He was married to Rebecca, the third daughter of Colonel William Dickson and Rebecca Pearson his wife. They had one son and one daughter. He was Clerk of the Peace for Colchester a few years. He died April 8th, 1848, aged 40 years, and his widow died at her daughter's house in New Jersey about the year 1867. Catherine, the only daughter of Robert and Susan Johnson, was born September 26th, 1784. She was married to Robert Anderson. They had two sons and two daughters. They settled in Cape Breton, where she and her husband died some time ago.

Hugh, the third son of Robert and Susan Johnson, was born October 6th, 1786. He was married to Elizabeth, the only daughter of Thomas Dickey and Elizabeth Scott his wife, November 22nd, 1811. He inherited the homestead half of his father's property. He died November 17th, 1841, aged 55 years. Thomas Dickey Johnson, their eldest son, was born October 16th, 1812. He was married to Susan, the second daughter of William Pearson and Nancy Dempsey his wife, June 23rd, 1836. Thomas Dunlap Johnson, their eldest son, was born November 6th, 1837. He was married to Margaret, the second daughter of William Putnam Archibald and Mary Jane Gourley his wife, October 16th, 1860. They have three sons and one daughter. Sarah, the only living daughter of Thomas and Susan Johnson, was married to Henry McLain, of Londonderry, February 15th, 1871. The remainder of their family died when they were young. Robert, the second son of Hugh and Elizabeth Johnson, was born February 28th, 1814. He was married to Janet, the eldest daughter of John H. Notting and Martha Kent, his wife, February 25th, 1843. They had two sons and five daughters. Elizabeth, the eldest daughter of Hugh and Elizabeth Johnson, was born November 10th, 1815. She was married to Samuel Pollock, of Lower Stewiacke, January, 1838. They had five sons and three daughters. Ann, their second daughter, was born October 10th, 1817. She was married to William Sterns McNutt February 4th, 1835. They had two sons and two daughters. She died November 27th, 1857, aged 40 years. George Scott, the third son of Hugh and Elizabeth Johnson, was born September 8th, 1819. He was married to Eunice, the eldest daughter of James D. Johnson and Miziann McNutt his wife, December 28th, 1841. Their only son, Alfred, left home and went to California, and was shot there by the Indians June 18th, 1870. Rachel, their third daughter, was born January 9th, 1823. She died unmarried July, 1845, aged 22 years. John, their fourth son, was born May 8th, 1827. He left Nova Scotia in the year 1852, and his friends have not heard from him since the year 1854. William, their fifth and youngest son, was born February 8th, 1829. He was married to Mary Jane, daughter of James D. and Miziann Johnson, May 14th, 1858. They had two sons and two daughters. He now resides in the house that his father purchased from John H. Notting. Rebecca, the youngest daughter of Hugh and Elizabeth Johnson, was born August 29th, 1832. She died unmarried December 15th, 1857, aged 25 years.

Stephen, the fourth son of Robert and Susan Johnson, was born June 5th, 1788. He was married to Nancy, the only daughter of Captain James Miller and Eleanor Mahan, his wife, July 27th, 1811. He inherited the half of his father's farm. He removed from there to Stewiacke, where he died December 26th, 1856, aged 68 years ; and his wife, Nancy, died November 25th, 1870, aged 86 years. Robert Johnson, their eldest son, was born in Truro, September 19th, 1818. He was married to Nancy Bryden, of Pictou, about 1842. They had four sons and three daughters. Mrs Johnson died in the year 1856, and he was married again to Mary Pratt, in 1858. James Charles, their second son, was born June 5th, 1824. He was married to Margaret, daughter of Daniel Archibald, Esq., and Rebecca Newcomb, his wife, July 4th, 1855. They have two sons and five daughters. He inherits what was his father's farm, on the Mountain of Stewiacke. Stephen, the youngest son of Stephen and Nancy Johnson, was born April 24th, 1826. He removed to the United States, and died there October 22nd, 1849, aged 23 years. Susan, the second daughter of Stephen and Nancy Johnson, was born August 21st, 1828. She was married to Robert Montieth, of Hants County, December 17th, 1862. Eleanor, their eldest daughter, was born November 7th, 1821. She was married to Robert Nelson, of Stewiacke, in the year, 1862.

Nancy, their youngest daughter, was born September 15th, 1830. She was married to Dr. Leander Barry. They had two sons. She died March 28th, 1870.

James, the fifth son of Robert and Susan Johnson, was born February 9th, 1790. He died a bachelor March, 1851, aged 61 years. Robert, the sixth and youngest son of Robert and Susan Johnson, was born October 21st, 1788. He was married to Rachel, the second daughter of Dumb John Johnson, October 12th, 1820. Margaret, their eldest daughter, was born June 2nd, 1821. She was married to William Boomer January, 1841. They had two sons. She died August, 1845, and her husband died. Thomas Johnson, their eldest son, was born February 1st, 1824. He was married to Mary Jane McCully, of Masstown, June 30th, 1851. They have five sons. He now resides on the same place that Lieutenant John Johnson and his son, Dumb John Johnson, lived and died. Susan, their second daughter, was born December 13th, 1825. She was married to Hugh Clarke April 18th, 1841. They had four sons and four daughters. She died Sept 9th, 1872, aged 47 years. John, their second son, was born July 31st, 1828. He removed to Portland, Me., and was married there to Elizabeth Archibald. They have four sons and three daughters. Hugh, their third son, was born October 3rd, 1830. He removed to the United States, and his people have not heard from him during eight years past. Isabell, their third daughter, was born December 18th, 1832. She died June 18th, 1858, aged 26 years. Henry, their fourth son, was born September 3rd, 1837. He was married to Mary Scott January 12th, 1864. They have four sons and one daughter. He died October 31st, 1872, aged 35 years. Catherine, their fourth daughter, was born July 1st, 1839. She was married to William Piers, of Wallace River, January 5th, 1859. They had one son and six daughters. Mary Jane, their fifth daughter, was born May 9th, 1841. She was married to James McDonald, of Pictou, December 7th, 1860. They had one son and two daughters. She died November 1st, 1870. Harriet, their sixth daughter, was born May 20th, 1843. She was married to Wentworth McDonald September 14th, 1867. They have two sons. Elizabeth, their seventh daughter, was born February 14th, 1845. She removed to United States. Mary, the eldest daughter of James and Elizabeth Johnson, was born in the year 1749. She was married to Adam Boyd. They had one daughter. She died May 15th, 1790, aged 41 years. Margaret, their second daughter, was born in the year 1751.

She was married to John Oughterson in the year 1774. They had three sons and three daughters. She died March 27th, 1791, aged 39 years. Rachel, the third daughter of James and Elizabeth Johnson, was born in the year 1752. She was married to James Rogers, of Shepody. Elizabeth, their fourth daughter, was born in the year 1754. She was married to James Rutherford February 15th, 1785. They had four sons and two daughters. She died about the year 1802.

Matthew, the third son of James and Elizabeth Johnson, was born in the year 1756, and was brought by his parents to Nova Scotia when he was five years old. He was married to Ruth, the fifth daughter of William Fisher and Eleanor Archibald, his wife, about the year 1782. They were the first persons who settled in Upper Stewiacke. They removed there in the fall of the year 1783, and lived one winter there, not having any neighbours nearer than Middle Stewiacke, a distance of seven miles. His farm was the same that is now owned by Eliakim Tupper, Esq., and his sons. At one time he had to go to Truro, a distance of nearly twenty miles, through the woods, and could not return the same day. His wife remained alone during his absence. At another time while he was absent, and his wife was alone, a bear came and tried to get their sheep from a small pen that was built up against the side of their log house. Mrs. Johnson went out with her dog and drove him off, and disappointed the bear of his prey. At another time Mr. Stewtly Horton, who was married to Hannah Fisher, sister of Mrs. Johnson, and settled at Musquodoboit, had been to Truro with his load of wheat on his back to the mill, and was returning home, he arrived at the north side of the Stewiacke River, in sight of the light from his brother-in-law's window, on the south side of the River, where he expected to lodge during the night. But before crossing the Bridge, which was only a fallen tree, he leaned himself back against the large root of a fallen tree to ease the load from his back and rest himself for a little before he would cross the River. In this position he sank into a sound sleep, and did not awake until the sun was shining clear the next morning far above the horizon. About the year 1792 he sold his farm to Eliakim Tupper, Esq. (this Mr. Tupper was grandfather of Eliakim Tupper, Esq., that now lives on it), and removed and settled at Musquodoboit. Some time after he exchanged farms with Mr. Thomas Ellis, and removed to Pembroke, where he died January 20th, 1825, aged 68 years, and his wife died August 8th, 1825, aged 62 years.

Margaret, the eldest daughter of Matthew and Ruth Johnson, was born August 14th, 1784.   She was married to James Dean, of Musquodoboit, May, 1805.   They had two sons and two daughters. She died September 11th, 1811, aged 27 years.   Elizabeth, their second daughter, was born in the year 1786.   She was married to James Guild, of Musquodoboit, November 10th, 1803.   They had five sons and seven daughters.   Mr. Guild died January 12th, 1862.

William, the eldest son of Matthew and Ruth Johnson, was born January 16th, 1788.   He died a bachelor, January 20th, 1819, aged 31 years.

James, their second son, was born March 13th, 1790.   He was married to Mary, daughter of John Johnson and Elizabeth Fulton, his wife, in the year 1813.   He inherited his father's property.   They had four sons and three daughters.   Mrs. Johnson died, and he was married again to Ann, daughter of John and Elizabeth Johnson, widow of the late Alexander Johnson, in the year 1830.   They had one son and two daughters.   He died March 12th, 1837, aged 47 years, and his widow died in the year 1844.   Adam, their third son, was born January 8th, 1792.   He died November 15th, 1794.

Alexander, their fourth son, was born December 8th, 1793.   He was married to Ann, daughter of John and Elizabeth Johnson, about the year 1816.   They had one daughter.   He died September 13th, 1818, aged 25 years.

Adam, their fifth son, was born December 8th, 1795.   He was married to Elizabeth, daughter of Adam Johnson and Elizabeth Fisher, his wife, October, 1830.   They had four sons and six daughters.   He died August, 1866, aged 70 years, and his wife died November 14th, 1858, aged 48 years.

John, their sixth son, was born July 8th, 1798.   He was married to Janet, daughter of Robert and Elizabeth Logan, April, 1825. They had five sons and four daughters.   He died December 12th, 1869, aged 71 years, and his wife died August 21st, 1863, aged 61 years.   David, their seventh son, was born March 11th, 1800.   He was married to Eunice Godfrey in the year 1831.   They had three sons and five daughters.   Matthew, their eighth son, was born April 28th, 1802.   He died January 16th, 1820, aged 18 years.   Robert, their ninth son, was born June 11th, 1804.   He died November 15th, 1834, aged 30 years.   Archibald Gammell, their tenth son, was born July 8th, 1807.   He died a young man.

James, the fourth son of James and Elizabeth Johnson, was born

October 16th, 1758.   He was married to Ann, daughter of James and Ann Fulton, of the Lower Village of Truro, December 10th, 1786. He followed the sea for a number of years, and during that time his family resided at Maitland.   About the year 1800 he quit the sea and removed to the south side of the River, in Middle Stewiacke, and settled on the farm upon which his youngest son, Samuel, and others now reside, where he died October 11th, 1842, aged 84 years.   His wife died January 15th, 1824, aged 59 years.   Jane, their eldest daughter, was born 1787.   She was married to William O'Brien, Esq., of Noel, October 1st, 1807.   They had one son.   She died shortly after.   James, their eldest son, was born 1789.   He died in 1801, aged 12 years.

Adam, the second son of James and Ann Johnson, was born May 14th, 1791.   He was married to Jane, the youngest daughter of James Fulton, Esq., and Margaret Campbell, of Bass River, February 17th, 1818.   He inherited a part of his father's farm at Middle Stewiacke, where he continued the whole of his life.   He died August, 1862, aged 71 years.   Ann Dick Johnson, their eldest daughter, was born December 18th, 1818.   She was married to William D. O'Brien, of Noel, February 9th, 1847.   They have two sons and five daughters. James, the eldest son of Adam and Jane Johnson, was born January, 1821.   He was married to Rossann Fulton, daughter of David Fulton and Mary Brown, of Bass River, March 5th, 1852.   They have three sons and one daughter.   He is settled at Bass River, where he carries on his business as blacksmith.   John Logan Johnson, their second son was born Sept. 25th, 1822.   He was married to Mary Jane, second daughter of Francis Creelman and Esther Fulton his wife, March 18th, 1855.   Margaret, the second daughter of Adam and Jane Johnson was born Sept. 3rd, 1824.   She was married to Moses Clark Brenton, March 17th, 1853.   They have three sons and two daughters.   George, their third son was born March 24th, 1827. He was married to Jane, daughter of Charles Corbett and Esther Rutherford his wife, Oct. 25th, 1856.   They have four sons and one daughter.   Samuel Johnson, their fourth son was born Feby. 20th, 1829.   He was married to Eleanor Grant June 29th, 1857.   They have three sons.   He is a Minister of the Gospel and settled over the Presbyterian Congregation of Harvey, N. B.   Andrew Johnson, their fifth son was born April 27th, 1832.   He was married to Susan O'Brien of Noel, Sept. 13th, 1860.   They have two sons.   He is settled in Truro Village where he carries on a large business at house building.

18

Agnes Johnson, their third daughter was born Decr. 13th, 1835. She was married to Thomas O'Brien of Noel, Novr., 1862. She died July, 1867, aged 31 years.

Margaret, the second daughter of James and Ann Johnson, was born March 14th, 1793. She was married to John D. Christie Feb. 8th, 1827. They had one son and one daughter. She died Nov. 29th, 1856, aged 63 years. Mr. Christie died May 11th, 1866, aged 82 years.

Ann, the third daughter of James and Ann Johnson, was born March 14th, 1795. She was married to John Logan, of Upper Stewiacke, Dec. 27th, 1813. They had seven sons and two daughters. She died Dec. 18th, 1830, aged 35 years. Mr. Logan died March 23rd, 1863, aged 74 years. Elizabeth Johnson, their fourth daughter was born Feby. 1st, 1797. She was married to Andrew O'Brien, of Noel, Dec., 1819. They had six sons and five daughters. She died Dec. 2nd, 1856, aged 59 years. Mary Johnson, their fifth daughter was born Dec. 11th, 1799. She is living still.

Susan Johnson, their sixth daughter was born Nov. 22nd, 1801. She was married to Andrew Creelman, Dec. 28th, 1824. They had five sons and four daughters. She died Jany. 11th, 1863, aged 61 years. Mr. Creelman died July 15th, 1867, aged 65 years.

Samuel, the third and youngest son of James and Ann Johnson was born Jany. 10th, 1807. He was married to Rebecca, daughter of Samuel Fulton and Rebecca O'Brien, his wife, of Bass River, March 10th, 1829. He inherits a part of what was his father's farm at Middle Stewiacke. Samuel Fulton Johnson, their eldest son, was born June 15th, 1830. He was married to Elizabeth O'Brien, of Noel, August 8th, 1859. He studied for the Ministry, and on Aug. 17th, 1859, he was ordained at Upper Stewiacke. He was sent by the Presbyterian Church of Nova Scotia to preach the Gospel to the heathen on the Island of Tana, in the South Sea. He sailed from Halifax with his partner in life November 8th, 1859, bidding adieu to his native land never to see IT, or any of his kindred again in this world. He died on Tana, January 21st, 1861, in the 31st year of his age. James William Johnson, their second son was born Feby. 11th, 1833. He studied for the Ministry, and is settled over a Congregation in Yorktown, in the State of New York. He was married there to Augusta A. Lasher, September 18th, 1866. Andrew, the third son of Samuel and Rebecca Johnson, was born October 11th, 1835. He was married to Rachel, daughter of John Gammell and

Sarah Tupper, his wife, January 15th, 1863. They have three sons and three daughters. Mary, their eldest daughter, was born May 22nd 1838. She died June 15th 1861. Isaac Johnson, their fourth son was born September 26th, 1849. He was engaged studying and teaching school for a few years before he died. He died February 9th, 1867. Oliphant Johnson, their fifth son, was born October 9th 1845. He removed to the United States and died there February 16th, 1869. Margaret Johnson, their second daughter, was born December 30th, 1842. Edward, their sixth son, was born January 15th, 1850. Frederick Johnson, their seventh son, was born Nov. 9th, 1847. Jotham Johnson, their eighth son, was born July 30th 1852.

William, the fifth son of James and Elizabeth Johnson, was born in the year 1759 and was brought by his parents to Nova Scotia when 2 years old. He was married to Sarah Miller November 15th, 1787, and shortly after this they removed to Upper Stewiacke and settled on the farm that Mr. James Cox now resides upon, and remained there about 10 years. He then sold his farm to Mr. Abraham Newcomb, and removed farther up the Stewiacke River, and settled on the farm that his grandsons David McG. and George Johnson now occupy. He died there December 10th, 1830, aged 61 years. His wife died March 3rd, 1821, aged 54 years.

Nancy, their eldest daughter, was born in the year 1788. She was married to Robert Rutherford about 1812. They had four sons and four daughters. She died June 2nd, 1849, aged 61 years. Her husband died July 26th, 1856, aged 75 years.

Elizabeth, the second daughter of William and Sarah Johnson, was born April, 1795. She was married to George McNaught, March 22nd, 1827. They had three sons and one daughter. She died June 5th, 1837, aged 42 years.

John Johnson, their eldest son, was born March 11th, 1797. He was married to Ann McGill, of the West River of Pictou, June 12th, 1822. They had two sons and one daughter. He inherited the half of his father's farm.

Robert Johnson, their second son, was born September 24th, 1800. He was married to Margaret Ann Bentley, December 20th, 1830. They had three sons and two daughters. He inherited the homestead half of his father's farm. He died September 20th, 1859, aged 59 years. Jane, their third daughter, was born June 10th, 1804. She was married to David Bentley, December 31st, 1823. They had four sons and three daughters. She died at Point Brule, June 6th, 1862. Sarah, their fourth daughter, was born March 5th, 1807. She was married to James, son of Henry Miller and Sarah Wright, his wife, December, 18—. They had two sons and three daughters. They settled on the Mountain, now called the Miller Settlement, where he reclaimed his farm from the forest. She died there October 1st, 1861, aged 54 years.

John, the sixth and youngest son of James Johnson, Senr., and Elizabeth Patterson, was born in the fall of the year 1760, and was brought by his parents to Nova Scotia in 1761. He was married to Elizabeth, daughter of James and Ann Fulton, of the Lower Village of Truro, about the year 1790. He went to Stewiacke and settled on the farm that his two grandsons John and Samuel Johnson now occupy. He died there, and his widow was married again to Robert Logan, July 1st, 1799. They had one son and one daughter. She died February 20th, 1827. Mr. Logan died Dec. 31st, 1833, aged 70 years. James Fulton Johnson, the only son of John and Elizabeth Johnson, was married to Ann, the fifth daughter of Samuel and Mary Creelman, November 13th, 1813. They had two sons (John and Samuel Johnson who now reside on the same farm that was owned by their father and their grandfather) and one daughter. He died September 14th, 1819, aged 28 years. His widow was married again to James Roddick, a Scotchman. They settled at the West River of Pictou. Mary, daughter of John and Elizabeth Johnson, was married to James, son of Matthew and Ruth Johnson 1813. They had four sons and three daughters. Ann, another daughter of John and Elizabeth Johnson, was married to Alexander, son of Matthew and Ruth Johnson, 1816. They had one daughter. This Alexander Johnson died in the year 1818, aged 25 years, and his widow was married again to James, son of Matthew and Ruth Johnson, 1830. They had one son and two daughters. She died in 1844. Her husband died March 12th, 1837, aged 47 years.

Hannah, the fifth daughter of James and Elizabeth Johnson, was born in Truro, June 23rd, 1762. She died unmarried about the year 1812, aged about 50 years. Jane, the eldest daughter of James Johnson and Margaret McRoberts, his second wife, was born in Truro April 4th, 1778. She was married to Samuel, son of John Hingley and Janet Archibald, his wife, in the year 1797. Samuel, their son was born August, 1799, three months after the death of his father. Samuel Hingley was married and has a family. They are settled at

Wallace River. Samuel Hingley, Senr., died May, 1799. His widow was married again to Joseph Crocket, of the Middle River of Pictou, in the year 1802. They had five sons and four daughters. She died October 11th, 1856, aged 78 years. Her husband died July 26th, 1853, aged 81 years. Sarah, the second daughter of James and Margaret Johnson, was born March 3rd, 1780. She was married to Daniel Hingley, of Kemptown, 1800. They had six sons and six daughters. Alison Johnson, their third daughter, was born in Truro, February 7th, 1782. She was married to John Warren, of Newport.

John Johnson, (who went by the name of Lieutenant Johnson), was born in Ireland, in the year 1711. He was married to Sarah Hogg about the year 1737. He come to Nova Scotia in the year 1761, with his wife and family, and his brother James, and his wife and family. They both settled in the Lower Village of Truro. They were Grantees of the Township. His house stood on the same place that the house now stands in which his greatgrandson Thomas Johnson 3rd lives. He was an active and leading man in public business. He was one of the seven who were elected as elders of the Presbyterian Church, of Truro, in the summer of the year 1770. It is said that for a considerable time after this date he, the Revd. Daniel Cock, and David Archibald, Esq., were the only three persons in Truro who owned and wore boots. He died December 2nd, 1793, aged 82 years. His wife died August 8th, 1796, aged 84 years.

Mary, their eldest daughter, was born in Ireland in the year 1738, and was brought by her parents to Nova Scotia when she was 23 years old. She was married to James Dunlap, December 6th, 1763. This was the first marriage in Truro after the settlement of the place by the British. They had six sons and three daughters, who appear among the Dunlaps. She died May 22nd, 1823, aged 85 years. Mr. Dunlap died December 5th, 1832, aged 92 years.

John, the eldest son of John and Sarah Johnson, was born in Ireland in the year 1741. He was deaf and dumb. He inherited his father's property in the Lower Village of Truro. He was very stout and robust. He was a Grantee of the Township, and outlived all the other Grantees and first settlers. He was married to Margaret Davison, December 10th, 1795. They had three sons and four daughters. He died November 11th, 1841, aged 100 years. His wife died March 23rd, 1869, aged 94 years. Sarah Johnson, their eldest daughter, was born March 31st, 1797. She was married to

John, son of Thomas Gourley and Jane Yuill, his wife, February 2nd, 1815. They had six sons and five daughters. Mr. Gourley died August 9th, 1836, aged 51 years. She was married again to William Soley, November, 1837. They had two sons. James Davison, the eldest son of John and Margaret Johnson, was born July 11th, 1799. He was married to Myziann McNutt, March 23rd, 1819. She died December 9th, 1872. Eunice, their eldest daughter, was born February 19th, 1821. She was married to George S., third son of Hugh and Elizabeth Johnson, December 28th, 1841. They had one son. Mary Jane, their second daughter, was born December 12th, 1823. She was married to John Johnson, May 4th, 1858. They have two sons and two daughters. Sophia, their third daughter, was born July 24th, 1826. She was married to Andrew Bland, of Wallace, April 9th, 1858. They have two sons and one daughter. Charles, the eldest son of James D. and Myziann Johnson, was born December 13th, 1828. He removed to California about the year 1850. He was married there to Armintha Hall. They have two sons and one daughter. William M., their second son, was born July 18th, 1831. He was married to Amelia, daughter of Joseph Wilson and Alice Barnhill, his wife, June 8th, 1858. They have sons and daughters. John Yuill Johnson, their third son, was born July 16th, 1834. He removed to California in the fall of the year 1865. Elizabeth, their fourth daughter, was born November 14th, 1837. She died March 22nd, 1854, aged 16 years. Ann, their fifth daughter, was born May 2nd, 1840. She died November 13th, 1854, aged 14 years. Margaret, their sixth and youngest daughter, was born August 24th, 1844. She was married to George Bland, of Wallace, December 31st, 1867. They have two sons. Samuel Sterns, their fourth and youngest son, was born June 6th, 1846. He was married to Lavinia Purdy, of Wallace, September, 1868. He inherits the homestead. Mary, the second daughter of John and Margaret Johnson, was born August 22nd, 1801. She was married to William McNutt, April 13th, 1820. They had seven sons and five daughters. She died January 2nd, 1866, aged 64 years. Rachel, their third daughter, was born July 8th, 1804. She was married to Robert, the youngest son of Robert and Susan Johnson, October 12th, 1820. They had four sons and seven daughters. John C. Johnson, their second son, was born June 11th, 1806. He was drowned in the Bay of Fundy, while engaged in codfishing. Thomas Johnson, third son of John and Margaret Johnson, was born June 22nd, 1809.

Sophia Johnson, their youngest daughter, was born August 1st, 1811. She was married to John Barnhill, May 4th, 1835. They had two sons and four daughters.

James, the second son of John and Sarah Johnson, was born in Ireland, June 4th, 1743, and was brought by his parents to Nova Scotia when he was 18 years old. He was a Grantee of the Township of Truro. He was married to Eleanor O'Brien, of Noel, in 1778. They settled first in the Lower Village of Truro. His house was on the west side of the road, opposite Rupert Dunlap's house. He sold his Right in Truro to William English, in the year 1798, and removed to Otter Brook, Stewiacke, and settled on the farm on which James Thomas Dunlap now resides. In 1806 he exchanged farms with Francis Creelman and removed to Debert, Londonderry, where he and his wife spent the remainder of their lives. He died January, 17th, 1829, in the 86th year of his age. His widow died July 13th, 1848, aged 89 years. Adam, their eldest son, was born in the year 1779. He was killed, when about two years old, by a log rolling over his body from his father's woodpile. John, their second son, was born in Truro in the year 1781. He followed the sea when he was a young man. He died of consumption, in the State of Maine, about the year 1810, being about 29 years old.

Timothy O'Brien Johnson, their third son, was born in Truro, December 17th, 1783. He was married to Eleanor, daughter of Samuel and Elizabeth McLellan, of Londonderry, June 11th, 1807. He purchased a farm on Salmon River from Mr. William Archibald, where he settled and spent the remainder of his life. On May 30th, 1825, he left home in the morning to float logs down the Salmon River to Archibald's Mill. He was engaged at this work during the day, and was last seen alive about sunset, under the lower Bridge, toiling to get a log from the deep water. He did not return home that night, and search being made for him the next morning, his body was found about half a mile below the Bridge, lying in the water on the falls of the River, at the head of the tide. His corpse was found by John J. Archibald and Alexander Miller, third, and was taken by them out of the water and laid on the bank of the River, until the Coroner, Nathaniel Marsters, was sent for ; an inquest was held, and the body was taken home by Mr. Thomas Nelson. His widow was left with six young children (the youngest about seven weeks old) to bemoan their sad bereavement. He was in the 42nd year of his age. His widow died May 2nd, 1850, aged 69 years.

Lavinia, their eldest daughter, was born January 1st, 1810. She was married to George Johnson, Esq., December 30th, 1828. He was the youngest son of Ralph and Hannah Johnson, who came from England in June 1817. Ralph Johnson died December 4th, 1831. His wife died December, 1843. Timothy, the eldest son of George and Lavinia Johnson was born March 10th, 1831. Ralph, their second son, was born February 12th, 1833. James William, their third son, was born May 3rd, 1835. Eleanor, their eldest daughter, was born April 28th, 1837. George Wren, their fourth son, was born August 29th, 1839. Hannah Jane, their second daughter, was born August 3rd, 1841. Robert J. N., their fifth son, was born September 24th, 1843. Richard Wesley, their sixth and youngest son, was born May 27th, 1848.

James, the eldest son of Timothy O'B. and Eleanor Johnson, was born April 27th, 1812. He was married to Rachel O'B., eldest daughter of John J. Archibald and Mary O'Brien, his wife, February 24th, 1845. They had two sons and four daughters. He inherits his father's farm on Salmon River, and took the management of it at the time of his father's death, when he was but 13 years old. Samuel George William, the second son of Timothy and Eleanor Johnson, was born July 2nd, 1817. He was married to Sarah Wiswell, June, 1841. They have sons and daughters. They removed to New Brunswick. Adam, their third son, was born March 18th, 1820.

John Johnson, their fourth son, was born March 20th, 1822. He was married to Mary McKenzie, of Greenfield, March, 1853. They had five sons and one daughter. Timothy, the fifth and youngest son of Timothy and Eleanor Johnson, was born April 6th, 1825. He died July 12th, 1846, aged 21 years. Adam, the fourth son of James and Eleanor Johnson, was born in the year 1786. He was married to Agnes Ryan in 1815. They removed to New Brunswick about the year 1817, where they reared their family, five sons and two daughters, and spent the remainder of their lives. Rachel, the eldest daughter of James and Eleanor Johnson, was born in the year 1790. She was married to Joshua Teed, of Wallace, in the year 1809. They had one daughter. Mr. Teed died, and his widow was married again to Samuel Campbell. They had five sons and five daughters. She died at Greenfield November, 1862, aged 72 years. Sarah, their second daughter, was born in 1792. She was married to Henry Ramsay in the year 1814. They had one daughter. They removed to St. John, N. B. She died there about the year 1840, and her husband died about the year 1818. Eleanor, their third daughter, was born in the year 1795. She was married to Samuel Lufkin in the year 1815. They removed to the United States. Robert, the fifth son of James and Eleanor Johnson, was born in the year 1797. He was married to Jane Young, in the early part of the year 1818. He followed the sea. He died in Halifax 1818. James, their sixth and youngest son, was born in the year 1799. He was married to Jane Young, widow of Robert Johnson, July 16th, 1822. They had eight sons and six daughters. Mrs. Johnson died April 16th, 1867.

Sarah, the second daughter of Lieut. John and Sarah Johnson, was born in the year 1745. She was deaf and dumb. She was married to John Mersor. Their house stood near the place on which Mr. Robert Hennesy now resides. They both died a considerable time ago, and left no issue. Rachel, the third daughter of John and Sarah Johnson, was born in the year 1846. She was married to Captain John McKeen, December 30th, 1769. They had four sons and two daughters. She died December 3rd, 1781, aged 45 years.

Adam, the third and youngest son of Lieut. John and Sarah Johnson, was born in Ireland in the year 1748, and was brought by his parents to Nova Scotia when he was thirteen years old. He was deaf and dumb. He was a stout, strong, robust man, and a good swimmer. On June 27th, 1771, when he and others were engaged fishing Salmon at the Board Landing, he got entangled in the net, and was drowned, aged 23 years.

CHAPTER XLII.

James Yuill, Esq , was born in Clydesdale, Scotland, in the year 1717, and Jane Bailey, his wife, was born in the year 1721. They were married about the year 1742. He carried on business there as a merchant ; and a part of his business was the manufacture and sale of snuff. He found his business in Scotland was not very profitable, so he removed to Boston, New England, in the year 1753, and there carried on the same business that he had followed in Scotland. He removed again to Old Barns, (now Clifton) in the year 1761. At the time that he and Mr. Alexander Nelson came to Truro, Nova Scotia, together, there were two old barns standing in the field east of

Mr. Ebenezer Archibald's house, and an old grist mill standing on the brook near John Yuill, Esqr.'s, shop. These buildings had been left by the French settlers, and this small village had no other name but Old Barns for more than eighty years. He still continued the sale of goods at Old Barns, and, as he said himself, he *kent* nothing about *cents* nor *per cents*, but his way of doing business was to sell his goods for just *double* they cost him. He was a Grantee of Truro Township. He, his son James, and Alexander Nelson, had their land laid off where they settled. Their land was about one and a quarter mile wide, along the Bay, and extended about four miles back. His house stood near the place that his grand son, John Yuill's stood. At this place he continued the remainder of his life. He died March 4th, 1807, aged 90 years. Jane his wife died January 11th, 1804, aged 83 years. They had several children who died young in Scotland. James, their son, was born in Scotland in the year 1752, and was brought by his parents to Boston when one year old, and from thence to Nova Scotia, when he was nine years old. His name is among the Grantees of the Township, although he was but thirteen years old at the date of the grant. He was married to Eleanor Mahon, of Londonderry, October 8th, 1776. He settled, and had his house on the same place where Mr. Charles Yuill now resides. In the fall of the year 1810, he started to go to Scotland to look after the business of the late Andrew Yuill, his father's brother, who had died there, having no children, and leaving a considerable property. He sailed from Pictou in a ship bound for Liverpool, England, and not long after, he took ill of a fever, and continued ill during the remainder of the passage. He arrived in Liverpool, and died about seven days after, on January 21st, 1811, aged 59 years. His wife died May 3rd, 1811, aged 52 years.

Jane Yuill, their eldest daughter, was born October 25th, 1777. She was married to James Laughead, in the year 1793.   Mr. Laughead purchased his farm from Charles Nelson in the year 1809, (at the time that Mr. Nelson removed to the Upper Village of Truro.) His house stood on the same place that the house now stands in which his grand son, Joseph Laughead now resides, at Clifton, where he died February 12th, 1850, aged 80 years. His wife died May, 1856, aged 78 years. John Laughead, their eldest son, was born July 26th, 1794. He was married to Margaret, daughter of Joseph McLellan, of Londonderry, July 20th, 1820. They had five sons and two daughters. Mrs. Laughead died September 8th, 1845. He was married again to Elizabeth, daughter of John Faulkner and Janet Moor his wife, September 14th, 1846. His second wife died February 29th, 1860. Eleanor, the eldest daughter of James and Jane Laughead, was born January 5th, 1796. She was married to James Totton, of the Folly Mountain, 1817. They had four sons and four daughters. James Laughead, their second son was born October 4th, 1797. He was married to Sarah, daughter of Samuel and Elizabeth McLellan, of Parrsboro, January 10th, 1822. They settled on the farm on which Mr. James Archibald now resides.

It may here be observed that this James Laughead, Junr., and his brother William, built a brigantine called the " Enterprise," in the years 1842 and 1843. In May, 1844, this vessel was loaded with Plaster at Pitchbrook, on the east side of the Shubenacadie River. She had twenty persons on board ; James Laughead, Junr., aged 46 years, his daughter Elizabeth, aged 21 years, William Laughead's wife and child, Maria, daughter of James Laughead, Senr., aged 23 years, James Noble, son of Robert and Eleanor Laughead, aged 14 years, Captain Allan, Mr. Atkins, first mate, Joseph Tidmon, second mate, Thomas Green, son of the late James Green, aged about 45 years. He (Thomas Green) left a wife and family. Matthew and William Green, sons of the late William Green, Matthew Green left a wife and three daughters ; Joseph Forbes, Thomas Keef, David Messenger, Mr. Blackwood, son of the Rev. Robert Blackwood, of Tatamagouche, Charles Tucker, Junr., of Truro, aged 18 years, William Hill Dill, second son of the late George Dill of Truro. He was a young lawyer about 25 years old ; Mahew, son of Eliakim Tupper, of New Glasgow, aged 23 years, and Alexander, youngest son of Alexander L. and Mary Archibald, aged 19 years. This vessel sailed from Spencer's Point, on the north side of the Bay, on May 22nd, 1844, and has not been heard from since, thus leaving a large circle of friends and relatives to mourn their loss.

Elizabeth, the eldest daughter of James Laughead, Junr., and Sarah his wife, was born December 1st, 1822. She was one who was lost in the " Enterprise." Mary Laughead, their second daughter, was born March 7th, 1825. She was married to Charles, fourth son of James and Sarah Yuill, December 31st, 1845. They had six sons and seven daughters. She died March 4th, 1870, aged forty-five years. Samuel Laughead, their eldest son, was born May 22nd, 1827. He was married to Lucinda, second daughter of William and Susan Creelman, December, 1852. He died July 9th, 1872, aged 45 years.

Jane, the third daughter of James and Sarah Laughead, was born September 10th, 1829. She was married to Charles Christie, January 30th, 1849. They had nine sons and four daughters. Charles Laughead, their youngest son, was born March 25th, 1832. He was married to Harriet, the youngest daughter of John and Jane Yuill, November 10th, 1856. They had two sons and one daughter. On September 23rd, 1869, their son Oscar was on a high part of his father's barn, when he fell on the barn floor, and was so much injured that he died in about ten hours. He was about 12 years old.

Robert, the third son of James Laughead Senr., and Jane, was born July 3rd, 1799. He was married to Ann, the youngest daughter of William and Ann Flemming, December 29th, 1825. She died September 25th, 1829, and left no issue. He was married again to Eleanor, eldest daughter of James and Sarah Yuill, January 5th, 1830. They had seven sons and five daughters.

Mary, the second daughter of James and Jane Laughead, was born June 12th, 1801. She was married to Jessie Gourley, 1820. They had one daughter. She died May 7th, 1821, aged 20 years. Mr. Gourley died March 27th, 1871, aged 77 years. William Laughead, their fourth son, was born April 23rd, 1803. He was married to Fanny Aljo, August 27th, 1833. They had three sons and three daughters. He inherited the homestead half of his father's farm. Mrs. Laughead and her youngest child were lost in the "Enterprise," May, 1844. He was married again to Hannah, daughter of Daniel S. and Dorothy Yuill, March 25th, 1851. They had three sons and one daughter. He died November 28th, 1865, aged 63 years. His second wife died June 17th, 1862, aged 33 years.

Susan Laughead, their third daughter, was born March 17th, 1805. She was married to William Creelman, December 9th, 1824. They had three sons and seven daughters. Joseph Laughead, their fifth son, was born December 23rd, 1806. He was married to Rebecca, daughter of James Archibald and Rosanna McKeen, his wife, January 10th, 1833. He inherits a part of his father's farm.

Elizabeth Laughead, their fourth daughter, was born September 17th, 1808. She died April 23rd, 1811.

Jane, their fifth daughter, was born January 17th, 1810. She died October 19th, 1827, aged 17 years.

Martha Laughead, their sixth daughter, was born October 25th, 1811. She was married to Samuel Creelman, December 25th, 1832. She died April 21st, 1835, aged 23 years.

Elizabeth Laughead, their seventh daughter, was born January 29th, 1815. She was married to William Rogers, of Shepody. They had one son and one daughter.

Catherine Laughead, their eighth daughter, was born December 4th, 1816. She was married to Alexander, son of William and Susan Archibald, January 10th, 1837. They had five sons and four daughters. She died in Musquodoboit, August 26th, 1869, aged 53 years.

Maria, their ninth daughter, was born April 7th, 1821. She was lost in the "Enterprize."

John, the eldest son of James and Eleanor Yuill, was born in Truro, May 22nd, 1779. He was married to Hannah, daughter of John and Mary Smith, February 3rd, 1803. He inherited what was his grandfather's property, where he spent the remainder of his life. He died October 4th, 1849, aged 70 years. His first wife died September 4th, 1817. Daniel Smith Yuill, their eldest son was born November 24th 1803. He was married to Dorothy, daughter of John and Martha Dunlap, of Stewiacke, February 11th, 1830. They had one son and four daughters. Mrs. Yuill died November 17th, 1857, aged 53 years. He was married again to Rachel, eldest daughter of Andrew and Nancy Yuill, October 19th, 1858. James the second son of John and Hannah Yuill, was born December 6th, 1806. He was married to Martha McCulloch, of Debert River, 1836. They had three sons and five daughters. Mary, the eldest daughter of John and Hannah Yuill, was born November 20th, 1809. She was married to David Chisholm of Londonderry, 1834. They had three sons and four daughters. Jane Yuill, their second daughter, was born November 21st, 1811. She was married to David Slack, September, 1838. They had one son and two daughters. Sarah Yuill, their third daughter, was born June 4th, 1813. She was married to Thomas son of William and Nancy Pearson, June 23rd, 1836. They had three sons and two daughters. She died April 9th, 1868, aged fifty-five years. Mr. Pearson died February 23rd, 1852, aged 38 years. Hannah Yuill, their fourth daughter, was born August 12th, 1817. She was married to John Smith Vance, July 13th, 1836. They had two sons and two daughters. She died July 4th, 1846, aged 29 years. John Yuill was married the second time to Jane McNutt of the Lower Village of Truro, August 10th, 1818. Myzian their eldest daughter, was born November 16th, 1819. She was married to William, son of Charles and Mary Nelson, December 25th,

1836. They had six sons and three daughters. Samuel Yuill, their eldest son was born March 14th, 1821. He was married to Agnes, Northup, March 14th, 1841. They had three sons and three daughters. He died March 25th, 1868, aged 47 years. William Grigor Yuill, their second son, was born August 12th, 1824. He was married to Elizabeth, the youngest daughter of Charles Tucker, Esq., and Mercy P. Polley his wife, February 1st, 1851. They had four sons and four daughters. Margaret Eleanor, their second daughter, was born September, 1829. She was married to Captain James O. Morrison, February 1848. They had five sons and three daughters. She died April, 1870, aged 40 years. Harriet, their third and youngest daughter was born February 2nd, 1833. She was married to William, son of James and Sarah Yuill, August 8th, 1850. Mr. Yuill removed to the United States and died there October 24th, 1850. She was married again to Charles, son of James Laughead, Jr., November 10th, 1856. They had two sons and one daughter.

William, the second son of James and Eleanor Yuill, was born April 25th, 1781. He was married to Jane Campbell of Londonderry. They settled at the Great Village. He died there September 29th, 1863, aged 82 years. His first wife died in 1818. He was married again to Eleanor, daughter of Thomas and Jane Gourley, February 11th, 1819. William, their only son, is living a bachelor. Eleanor Yuill, their only daughter, was married to Samuel O'Brien of Noel. They had a numerous family. She died some time ago. Thomas, the eldest son of William and Eleanor Yuill, was born March, 1821. He was married to Jane McNutt. They had one son and three daughters. He removed to the United States, and died there. James Yuill, their second son was born in 1823. He died in 1844. John Yuill, their third son, was born in 1825. He was married to Margaret Thompson. They had sons and daughters. Robert Barry Yuill, their fourth son was married to Mary Smith. They had three sons and one daughter. He removed to the United States. He died at Arizona, July, 1871. Joseph Yuill, their fifth son, was married to Amelia Corbett. They had four sons and two daughters. Susan Yuill, their only daughter, was married to Nelson Chisholm. They removed to California.

James, the third son of James and Eleanor Yuill, was born January 10th, 1783. He was married to Sarah, the youngest daughter of Major John Archibald and Margaret Fisher, August 29th, 1809. He inherited the homestead part of his father's property at Old Barns.

He died there September 7th, 1863, aged 80 years. His wife died August 2nd, 1866, aged 75 years.

George Yuill, their eldest son, was born August 12th, 1810. He was married to Jane, second daughter of Joseph Crowe and Mary Vance his wife, July 9th, 1839, They had one son and one daughter. Eleanor, their eldest daughter was born December 28th, 1811. She was married to Robert Laughead, January 5th, 1830. They had seven sons and five daughters. Margaret, their second daughter, was born November 20th, 1813. She was married to Robert O. Christie, December 30th, 1831. They had five sons and two daughters. Mr. Christie died March 22nd, 1867. Susannah, their fourth daughter, was born June 27th, 1815. She was married to Isaac Christie, December, 1834. They had one son and eight daughters. She died September 17th, 1863, aged 48 years. Sarah Ann, their fourth daughter, was born October 13th, 1817. She was married to John Blackie, January 14th, 1836. They had four sons and two daughters.

James Yuill, their second son, was born May 3rd 1819. He died when he was young. John Yuill, their third son, was born December 12th, 1820. He was married to Barbara Henderson, February 7th, 1843. They had one son and three daughters. He holds a commission of the Peace, and is Captain of a company of the Militia. Eliza Jane, their fifth daughter, was born December 1st, 1822. She was married to Richard Christie, December 31st, 1842. They had six sons and four daughters. She died June 20th, 1872. Charles Yuill, their fourth son was born July 15th, 1824. He was married to Mary, daughter of James Laughead, Junr., December 31st, 1845. They had six sons and seven daughters. Mrs. Yuill died March 5th, 1870. He was married again to Sarah Yuill, December 15th, 1870. He resides on the same place on which his father and grandfather resided. William Yuill, their fifth son was born October 20th, 1826. He was married to Harriet Yuill, August 9th, 1850. He died suddenly October 24th, 1850. Alexander Yuill, their sixth son, was born September 25th, 1828. He was married to Mary Helpert, of Halifax, October 17th, 1854. They had one son and four daughters. He is settled at Debert River, where he carries on the blacksmith work. Ruth, their sixth daughter, was born March 11th, 1830. She was married to Isaac, the fifth son of James M. and Margaret McCurdy, of Musquodoboit, July 29th, 1851. They had six sons and three daughters. Mr. McCurdy died March 31st, 1867, aged 41 years. Maria, their seventh daughter, was born March 11th, 1833. She was married to Joseph Howe Archibald, March 15th, 1864. They had one son and one daughter. They have removed to California. Mary L., their eighth daughter, was born August 5th, 1835. She was married to John M. Atkins, December 25th, 1855. They have three daughters.

George, the fourth son of James and Eleanor Yuill, was born February 8th, 1785. He was married to Susannah, daughter of William and Mary Forbes, November 16th, 1826. He settled on the farm that had been owned by James Rutherford, and afterwards by Thomas Crowe, Senr. Mrs. Yuill died September, 1845. Eleanor and Sarah, their twin daughters, were born December 1st, 1827. Eleanor was married to George, son of William and Mary Creelman, October 3rd, 1856. They have three sons and two daughters. Sarah, the other twin daughter, was married to Charles Yuill, December 15th, 1870. Isaac, the only son of George and Susan Yuill, was born January 5th, 1836. He was married to Eleanor, daughter of William and Sarah Cox, of Upper Stewiacke, May 22nd, 1862. They have two sons and one daughter. He inherits his father's farm at Beaver Brook, Clifton.

Andrew, the fifth son of James and Eleanor Yuill, was born May 16th, 1787. He was married to Rachel, daughter of Capt. John and Rachel McKeen, October 22nd, 1811. He inherited a part of his father's farm. Mrs. Yuill died April 18th, 1813. He was married again to Nancy, the third daughter of Isaac and Elizabeth Miller, December 1st, 1814. She died April 15th, 1822, aged 35 years. Thomas, the only son of Andrew and Rachel Yuill, was born August 18th, 1812. He was married to Mary, the eldest daughter of James and Sarah Crowe, July 11th, 1854. He inherits a part of his father's farm. Rachel, the eldest daughter of Andrew and Nancy Yuill, was born January 9th, 1816. She was married to Daniel Smith Yuill, October 19th, 1858. Vashti, their second daughter, was born August, 16th, 1817. Elizabeth, their third daughter, was born August, 1819. She was married to John Miller, of New Glasgow, June 27th, 1871.

Samuel, the sixth son of James and Eleanor Yuill, was born October 21st, 1789. He was married to Margaret daughter of James Corbett and Elizabeth Marsh, his wife, of Five Islands, July 21st, 1812. He inherited a part of his father's property, at Clifton, where he spent the whole of his life. He died May 13th, 1868, aged 78 year. Elizabeth, their eldest daughter, was born July 26th, 1814. John Corbett Yuill, their eldest son, was born April 17th, 1817. He was married to Martha, daughter of Joshua Corbett and Eleanor Yuill, his wife, of Five Islands, July, 1848, They have one son and three daughters. He inherits a part of his father's farm. Joseph Yuill, their second son, was born June 30th, 1819. He learned the blacksmith trade with William Hall, of Truro, and carries on his business at Clifton. He was married to Martha, daughter of William and Agnes Miller, of Five Islands, October 11th, 1842. They had five sons and three daughters. Sarah Yuill, their second daughter, was born August 19th, 1821. She was married to Christopher Dillman, of Musquodoboit, June 18th, 1858. James Yuill, their third son, was born October 15th, 1823. He was married to Catherine daughter of Jacob Dillman and Margaret McKenzie, his wife, of Musquodoboit, September 26th, 1848. They had three sons and two daughters. He settled up the Beaver Brook. Eleanor, their third daughter, was born February 9th, 1826. She was married to William Elliott, of Chiganoise, July 25th, 1848. They had three sons and three daughters. Zeuriah Yuill, their fourth daughter, was born March 7th, 1829. She was married to David Rude, of Chiganoise. Louisa, their fifth daughter, was born October, 1831. She was married to George Burgess, December 27th, 1860. Hezekiah Yuill, their fourth son, was born September 30th, 1833. He was married to Eliza Margaret, daughter of Christopher Dillman and Catherine Dunbrack, his wife, November 1st, 1860. They have one son and two daughters. He inherits the homestead part of his father's farm.

Elizabeth, the second daughter of James and Eleanor Yuill, was born May 23rd, 1792. She was married to John. L. Fisher in the year 1812. She died shortly after. Eleanor Yuill, their third daughter, was born April 1st, 1795. She was married to Joshua Corbett in the year 1812. They had five sons and five daughters. Mr. Corbett died 1868.

Jacob, the seventh and youngest son of James and Eleanor Yuill, was born October 13th, 1802. He was married to Susan, daughter of Daniel Urquhart, of Portaupique, August 15th, 1822. He settled on the farm upon which the Messrs. McCurdys now reside, near the shore at Clifton. Eleanor Jane, their eldest daughter, was born March 17th, 1824. She was married to John Knight, of Portaupique, April, 1867. Mary Ann, their second daughter, was born February 22nd, 1826. She was married to Capt. William McDuffey,

February, 1851. They had four sons and three daughters. James, their eldest son, was born December 21st, 1828. He was drowned from a vessel that was lost on the rocks at Grand Manan, in the Bay of Fundy, in March, 1849. Amelia Yuill, their third daughter, was born December 12th, 1833. She was married to William Smith Cox, August 7th, 1855. They have two sons and two daughters.

Daniel, the second son of Jacob and Susan Yuill, was born December 19th, 1835. It may here be observed that Mr. Yuill and his son Daniel were crossing the Shubenacadie River in a boat, in the spring of the year 1845, when he was removing from his farm at Old Barns to the County of Hants. He had in the boat with him his seed wheat, some of his farming utensils, and a pair of oxen fastened to the boat to make them swim across the River. The oxen upset the boat and threw all in the River. His son, then in the tenth year of his age, was drowned. Mr. Yuill held on by the oxen until they swam ashore, and was in this way delivered from his perilous situation. William Yuill, their third son, was born May 16th, 1837. He was drowned in August, 1854, being thrown overboard by the boom of a vessel in the Bay of Fundy. David Yuill, their fourth son, was born January 20th, 1839. He was married to Claressa, only daughter of the late Joseph Russell and Sarah Conley, his wife, February, 1865. They have one son and two daughters. Sarah Yuill, their fourth daughter, was born June 11th, 1840. She removed to the United States and was married there to Samuel H. H. Humphrey, of Peabody, Mass., September 27th, 1781. Nancy Yuill, their fifth daughter, was born July 16th, 1841. She was married to Captain Caleb Atkins, September 1860. They have one son and one daughter. George Yuill, their fifth son, was born in 1843. He left Truro for California, April 2nd, 1867, and arrived at Sacramento in May. On the 25th of October, same year, while out on a duck hunting excursion on a lake, in a boat alone, he was shot by the accidental discharge of his own gun. Jane, the only daughter of James Yuill, Esq., was born in Boston in 1857. She was married to Thomas Gourley. They had seven sons and six daughters.

CHAPTER XLIII.

Robert Hunter was one of the first settlers of Truro, and was a Grantee of the Township. His house stood near the place that Mr. S. S. Nelson's store now stands. He was one of the first elders of the Presbyterian Church of Truro, who were chosen in the summer of the year 1770. He died February 7th, 1810, aged 77 years. He outlived the rest of the elders who were chosen at the same time he was. His wife died October 14th, 1807, aged 74 years. He was born in Ireland in the year 1733. He came out to New England when he was young, and was married there to Esther Moore, about the year 1756. They removed to Nova Scotia in the spring of the year 1760.

Letitia, their eldest daughter, was born in New England in the year 1755. She was married to Caleb Putnam, of Maitland, 1775. William, their eldest son, was born February 1st, 1779. He was married to Jane McKenzie, September 20th, 1817. They had six sons and three daughters. He was drowned in the Shubenacadie River, November 10th, 1840, in the 61st year of his age. Esther, the second daughter of Caleb and Letitia Putnam, was born March 14th, 1781. She was married to Robert, eldest son of Gavin Johnson and Elizabeth Hunter, his wife, 1803. They had one son and three daughters. They removed to Ohio, U. S., in the year 1805. Elizabeth Putnam, their eldest daughter, was born September 7th, 1776. She was married to Robert Brydon, 1799. They had two sons and three daughters. She died September, 1832, aged 56 years. Her husband died at Tatamagouche about 1856. Mary Putnam, their third daughter, was born August 7th, 1783. She was married to James Douglas, December, 1807. They had four sons and one daughter. She died January, 1870, aged 86 years. Mr. Douglas died April, 1842. Caleb Putnam, their youngest son, was born July 12th, 1785. He was brought up at his grandfather Hunter's, after the death of his mother. He was married to Catherine McDougall, October 1815. They had four sons and three daughters. He died August, 1850, aged 65 years. His widow died in 1850. Caleb Putnam's first wife died in 1785. He was married to Jane Fulton in 1787. They had two sons and six daughters. He died Sept., 1838.

Elizabeth, the second daughter of Robert Hunter and Esther Moore, was born in New England in the year 1759. She was married to Gavin Johnson, a Scotchman, December 7th, 1780. Mr. Johnson was a school teacher. He lived in a house that adjoined the house Mr. William Bowlan now resides in at west end. He was Town Clerk from about the year 1790 to 1798. A few years after this date he removed to Ohio, U. S., and about the year 1805 he returned to Truro on a visit, and it is said that he persuaded his brother-in-law, John Hunter, to go with him to Ohio. They went in 1815, and after the death of Mr. Hunter, Johnson and his family got his property, which was considerable. Mr. Johnson and his family both died there a number of years ago. Robert Hunter, the eldest son of Gavin and Elizabeth Johnson, was born in Truro, December 29th, 1781. He was married to Esther, daughter of Caleb and Letitia Putnam, 1803. He removed to Ohio, U. S., in 1815. They had one son and three daughters. William Johnson, their second son, was born in Truro, October 22nd, 1783. He was a house joiner. He was married to Elizabeth, daughter of David and Eleanor Taylor, October 8th, 1807. He owned the half of what was Mr. Taylor's farm, being the same that Mr. John Hattie now owns. He built the house in which Mr. Hattie now lives. He sold out and went with his father and the rest of the family to Ohio in 1815. He and his wife both died there some time ago. John Johnson, their third son, was born December 16th, 1785. Thomas Johnson, their fourth son, was born October 3rd, 1788. He died when young. Archibald Johnson, their fifth son, was born July 27th, 1791. He was a minister of the Gospel in the United States. Gavin Roat, their sixth son, was born March 22nd, 1796. Grizzel Roat Johnson, their daughter, was born March 10th, 1794.

John Hunter, the only son of Robert and Esther, was born in 1761. He inherited his father's property in Truro until 1806. He then exchanged farms with William Smith and removed to Middle Stewiacke, to the farm that John Putnam lived and died upon. He sold out there to Timothy Putnam, in 1815, and removed to Ohio. He died there a bachelor some time ago.

Janet, the third daughter of Robert and Esther Hunter, was born in Truro, January 18th, 1763. She was married to Timothy Putnam about the year 1785. They settled at Middle Stewiacke, on the farm which Mr. David Fisher now occupies, where they spent the remainder of their lives. She died February 26th, 1841, aged 78 years. Mr. Putnam died October 9th, 1840, aged 84 years.

Letitia Putnam, their eldest daughter, was born in the year 1786.

She was married to James Rutherford, Senr., 1808. They had one son and six daughters. She died April 27th, 1824, aged 38 years.

Robert, the eldest son of Timothy and Janet Putnam, was born July, 1788. He was married to Jane, daughter of William and Mary Cox, of Upper Stewiacke, January, 1814. He resided on the farm on which his son William now lives.

Eleanor, the eldest daughter of Robert and Janet Putnam, was born October 27th, 1814. She was married to Robison Rutherford. Jane Putnam, their second daughter, was born June 20th, 1817. She was married to William Fisher. They had sons and daughters. Mrs. Putnam died July 7th, 1817. He was married again to Elizabeth, third daughter of William and Ann Flemming, July, 1821. They had three sons and two daughters. He started to go to New York for the improvement of his health, and died on board the vessel in New York harbour, July 10th, 1839, aged 51 years.

Timothy, the second son of Timothy and Janet Putnam, was born October 26th, 1790. He was married to Ruth, the youngest daughter of Adam and Eleanor Dunlap, February 14th, 1828. They had six sons and six daughters. He inherited his father's farm. He died July 17th, 1852, aged 62 years. Mrs. Putnam died August 7th, 1851, aged 49 years.

John, the third son of Timothy and Janet Putnam, was born May, 1793. He was married to Jane, daughter of John Corbett and Mary Flemming, January, 1820. He settled on the farm that William Kennedy first settled on in 1780, and was afterwards owned by William Smith and John Hunter. They had three sons and six daughters. He died November 14th, 1870, aged 77 years. His wife died October 24th, 1857, aged 62 years. Esther, the second daughter of Timothy and Janet Putnam, was born December 31st, 1796. She was married to James Barnhill, March 17th, 1818. They had three sons and five daughters. She died May 3rd, 1868, aged 72 years. Elizabeth, the youngest daughter of Timothy and Janet Putnam, was born 1799. She was married to James Dunlap, February, 1820. She had one son. She died suddenly, April 14th, 1821, aged 22 years.

Alice, the fourth daughter of Robert and Esther Hunter, was born in Truro, July 18th, 1766. She was married to Alexander Barnhill in 1785. They had two sons and three daughters. She died December 22nd, 1831, aged 65 years. Her husband died September 22nd, 1813, aged 47 years. Margaret Hunter, their fifth daughter, was born in Truro, August 4th, 1769. She was married to Samson,

son of Samson Moore and Martha Archibald, his wife, December 31st, 1795. They had one son and one daughter. She died in 1816, aged 47 years. Her husband died in 1818, aged 51 years. Esther, the youngest daughter of Robert and Esther Hunter, was born June 10th, 1772. She was married to William Smith, February 28th, 1793. They had four sons and three daughters. She died May 10th, 1835, aged 63 years. Her husband died November 3rd, 1853, aged 86 years.

CHAPTER XLIV.

Andrew Gammell was another of the first settlers of Truro. He was a Grantee of the Township. His front land was in the Lower Village, where he resided during the remainder of his life (being the same place that Mr. Robert O. Christie owned). On March 8th, 1769, while he was chopping in the woods, he was unfortunately killed by the falling of a tree. He was married to Elizabeth Thomson before they came to Nova Scotia. John Gammell, their eldest son, was born before they came to Nova Scotia. His name is among the Grantees of Truro Township. It is said that he left home to follow the sea, and was never heard from.

Archibald Gammell, their second son, was born before they came to Nova Scotia. He was married to Sarah, daughter of William Fisher and Eleanor Archibald, November 15th, 1782. He resided on the north side of Salmon River, and had his house on the upland which Mr. John Hattie now owns. He continued there until about the year 1790. He then removed to Upper Stewiacke, and settled on the farm that is now owned by Mr. William Cox, on the interval on the north side of the River. He died there in 1835, aged about 75 years. His wife died date unknown. Betty Thomson Gammell, their eldest daughter, was born November 19th, 1783. She was married to Thomas Skeed. They had sons and daughters. They removed to the United States and died there some time ago. Eleanor Gammell, their second daughter, was born in Truro, January 10th, 1785. She was married to William, son of James Dickey and Elizabeth Kennedy, in 1808. They had two sons and two daughters. Mr. Dickey died February 21st, 1872, aged 86 years.

John, the only son of Archibald and Sarah Gammell, was born in

Truro, March 26th, 1787. He inherited his father's farm until nearly the close of his life. He was Precentor in the Church of Upper Stewiacke for more than fifty years. He was married to Elizabeth, daughter of James and Janet Kennedy, in 1807. They had one son and two daughters. He died September 4th, 1863, aged 76 years. His wife died April 19th, 1870, aged 79 years. Margaret, the third daughter of Archibald and Sarah Gammell, was born in Truro, April 20th, 1789. She was married to David, son of David and Martha Fisher, of Middle Stewiacke, in 1811. They had four sons and four daughters. Ruth Gammell, their fourth daughter, was born in Stewiacke in 1791. She was married to Gilbert Rutherford, in 1813. They had one son. Sarah Gammell, their fifth daughter, was born in 1793. She was married to John W. Henry, of Musquodoboit. They had two sons and five daughters. She died April, 1869, aged 76 years. Hannah Gammell, their sixth daughter, was born in 1795. She was married to Thomas Cousins, in the year 1815. They removed to the United States.

Andrew, the third son of Andrew and Elizabeth Gammell, was born November 28th, 1763. He died young.

Robert Gammell, their fourth son, was born April 24th, 1765. He was married to Margaret, one of the twin daughters of William and Janet Kennedy, February 16th, 1792. He settled on the farm on which his grandson, Robert Gammell, now resides. This was the first marriage that was in Middle Stewiacke. He was a very worthy man, and was an elder in the Presbyterian Church of Stewiacke for a long time. He assisted in erecting three Churches in Upper Stewiacke. Mrs. Gammell died October 21st, 1811, aged 43 years. He was married again to Phœbe Ann, daughter of David McCollum, Senr., and Margaret Moore, June 20th, 1816. He died November 7th, 1853, aged 88 years. His widow died April 8th, 1859, aged 82 years. Andrew, the eldest son of Robert and Margaret Gammell, was born February 17th, 1794. He died March 11th, 1815, aged 21 years. Elizabeth, their eldest daughter, was born August 7th, 1797. She died January 13th, 1813, in the 16th year of her age.

William, the second son of Robert and Margaret Gammell, was born May 30th, 1799. He was married to Janet, daughter of Hugh Logan and Elizabeth E. Archibald, December 31st, 1822. They had four sons and five daughters. She died February 12th, 1843, aged 42 years. He was married again to Susan, daughter of John Dunlap and Martha Putnam, March 30th, 1844. They had one son and one daughter. He inherited his father's property. He was an elder in the Church, and a Justice of the Peace for some time before he died. He died of consumption, August 21st, 1848, aged 49 years.

John Gammell, their third son, was born July 19th, 1801. He was married to Sarah, daughter of Samuel Tupper, Esq., and Rachel Dunlap, in 1826. They had three sons and seven daughters. He settled on the farm on which the Hon. Samuel Creelman now resides. He died there July, 1861, aged 60 years. His widow died October 11th, 1846, aged 40 years. Margaret, daughter of Robert and Margaret Gammell, was born July 25th, 1809. She died young. Jane, daughter of Robert and Margaret Gammell, was born May 3rd, 1804. She was married to Ebenezer Fulton, Esq., March 25th, 1824. They had three sons and one daughter. She died November 30th, 1836, aged 32 years.

CHAPTER XLV.

William Kennedy was one of the first settlers of Truro, and a Grantee of the Township. His house lot was on the west side of the street running from Queen Street to the interval. Temperance Hall now partly occupies the site. His front wood lot, so called, is the one upon which Samuel Rettie, Esq., Dr. Samuel Muir, and a number of others, now reside. In the year 1768, he sold his house lot to Robert Hunter, his front wood lot to George Scott, and removed to Pictou. He built the first frame house that was in Pictou town. In 1776, he sold out in Pictou, and returned to Truro. In 1780, he removed and settled at Middle Stewiacke, on the farm which Mr. John Putnam afterwards owned. He was there one year without any neighbour. In the spring of the year 1781, Mr. Samuel Teas, who had recently come from Ireland, settled on the south side of the river, nearly opposite to his place. (The first settlers of Middle Stewiacke had their path or road through the woods from Truro, running along Young Street, up over the high land, passing through what is now Mr. Joseph Marshall's farm in Upper Brookfield and entering, Stewiacke at Mr. Kennedy's). He continued to reside on this farm, enduring the hardships of settling in the woods, until the infirmities of old age came upon him. He then divided his farm between his three sons, James, Robert and John, and went to the South Branch to live, with his eldest daughter, Elizabeth, who was then the widow Dickey. When she married the second time, he removed to his son James', who then lived on the place which Mr. Jacob Layton recently occupied at Upper Stewiacke Village, where he died October, 1816. His wife died in 1813. He was married before he came to Nova Scotia, about the year 1758.

William, the eldest son of William and Janet Kennedy, was born in 1759. In February, 1792, he started from his father's house in Middle Stewiacke, and went up the river on the ice, with the intention of crossing from the South Branch to Musquodoboit, to see Miss Ann Archibald, daughter of John and Alice Archibald, to invite her and some others of the family to a wedding at his father's house, the time Robert Gammell was married to his sister Margaret. When he got up about the mouth of the South Branch, the ice gave way with him, and he was drowned. Elizabeth, the eldest daughter of William and Janet Kennedy, was born in Truro, October 25th, 1761. It is said that she was the first who was born in Truro, after the settlement of the place by the British. She was married to James, son of Adam and James Dickey. They had three sons and two daughters, On August 22nd, 1793, Mr. Dickey was drowned, as described in another place. She married again to Adam Dunlap, September 28th, 1805. Mr. Dunlap died May 25th, 1808. She was married again to Mr. George McConnell, of the West River of Pictou. She died about the year 1815.

James Kennedy, their second son, was born in Truro, November 17th, 1763. He was married to Janet, daughter of Adam and Janet Dickey, in 1790. He inherited the homestead and middle part of his father's farm. About the year 1800, he exchanged farms with William Smith, and removed to Upper Stewiacke, where he spent the remainder of his days. They had five sons and three daughters. He died May 24th, 1845, in the 82nd year of his age. His wife died July, 1825.

Robert, the third son of William and Janet Kennedy, was born in Truro, August 1st, 1766. He was married to Mary Woodworth, December 28th, 1797. He inherited the east side of his father's farm, being that part on which Mr. William F. Putnam now resides. He sold this farm, and removed to Upper Stewiacke, and settled on the farm that is now owned by David McG. Johnson, Esq. He sold out and removed again to Mosquito Cove, where his grandson now resides.

They had five sons and three daughters. He died in October, 1834, aged 68 years, His widow died June 10th, 1853.

Margaret and Jane, twin daughters of William and Janet Kennedy, were born in Pictou in 1768. Margaret was married to Robert Gammell, February 16th, 1792. Their family appears among the Gammells. She died October 21st, 1811, aged 43 years. Her husband died November 7th, 1853, aged 88 years. Jane, the other twin daughter, was married to James, eldest son of James and Mary Dunlap, in 1794. They had two sons and one daughter. Her husband died October, 1809, aged 42 years.

John, the youngest son of William and Janet Kennedy, was born in Pictou, in 1770. He was married to Ann, daughter of John Archibald and Alice Moore, of Musquodoboit, in 1795. He inherited the west side of his father's farm, being the same that John Putnam, Jr., now occupies. He died there May 2nd, 1817. His widow was married again to David Dickey, of Musquodoboit, February, 1823. Mr. Dickey died November, 1852. She died at her son William's house, in Pleasant Valley, October, 1858, aged 86 years. William, the eldest son of John and Ann Kennedy, was born October 4th, 1796. He was married to Mary, daughter of William Carter and Nancy Cox, of Brookfield, February 7th, 1823. They had eight sons and one daughter. They are living at date (November, 1872) on the farm that he reclaimed from the forest in Pleasant Valley. Alice Kennedy, their eldest daughter, was born 1798. She was married to William Moore, of Brookfield, March, 1820. They had one son and two daughters. Mr. Moore died September, 1856, aged 60 years. She was married again to James Murphy, of Musquodoboit. Mr. Murphy died, and she is now living a widow   Jane Kennedy, their second daughter, was born 1800. She was married to Daniel Carter, January, 1823. They had eight sons and one daughter. John, the second son of John and Ann Kennedy, was born April 6th, 1802. He was married to Eleanor McBride, January 1st, 1835. They had two sons and two daughters. Mrs. Kennedy died December 11th, 1861. David Kennedy, their third son, was born 1804. He was married to Hannah Aikens, March 1832. They had three sons and three daughters. He died July, 1845. His wife died May, 1845. James Kennedy, their fourth son, was born 1806. He was married to Elizabeth Cotton, of Lower Stewiacke, March 1842. They had four sons and four daughters. He reclaimed his farm from the forest in Pleasant Valley. He died there January 9th, 1870. Hugh

Kennedy, their fifth son, was born 1808. He was six feet five inches in height, and very slender. He died a bachelor, May 1830, aged 22 years.

CHAPTER XLVI.

Charles Cox was another of the first settlers of Truro, and a Grantee of the Township. His interval lot extended from Salmon River south, to the upland east of John Caldwell's lot at Caldwell's Bridge, so called, on the road leading up Salmon River. On this lot he built his first house, and, after the great freshet in 1792, he found it not very safe to reside on the interval. He built his next house on the front end of his wood lot on the upland, being the same on which Robert Archibald now resides. He owned about forty acres more of interval on the north side of the River, called the Island, that is now owned by Mr. Edward Archibald and others. He was married to Eleanor Stewart, about the year 1807. (A stone that is supposed to be at his grave has spawled off so that neither letter nor figure is now legible.) After the death of Mr. Cox, his widow removed to Stewiacke, where she spent the remainder of her life. She died at the house of her son William, December, 1822. Her remains were brought to Truro and interred in the Truro Cemetery.

William, the eldest son of Charles Cox and Eleanor Stewart, his wife, was born in 1757, and was brought by his parents to Nova Scotia when he was five years old. He was married to Mary, the eldest daughter of John and Mary Smith (who had come from Scotland a few years before), January 26th, 1786. They removed to Upper Stewiacke in the spring of the year 1792, and settled on the farm that his grandson, Francis Cox, now resides upon, where they spent the remainder of their days. He died there, January 24th, 1844, aged 86 years. His widow died February 2nd, 1850, aged 86 years. Daniel Smith Cox, their eldest son, was born in Truro, October 30th, 1786. He was married to Amelia Smith, March 10th, 1810. They settled on the south part of the interval that was his father's. Mrs. Cox died there September 2nd, 1857, aged 68 years. Mr. Cox died January 28th, 1873, aged 86 years.

John Smith Cox, the eldest son of Daniel S. and Amelia Cox, was born in Stewiacke, January 19th, 1811. He removed to New Brunswick, and was married there to Lydia Connell, June 6th, 1842. They had one son and four daughters. Mrs. Cox died December 17th, 1855. He was married again to Frances Smith, of New Brunswick, July 5th, 1857. She died February 2nd, 1861. He returned to Stewiacke, and has been nearly three years laid aside on account of illness. Daniel Smith Cox, their second son, was born April 23rd, 1818. He was married to Mary Ellis, of Shubenacadie, 1842. They had two sons and three daughters. He died in Truro, May 3rd, 1869, aged 51 years.

Mary, the eldest daughter of Daniel S. and Amelia Cox, was born January 20th, 1813. She was married to Alexander M. Lydiard, of Halifax, October, 1834. They had five sons and one daughter.

William Cox, their third son, was born December 23rd, 1820. He was married to Elizabeth Green, September, 1852. They had one son and two daughters. Sarah Cox, their second daughter, was born October 17th, 1823. She remains at home with her aged father and afflicted brother. Charles Cox, their fourth son, was born May 3rd, 1827. He was married to Mary, daughter of James Dunlap and Christiann Aikens, 1853. They had one son and one daughter. Mrs. Cox died July 22nd, 1869. Jotham Blanchard Cox, their fifth son, was born August 21st, 1830. He was married to Susan, daughter of James and Christiann Dunlap, April 22nd, 1858. They had one son and three daughters. George Russell Cox, their sixth son, was born June 5th, 1833. He was married to Eleanor, daughter of James and Christie Dunlap, December 25th, 1861. They had three sons and one daughter.

Eleanor, the eldest daughter. of William and Mary Cox, was born in Truro, December 1st, 1788. She was married to William Rutherford, Esq., February 5th, 1807. They had one son and three daughters. She died January 15th, 1813, aged 24 years. Mr. Rutherford died October 19th, 1856. Mary, the second daughter of William and Mary Cox, was born in Truro, May 20th, 1791. She was married to Samuel Creelman, January, 1809. They had one daughter. She died December 28th, 1813, aged 24 years. Jane Cox, their third daughter. was born in Stewiacke, 1793. She was married to Robert Putnam, January, 1814. They had two daughters. She died July 7th, 1817, aged 24 years. Mr. Putnam died July 10th, 1839.

John, the second son of William and Mary Cox, was born June

8th, 1796. He was married to Margaret, the youngest daughter of Francis and Esther Creelman, December 25th, 1821. He inherited the homestead and a large part of his father's farm, where he spent his life. He died April 24th, 1867, aged 71 years. Mary Cox, their eldest daughter, was married to James, the only son of James Dunlap and Elizabeth Putnam, Feb'y, 4th, 1846. They have two daughters. Esther Cox, their second daughter, was born September, 1829. She was married to David McG. Johnson, Esq., December 24th, 1850. They have five sons and four daughters. John, the eldest son of John and Margaret Cox, was born March 2nd, 1827. He was married to Elizabeth, daughter of James and Christiann Dunlap, December, 1851. They had one son. Mr. Cox, on January 26th, 1853, was engaged with a number of others threshing grain with a machine. They put a young horse into the team. The whole team took fright, and commenced to go round furiously. In attempting to stop them, he put a handspike into the wheel of the machine, which broke the wheel in an instant, and a piece of the wheel struck him on the head, which caused immediate death. He left a young widow and one son to lament their sad bereavement. Francis Cox, their second son, was born January 3rd, 1832. He was married to Catherine, daughter of John and Susan Creelman, December 27th, 1860. They have six sons. He inherits the farm that was his father's, and his grandfather's before him. Hugh Graham Cox, their third son, was born March 3rd, 1835. He was married to Elizabeth, daughter of James Creelman and Martha Cox, March 8th, 1861. They have one son and four daughters. He settled north of the meadow near Otter Brook. William Cox, their fourth son, was born June 23rd, 1837. He was married to Jane Kennedy, December 31st, 1861. They had two sons and one daughter. Mrs. Cox died August 24th, 1869. Samuel Cox, their fifth son, was born May 23rd, 1842.

Charles, the third son of William and Mary Cox, was born August 22nd, 1798. He was married to Janet Newcomb, March, 1820. Mrs. Cox died January 6th, 1867, aged 67 years. He was married again to Sarah Young, widow of the late John Walker, January 23rd, 1871. Ann, the eldest daughter of Charles and Janet Cox, was born in 1820. She died unmarried, April 26th, 1833, aged 32 years. Mary Jane Cox, their second daughter, was born April 14th, 1822. She was married to the Rev. Obed Chute, March 30th, 1850. They had five sons. Elizabeth Cox, their third daughter, was born July 15th, 1823. She was married to James Bentley, January, 1851.

They had three sons. On April 26th, 1858, Mr. Bentley was going to Halifax in the cars. When they arrived at Richmond station, in stepping from the cars to the platform, while the cars were in motion. he fell, and was crushed between the car and the platform, which caused immediate death. William, the eldest son of Charles and Janet Cox, was born March 17th, 1827. He was married to Rebecca Delaney, of Londonderry, December 28th, 1852. They have two sons and one daughter. Rosanna, the fourth daughter of Charles and Janet Cox, was born August 4th, 1829. She was married to L. J. Walker, Merchant of Truro, December 30th, 1852. Abraham, the second son of Charles and Janet Cox, was born April 14th, 1832. He was married to Olivia, daughter of Adam and Hannah Rutherford, March, 1857. They had one daughter. Mrs. Cox died March 18th, 1860. He was married again to Susan, daughter of Abraham and Margaret Bentley, May 29th, 1862. They have four sons and one daughter. Charles and Margaret, twin son and daughter of Charles and Janet Cox, were born October 14th, 1824. Margaret is yet unmarried. Charles was married to Sarah Scott, of Guysborough, May 7th, 1860. They had one son and two daughters. Mrs. Cox died January 7th, 1867. He was married again to Margaret, daughter of Hugh Logan and Elizabeth Archibald, of Cumberland, April 1st, 1868. They had one daughter. He died June 21st, 1871, aged 36 years. Elmina Cox, their sixth daughter, was born September 23rd, 1837. She was married to Samuel Rettie, Esq., of Truro, May 14th, 1860. They had sons and daughters. James Cox, their fourth and youngest son, was born February 25th, 1841. He was married to Amanda Banks, of Lower Stewiacke, June, 1865.

Hugh Graham, the fourth son of William and Mary Cox, was born February 24th, 1801. He was married to Eliza, daughter of Eddy Tupper and Ann Fulton, February 5th, 1824. Eleanor, their only daughter, was married to Samuel Ashmore Creelman. They had two sons and five daughters. Mr. Creelman died May 11th, 1870, aged 50 years.

William, the fifth son of William and Mary Cox, was born February 5th, 1804. He was married to Sarah, daughter of John Dunlap and Martha Putnam, February 15th, 1827. Martha Dunlap Cox, their eldest daughter, was born January 7th, 1828. She was married to Andrew Logan, October 20th, 1853. They had four sons and three daughters. William Smith Cox, their eldest son, was born May 31st, 1831. He was married to Amelia Yuill, August 7th, 1855.

They had two sons and two daughters. He carries on tanning and currying on Elm Street, Truro. Margarat Jane Cox, their second daughter, was born July 13th, 1833. She was married to Joseph Peppard, of Londonderry, November 7th, 1854. They have sons and daughters. John Dunlap Cox, their second son, was born March 22nd, 1837. He removed to California. Susan Dunlap Cox, their third daughter, was born January 8th, 1835. She was married to John Robert Loughead, of Clifton, October 18th, 1853. They have sons and daughters. Eleanor Cox, their fourth daughter, was born June 19th, 1839. She was married to Isaac Yuill, May 22nd, 1862. They have sons and daughters. Amos Cox, their third son, was born September 13th, 1841. Francis C. Cox, the fourth son of William and Sarah Cox, was born May 9th, 1844. He was married to Elizabeth Brown, May 10th, 1869. William Cox's wife, Sarah, died May 10th, 1855, aged 49 years. He was married again to Mrs. Elizabeth Hunt, May 13th, 1860. Frederick W. B. Cox, their only son, was born December 1st, 1862.

George, the sixth and youngest son of William and Mary Cox, was born September 10th, 1810. He was married to Ann, daughter of Charles Blackie and Letitia Deyarmond, February 23rd, 1832. Mr. Cox died March 1st, 1860, aged 50 years. William Cox, their eldest son, was born May 5th, 1833. He was married to Janet Brown, of Musquodoboit, December 10th, 1862. They have two sons and three daughters. Charles Cox, their second son, was born August 18th, 1835. He was married to Agnes Fisher, August 9th, 1859. They had two sons and four daughters. John Smith Cox, their third son, was born April 21st, 1838. He was married to Esther, daughter of Robert Cox and Margaret Putnam, of Hants County, March, 1866. They have two sons and one daughter. Mary Cox, their eldest daughter, was born October 17th, 1840. She was married to George Prescott Henry, of Musquodoboit, July 14th, 1864. They have two daughters. Duncan Cox, their fourth son, was born December 25th, 1841. He was married to Esther Kennedy, November 29th, 1870. They have one daughter. Letitia Cox, their second daughter, was born December 1st, 1845. She was married to William, son of Anthony Bonnell and Mary Vance, April 25th, 1865. They have three daughters. Ellen Jane Cox, their third daughter, was born February 25th, 1848. She was married to Thomas, son of George S. Rutherford and Margaret Howard, January 20th, 1870.

Elizabeth Cox, their fourth daughter, was born August 5th, 1850. Margaret Cox, their fifth daughter, was born January 20th, 1852.

Eleanor, the eldest daughter of Charles and Eleanor Cox, was born in the year 1760. She was married to Daniel Moore in 1780. They had five sons and two daughters. They were the first who settled in Brookfield, about the year 1785. She died at Brookfield in 1851, aged 91 years. She was deprived of sight for a number of years before her death. Mr. Moore died at Brookfield in February, 1826, aged 72 years.

Charles, the second son of Charles and Eleanor Cox, was born in the year 1762. He was married to Agnes Thomson, about the year 1783. He was one of the eight who first settled in Upper Stewiacke, in the spring of the year 1784. His farm laid east of his brother William's. His house was on the south side of the interval. A part of his place is now owned by William Creelman. He continued on this place for a number of years. He then removed to the upper part of the settlement, where his three sons, William, Andrew and Robinson, continued the remainder of their lives. He died there July 17th, 1818, aged 56 years. His widow died of Small pox, February 2nd, 1828, aged 66 years.

Charles, the eldest son of Charles and Agnes Cox, was born November 24th, 1784. He was married to Mary Marsh, of Economy, November 24th, 1810; and he was killed by falling from a horse, November 24th, 1860. John Cox, their eldest son, was born August 22nd, 1816. He was married to Mary Jane, daughter of Jacob Dillman and Margaret McKenzie, of Musquodoboit, 1851. Archibald Thomson Cox, their second son, was born June 20th, 1818. He removed to the United States, and was married there to Martha Lightbody, of Masstown, Londonderry, December 17th, 1850. They have two sons and two daughters. He worked at shipwork about the Bay, and in the United States for a number of years. He is now settled at Clifton, on the farm that was owned by Captain Richard Christie. Charles Cox their third son, was born March 30th, 1820. He removed to the United States some time ago, where he is married and has a family. William Cox, their fourth son, was born in 1822. He removed to New York, where he died a bachelor in 1869, aged 47 years. Eleanor Cox, their eldest daughter, was born in June, 1824. She was married to James Tuttle, of Wallace River, June, 1853. They had three sons and three daughters. James Cox, their fifth son, was born in the year 1827. He removed to California about the year 1850. Some time after, while working in a saw mill, he got his hand hurt. In consequence of bad treatment, he had to get it cut off. He became quite wealthy, and died there a bachelor March 20th, 1871, aged 44 years. Andrew Cox, their sixth son, was married to Nancy, daughter of James McCulloch and Eleanor Andrews, his wife. They have three sons and one daughter. Nancy Cox, their second daughter, was married to Jacob Dillman, of Musquodoboit, September 24th, 1848. They had seven sons and five daughters. Rachel Cox, their third daughter, was married to George Notall, of Gay's River. They had two daughters. Isaac Cox, their seventh son, was born January 25th, 1833. He removed to Massachusetts, U. S., and was married there to Catherine Holton, April 10th, 1856. They have two sons and two daughters. He is now settled at Maitland.

Archibald, the second son of Charles Cox, Senr., and Eleanor Stewart, was born December 17th, 1786. He was married to Mary Alexander, of Hants County, April 2nd, 1812. He removed from Stewiacke to Selma, Hants' County, in 1816, where he and his sons have carried on a large business at building and sailing ships. His wife died there, December 22nd, 1868, aged 72 years. Charles Cox, their eldest son, was born April 17th, 1815. He was married to Hannah, daughter of John Douglass, of Maitland, November 29th, 1840. Mrs. Cox died October 3rd, 1841. He was married again to Margaret, daughter of John Graham, February 15th, 1843. They had five sons and three daughters. Mrs. Cox died April 22nd, 1863. He was married again to Susan Matthew, of England, January 9th, 1870. He inherits the homestead part of his father's farm, where he carries on a large business of farming, merchandise, building, and sailing vessels. Robert, the second son of Archibald and Mary Cox, was born May 22nd, 1817. He was married to Margaret, daughter of Caleb Putnam and Catherine McDougall, his wife, November, 1842. They had four sons and three daughters. He died January 31st, 1868, aged 50 years. Archibald Cox, their third son, was born February 14th, 1823. He was married to Elizabeth, daughter of David Smith and Mary Graham, his wife, September, 1848. They have two sons and three daughters. He removed with his family, a few years ago, to Liverpool, England. He removed again to Antwerp in 1872. William Cox, their fourth son, was born August 4th, 1828. He was married to Rebecca Ann, daughter of David and Mary Smith, July, 1856. They had two sons and six daughters. Mrs. Cox died

20

December 31st, 1871, aged 37 years. He was married again to Eliza-beth Goodwin, June 15th, 1872. John Cox, their fifth son, was born August 12th, 1837. He died at sea, of yellow fever, February 25th, 1856. Mary the, eldest daughter of Archibald and Mary Cox, was born August 10th, 1819. She was married to Captain Isaac Dart, May 17th, 1843. They had four sons and three daughters. Mr. Dart died in Liverpool, England, June 14th, 1867. Sarah Cox, their second daughter, was born December 27th, 1821. She was married to James Dunn, December 8th, 1847. They had four sons and three daughters. Martha, their third daughter, was born June 1st, 1826. She was married to Captain John Graham, October 9th, 1848. They had seven sons and three daughters. Nancy Cox, their fourth daughter, was born May 20th, 1831. She was married to William, son of James Creelman and Martha Cox, his wife, of Upper Stewiacke, May 26th, 1859. They have two sons. Elizabeth Cox, their fifth daughter, was born September 17th, 1833. Jane Cox, their sixth daughter, was born May 9th, 1835. She was married to John, son of Thomas and Letitia Crow of Clifton, November 29th, 1863. They have three sons and one daughter.

Mary, the eldest daughter of Charles and Agnes Cox, was married to Robert Fisher, of Middle Stewiacke.

William, the third son of Charles and Agnes Cox, was born June, 1796. He was married to Sarah, the fourth daughter of William and Esther Fisher of Truro, January 20th, 1822. Mrs. Cox died June 19th, 1823. He was married again to Olivia Thomson, Febru-ary 24th, 1824. They had two sons and one daughter. Mr. Cox died of small pox, January 20th, 1828. His widow was married again to Eleazar B. Dickey, December 31st, 1833. They had two sons and four daughters.

Andrew, the fourth son of Charles and Agnes Cox, was married to Nancy Thomson, October 3rd, 1829. They had four sons and six daughters. He died January 4th, 1863. Martha Cox, their second daughter, was married to James Creelman, February, 1822. They had five sons and three daughters. She died January 17th, 1856. Robison Cox, their fifth son, was married to Mary Campbell, eldest daughter of James Creelman and Margaret Graham, his wife, in 1830. They had five sons and five daughters. He died November, 1871.

Esther, the second daughter of Charles and Eleanor Cox, was born in Truro, April 17th, 1764. She was married to David Archibald, 4th, February 14th, 1788. They had four sons and five daughters. She died November 13th, 1837, aged 73 years. Mr. Archibald died July 11th, 1830, aged 68 years. Margaret, their third daughter, was born June 24th, 1766. She was married to a Mr. Tulle. They removed to the United States long ago. We know nothing of her descendants.

John, the third son of Charles and Eleanor Cox, was born in Truro, October 12th, 1768. He was married to Rebecca McArthur, of Shubenacadie, September 4th, 1807. He inherited his father's farm in Truro for a time, and after that he built a house on the same place that his son David now resides, where he spent the remainder of his days. He died November, 1855, aged 87 years. His wife died April, 1839. John Barnhill Cox, their eldest son, was born in Truro, January 17th, 1809. He removed to New Brunswick when he was a young man, and married there. Mary Cox, their eldest daughter, was born May 14th 1811. She removed to New Brunswick about the year 1845. She was married there. Esther Archibald Cox, their second daughter, was born October 22nd, 1813. She was married to Alexander Chisholm, of New Glasgow. They had three sons and three daughters. Duncan McArthur Cox, their second son, was born October 22nd, 1815. He was lost at sea. David Archibald Cox, their third son, was born April 21st, 1818. He was married to Eunice Budd. of Cumberland, February, 1843. They had three sons and seven daughters. He inherits his father's place. Charles Cox, their fourth son, was born June 2nd, 1820. He followed the sea for a number of years. He was married in Boston. They had two sons and one daughter. He was lost in Boston Harbour about 1860. Eleanor Cox, their third daughter, was born January 28th, 1823. She was married to William Kennedy, Junr., of Pleasant Valley, 1850. They have two sons and two daughters. Sarah Cox, their fourth daughter, removed to New Brunswick. Jane Cox, their fifth daughter, removed to Boston and married there.

Mary Cox, the fourth daughter of Charles and Eleanor Cox, was born in Truro, November 19th, 1770. She died May 7th, 1791, aged 20 years, Elizabeth Cox, their fifth daughter, was born February 5th, 1773. She was married to John Hamley. They had three sons and one daughter. He settled on the old road between Brookfield and Stewiacke. They removed to Canada about the year 1830.

Agnes, the sixth and youngest daughter of Charles and Eleanor Cox, was born in Truro, March 11th, 1775. She was married to William Carter, of Onslow, March 22nd, 1797. They settled in

Brookfield, where he reclaimed from the forest the farm upon which his son George now resides. The Railway station, and a number of other buildings now occupy a part of this same farm. Mr. Carter died January, 1832. He was the first who was buried in the Brookfield Cemetery. His widow died September, 1861, aged 86 years. Daniel Carter, their eldest son, was born August 12th, 1797. He was married to Jane Kennedy, January, 1823. They had eight sons and one daughter. Mary Carter, their eldest daughter, was born November 17th, 1798. She was married to William Kennedy, February 7th, 1823. They had eight sons and one daughter. John Carter, their second son, was born June 9th, 1800. He was married to Agnes Hamilton, November 19th, 1827. They had five sons and four daughters. Mrs. Carter died, and he was married again to Margaret Philips, January, 1867. They had one son and one daughter. Charles Carter, their third son, was born August 10th, 1802. He was married to Agnes Oughterson, December 2nd, 1829. They had two sons. Mr. Carter died. William Carter, their fourth son, was born May 10th, 1804. He died a bachelor, suddenly, January, 1826. George Carter, their fifth son, was born February 5th, 1806. He was married to Elizabeth Conley. They had two sons and eight daughters. He inherits a part of his father's farm at Brookfield. Robert Carter, their sixth son, was born May 30th, 1808. He was married to Eleanor Conley. They had four sons and three daughters. Edward Carter, their seventh son, was born February 11th, 1810. He was married to Margaret Oughterson, December 21st, 1832. They had four sons and three daughters. They removed to the United States about the year 1840. He died there about the year 1862. Agnes Carter, their second daughter, was born March 2nd, 1812. She was married to Thomas Hamilton, April 8th, 1830. They had three sons and four daughters. Mr. Hamilton died July 14th, 1868, aged 71 years. Eleanor Carter, their third daughter, was born June 2nd, 1814. She was married to John Newton. They had three sons and three daughters. She died in Halifax about 1852. Lucilla Carter, their fourth daughter, was born August 18th, 1816. She was married to David Fisher. They had five sons and one daughter. She died 1864. Margaret Carter, their fifth daughter, was born February 14th, 1818. She died unmarried November, 1866.

George, the fourth and youngest son of Charles and Eleanor Cox, was born June 2nd, 1777. He died a bachelor.

CHAPTER XLVII.

Adam Dickey was among the first settlers of Truro, and was a Grantee of the Township. He built his first house on the north side of the interval road, between Charles Cox's lot and John Caldwell's, at Caldwell's Bridge, so called. He owned the farm that Mr. David Fulton now resides upon, where he resided for a number of years, in a house that stood nearly opposite Mr. Samuel J. Blair's house. He was married to Janet Scovil, of New England, 1751. Mr. Scovil, Janet's father, lived until he was 116 years old, and walked 30 miles in one day, a week before he died.

David Dickey, their eldest son, was born in Massachusetts, U. S., in 1752. He was married to Martha, daughter of Ephraim Howard and Sarah Blair, his wife. They had four sons and four daughters. He settled at Lower Stewiacke, south of the river and interval, and on the west side of the old Halifax road. On this place he spent the remainder of his days. He was drowned from a boat on the Shubenacadie River, October, 1818. His first wife died in 1807. He was married again to Mrs. Rebecca Rowland. They had one son and two daughters. Janet the eldest son of David and Martha Dickey, was on a load of hay when she was small, and fell and the wheel went over her body. She was not missed by her father until he went to his barn. He returned to look for his child and found her dead. Mr. Dickey's second wife died April 7th, 1866, aged 84 years.

James, another son of Adam and Janet Dickey, was married to Elizabeth, the eldest daughter of William and Janet Kennedy, about the year 1781. They had three sons and two daughters. He settled at the South Branch of Stewiacke. He and William Putnam built the first mill that was built there. On August 22nd, 1793, Mr. John Johnson came with his grain to the mill; Mr. Dickey left his house, which stood on the west side of the Branch, to go to the mill, which was on the east side. His son James, who was about eight or ten years old, went with him; as they were crossing the stream on a raft made of poles, it was supposed that the boy fell into the stream, and the father went in to try and save his son. In a short time after they were found both drowned. Mr. Dickey was a good swimmer. He left a widow and four young children to bemoan their sudden and sad bereavement. William Dickey, their son, was born in 1784. He was married to Eleanor, second daughter of Archibald and Sarah Gammell. They had two sons and two daughters. He died February 21st, 1872, aged 87 years. Adam Dickey, their other son, was born 1786. He was married to Elizabeth McNutt, of Lower Stewiacke, in 1812. They had one son and one daughter. They removed to St. Andrews, N. B., about the year 1814. He died there some time ago.

William, the third son of Adam and Janet Dickey, was born 1761. He was married to Hannah, daughter of Ephraim Howard and Sarah Blair, about 1788. They had two sons and five daughters. They settled on the south side of the River at Lower Stewiacke. He died there January 1846, aged 84 years. His widow died May, 1854, aged 95 years. Mary, the eldest daughter of Adam and Janet Dickey, was married to Thomas Croker. They had three sons and five daughters. He was one of the eight who settled first in Upper Stewiacke, in the spring of 1784. Mr. Croker died there January 14th, 1829, aged 78 years. Eleanor, the second daughter of Adam and Janet Dickey, was born in 1754. She was married to David Whidden, September 29th, 1774. They had three sons and one daughter. She died at Maitland, August 1st, 1828, aged 74 years. Mr. Whidden died October 1st, 1824, aged 76 years.

Janet, third daughter of Janet and Adam Dickey, was married to James Kennedy in 1790. They had five sons and three daughters. She died July, 1825. Mr. Kennedy died in Upper Stewiacke, May 28th, 1845, aged 82 years. Isabell, their fourth daughter, removed to the United States, and was married there to a Mr. Anderson. Elizabeth Dickey, their fifth daughter, was born in Truro, January 23rd, 1763. She was married to Isaac Miller, December 12th, 1782. They had three sons and six daughters. She died December 20th 1803, aged 40 years. Mr. Miller died November 4th, 1825, aged 75 years. Mr. Dickey's first wife, Janet, died. He was married again to Margaret, daughter of John Fulton and Sarah Wright, November 19th, 1782. Sarah Wright Dickey, their only daughter, was born October 1st, 1783. She was married to Alexander, second son of David and Martha Fulton, of Stewiacke, November 28th, 1815. They had three sons and one daughter. She died August 18th, 1863, aged 80 years. Mr. Fulton died July 22nd, 1825. Adam Dickey died April 6th, 1800. His second wife, Margaret, died December 5th, 1825, aged 76 years.

David Dickey (brother of Adam) was another of the first settlers of Truro, and a Grantee of the Township. He was married before he came to Nova Scotia. David and Samuel, twin sons of David and Mary Dickey, were born in Truro, April 29th, 1763. Samuel died when he was young. David was married to Ruth Wetherby. They had six sons and three daughters. He settled in Musquodoboit, on the farm now occupied by Mr. Dickey, son of Thomas Dickey, of Middle Stewiacke. He was generally known by the name of Yankee Davie. Ruth, his first wife, died in 1816. He was married again to Ann, daughter of John and Alice Archibald, widow of the late John Kennedy, of Middle Stewiacke, February, 1823. He died November, 1852, aged 89 years. His widow died at Pleasant Valley, October, 1868, aged 86 years.

Robert Dickey (brother of Adam and David), was another of the first settlers of Truro, and Grantee of the Township. His house was on the north side of the road, and east of Charles Cox's lot. It is now owned by Messrs. Watsons. Martha Dickey, their only daughter, was born in the year 1756. She was married to David Fisher about the year 1776. They had eight sons and three daughters. She died December 22nd, 1848, aged 87 years. Her husband died in Middle Stewiacke, March 18th, 1834, aged 82 years.

CHAPTER XLVIII.

Charles McKay was another Grantee of Truro Township. He was married to Agnes Dickey before they came to Nova Scotia. John, their son, was born in Truro, January 31st, 1763. David McKay, their son, was born in Truro, April 25th, 1765. Mr. McKay and family returned to New England. He left his back lands in Truro undisposed of, and others have taken possession of them, and settled on some of them.

CHAPTER XLIX.

John Fulton was another of the early settlers of Truro, and a Grantee of the Township. His house lot was the one on which the Presbyterian Church now stands, extending north to the interval. His front wood lot was on the east side, adjoining Young Street. He was born in Ireland, in the year 1728. He was married to Sarah Wright in New England, in the year 1748. John Fulton, their eldest son, was born in New England, in the year 1753. He inherited his father's farm in Truro Village. He purchased Adam Dickey's farm, and lived on it for a number of years, in the house that stood nearly opposite Mr. Samuel J. Blair's, on the interval of Salmon River. He built a new house in the village, which is still standing, west of Mr. James A. Hamilton's. He removed into this house about the year 1812, where he died a bachelor November 20th, 1833, aged 80 years. He owned considerable of property at the time of his death. John Fulton, Senr., died September 6th, 1810, aged 82 years. His wife died December 15th, 1799, aged 74 years.

Margaret, the eldest daughter of John and Sarah Fulton, was born in 1749. She was married to Adam Dickey, November 19th, 1782. They had one daughter. She died December 5th, 1825, aged 76 years. Her husband died April 6th, 1800. Sarah, the second daughter of John and Sarah Fulton, was born in 1756. She was married to James McLellan. Jane, their third daughter, was born in 1759. She was married to John Boggs, about the year 1783. They had one son and one daughter. She died April 20th, 1792, aged 32 years. Mary Fulton, their fourth daughter, was born in Truro, January 1st, 1762. She was married to Daniel Drew, about the year 1783. They had sons and daughters. Mr. Drew lived in a house that stood near the place on which Mr. John A. Tucker now resides. Mrs. Drew died February 11th, 1800, aged 38 years.

David Fulton, their second son, was born in Truro, June 25th, 1765. He removed with seven others, and settled in Upper Stewiacke, in the spring of the year 1784. He settled on the farm on which Alexander Steel now resides. He was married to Martha, daughter of John Ellis, November 8th, 1787. Sarah Fulton, their eldest daughter, was born October 8th, 1788. She died unmarried, August 31st, 1818, aged 30 years. Elizabeth, the second daughter of David and Martha Fulton, was born in Stewiacke, December 15th, 1789. She was married to John Dean, of Musquodoboit. They had five sons and three daughters. She died in August, 1858, aged 68 years. Mr. Dean died in June, 1843. John Fulton, their eldest son, was born September 10th, 1791. He inherited a part of his father's farm. He died a bachelor November 3rd, 1855, aged 64 years.

Alexander Fulton, their second son, was born October 26th, 1793. He was married to Sarah Wright, only daughter of Adam and Margaret Dickey, of Truro, November 28th, 1815. He removed to Truro, and took his uncle, John Fulton's, farm, where he continued the remainder of his life. He died in Truro, July 22nd, 1825, aged 31 years. His widow died at her son's, Adam Fulton, of Stewiacke, August 18th, 1863. Her remains were brought to Truro and interred beside the remains of her husband.

Margaret, the eldest daughter of Alexander and Sarah Fulton, was born January 22nd, 1817. She was married to David, son of Jacob Wright and Mary Fulton, January 16th, 1854. David, the eldest son of Alexander and Sarah Fulton, was born December 8th, 1818. He was married to Eliza Johnson, of Stewiacke, January 14th, 1841. They have three sons and two daughters. He inherits a part of what was his grandfather's farm. John, the second son of Alexander and Sarah Fulton, was born March 23rd, 1821. He died August 26th, 1822. Adam, their third son, was born February 28th, 1824. He was married to Janet Power, March 5th, 1850. They had two sons and five daughters. He inherits what was his father's farm in Upper Stewiacke. Jane, the third daughter of David and Martha Fulton, was born June 1st, 1796. She was married to Charles Dean, of Musquodoboit, April, 1840. They had two daughters. She died July, 1860, aged 64 years. Mary Fulton, their fourth daughter, was born November 20th, 1798. She was married to Jacob Wright, December 7th, 1825. They had three sons and three daughters. She died August 12th, 1854, aged 55 years. Martha Fulton, their fifth daughter, was born October 16th, 1801. She died August 15th, 1818, aged 17 years. David Fulton, their third son, was born June 8th, 1804. He was married to Hannah Prescott, daughter of Hugh Graham and Janet Kennedy, March, 1844. They had nine sons and three daughters. They reside on the south side of the interval, opposite Upper Stewiacke Village. Rebecca, the sixth and youngest daughter of David and Martha Fulton, was born October 30th, 1810. She was married to George Steel (an Englishman), March 3rd, 1830.

They had two sons and two daughters. They now inherit what was her father's farm, in Upper Stewiacke. Samuel, the third and youngest son of John and Sarah Fulton, was born in 1767. He removed to Ohio, U. S., when he was a young man, and has not been heard from since.

CHAPTER L.

The Township of Londonderry, New Hampshire, was settled previous to the year 1718 by sixteen families. On the 26th of March, 1718, a petition was signed by three hundred and nineteen persons, of Londonderry, Ireland, to Samuel Suitte, Governor of New England, asking him to protect them and their families. These persons arrived in New Hampshire the same year ; and a large number of them were the forefathers of those who first settled Colchester and other parts of Nova Scotia. Among them, we find the names of Cook, Dunlap, Blair, Paterson, Wilson, Campbell, Wright, King, Christie, McKeen, Smith, Henderson, Boyd. Johnson, Flemming, Murdoch, Alexander, Craig, Kennedy, Hunter, Watson, Millar, Caldwell, Moor, and Thompson.

On April 12th, 1719, the first sermon was preached to these settlers of Londonderry, N. H., by the Rev. James McGregor, under the wide-spreading branches of a venerable oak, which, for more than a century after, marked the spot. Then, for the first time, did this wilderness and solitary place, over which savage tribes had roamed for centuries, resound with the voice of prayer and praise, and echo the sound of the glorious Gospel. The text was chosen from Isaiah 32nd chapter and 2nd verse—"And a man shall be as a hiding-place from the wind, and a covert from the tempest ; as rivers of water in a dry place ; as the shadow of a great rock in a weary land."

James McKeen, ancestor of all the McKeens that came to New England and Nova Scotia, lived in the North of Ireland. He was a staunch Protestant, and took an active part in the defence of Londonderry in the years 1688 and 1689. He and his brother John were partners in business. They resided in Ballymony, and became comparatively wealthy.

James McKeen, his eldest son with his second wife, Annis

Cargill, and family, came to America in the year 1718, and settled in Londonderry, New Hampshire. Here he was an active, leading man for many years. He was the first Justice of the Peace in Londonderry; his Commission is dated April 29th, 1720, and was in a state of good preservation in 1850, in the possession of his grandson, Rev. Silas McKeen of Bradford, Vermont. He was born in Ireland in the year 1666, and died in Londonderry, N. H., November 9th, 1756, in the nintieth year of his age. His widow, Annis Cargill, died August 8th, 1782, aged 93 years.

John, the eldest son of James and Annis McKeen, was born in Ballymony, Ireland, April 13th, 1714. He was an elder in the Presbyterian Church in Londonderry, N. H. He was a representative in the Legislature, and held several other civil offices in the town. He married Mary McKeen, daughter of his uncle John, and had a large family.

James McKeen, their eldest son, was married to Miss Cunningham. Soon after their marriage they removed to Peterborough, where he died in 1790. His son Levi McKeen removed to the State of New York, 1790, where he went by the name of Judge McKeen for many years. He filled a number of responsible offices in the State.

Rev. Joseph McKeen, D. D., was the third son of John McKeen, and grandson of James McKeen, Esq., who emigrated to New Hampshire, 1718. He was born in Londonderry, N. H., October 15th, 1757. When quite young he manifested a strong desire to obtain a liberal education. With this end in view, he continued to prosecute his studies until the year 1775, when he joined the army as a private soldier to fight for independence. After the war was over, he again resumed his studies; and, in a short time, was licensed by the Presbytery of Londonderry to preach the everlasting Gospel. After preaching some time in Boston, he was called to take charge of a congregation in Beverly, Mass. He accepted the call, and was ordained in May, 1785. Here he continued to labour as a minister of Christ for seventeen years, when he was called to the office of President of Bowden College. His inauguration took place on the second day of September, 1802. There being no church in the village, the people used to assemble in a *grove*, not idolatrously, we presume; and then he would conduct the worship of God, under the blue canopy of heaven, shaded from the scorching sun by the beautiful trees, grander than any modern church.

Dr. McKeen was, in person, above the ordinary stature, and of noble appearance. He was dignified, yet simple, gentle and affable in his manners. His walk and conversation, in the church and in the world, were becoming and consistent. As a public speaker, his voice was clear and strong. He managed the affairs of the college in such a way as to give general satisfaction, until September, 1805, when he was laid aside by illness. He bore his sickness with Christian submission and fortitude. Towards the close of his life, the fifty-first Psalm was his favourite subject of meditation and conversation. Deeply sensible of past sins, he relied on the free and sovereign grace of God in Christ Jesus. He fell asleep in Jesus, July 15th, 1807, aged 52 years.

John, the brother of James McKeen, Esq., intended to emigrate with him. He died, however, a short time before the vessel sailed. His widow, Janet, with her four children, came to America with James.

Her son, John McKeen, Esq., was another of the early settlers of Truro. He was a Grantee of the Township. Two of his sons, William and John, were Grantees also. Their three house lots were adjoining each other, and are now owned by Jas. F. Blanchard, Esq., J. L. Crow, Esq., Dr. Charles Bent, Mr. George Gunn, James Berrell, Esq., Mr. Charles B. Archibald, and a number of others, extending the same breadth north to the interval. They all resided on these lots for a short time. John McKeen, Esq., was born in Ireland in the year 1700. His wife, Martha Cargill, was born in 1707. They were married in 1741, and had three sons and two daughters, who came to Nova Scotia with them in the year 1760. Mr. and Mrs. McKeen both died in one day, December 30th, 1767.

William, the eldest son of John and Martha McKeen, was born in 1745. He was married to Ann, the second daughter of David Archibald, Esq., and Elizabeth Elliott, October 3rd, 1771. He sold out his property in the Village about the year 1780, and purchased the Mill site and Mills which were owned by Alexander Miller and Capt. John Morrison. Here he resided and carried on Milling until the spring of the year 1815. He then sold out in Truro to Mr. John McDougall, and removed to Musquodoboit, where he continued a number of years. He died there in 1826. His wife was deprived of her sight for a number of years before they left Truro. She died at Mabou, Cape Breton, in the house of her son Samuel in 1836, aged 84 years. Martha, the eldest daughter of William and Ann McKeen, was born in Truro, September 26th, 1772. She died February 5th,

1773. He followed the sea when he was a young man. He served some time on board a ship of war as carpenter. He returned home about the year 1811. He was married to Isabell Thomson in 1812. They settled beside the old Halifax road, about three miles south of Gay's River, where they kept an inn, and spent the remainder of their lives. He died there June, 1857, aged 83 years. His wife died in Halifax, July 16th, 1834, Eliza Ann McKeen, their eldest daughter, was born May 28th, 1813. She was married to James Etter of Halifax, August 7th, 1834. They had five sons and three daughters. They settled at Shubenacadie, where he died July, 1869. Margaret McKeen, their second daughter, was born March 25th, 1815. She was married to Samuel Kerr, April, 1846. They had two sons and three daughters. William McKeen, their eldest son, was born February, 1817. He was married to Jane Keys. They had three sons and six daughters. James Alexander, the second son of John and Isabell McKeen, was born in 1819. He died a bachelor in 1848. Isabell Thomson McKeen, their third daughter, was born March 10th, 1821. She was married to William, the eldest son of David and Martha Whippie, of Onslow, November 7th, 1839. They had three sons and eight daughters. John McKeen, their third son, was born May 20th, 1824. He learned the trade of saddler and harness maker with John McKeen, of Mabou, C. B. He removed to the United States, was married there, and had two sons and one daughter. On May 12th, 1859, some man forced into his shop, dragged him to the door, and stabbed him with a knife, causing instant death. His wife died about the year 1861. David McKeen, their fourth son, was born October, 1826. He was married to Elizabeth Irvin, of Musquodoboit. They had four sons and two daughters. Mrs. McKeen died, and he was married again to Isabell Irvin. They had three sons and one daughter. Caroline McKeen, their fourth daughter, was married to Adam Benvey, of Mabou, C. B., August, 1860. Livinia L. McKeen, their fifth daughter, removed to the United States, and was married there to Frank Taylor. They had three daughters. Mr. Taylor died, and she was married again to William Mullon. Martha, the eldest daughter of John McKeen, Esq., was born in 1742. She was married in the States, and remained there.

David, the second son of William and Ann McKeen, was born in Truro, July 31st, 1775. He was married to Diana Huchinson, 1801. They settled at Musquodoboit. He carried on milling at the same place that James and Matthew Archibald's mills now stand. His first wife died there in February, 1811. He was married again to Susan, daughter of John and Ann Logan, of Truro, 1811. She died, of consumption, in 1813. He was married the third time to Lucy, daughter of Ebenezer Hoar and Catherine Downing, of Onslow, widow of the late Thomas Taylor, March, 1818. He died in July, 1824. After his death, his widow and children returned to Truro, and resided on her first husband's farm, until about the year 1843. She then removed to Pictou town with her sons, Thomas and Ebenezer McKeen, where she died October 4th, 1847. John, the eldest son of David and Diana McKeen, was born May 7th, 1802. He served with Mr. Alexander Knight, of Truro, and learned the trade of saddle and harness making. He removed to Mabou. C. B. He was married there to Grace Smith, November 9th, 1826. They had four sons and four daughters. Mrs. McKeen died February 13th, 1870. William McKeen, their second son, was born May 27th, 1804. He removed to Mabou also. He was married there to Rebecca Smith, about the year 1830. They had two sons and seven daughters. He died there March 26th, 1867. David McKeen, their third son, was born August 6th, 1806. He was married to Susan Higgins, of Musquodoboit, January 5th. 1831. They had seven daughters. Mr. McKeen, Joseph Parker, James Higgins and John Read, went together to a lake south of Musquodoboit to fish. By some means they were thrown from their boat or raft into the lake, and were all found drowned, June 13th, 1851. Ann, the only daughter of David and Diana McKeen, was born June 4th, 1808. She died at Mabou, C. B., February, 1827, aged 19 years.

Susan, the only daughter of David and Lucy McKeen, was born June, 1819. She was married to Thomas Nelson, of Musquodoboit, in 1840. They had one son and two daughters. She died about the year 1848. Thomas, the eldest son of David and Lucy McKeen, was born in 1821. He learned the trade of tanning and shoe] making with Major A. L. Archibald, of Truro. He removed to Pictou town, and carried on his business there for a number of years. He then removed to Cape Breton, where he still resides. He was married in Pictou to Mary Roach, May, 1849. They had four sons and seven daughters. Ebenezer McKeen, their second and youngest son, was born in 1823. He removed to Pictou with his mother and brother Thomas. He died there June, 1847, aged 24 years.

Margaret, the second daughter of William and Ann McKeen, was born in Truro, September 18th, 1777. She died when young.

James, their third son, was born April 10th, 1779. He removed to Cape Breton, and was married to Eliza Scott, of Musquodoboit, August, 1824. They had four sons and two daughters. He died at Mabou, C. B., in 1847, aged 68 years. His widow and family removed to the United States. Mrs. McKeen died there in 1853. Elizabeth, the third daughter of William and Ann McKeen, removed to Musquodoboit with her parents and family. She died there unmarried, July 1851. Margaret McKeen, their fourth daughter, was born in Truro, 1786. She was married to Robert Higgins, of Musquodoboit. They had two sons and two daughters. She died July, 1860.

William McKeen, their fourth son, was born in Truro, August 18th, 1789. He left home when a young man and went to Pictou for a while, when the timber trade was brisk there. He returned and went to Musquodoboit, where he was married to Elizabeth McDougall, July, 1811; and, soon after, they removed to Mabou, C. B., where he carried on a large business as a merchant and farmer. They had five sons and six daughters. His first wife died December 18th, 1834. He was married again to Christiann Smith in April, 1835. They had five sons and seven daughters. He was a member of the Legislative Council of Nova Scotia for a number of years before his death. He died May 17th, 1865, aged 76 years. Martha McKeen, their fifth daughter, was born in 1792. She was married to Samuel Benvey, of Musquodoboit, about 1820. They had five sons and five daughters. Mr. Benvey died in March, 1841, aged 50 years. A few years after the death of her husband, she removed with her family to Cape Breton.

Samuel, the fifth and youngest son of William and Ann McKeen, was born in Truro, August 25th, 1794. He removed with his parents and the rest of the family to Musquodoboit, in 1815. He was married there to Jane Higgins, in 1818. They had four sons and two daughters. He removed to Cape Breton. His wife died there April 10th, 1865. He was married again to Mrs. Mary Ross, of Margaree, March, 1871.

John, the second son of John and Martha McKeen, was born before they came to Nova Scotia, in 1747. In the after part of his life, he went by the name of Captain McKeen. He was married to Rachel, daughter of Lieut. John and Sarah Johnson, December 30th, 1769. He resided a large portion of his life in a house which stood near the place where Mr. Tremain now resides. Mr. William Logan, his neighbour, was passing the house of Mr. McKeen, who was busily engaged chopping wood. Mr. Logan said to him, you are hard at work this morning, Mr. McKeen. Mr. McKeen replied : " O yes ; it has become a second nature for me to work." Mr. Logan replied : I'm glad of it, for it was never your first. His first wife, Rachel, died December 3rd, 1781. He was married again to Rachel Duncan, widow of the late Samuel Archibald, 2nd, February 12th, 1783. In his old days, he removed to St. Mary's, to live with his youngest son, William, and his wife remained in Truro. Once he said that he travelled all the way from St. Mary's to Truro to see his wife, and when he came he could not see her. He had lost his sight a few years before. He died at St. Mary's. His second wife died in Truro, January 20th, 1814. aged 71 years.

John, the eldest son of Captain John and Rachel McKeen, was born in Truro, December 30th, 1770. He was married to Elizabeth, the third daughter of Dr. John Harris and Elizabeth Scott, December, 1798. (They were the first whom Mr. Waddell married after he came to Truro.) He settled and cleared a small part of the farm that Mr. Hugh Clarke now resides upon. He sold this farm to Samuel Clark in 1805. He removed to St. Mary's, and continued there until 1817. He then removed to Tatamagouche Mountain, where he and his sons reclaimed their farms from the forest. He died there October 17th, 1854, aged 84 years. His wife died there January 6th, 1820, aged 45 years. Rachel McKeen, their eldest daughter. was born January 13th, 1800. She was married to Hiram Downing, December 31st, 1829. They had two sons and two daughters. She died March, 1835, aged 35 years. John McKeen, their eldest son, was born May 31st, 1802. He inherited a part of his father's property on Tatamagouche Mountain, where he died a bachelor October 20th, 1857, aged 55 years. Sarah McKeen, their second daughter, was born January 14th, 1804. She was married to Peter Teed, Esq., of Wallace, December, 1827, She died March, 1856, aged 52 years. On November 12th, 1848, Mr. Teed was burned to death in his barn, trying to save a waggon. Martha McKeen, their third daughter, was born November 22nd, 1806. She was married to Richard Wooden (a school teacher), November 13th, 1824. They had three sons and three daughters. She died April, 1865, aged 58 years. Her husband died October, 1858. William McKeen, their second son, was born October 16th, 1808. He was married to Amelia, the third daughter of James Drysdale and Nancy Brown, March, 1833. Mrs. McKeen died July 3rd, 1833, aged 16 years. He was married again to Jane, daughter of George and Sarah Crow, February, 1837. He died October 16th, 1846, aged 38 years. His widow died in 1848. Eliza McKeen, their fourth daughter, was born May 25th, 1810. She was married to John, the eldest son of Joseph Mahon and Margaret Crow, December 24th, 1833. They had three sons and two daughters. Mr. Mahon died October 10th, 1858. Margaret McKeen, their fifth daughter, was born April 25th, 1812. She was married to John, the eldest son of James and Nancy Drysdale, March 20th, 1845. They had three sons and one daughter. They reside on Tatamagouche Mountain. Maria McKeen, their sixth daughter, was born February 28th, 1815. She was married to Adam Armstrong, of Chiganoise, March 20th, 1851. They had one son. Mr. Armstrong died February 28th, 1864. Susan, their seventh daughter, was born April 6th, 1817. James McKeen, their third and youngest son, was born May 17th, 1819. He was married to Abigail, daughter of George and Sarah Crow, March 20th, 1845. They had sons and daughters. He resides on Tatamagouche Mountain.

Martha Cargill, the eldest daughter of Captain John and Rachel McKeen, was born in Truro, October 26th, 1772.

James, the second son of Captain John and Rachel McKeen, was born in Truro, November 28th, 1774. He died April 19th, 1791, aged 16 years. Samuel McKeen, their third son, was born April 17th, 1777. He was married to Sarah, daughter of John and Ann Logan, June 16th, 1803. They had three sons and one daughter. About the year 1845, as he was riding home on horseback, he fell from his horse, and was taken up dead. His widow died in 1866, in St. Mary's, where they had resided from about the time they were married.

Adam McKeen, their fourth son, was born in Truro, September 17th, 1779. He was married to Janet, the eldest daughter of David and Eleanor Taylor, August 15th, 1805. They had four sons and four daughters. They removed to St. Mary's, where they settled, and spent the remainder of their days. He died there, and Mrs. McKeen died. Rachel, the youngest daughter of John and Rachel McKeen, was born December 3rd 1781. She was married to Thomas Johnson, of the Lower Village of Truro, September 20th, 1804. They had two sons. Mr. Johnson died in 1809. She was married again to Andrew Yuill, October 22nd, 1811. They had one son. She died April 18th, 1813, aged 31 years. William, the only son of John

McKeen and Rachel Archibald, his second wife, was born in Truro, June 4th, 1786. He settled at St. Mary's. He was married there to Miss Kirk, in 1812. They had sons and daughters. He died about 1862.

David the third son of John McKeen, Esq., and Martha Cargill, was born in 1749. He was married to Janet, daughter of Captain Matthew Taylor and Elizabeth Archibald, October 22nd, 1773. After the death of James Fulton, and the removal of his sons to Stewiacke and elsewhere, he purchased their place in the Lower Village of Truro, being the place that Charles Crow now resides upon, also the lot that Samuel Soley now resides upon. Here he settled, and built a mill up the brook. Shortly after, a heavy freshet came and carried it away, which discouraged him so much that he removed to St. Mary's, and settled on the farm on which Mr. Samuel Archibald now resides, two miles up the West River, above the Forks. He settled there in 1802. In August, 1818, he came to Truro to have a cancer cut out of his lip. The operation was successfully performed, and he returned home, apparently quite well; but, about eleven years after, it broke out again, and he died in 1830. His wife died in 1820. John Cargill McKeen, their eldest son, was born in Truro, April 15th, 1775. He was married to Sabrina, daughter of Colonel Atwater, of Guysborough, November 1st, 1808. They had seven sons and one daughter. He settled at Stillwater, St. Mary's, where he spent the remainder of his life. He died there in 1852, aged 77 years. His wife died there about 1860. Matthew, the second son of David and Janet McKeen, was born in Truro, March 11th, 1777. He died November 17th, 1790, aged 13 years. William McKeen, their third son, was born February 10th, 1779. He died in the Lower Village in 1798. Elizabeth, the eldest daughter of David and Janet McKeen, was born in Truro, February 2nd, 1781. She was married to James McLain, about 1804. They settled for a time on the south-west side of the St. Mary's River, at the Forks. Rosannah McKeen, their second daughter, was born in Truro, November 30th, 1783. She was married to James, third son of James Archibald, Esq., and Rebecca Barnhill, October, 1808. They had one son and two daughters. She died October 30th, 1814, aged 31 years. Samuel McKeen, their fourth son, was born in Truro, February 11th, 1786. He was married to Elizabeth, daughter of John and Nancy Taylor, of St. Mary's, June, 1809. They had two sons. Mrs. McKeen died in 1814. He was married again to Miss Glencross, in 1815. He settled up the West

River of St. Mary's. He died there about the year 1826, aged 40 years. His wife died there too. David McKeen, their fifth son, was born in Truro, May 22nd, 1788. He was married to Miss McKenzie in 1811. They had sons and daughters. He removed to Ohio, U. S., with his family, about the year 1820. Robert, the sixth son of David and Janet McKeen, was born in the Lower Village of Truro, in 1790. He became somewhat insane. Shortly after James Archibald was married to his sister, Rosannah, and had removed to Stewiacke, his attachment to his sister was so strong that he started from St. Mary's and found his way through the woods to Stewiacke. His friends followed him ; and. when taking him home again, he got away from them into the woods, and was never heard of after. He was 19 years old at the time. James McKeen, their seventh son, was born in 1792. He removed to Ohio, U. S., when he was a young man. Matthew McKeen, their eighth son, was born in 1794. He removed to Ohio, U. S., when he was a young man. Margaret, daughter of John and Martha McKeen, was born in 1751, before they came to Nova Scotia. She was married to James Fisher, February 12th, 1772. They had two sons and three daughters, born in Truro. They removed to St. Mary's. She died there in 1817. Her husband died in the year 1812.

CHAPTER LI.

William Fisher was among the early settlers of Truro. He was born in Londonderry, Ireland, in 1716. He was married to Eleanor Archibald about the year 1743. They removed to Londonderry New Hampshire, about this time. They removed again to Truro with the Archibalds and others, in December, 1762. He was a Grantee of the Township. He was the first Town Clerk of Truro after it was settled by the British. He was one of the seven elders of the Church who were elected in the summer of the year 1770. He took his seat in the House of Assembly June 6th, 1770, and represented Truro five years. He resided on the interval of Salmon River. His house stood near the place that Thomas Blair's house now stands. He died there June 6th, 1777, aged 61 years.

John Fisher, their eldest son, was born in New Hampshire, March

4th, 1744. He came with his parents to Nova Scotia. He was a Grantee of Truro. He was married to Elizabeth Cowley in 1763. He was one of the seven who removed to Upper Musquodoboit in the spring of the year 1784. Shortly after they settled in Musquodoboit there was a moose crossing the field of this Mr. Fisher ; his wife took the gun and shot and wounded him so badly that the men followed after and got him. He died at Musquodoboit, March 2nd, 1818, aged 74 years. His widow died November 6th, 1826, aged 83 years. Josiah Fisher, their eldest son, was born in Truro, September, 1764. Eleanor Fisher was born February 14th, 1767. Janet Fisher, their second daughter, was born July 5th, 1769. Margaret Fisher, their third daughter, was born August 22nd, 1771. Elizabeth Taylor Fisher, their fourth daughter, was born June 2nd, 1773. William Handcock Fisher, their second son, was born June 29th, 1775. Sarah Milliken Fisher, their fifth daughter, was born June 25th, 1777. Hannah Fisher, their sixth daughter, was born August 27th, 1779. Ruth Fisher, their seventh daughter, was born July 29th, 1781. They had two other daughters. George Fisher, their third son, was born, lived and died in Musquodoboit. Robert Fisher, their fourth and youngest son, was born April 28th, 1790. He was married to Susan K. Dean, April 1st, 1829. They had sons and daughters. They now (January, 1873) reside near the Shubenacadie River, on the east side.

James, the second son of William and Eleanor Fisher, was born in 1746. He was married to Margaret, daughter of John Mc-Keen, Esq., and Martha Cargill, February 12th, 1772. He was a Grantee of Truro, although he was but nineteen years old at the date of the grant. He was one of the seven who removed to Upper Musquodoboit in the spring of the year 1784. He removed again to St. Mary's, where he spent the remainder of his days. He died there about the year 1812, aged 66 years. His wife died about the year 1817. William Fisher, their eldest son, was born in Truro, December 30th, 1772. Martha Fisher, the eldest daughter, was born January 11th, 1775. Eleanor Fisher, their second daughter, was born in Truro, February 10th, 1777. John McKeen Fisher was born in Truro, May 15th, 1779. Jane Fisher, their third daughter, was born in Truro, May 5th, 1781.

Samuel, the third son of William and Eleanor Fisher, was born in New Hampshire in 1750. He came with his parents to Nova Scotia. He was a Grantee of Truro Township. He was married to Mary

Langell, December 24th, 1778. He removed to Musquodoboit with his two brothers in the spring of the year 1784. Sarah Fisher, their eldest daughter, was born in Truro, June 23rd, 1779. Mary Fisher, their second daughter, was born in Truro, May 8th, 1781. They had three sons and three daughters after they left Truro.

David, the fourth son of William and Eleanor Fisher, was born in New Hampshire in 1752. He was brought by his parents to Nova Scotia when he was ten years old. His name is among the Grantees of Truro Township, although he was but thirteen years old at the date of the grant. He was married to Martha, the only daughter of Robert Dickey, about the year 1776. They had eight sons and three daughters. They removed to Middle Stewiacke in the fall of the year 1782 (when their second son, Robert, was about one and a half years old). They settled on the same farm that their son Alexander now resides upon, on the south side of the River. He died there, March 18th, 1831, aged 82 years. His widow died December 22nd, 1843, aged 87 years.

William, the fifth son of William and Eleanor Fisher, was born in New Hampshire in 1756. He was brought by his parents to Nova Scotia when he was six years old. He was married to Esther, daughter of John and Mary Logan, February 14th, 1786. He inherited his father's farm, on the interval of Salmon River. He died there in 1811, aged 55 years. His widow was married again to James Archibald, Esq., in 1820.

John Logan Fisher, their eldest son, was born February 19th, 1787. He inherited a part of his father's farm for a few years. He built his first house on the same place that Mr. Daniel Cock's house now stands. He was married to Elizabeth, the second daughter of James and Eleanor Yuill, of Old Barns, in 1812. She died a short time after. He was married again to Esther, the eldest daughter of William and Ann Flemming, of Truro, August 29th, 1816. They had four sons. He died Decr. 28th, 1863, in the 77th year of his age.

William, the second son of William and Esther Fisher, was born in Truro, April 23rd, 1789. He learned the blacksmith trade. He removed to Musquodoboit, and was married there to Kezia Holdman, in 1810. She died in Truro, June 14th, 1818, aged 28 years. He removed to Pictou Town, where he carried on his business for a number of years. He died there. Eleanor, the eldest daughter of William and Esther Fisher, was born in Truro, June 12th, 1791. She was married to George McNaught, of Upper Stewiacke, December

13th, 1839. She died August 27th, 1872, aged 81 years. Mary Fisher, their second daughter, was born June 17th, 1793. She was married to Alexander Ellis, of Stewiacke, December, 1815. They had four sons and four daughters. She died January, 1869, aged 75 years.

Edward Logan Fisher, their third son, was born August 26th, 1795. He inherited his father's farm for a few years. He then removed to Upper Stewiacke. He was married there to Mary Winton, in 1826. They had seven sons and four daughters. He died August 27th, 1872, aged 77 years. His wife died January 14th, 1849. Nancy Fisher, their third daughter, was born November 26th, 1799. She was married to John McDonald. They settled in Georgetown, P. E. I. They had two sons and two daughters. They removed to the United States, where he died. She returned to the Island again, where she died in the year 1866, aged 67 years. Sarah Fisher, their fourth daughter, was born March 26th, 1801. She was married to William, son of Charles Cox and Nancy Thomson, January 20th, 1822. She died June 21st, 1823, aged 22 years. Mr. Cox was married again to Olivia Thomson, February 24th, 1824. They had two sons and one daughter. Mr. Cox died of small pox January 20th, 1828. His widow was married again to Eleazar B. Dickey, December 31st, 1833. They had two sons and four daughters. Janet Fisher, their fifth daughter, was born May 24th, 1803. She died May 10th, 1807. James Fisher, their fourth son, was born July 26th, 1806. He was married to Esther Millan. They had one son and two daughters. He now resides in Musquodoboit, where he carries on blacksmith work.

Margaret, the eldest daughter of William and Eleanor Fisher, was born in 1747. She was married to John Archibald, second, March 4th, 1772. They had five sons and five daughters. She died May 12th, 1809, aged 62 years. Mr. Archibald died October 15th, 1813, aged 66 years.

Elizabeth, the second daughter of William and Eleanor Fisher, was born in 1754. She was married to James Hughes. They had one son and one daughter. This daughter was married to James D. Nash, August 15th, 1805, They had seven sons and seven daughters. John D. Nash, Esq., of Halifax, was their eldest son. Mr. Nash died in Truro, October 16th, 1837. His widow was married again to Robert Fisher, of Middle Stewiacke. Hannah Fisher, their third daughter, was born in 1758. She was married to Stewtly Horton. They removed to Musquodoboit with her three brothers, in the spring

of the year 1784, where they settled and spent the remainder of their
lives. Sarah Fisher, their fourth daughter, was born, in 1760. She
was married to Archibald Gammell, November 15th, 1782. They
had one son and six daughters. They removed to Upper Stewiacke,
about the year 1790, where they spent the remainder of their days.
Ruth Fisher, their fifth daughter, was born in Truro, February 7th,
1763, about two months after they arrived in Truro. She was married
to Matthew Johnson, of the Lower Village of Truro, in 1782. They
had seven sons and two daughters. They removed to Stewiacke in
the fall of the year 1783. She died at Pembroke, August 8th, 1825,
aged 62 years. Mr. Johnson died there January 20th, 1825, aged 68
years. Alexander McNutt Fisher, their sixth son, was born in Truro,
July 2nd, 1765. He had a part of his father's farm on the interval.
He sold it, and removed to Musquodoboit, where he spent the
remainder of his life. He was married to Janet, daughter of Robert
and Hannah Archibald, widow of the late William Logan, in 1798.
They had two sons and one daughter. Eleanor Fisher, their sixth
daughter, was born in Truro, August 23rd, 1767. She was married
to Robert Logan, in 1788. They had one son and one daughter.
She died in Stewiacke in 1792. He was married again to widow
Johnson in 1801. They had one son and one daughter. Mr. Logan
died December 31st, 1833, aged 70 years.

CHAPTER LII.

John Jeffrey was another of the first settlers of Truro, and one of
the Grantees of the Township. He resided on his front land in the
Lower Village. His house stood in William McNutt's field, north of
the meeting house. He was married to Mary Trevois, Feb'y, 1779.
Mr. and Mrs. Jeffrey died when their children were young. Mary
Jeffrey was born in Truro, December 9th, 1779. She was married to
William Brownrig, in 1797. They had three sons and two daughters.
Mr. Brownrig was lost at sea, from a vessel bound for the West
Indies with a cargo of lumber and horses, in 1810. She was married
again to William English. They had one daughter, who is now
the wife of William McLain, of Truro. Mr. English died, and she
removed to Pictou town, and died there January 19th, 1857, aged 77

years. Jane Jeffrey, their second daughter, was born in Truro, September 8th, 1781. She was married to John Herron, of the Lower end of Onslow. They had two sons and four daughters. She died in 1870. Mr. Herron died, too. Elizabeth Jeffrey, their third daughter, was born May 5th, 1783. She was married to Mr. McLearn, of Hants County. Mr. McLearn died. She was married again to Hugh Forbes, of the same place. She died there in April, 1871, aged 88 years. John Jeffrey, their eldest son, was born April 5th, 1784. He was married to Janet, daughter of James Dickey and Elizabeth Kennedy. They had five sons and three daughters. He settled at South Branch of Stewiacke. He died at Brookfield April, 1864, aged 85 years. His wife died there, too. Sarah Jeffrey, their fourth daughter, was born May 28th, 1786. She went with William Long and family to Ohio, U. S. Margaret Jeffrey, their fifth daughter, was born January 1st, 1788. She was married to John Boomer, of Brookfield. They had six sons and two daughters. She died August, 1831, aged 43 years. Mr. Boomer died June 15th, 1856. Margaret Jeffrey was brought up, and married at the house of Mr. William Smith, of Truro. Joseph Jeffrey, their youngest son, was born June 27th, 1790. He stopped a considerable time at Mr. Smith's also. He enlisted and went off with the soldiers in 1811. He never returned.

CHAPTER LIII.

James Gourley was another of the first settlers of Truro, and a Grantee of the Township. He resided on his front lands in the Lower Village, where he spent the remainder of his life. He died there about the year 1790. His wife, Catherine Stevenson, died July 5th, 1804, aged 90 years. He was married and had several children before they came to Nova Scotia. John Gourley, their eldest son, was born in 1751. He was brought by his parents to Truro. He was a Grantee of the Township, although he was but fourteen years old at the date of the grant. He was lost at sea when he was a young man.

Thomas, the second son of James and Catherine Gourley, was born in New England, in 1752. He came with the family to Truro in 1761. His name is among the Grantees for the Township, being but twelve years old at the date of the grant. He was married to Jane, the only daughter of James Yuill, Esq., and Jane Bailey, in 1779. He inherited a large part of his father's property in the Lower Village, where he spent the remainder of his life. On April 14th, 1821, he was engaged building a breakwater to secure the bank of the marsh above the Board-landing, when he fell and was taken up dead, being 68 years old at the time. His widow died February 15th, 1828, aged 71 years. Thomas Gourley, their eldest son, was born in Truro, in 1780. He was married to Mehitable, daughter of William and Dorothy Putnam, of Stewiacke, July 19th, 1809. They resided for a short time in a house which stood at the Board-landing. They removed and lived a short time in a house that stood where James N. Crow, Esq., now resides. They removed again, in the year 1814, to the South Branch of Stewiacke, where they spent the remainder of their lives. They had three sons and five daughters. He died November 8th, 1843, aged 63 years. His widow died in September, 1869. James, the second son of Thomas and Jane Gourley, was born in 1782. He was married to Elizabeth Totton, of Chiganoise, in 1810. They removed to Pictou town, and kept a house of entertainment. They had one son and two daughters. He died in 1832, aged 50 years. His widow was married again. She died in 1860. Susan, the eldest daughter of Thomas and Jane Gourley, was born January 2nd, 1784. She was married to Hugh Dunlap, January 24th, 1805. They had two sons and six daughters. She died at Stewiacke, November 22nd, 1857, in the 74th year of her age. Her husband died September 6th, 1852, aged 79 years.

John, the third son of Thomas and Jane Gourley, was born December 30th, 1784. He was married to Sarah, the eldest daughter of Dumb John Johnson and Margaret Davison, February 2nd, 1815. He inherited the half of his father's farm. He died August 9th, 1836, aged 51 years. Robert, the eldest son of John and Sarah Gourley, was born November 12th, 1815. He removed to the State of Illinois He was married there, and had one son and one daughter. He died there December 18th, 1849, aged 34 years. John Gourley, their second son, was born March 5th, 1817. He removed to Shepody, where he died December 10th, 1841, aged 24 years. Mary Gourley, their eldest daughter, was born February 17th, 1819. She was married to Joseph Peppard, of Londonderry. They had five sons and four daughters. Mr. Peppard died April, 1866. Thomas Gourley, their third son, was born July 10th. 1821. He learned the blacksmith trade with Mr. William McLeod. He was married to Margaret Hamilton, of Onslow. Mrs. Gourley died October, 1868. He was married again to Mary Hutchison, recently from England, July 20th, 1870. James Gourley, their fourth son, was born February 2nd, 1823. He learned the carpenter trade with Samuel J. Blair, of Truro. He was married to Mary Ann Bentley, of Stewiacke, June, 1856. They had two sons and two daughters. He and his brother Thomas settled at Great Village, Londonderry, where they carry on a considerable business as merchants and shipowners. George Gourley, their fifth son, was born April 10th, 1825. He learned the tanning business, and carried it on for a while at Great Village. He died there January 12th, 1856, aged 30 years. William Gourley, their sixth son, was born March 17th, 1827. He died September, 1828. Rachel Gourley, their second daughter, was born April 20th, 1829. She removed to the United States, and was married there to Augustus F. Garland, October, 1856. They had one son. He died in 1859. Margaret Gourley, their third daughter, was born July 20th, 1831. She was married to Isaiah Peppard, May 4th, 1854. She died May, 1855. Hannah Gourley, their fourth daughter, was born September 1st, 1833. She was married to James Bland, of Wallace, in the United States in 1853. They have four sons. Sarah Gourley, their fifth daughter, was born August 29th, 1835. Sarah Johnson, widow of John Gourley, was married to William Soley, November, 1837. William Lawson Soley, their eldest son, was born March 12th, 1838. He was married to Sarah, daughter of George S. and Esther Dickey, April, 1865. They have one son. They have removed to the United States. John Soley, their second son, was born April 29th, 1841. He was married to Margaret Cormick, of Chatham, New Brunswick, May, 1869. They have one son and one daughter.

Stephen, the fourth son of Thomas and Jane Gourley, was born in 1786. He died January, 1808, aged 21 years. Margaret Gourley, their second daughter, was born in 1789. She died of consumption in the fall of the year 1815. Jane Gourley, their third daughter, was born in 1791. She and her brother Stephen died of Typhus fever, January, 1808, and were both interred at one time. Jesse Gourley, their fifth son, was born November 15th, 1793. He was married to Mary, the second daughter of James and Jane Laughead, November 8th, 1819. Mary Jane, their only daughter, was born May 8th, 1821. She was married to William P. Archibald, January 30th,

1838. They had five sons and four daughters. Mrs. Archibald died February 27th, 1857, aged 36 years. Mrs. Gourley died May 8th, 1821, the same day that her only daughter was born. He was married again to Eunice McNutt, June, 1825. Margaret Gourley, their only daughter, was born September 9th, 1827. She was married to James N. Crow, Esq., April 8th, 1845. They have four sons and one daughter. They inherit what was her father's property. Mr. Gourley, on the 27th day of March, 1871, was engaged chopping wood at his door. He fell, and when taken up a few minutes after, life had departed. He was in the 78th year of his age. Eunice, his second wife, died May 8th, 1862, aged 56 years. Catherine, the fourth daughter of Thomas and Jane Gourley, was born 1795. She was married to Mr. Casey, October, 1828. They had one daughter. Mr. Casey died, and she was married again to Mr. Wedgewood, April, 1838. She died November 3rd, 1867, aged 72 years. William Gourley, their sixth son, was born in 1796. He died when he was about six years old. Robert Gourley, their seventh son, was born 1797. In 1815 he was at Pictou attending the Academy, and he walked home to attend his brother's wedding. He returned to Pictou, and very shortly after took ill. He died there March 5th, 1815, aged 18 years. His body was brought home for interment. Eleanor Gourley, their fifth daughter, was born March 17th, 1799. She was married to William Yuill, of Great Village, Londonderry, February 11th, 1819. She had five sons and two daughters. Mr. Yuill died September 29th, 1863, aged 82 years. Hannah Gourley, their sixth daughter, was born March 11th, 1801. She was married to James Dunlap, March 16th, 1826. They had one son and one daughter. Mr. Dunlap died March 5th, 1856, aged 55 years.

William Gourley, the fourth son of James and Catherine Gourley, was born in New England in 1756, and brought by his parents to Truro when he was six years old. He was married to Lydia Hamilton in 1777. He resided in the Lower Village; his house stood beside the road south of the school house. He followed the sea, and was drowned in 1799. Catherine Gourley, their eldest daughter, was born in Truro, October 29th, 1779. She was married to Vinton Taylor. They had two sons and two daughters. They removed to Ohio, U. S. John, the second son of William and Lydia Gourley, was born August 22nd, 1781. He was married to Elizabeth, the second daughter of Samuel Tupper, Esq., and Hannah Archibald, in 1807. They had two sons and four daughters. He settled at the South Branch of Stewiacke. He died there. Hannah Gourley, their second daughter, was born in Truro, August 11th, 1783. She was married to Mr. McCabe, of River John. They had three sons and three daughters. She died in 1863. Elizabeth Gourley, their third daughter, was born October 30th, 1785. James, the eldest son of William and Lydia Gourley, was born November 7th, 1778. He was married to Susanna Carter, of Onslow, March 7th, 1799. They had five sons and one daughter. He was a sea Captain. He died at Brookfield, January, 1852. His widow died November, 1858. Samuel Gourley, their third son, was born in 1788. He was a carpenter by trade. He removed to Cumberland, and was married there to Isabell Copps, in 1815. They had two sons and three daughters. He died in 1856.

Peter, the fourth and youngest son of William and Lydia Gourley, was born in Truro in 1797. He was a mason by trade. He settled at the South Branch of Stewiacke. He was married there to Catherine McCulloch, about 1840. They had three sons and two daughters. He died December 18th, 1870, aged 73 years.

Susannah, the only daughter of James and Catherine Gourley, was born in New England in 1758. She was married to Robert Johnson, December 2nd, 1778. They had six sons and one daughter; these appear among the Johnsons. She died July, 1844, aged 86 years. Mr. Johnson died April 4th, 1815, aged 68 years.

Jesse Gourley, the third son of James and Catherine Gourley, was born in New England in 1754. He removed to Lower Stewiacke with his brother Stephen, where he spent the remainder of his life. He died there a bachelor, May 20th, 1830, aged 76 years.

Stephen, the fifth and youngest son of James and Catherine Gourley, was born in 1760, and was brought by his parents to Truro in 1761. He built a house for an Inn at the Board-landing, where there was considerable shipbuilding carried on at the time. He was married to Hannah Swinburn, widow of the late Alexander Kent, in 1797. They removed then to Lower Stewiacke, and settled on the farm that his grandson, Robert J. Pollock, Esq., now resides upon, where he kept an Inn. His house stood on the west side of the road leading from Truro to Halifax, where Mr. Pollock's barn now stands. He lost one of his hands by some means when he was a young man. He died February 15th, 1829, aged 68 years. His widow died January 31st, 1831, aged 75 years. Susannah, the only daughter of Stephen and Hannah Gourley, was born at Lower Stewiacke, November 27th, 1798. She was married to William Pollock, January, 1820. They had three sons and one daughter. Mr. Pollock died May 15th, 1827. She was married again to Robert Hill, July 3rd, 1828. They had three sons and five daughters. Mr. Hill died August 23rd, 1851, aged 56 years.

The above named Alexander Kent was brother of Jas. Kent, Esq., of the Lower Village of Truro. He was an officer in the British army, and had been some time in Fredericton, N. B., with his wife and family. He was about to leave the army, and went to the West Indies to secure his pension. He died there, leaving a widow and three sons in Fredericton. Mr. Kent, of the Lower Village, went and brought her and her family to the Lower Village. She lived in the house that James Kent, second, afterwards lived in, until she was married. Their son James settled in Musquodoboit. He was Colonel of the first battalion of Colchester Militia many years. He was married to Christiann Guild. They had four sons and five daughters. He died November, 1864. His wife died June, 1863. Their son, Alexander Kent, settled in Musquodoboit also. He was married to Elizabeth Horton. They had five sons and six daughters. He died November, 1871. Their son, Samuel Kent, settled in Lower Stewiacke. He was married to Mary Pollock in 1815. They had two sons and three daughters. Mrs. Kent died about 1864.

CHAPTER LIV.

Samson Moore was among the early settlers of Truro, and was a Grantee of the township He was born in Ireland in 1730. He emigrated to New England, and from thence to Nova Scotia, in 1762. He was married to Martha Archibald in 1754. He settled in the Lower Village. His house stood near the place where Mr. Rupert Dunlap now resides. He was drowned in the Bay near Salter's Head, out of a boat, in 1782, aged 52 years.

James Moore, their eldest son, was born in 1755. He was brought by his parents to Truro when he was seven years old. His name is among the Grantees of the Township, although he was but 10 years old at the date of the grant. His front land adjoined his father's, being the same that James D. Johnson and sons now reside upon. He was married to Margaret Pollock, in 1783. He settled near the Shubenacadie River, at the carrying place, so called. (This place took its name from the fact that when the people were passing up and down the River in their boats or canoes, they would take them out of the water and carry them over a narrow piece of land about three rods in breadth, to the River again, to save them going one mile round by the River.) Here he spent the remainder of his life.

Jane, the eldest daughter of James and Margaret Moore, was born in 1784. She was married to James Parker of Cornwallis. They had four sons and three daughters. Mr. and Mrs. Parker both died a number of years ago. Mrs. Moore died, and he was married again to Susan, daughter of Samuel and Janet Teas, of Stewiacke, in 1787. Martha, the eldest daughter of James and Janet Moore, was born in 1788. She was married to Samuel Moore, of Gays River. They had one daughter. Mr. Samuel Moore died about 1857.

Daniel Moore, their eldest son, was born about 1790. He was married to Jane, daughter of William M. and Jane Nelson, January, 1829. They had three sons and four daughters. He died April, 1863, aged 73 years.

Margaret, the second daughter of James and Susan Moore, was born in 1792. She was married to James Philips, October 15th, 1811. They had four sons and five daughters. She died July 26th, 1867, aged 75 years. Mr. Philips died December 23rd, 1830, aged 43 years. Mary Moore, their third daughter, was born in 1793. She was married to John Philips, February 17th, 1817. They had four sons and three daughters. She died February, 1864, aged 71 years. Mr. Philips died December, 1866, aged 76 years. Elizabeth Moore, their fourth daughter, was born 1795. She was married to Henry Hughes. They had three sons and three daughters. Isabell Moore, their fifth daughter, was born in 1797. She was married to Samuel Creelman, of Prince Port, December 9th, 1821. They had one son. She died in 1824. Mr. Creelman died January 8th, 1867, aged 72 years.

James Moore, their second son, was born in 1798. He died about 1818. Samuel Moore, their third son, was born in 1800. He was married to Margaret Gunn. They had two sons and two daughters. He died June 1844. Susan Moore, their sixth daughter, was born in 1802. She was married to William Philips, February 28th, 1822.

They had four sons and six daughters. She died March, 1866. Mr. Philips died June, 1851.

David, their fourth son, was born 1803. He was married to Margaret McKay. They had three sons and four daughters. George Moore, their fifth son, was born in 1805. He was married to Elizabeth, daughter of Samuel Frame and Jane McDonald. They had two sons and three daughters. Dorothy Moore, their seventh daughter, was born in 1807. She died unmarried. Alice Moore, their eighth daughter, was born in 1809. She was married to James Nelson, October, 1828. They had two sons and one daughter. She died March 21st, 1834. William Moore, their sixth son, was born 1811. He was married to Janet McKay. They had one son and two daughters.

John, the second son of Samson and Martha Moore, was born in New England in 1757. He was brought by his parents to Nova Scotia. He was drowned, by the upsetting of a boat, in 1782, when he was 25 years old. Eleanor, the eldest daughter of Samson and Martha Moore, was born in 1761. She was married to John McCabe in 1779. (He was the eldest son of James McCabe, who came from Philadelphia in the ship "Hope," and settled in Pictou in June, 1767.) They settled in Loch Broom, Pictou. They had six sons and seven daughters. She died in 1848, aged 87 years. Mr. McCabe died about 1838.

David, the third son of Samson and Martha Moore, was born in Truro, April 1st, 1763, about four months after they arrived in Nova Scotia. He removed to Cumberland County. He was married there to Catherine Taylor, February 17th, 1801. He returned again to Truro. He died at Old Barns, April 20th, 1849, aged 86 years. His widow died November 4th, 1851, aged 68 years. Martha Moore, their eldest daughter, was born March 22nd, 1802. She was married to Edward Flinn. They had one son and one daughter. She died in Cape Breton, in 1850. Eleazer Moore, their eldest son, was born in Cumberland, September 24th, 1803. He removed to the State of Maine, and was married there. They had one daughter. Mrs. Moore died there, and he was married again to widow Ellenwood, in 1856. Janet Moore, their second daughter, was born in Parrsborough, December 24th, 1804. She was married to Israel Barker, of Cumberland, in 1832. They had seven sons and seven daughters. Mr. Barker died in 1861. His widow removed to the United States. Samson Moore, their second son, was born in Truro, June 6th, 1806.

He was married to Miss Jeffers, of Cumberland, in 1830. They had four sons and two daughters. Alice Moore, their daughter, was born August 29th, 1808. She was married to Charles Jarvis, of Cumberland, June 1835. They had four sons and five daughters. Susan, their fourth daughter, was born September 24th, 1810. She was married to Charles Skinner, of Debert River, January 10th, 1832. They had five sons and six daughters. Eleanor, Moore, their fifth daughter, was born March 7th, 1812. She was married to Joseph Atkison, of Cumberland, in 1836. They had two sons and six daughters. John P. Moore, their third son, was born June 25th, 1813. He was married to Margaret Stevens, widow of the late Thomas McElhenney, of Onslow, March 26th, 1838. Mrs. Moore died October 2nd, 1861, aged 67 years. He was married again to Lydia Ann, Jenks, March 31st, 1866. They have one son. He is settled in Truro Village, where he carries on business as a fuel merchant and grocer. Esther Moore, their sixth daughter, was born May 30th, 1815. Margaret Moore, their seventh daughter, was born March 23rd, 1817. She was married to Dr. Robert Key. They had one son and two daughters. She died at Prince Edward Island, January, 1858. Mr. Key died the same day. Catherine Moore, their eighth daughter, was born October 23rd, 1818. She was married to James Good, of Princeport, January 16th, 1840. Mary Ann Moore, their ninth daughter, was born July 17th, 1820. She was married to Henry Good, in 1836. They had two sons. Ur. Good was drowned November 12, 1842. She was married again to John Waddell, of Hants County, June, 1844. They had six sons and two daughters. She died May 10th, 1864. Sarah Moore, their tenth daughter, was born March 29th, 1822. She was married to John Johnson. They had one son. Mr. Johnson died. James Moore, their fourth son, was born July 31st, 1824. He was married to Elizabeth Colter, March, 1858. Mrs. Moore died in October, 1867. He was married again to Catherine McInnis, May 14th, 1871.

Alice, the second daughter of Samson and Martha Moore, was born March 16th, 1766. She was married to William Philips, December 16th, 1786. They settled beside the Shubenacadie River, where some of their grandsons now reside. She died there January 1st, 1815. Mr. Philips was married again to Elizabeth Munro, October 15th, 1815. He died December 28th, 1830. James, the eldest son of William and Alice Philips, was born August 30th, 1787. He was married to Margaret, second daughter of James and Susan

Moore, October 15th, 1811. He inherited a part of his father's farm. He died December 23rd, 1830. His widow died July 26th, 1867. aged 75 years. Jane Philips, their eldest daughter, was born September, 1812. Susan, their second daughter, was born December, 1815, William, their eldest son, was born October 13th, 1818. He inherited his father's farm. Isabell, their third daughter, was born April 5th, 1821. Martha, their fourth daughter, was born December 30th, 1823. They had three sons and one daughter besides these. Their son, John, came to his death by falling from a load of hay on a pitchfork. Isabell, the only daughter of William and Alice Philips, was born March 8th 1789. She was married to Robison Nelson, December 31st, 1807. They had one son and ten daughters. John Philips, their second son, was born October 4th, 1790. He was married to Mary, the third daughter of James and Susan Moore, February 17th, 1817. They had four sons and three daughters. He died December, 1866. His wife died February, 1864, aged 71 years. William, the third son of William and Alice Philips, was born in 1792. He was married to Susan, the sixth daughter of James and Susan Moore, February 28th, 1822. They had four sons and six daughters. He inherited a part of his father's property. He died June, 1851. His widow died March, 1866.

Samson, the fourth son of Samson and Martha Moore, was born December 9th, 1767. He was married to Margaret, fifth daughter of Robert and Esther Hunter, December 31st, 1795. He inherited his father's farm in the Lower Village of Truro. Robert Moore, their eldest son, was born in 1796. He died of consumption in 1816. Mrs. Moore died in the same year, of the same complaint. Margaret Moore, their daughter, was born in 1798. She died at the house of her uncle, William Smith, in 1817, of the same complaint. Mr. Moore died in 1818.

Daniel, the fifth son of Samson and Martha Moore, was born May 1st, 1770. He was married to Jane, third daughter of Alexander and Margaret Nelson. They had one son and two daughters. Mr. Moore was lost at sea.

Joseph Moore, brother of Samson Moore, was among the early settlers of Truro, and was a Grantee of the Township. His house lot was the whole of the Upland east of Walker Street. The hill on which George Reading, Esq., now resides, was long known as " Joe Moore's Hill." He had but one son ; he was a watchmaker, and

22

removed to the United States. He had a number of daughters ; some of them were married and went to New Brunswick, and some to the United States. We know nothing about them at present.

CHAPTER LV.

James Downing was another of the first settlers of Truro, and a Grantee of the Township. He resided on his front land in the Lower Village, where he and his wife spent the remainder of their days. He died October 28th, 1776. His widow died December 31st, 1801. He was married to Janet Montgomery, in New England, in 1749. Mary, their eldest daughter, was born in New England in 1750, and was brought by her parents to Nova Scotia when she was ten years old. She was married to William, the eldest son of Capt. William Blair and Jane Barns, about the year 1770. Her descendants appear among the Blairs. She died November, 1817, aged 67 years. Mr. Blair died March, 1848, aged 91 years. Janet Downing, their second daughter, was born in 1753. She was married to Joshua Higgins. They had three sons and three daughters. They resided at Lower Onslow, where they both died some time ago. James Downing, their only son, was born in New England in 1758. He was married to Margaret, the second daughter of John Dickson, Senr., and Margaret Burn, November 22nd, 1787. They had two children. He died July 21st, 1789. His wife died February 15th, 1790. Catherine Downing, their third daughter, was born on board the vessel that they came in to Nova Scotia, a short time before they anchored at Savages Island, in the spring of the year 1760. She was married to Ebenezer Hoar, January 5th, 1775. They had two sons and ten daughters. They resided on the same place that their youngest son, James Hoar, now resides, in Onslow. She died of fever, August 30th, 1819, aged 59 years. Mr. Hoar died of the same fever, August 2nd. 1819, aged 61 years. Nancy Downing, their fourth daughter, was born in Truro, January 23rd, 1762. She was married to John, second son of Capt. William Blair and Jane Barns, in 1781. They had five sons and three daughters, who appear among the Blairs. She died January 9th, 1829, aged 67 years, and Mr. Blair died October 5th, 1847, aged 88 years.

William Downing (brother of James) was another of the first settlers of Truro, and a Grantee of the Township. He was married to Mary Logan, sister of John and William Logan, in 1768. He was the third person who settled in Brookfield, about the year 1787, on the farm which was afterwards owned by John Hamilton, and is now owned by Robert Hamilton, Esq., his brother John, and their sons. He continued in Brookfield but a few years. He returned to Truro Village, and resided near the Messrs. Logan for a few years. His wife died there in 1793. He was married again to Ruth Hoar, widow of the late William P. Whippie, December 26th, 1793. He resided on the Whippie place, near Robert Turner Blair's, in Onslow. He died there June, 1816. His widow died December 8th, 1848, aged 92 years.

John, the eldest son of William and Mary Downing, was born in Truro, April 5th, 1769. He was married to Esther Lynton, June 30th, 1795. He settled east of the Chiganoise River, where he spent the remainder of his life. He died there February, 1826, aged 57 years. His wife died September 11th, 1829. James Downing, their eldest son, was born June 21st, 1797. He was married to Sarah Thomas, October 21st, 1825. They had three sons and three daughters. He died May, 1855, aged 58 years. Robert Downing, their second son, was born August 9th, 1801. He was married to Eliza Ray, of Shepody, September 2nd, 1829. They had five sons and three daughters. He inherited a part of what was his father's farm. He died March 24th, 1868, aged 67 years. John Downing, their third son, was born September 17th, 1803. He was married to Letitia, the eldest daughter of Richard Blackie and Margaret Barnhill, April 10th, 1831. They had one son and one daughter. Mrs. Downing died February, 1844. He was married again to Nancy Hughes, widow of the late Matthew Green, July 22nd, 1848. They had one son and two daughters. George Downing, their fourth son, was born March 16th, 1805. He was married to Margaret Johnson, of Pleasant Valley, November 4th, 1829. They had two sons and six daughters. Elizabeth Downing, their only daughter, was born August 1st, 1799. She was married to John Hollice, December, 1831. They had three sons and four daughters. They removed and settled at Goose River, in Cumberland County. She died there April, 1869.

Janet Downing, the eldest daughter of William and Mary, was born in Truro, August 30th, 1770. She was married to William

Davison, November 16th, 1789, by Dr. John Harris, who was then authorized to perform the ceremony of marriage. It was so dark on this wedding day that candles were lighted at two o'clock in the afternoon, to give them light to attend to the work in the house, and this day is spoken of yet by the old people of Brookfield as the dark day. On March 2nd, 1790, Mrs. Davison died, in the twentieth year of her age. The first marriage and first death which took place in Brookfield was in the house of Mr. William Downing. Mary, the second daughter of William and Mary Downing, was born in Truro, May 2nd, 1772. She was married to Thomas Wetherby, of Londonderry, November 12th, 1794. They had three sons and two daughters. Catherine Downing, their third daughter, was born in Truro, May 9th, 1774. She was married to Barnabas O'Brien, of Chiganoise, November 23rd, 1793. They had three sons and five daughters. She died April, 1869, aged 94 years, and Mr. O'Brien died about 1834. Sarah Downing, their fourth daughter, was born July 22nd, 1778. She was married to William Wetherby. They had three sons and one daughter. William Logan Downing, their second son, was born in Truro, November 21st, 1780. He was a shoemaker by trade. He removed to Hants County, and was married there to Miss Porter, of Windsor. James Downing, the eldest son of William and Ruth, was born in Onslow, September 22nd, 1794. He was a blacksmith by trade. He was married to Dorothy, third daughter of Simeon and Dorothy Whidden, of Middle Stewiacke, July 20th, 1818. They had two sons and four daughters. They inherited a part of her father's farm at Stewiacke. He died there June 1st, 1840, aged 45 years. His widow died September 4th, 1850, aged 56 years. Hiram, the second son of William and Ruth Downing, was born in Onslow, January 22nd, 1800. He removed and settled on Tatamagouche Mountain. He was married there to Rachel, the eldest daughter of John and Elizabeth McKeen, December 31st, 1829. They had two sons and two daughters. Mrs. Downing died in 1836. He was married again to Nancy Vincen. They had four sons and one daughter. He died there December, 1869, aged 72 years. His widow died January, 1871.

CHAPTER LVI.

Joshua Lamb was among the early settlers of Colchester. He was a Grantee of Onslow Township. He resided on the place on which Augustus McCurdy now resides. He was Representative of Onslow, and Registrar of Deeds a few years. He sold his property in Onslow in 1777 to Robert Catherwood, and returned to New England. James Blair was married to Robert Catherwood's daughter Isabell July 20th, 1792. They inherited her father's property a large part of the remainder of their lives. Mr. Lamb was married to Mary Brooks,. September 11th, 1766. They had two sons and two daughters, born in Onslow.

CHAPTER LVII.

James Whidden was among the first settlers of Truro. He was a Grantee of the Township. His house lot was that on which Mr. Thomas M. Crowe and son now reside. He owned the interval on the west side of the marsh road that Dr. C. Bent now owns. He was married and had four sons before he came to Nova Scotia. His wife died and he was married again to Mary Guild, widow of the late Jacob Lynds, of Onslow. He died December 13th, 1790. His widow returned to her son Thomas Lynds' house, at North River. John, the eldest son of James Whidden and his first wife, settled in Cornwallis; he was a leading man there. He was Justice of the Peace and Judge of the Court of Common Pleas for Kings County. He died there September 14th, 1794. Sarah, his second daughter, was drowned at the Board-landing, near Truro, August 12th, 1770, aged 17 years. Elizabeth Whidden, another daughter, was married to the Rev. Hugh Graham, 1792. Mr. Graham was married in Scotland to Elizabeth Brown, a short time before they left. The first time that the Rev. Hugh Graham preached in Middle Stewiacke was on the first day of the week, the first day of the month, the first day of the year, and the first day of the present century.

David, the second son of James Whidden, Senr., was born in New

England, in 1749. He came with the rest of the family to Truro.
He was a grantee of the Township, although he was but 16 years old
at the date of the grant. He was married to Eleanor, second daughter
of Adam and Janet Dickey, September 29th, 1774. He inherited his
father's property in Truro. In 1795 he sold his property in Truro,
and removed to Maitland, where he spent the remainder of his life.
He died October 1st, 1825, aged 76 years. His widow died August
10th, 1828, aged 74 years. James Whidden, their eldest son, was
born in Truro, July 8th, 1775. He was married to Abigail Brown in
1804. They had five sons and five daughters. He carried on a large
business at Maitland as merchant and ship builder. He died June
3rd, 1830, aged 55 years, His widow died June 26th, 1867, aged 88
years. John Hancock, the second son of David and Eleanor Whidden,
was born in Truro, February 13th 1777. He died a bachelor, at
Maitland. David Whidden, their third son, was born in Truro, April
2nd, 1779. He followed the sea, and was lost when he was a young
man. Abigail Whidden, their daughter, was born in Truro, November
10th, 1780. She was married to William Frieze in 1801. They had
one son and three daughters. She died at Maitland, January 4th,
1808, aged 27 years. Mr. Frieze died January 14th, 1843, aged 68
years.

Samuel, the third son of James Whidden and his wife, was born
in New England in 1752. He came with his parents and family to
Nova Scotia in 1760. He was married to Abigail Newcomb, July
15th, 1774. He settled on the interval of Salmon River, on the same
farm on which Timothy Johnson now resides. He died July 10th,
1821, aged 69 years. His wife died March 11th, 1815, aged 57 years.
Elizabeth Whidden, their eldest daughter, was born March 29th,
1775. She was married to Richard Pyke, in 1798. She died, and
Mr. Pyke was drowned by being upset from a boat while crossing the
Shubenacadie River, about the year 1804. Samuel Pyke, their eldest
son, was born 1799. He was married to Martha, daughter of James
and Janet Kennedy, January, 1834. They had two sons and two
daughters. They settled for a time in Smithfield, Stewiacke. He
died September, 1867. Richard, the second son of Richard and
Elizabeth Pyke, was born May 4th, 1801. He was married to
Eleanor, second daughter of James and Nancy McCabe, of Greenfield,
January, 1834. They had three sons and two daughters. He settled
in Smithfield, Stewiacke. Rebecca, the only daughter of Richard and
Elizabeth Pyke, was born 1803. She was married to David, the

youngest son of Simeon Whidden and Dorothy Blair, January, 1821. They had three sons and three daughters. They are settled in Smithfield, Stewiacke.

Abigail, the second daughter of Samuel and Abigail Whidden, was born in Truro, December 7th, 1776. She removed to Maitland, to keep house for her uncle, David Whidden. She was married there to Robert O'Brien of Noel, November 23rd, 1802. They had two sons and five daughters. She died in 1857, aged 80 years. Mr. O'Brien died about the year 1849.

Eddy Whidden, their eldest son, was born February 16th, 1778. He was married to Sarah, daughter of Samuel Fisher and Mary Tupper of Stewiacke, in 1807. They had five sons and five daughters. He settled in the woods at Greenfield, on the same farm on which Mr. Ralph McCabe now resides, being five miles from any neighbours. Upon one occasion while they were living in this lonely situation in the woods and the snow was very deep, Mrs. Whidden not being very well one morning he started and took his cattle with him to try and make a track in the snow, so that some person might get to his house to be with her ; but he failed in getting a track made through the deep snow. He returned home at night much fatigued, when his wife presented him with two sons that had been born during the day. He removed to New Annan. where he died in 1858, aged 80 years. His wife died December, 1835. Sarah, the third daughter of Samuel and Abigail Whidden, was born December, 29th, 1779. She died unmarried in 1797. Eleanor Whidden, their fourth daughter, was born April 5th, 1783. She was married to Dan Bentley of Stewiacke February 10th, 1810. They had one son and two daughters. She died at Stewiacke June 2nd, 1836, aged 53 years. Mr. Bentley died September 4th, 1865. Mary Whidden, their fifth daughter, was born June 29th, 1785. She was married to John Bartlett in 1812. They had five sons and two daughters. They settled on Onslow Mountain, where she died February 12th, 1839. Mr. Bartlett died August 18th, 1837.

Nancy Whidden, their sixth daughter, was born December 24th, 1787. She was married to James McCabe of Pictou, September, 1807. They settled in Greenfield, on the same place that their son James now resides. She died there April 24th, 1858, aged 70 years. Mr. McCabe died December 28th, 1861, aged 80 years.

John McCabe, their eldest son, was born September 10th, 1808. He was married to Rebecca McLellan, of Economy, January, 1835.

They had five sons and five daughters. They removed to Economy, where Mrs. McCabe died March 8th, 1865. He was married again to Ann Ward, September, 1867. Samuel McCabe, their second son, was born April 15th, 1810. He was married to Elizabeth, daughter of John and Mary Bartlett, of Onslow Mountain, March 21st, 1839. They had five sons and five daughters. Mary McCabe, their eldest daughter, was born August 25th, 1812. She was married to William Staples, of Lower Onslow, March 23rd, 1848. They have one daughter.

Eleanor, the second daughter of James and Nancy McCabe, was born June 3rd, 1815. She was married to Richard Pyke, of Smithfield, January, 1833. They have three sons and one daughter. James McCabe, their third son, was born July 6th 1817. He was married to Abigail, daughter of James Downing and Dorothy Whidden, January 20th, 1842. They had four sons and four daughters. He inherits his father's farm in Greenfield. Dan McCabe, their fourth son, was born June 9th, 1819. He was married to Susan McCarnia, in 1852. They had two sons and one daughter. Mrs. McCabe died in 1857. He was married again to Mary McCarnia. They have two daughters. Edward McCabe, their fifth son, was born April 3rd, 1821. He was married to Sarah Higgins, of Musqudoboit, December 20th, 1843. They had seven sons and two daughters. He carries on the blacksmith business at Musquodoboit. Abigail McCabe, their third daughter, was born March 23rd, 1823. She was married to George Higgins of Musquodoboit, December 4th, 1845. They had three sons and three daughters. Asa McCabe, their sixth son, was born March 7th, 1825. He was married to Dorothy, daughter of James and Dorothy Downing, of Stewiacke, February 29th, 1848. They had two sons and four daughters. He reclaimed his farm from the forest where he resides. Ralph McCabe, their seventh son, was born July 27th, 1827. He was married to Jane, daughter of James and Dorothy Downing, of Stewiacke, June 3rd, 1852. They had five sons and five daughters. He now owns and resides on the farm that Eddy Whidden settled on.

Samuel, the second son of Samuel and Abigail Whidden, was born August 13th, 1790. He was married to Sarah, the only daughter of Thomas Stevens and Nancy Elliot, February, 1811. He settled first in Greenfield. He settled again in Harmony, where his wife died, April 21st, 1842. He was married again to Elizabeth McMullon, of Stewiacke, January 31st, 1844. He sold out in Harmony, and built the house that Robert Dinsmore recently lived in. He died there February 16th, 1862, aged 71 years. Elizabeth Whidden, their eldest daughter, was born December 6th, 1811. She was married to Joshua Higgins, of New Annan. They had six sons and four daughters. Abigail Whidden, their second daughter, was born January 26th, 1814. She died unmarried, November, 1846, aged 32 years. Nancy Whidden, their third daughter, was born May 26th, 1816. She was married to Elisha Logan in May, 1842. They had five sons and two daughters. She died December 27th, 1865, aged 49 years. Mr. Logan died September 27th, 1870, aged 54 years. Sarah Whidden, their fourth daughter, was born August 10th, 1818. She was married to William Smith. They had one son. Mr. Smith died, and she was married again to Robert Hill, of Londonderry. They had one son and two daughters. She died in April, 1864, aged 46 years. Eleanor Whidden, their fifth daughter, was born June 20th, 1821. She was married to Abiather Blair, December 27th, 1842, They had eight sons and two daughters. James, the eldest son of Samuel and Sarah Whidden, was born July 27th, 1823. He died a bachelor, April 7th, 1865, aged 41 years. John Whidden, their second son, was born January 26th, 1826. He removed to the United States. He was married there to Mary McCarthany. They had three sons and one daughter. He died in 1863, aged 37 years. Mary Jane Whidden, their sixth daughter, was born September 22nd, 1828. She was married to John Stewart, of Londonderry, September 12th, 1855. They had one son and four daughters.

James, the third son of Samuel and Abigail Whidden, was born in 1796. He was married to Hannah, daughter of Ralph and Hannah Johnson, December, 1820. (Mrs. Whidden was born in England, July 16th, 1801). They settled first at Greenfield. He died at Onslow, Sept. 5th, 1870, aged 75 years. Ralph Whidden, their eldest son, was born March 20th, 1822. He was married to Bridget Stone, of Tatamagouche, February, 1850. They had four sons and five daughters. Samuel Whidden, their second son, was born March, 1824. He removed to New Brunswick. He was married there to Ruth Ann Crooks. They had four sons and five daughters. They now reside in the State of Maine. Abigail Whidden, their eldest daughter, was born in Greenfield, May 8th, 1827. She was married to James Archibald, January 8th 1847. They had two sons and four daughters. Mr. Archibald died at North River, June 4th, 1871, aged 47 years. Margaret Whidden, their second daughter, was born December, 1831. Hannah Whidden, their third daughter, was born March 16th, 1835. She was married to William Wade, of New Brunswick. They had one son and one daughter. She died in the State of Maine, April 8th, 1867, aged 32 years. Mary Whidden, their fourth daughter, was born March 16th, 1838. She was married to George Smith, of Onslow, December 27th, 1869. They have one daughter. James Whidden, their third son, was born in September, 1841. He was married to Margaret Adams, of River John, January, 1869. They have two daughters. William Whidden, their fourth son, was born April 17th, 1844. He removed to California. Wren Whidden, their fifth son, was born July 15th, 1846.

Phebe, the youngest daughter of Samuel and Abigail Whidden, was born February 18th, 1799. She was married to Ralph Johnson, of Greenfield. They had three sons and two daughters. She died July 28th, 1842, aged 43 years.

Simeon, the fourth son of James Whidden, Sen., was born in New England, in 1754, and was brought by his parents to Nova Scotia when he was about six years old. He was married to Dorothy, the fourth daughter of Captain William Blair and Jane Barns, about the year 1775. They settled in Middle Stewiacke about the year 1782. His farm laid on the west side of James Archibald's, which is now owned by the Messrs. Rutherford. In January, 1800, he was loading logs in the woods, when a log rolled on him and broke his leg. He lived but three days after. His widow died November, 1827, aged 74 years.

James, the eldest son of Simeon and Dorothy Whidden, was born in 1778. He was married to Jane, third daughter of James Fisher and Margaret McKeen, of Musquodoboit. They had five sons and five daughters. They removed to Canada some time ago. He died there. His wife and two daughters died there in 1852. Mary, the eldest daughter of Simeon and Dorothy Whidden, was born in 1780. She was married to William, the eldest son of James and Margaret Fisher, of Musquodoboit. They had sons and daughters. They removed to St. Mary's. Sarah Whidden, their second daughter, was born in 1782. She was married to John Higgins, of Musquodoboit, in 1807. They had four sons and four daughters. She died February 11th, 1871, aged 89 years. Mr. Higgins died in March, 1869.

William, the second son of Simeon and Dorothy Whidden, was born in 1784. He was married to Mary McLain, of Pictou. They had five sons and five daughters. He removed and settled at St.

Mary's. He died in February, 1857, aged 73 years. His wife died in 1842.

Simeon, the third son of Simeon and Dorothy Whidden, was born May 17th, 1786. He was married to Susan Harris, of Sydney, C. B., in 1812. They resided in Cape Breton, Stewiacke, Dartmouth and Truro. He died in Truro, October 25th, 1859, aged 73 years. His wife died in Truro, April 10th, 1859, aged 73 years. George, the eldest son of Simeon and Susan Whidden, was married to Abigail Jane, daughter of Robert and Esther Whidden, December 22nd, 1840. They had two sons and three daughters. James, the second son of Simeon and Susan Whidden, removed to the United States. He is married there. Mary Whidden, their eldest daughter, was married to Kennedy Archibald, December 22nd, 1840. They had six sons and four daughters. Abigail Whidden, their second daughter, was married to Johnson Archibald, October 9th, 1845. They had three sons and four daughters. John Whidden, their third son, was married to Sophia Graham, in 1846. They reside in Dartmouth. They had sons and daughters. Simeon, the fourth son of Simeon and Susan Whidden, was married to Harriet Reeves in 1845. They had four sons and three daughters. They reside in Halifax. Sarah, the third daughter of Simeon and Susan Whidden, was married to Charles Hall, September 23rd, 1846. They had three sons and two daughters. Susan, the fourth daughter of Simeon and Susan Whidden, was born December 24th, 1834, She was married to Roderick McKinnon, December 8th, 1859. They had two sons and two daughters.

Robert, the fourth son of Simeon and Dorothy Whidden, was born April 2nd, 1788. He was married to Esther, second daughter of Francis Creelman and Esther Campbell, November 9th, 1813. He inherited a part of his father's farm. He died April 1st, 1834, aged 46 years. Hannah Whidden, their eldest daughter, was born July 26th, 1815. She was married to Samuel Frame, December 22nd, 1838. They had three sons and five daughters. They removed to the United States, where he and his wife both died some time ago. Abigail Jane Whidden, their second daughter, was born February 7th, 1818. She was married to George Whidden, December 22nd, 1840. They had two sons and three daughters. Matthew Whidden, their eldest son, was born in December, 1820. He was married to Janet, daughter of William and Martha Ellis, November, 1844. They had two sons and one daughter. They removed to the United States Mary Whidden, their third daughter, was born in 1822. She removed to the United States. She was married there to Rufus Young. They had two sons and one daughter. Simeon Whidden, their second son, was born in 1824. He was married to Eliza Frame. They had two sons. They removed to the United States. Mrs. Whidden died there in 1853. He was married again to Hannah, daughter of Robert Higgins, of Onslow. She lived but a short time after they were married. Esther Whidden, their fourth daughter, was born in 1826. She was married to William, son of Chas. Carter and Agnes Oughterson, in 1855. They had four sons and three daughters. They reside in Brookfield. Robert Kirk Whidden, their third son, was born in 1828. He was married to Margaret Boomer. They removed to California. They had one son and two daughters. James Smith Whidden, their fourth son, was born in March, 1830. He removed to the United States. He was twice married there. He died there some time ago. Margaret Whidden, their fifth daughter, was born April 6th, 1832. She removed to the United States. She was married there to Harris Merril. They had three daughters. David Whidden, their fifth son, was born March 5th, 1834. He removed to the United States. He was married there to Elizabeth Babcock. They have one daughter.

John, the fifth son of Simeon and Dorothy Whidden, was born in 1792, and was married to Miss Symonds, of Antigonish. They had a family. He was a Baptist minister, settled in Antigonish, and died there.

Dorothy, the third daughter of Simeon and Dorothy Whidden, was born May 29th, 1794. She was married to James Downing, July 20th, 1818. They had two sons and four daughters. She died September 5th, 1850. Mr. Downing died June 1st, 1840, aged 45 years. David Whidden, their sixth son, was born in 1796. He was married to Rebecca Pyke, January, 1821. He was one of the first that settled in Smithfield in 1825. Richard Whidden, their eldest son, was born December 13th, 1821. He was married to Abigail Bartlet, of Onslow Mountain, December 31st, 1845. They had one son. Samuel Whidden, their second son, was born November, 1825. He was married to Rebecca Smith, of St. Mary's, December, 1856. They had two sons and three daughters. Elizabeth Whidden, their eldest daughter, was born in 1827. She died in 1858. Eleanor Whidden, their second daughter, was born in 1829. She was married to Hugh Whidden, of St. Mary's, November 4th, 1854. They had sons and daughters. He died February, 1872. Jane Whidden, their third daughter, was born in 1831. Dorothy Whidden, their fourth daughter, was born in 1833. She was married to Henry Smith, of St. Mary's, in 1858. They had three sons and four daughters. David Whidden, their youngest son, was born in 1836. He was married to Mary McCabe, of Greenfield, February 12th, 1865. They had three daughters.

Jane, the fourth daughter of Simeon and Dorothy Whidden, was born January 22nd, 1798. She was married to James Reed, May 12th, 1817. They had eight sons and five daughters. Mr. Reed came from Scotland in 1815. He settled in Musquodoboit. He died October 21st, 1870, aged 73 years, Abigail, the fifth daughter of Simeon and Dorothy Whidden, was born in 1799. She died unmarried.

CHAPTER LVIII.

James Kent was born in Alloa, Scotland, in 1749. He came out to Halifax when he was a young man. He was married to Margaret Williams in 1774. He settled at Lower Stewiacke, on the farm that Robert Pollock, Esq., now resides upon ; he continued there until 1782. He then removed to Truro, and settled on the farm that Alexander U. Cutton now resides upon. He was a Justice of the Peace, and always forward in public business. He died October 31st, 1825. His widow died January 26th, 1829, aged 76 years.

James Kent, their eldest son, was born in Lower Stewiacke, May 1st, 1777. He was married to Eleanor, second daughter of William and Hannah Dickey, December 26th, 1811. He resided in a house which stood on the hill west of William McNutt, Esq's. He died there December 29th, 1834. William, the eldest son of James and Eleanor Kent, was born June 5th, 1813. He was married to Patience Joyce, July 17th, 1837. They had two sons and three daughters. He inherits a part of his father's farm. James Flemming Kent, their second son, was born December 4th, 1815. He removed to the United States in 1843. He was married there to Caroline Potter. They had one daughter. Mrs. Kent died in 1857. His friends have not heard from him since 1868. Robert Kent, their third son, was born March 24th, 1818. He left home in 1838. He has followed the whale fishing since. He was married in Nantucket in 1856. They had two daughters. Alexander Kent, their fourth son, was born November 6th, 1821. He was married to Nancy Archibald, August 10th, 1854. They had two sons and five daughters. Mrs. Kent died March 4th, 1866. He was married again to Mary Jane Wright, widow of the late Rand Kennon. They had one son and two daughters. Sarah Kent, their eldest daughter, was born July 2nd, 1824. She removed to the United States in 1856. She was married there to Furmon Mack, in 1857. They had one son and three daughters. She died there September, 1868, and her husband died August, 1872. Susannah Kent, their second daughter, was born January 14th, 1826. She was married to John McClure, January 25th, 1853. They had five sons and two daughters. Martha Kent, their third daughter, was born March 6th, 1833. She died April 5th, 1854.

Alexander, the second son of James and Margaret Kent, was born in Lower Stewiacke, May 1st, 1779. He was married to Jane, the eldest daughter of John and Nancy Christie, January 27th, 1803. He settled on the farm that William Cock now resides upon in the Lower Village. He was a wheelwright, cabinet maker, house joiner, and shipbuilder. In 1818 he built a brig, called the Oliphant, for Capt. Richard Christie. Capt. Christie went to England in her, and in the spring of 1820 he brought out a considerable number of passengers from the North of Ireland ; among these were Mr. Samuel Craig and family. On May 6th, 1820, Mrs. Craig was delivered of a son on board of the brig on her passage from Ireland ; they named him for the Captain, Richard Christie Craig. Mr. R. C. Craig is now a merchant in Truro Village, and a strong advocate for the cause of temperance. He has attended nearly four hundred temperance meetings. Mr. Kent was a worthy man ; he was forward in public business, both religious and secular ; he held a Commission of the Peace for more than forty years, and the example he set was worthy of imitation. He and his wife lived together nearly seventy years. He died July 24th, 1872, aged 93 years. His wife died June 1st, 1872, aged 90 years.

Margaret, the eldest daughter of Alexander and Jane Kent, was born in Truro, August 13th, 1804. She was married to John Dickson, Esq., December 21st, 1826. They had two sons and three daughters. Nancy Kent, their second daughter, was born October 28th, 1806. She was married to Jotham B. Waddell, April 6th, 1830. They had five sons and three daughters. She died August 14th, 1852, aged 46 years. Mary Kent, their third daughter, was born March 25th, 1809. She was married to William Flemming, March 11th, 1828. They had five sons and four daughters. Mr. Flemming died January 24th, 1873, aged 70 years. James Kent, their only son was born October 12th, 1811. He was married to Sarah, daughter of Alexander and Mary Archibald, January 10th, 1833. They had one son and five daughters. Mrs. Kent died June 8th, 1847, aged 33 years. He was married again to Mary, daughter of Samuel and Mary Dunlap, June, 1858. They have one son and two daughters. Martha Kent, their fourth daughter, was born March 4th, 1814. She was married to Timothy Archibald, January 1st, 1835. They had four sons and three daughters. Rebecca Kent, their fifth daughter, was born November 10th, 1816. Susan Jane Kent, their sixth daughter, was born September 18th, 1818. She was married to Ezekiel Sibley, October 15th, 1839. They had five sons and one daughter. She died March 7th, 1864. Anna Kent, their seventh daughter, was born June 6th, 1821. She was married to James McDonald, of Pictou, November 12th, 1857. Mr. McDonald was accidentlly shot at Lunenburg, November 22nd, 1861.

John, the third son of James and Margaret Kent, was born at Lower Stewiacke, in 1781. He was married to Janet, eldest daughter of James McCurdy and Agnes Archibald, November 6th, 1806. He settled on the farm on which John Corbett had resided. He died January 5th, 1829, and his widow died September 1st, 1870, aged 84 years. Martha Kent, their eldest daughter, was born January 19th, 1808. She was married to John H. Notting, September 29th, 1825. The had one son and two daughters. Sarah Kent, their second daughter, was born November 20th, 1809. She was married to John G. Nelson, March 12th, 1831. They had five sons and two daughters. She died in 1845. James Kent, their eldest son, was born September 9th, 1811. He died May 1st, 1833. Susannah Kent, their third daughter, was born October 26th, 1813. She was married to William Brydon. They had one daughter. Mr. Brydon died at Tatamagouche, October, 1842. She was married again to Charles Ryley. John Kent, their second son, was born July 14th, 1815. He was married to Sarah L. Archibald, April 7th, 1835. They had four sons and three daughters. He inherited his father's farm. Mary Jane Kent, their fourth daughter, was born July 20th, 1817. She died June 24th, 1837. Alexander Kent, their third son, was born August 21st, 1819. He was married to Olivia Archibald. They had four sons and two daughters. He inherits a part of his father's farm. Robert William Kent, their fourth son, was born November 5th, 1821. He was married to Sarah, daughter of Alex. and Mary Conkey, December 29th, 1844. Mrs. Kent died September 12th, 1871. He was married again to Barbara Wilson, widow of the late Alexander Blair, September 26th, 1872. Edward Kent, their fifth son, was born December 25th, 1823. He removed to Tatamagouche, where he carried on a considerable business at shipbuilding and merchandise. He was married to Jessie Williamson. They had five sons and four daughters. He died in May, 1870. Daniel Kent, their sixth son, was born February 14th, 1826. He was married to Ruth Stevens, September, 1850. They had five sons and five daughters. He now resides at Great Village, Londonderry.

Martha, the eldest daughter of James and Margaret Kent, was born in Truro, August 1st, 1783. She was married to James Flemming, Esq., of Londonderry, in 1804. He inherited his father's property at the Folly. He died December 31st, 1839, aged 61 years. His wife died August 20th, 1837. They left no children. Margaret, the second daughter of James and Margaret Kent, was born August 1st, 1787. She was married to James Fulton, of Stewiacke, in 1810. They had five sons and three daughters. She died at Londonderry, February 1st, 1870. Mr. Fulton died March 18th, 1829.

Robert, the fourth son of James and Margaret Kent, was born June 4th, 1791. He was married to Anner, third daughter of Capt. William and Anner Cock, December 31st, 1818. He inherited his father's farm for a few years. He died January 3rd, 1867. James Kent, their eldest son, was born January 17th, 1820. He removed to the United States. He was married there to Rebecca Hall. They had four children, who all died young. Mrs. Kent died in 1865. William Kent, their second son, was born April 27th, 1822. He removed to the United States. He was married there to Elizabeth Perkins. They had one son and one daughter. John Kent, their third son, was born August 2nd, 1824. He was married to Charlotte Norris, of Princeport, January 15th, 1851. They had five sons and four daughters. Elizabeth Kent, their eldest daughter, was born February 10th, 1827. She was married to James Cutton, of Onslow, June, 1850. They had five sons and two daughters. Mr. Cutton died in King's County, September, 1869. Margaret Kent, their second daughter, was born June 25th, 1829. Adelaide Kent, their third daughter, was born December 12th, 1832. She was married to Avret Ally, March, 1861. They have one son. They reside in the

United States. Anna Kent, their fourth daughter, was born May 20th, 1834. She removed to the United States. She was married there to Dominick Fumigally, in 1858. They had two sons and three daughters. Martha Kent, their fifth daughter, was born April 4th, 1838. She removed to the United States. Susan Blair Kent, their sixth daughter, was born November 10th, 1840. She removed to California. She was married there to Henry Helling. They had one son and one daughter. David Lynds Kent, their fourth son, was born August 18th, 1843. He removed to California. He was married to Mary Ashley. They had two sons and one daughter. Henry Peter Kent, their fifth son, was born April 23rd, 1845. He was married to Mary Nelson, April 6th, 1869. They removed to the United States.

Susan, the third daughter of James and Margaret Kent, was born August 28th, 1796. She was married to William Blair, 3rd, November 19th, 1819. They had three sons. She died February 7th, 1864. Mr. Blair died August 9th, 1834, aged 39 years.

CHAPTER LIX.

Robert Hamilton was born in Armagh, Ireland, November 8th, 1734, and Agnes Ferguson, his wife, was born March 5th, 1739. They were married about the year 1757. They removed to Nova Scotia in the summer of the year 1771, and settled in Truro, on the farm on which Mr. David Cameron now resides. He died there December, 1814, aged 80 years, and his widow died at Upper Stewiacke, 1835, aged 96 years.

William Hamilton, their eldest son, was born in Ireland, December 28th, 1758, and was brought by his parents to Nova Scotia when he was in the 13th year of his age. He was married to Louisa Thomson, daughter of Aaron Thomson, of Onslow, January 29th, 1789. He had been living in Brookfield and clearing his farm four or five years before he was married, and they resided there the remainder of their lives. He died there January 20th, 1838, aged 79 years, and his widow died December 10th, 1846, aged 79 years.

Sarah Hamilton, their eldest daughter, was born April 14th, 1791. She was married to Adam Miller, third son of Isaac Miller

23

and Elizabeth Dickey, March 12th, 1829. They have three daughters. Agnes Hamilton, their second daughter, was born July 7th, 1793. She was married to Captain Samuel Soley, of the Lower Village of Truro, July 29th, 1813. They had seven sons and two daughters.

Aaron Hamilton, their eldest son, was born Jany. 30th, 1796. He was married to Nancy Boomer, daughter of Joseph and Jane Boomer, September 25th, 1820. He settled on the farm that his son William now resides upon, west of the Brookfield station, where he and his wife spent the remainder of their lives. He died there March 10th, 1844, aged 48 years, and his wife died April 28th, 1844, aged 55 years. William Hamilton, their eldest son, was born June 9th, 1821. He was married to Margaret Jeffers, April, 1848. They had three sons and one daughter. Mrs. Hamilton died March 17th, 1864, and he was married again to Martha Jane Withrow, March 3rd, 1868. He inherits what was his father's farm. They had one son. James Joseph, the second son of Aaron and Nancy Hamilton, was born October 8th, 1822. He was married to Margaret Williams, May 13th, 1852. They had two sons and four daughters. He removed and settled at Point Brule, May, 1867. He has held a Commission of the Peace several years. Mary, the eldest daughter of Aaron and Nancy Hamilton, was born July 7th, 1827. She removed to the State of Maine, and was married to James Wright, an Englishman. They had one son and one daughter. Louisa, the second daughter of Aaron and Nancy Hamilton, was born July 7th, 1829. She removed to South Boston, and died there October 1st, 1850, aged 21 years. Elizabeth, the third daughter of William and Louisa Hamilton, was born May 24th, 1798. She was married to John Conley, February 13th, 1824. They had two sons and two daughters. She died June 18th, 1834, aged 36 years.

Robert, the second son of William and Louisa Hamilton, was born April 30th, 1800. He was married to Sophia, the eldest daughter of Peter and Mehetabel Stevens, March 10th, 1825. He inherited a part of his father's farm in Brookfield, and built the two story house in which Mr. Robert Dinsmore now resides. He died at North River, January, 1857, aged 56 years. Peter Stevens Hamilton, their eldest son, was born in Brookfield, January 3rd, 1826. He studied the law, and now resides in Halifax. He was married to Anne, daughter of Thomas I. Brown, Esq., and Rachel Pearson, December 8th, 1849. They had three sons and two daughters. Louisa, the eldest daughter of Robert and Sophia Hamilton, was born March 3rd, 1828. She died October, 1835, aged seven years. Mehetabel, their second daughter, was born June 30th, 1830. She removed to Boston, and was married there to Alexander Fraser. They had two sons and one daughter. Edmond W. Hamilton, their second son, was born January 18th, 1835. He was married to Nancy Harriet, daughter of Simeon H. Blair and Janet McCurdy, September 21st, 1858. They had one son and three daughters, besides several others that died young. George R. Hamilton, their third son, was born May 16th, 1839. He removed to British Columbia. Helen Mercy, their third daughter, was born February 27th, 1837. She was married to John McCullion, of Pugwash. They had two daughters. She died June 11th, 1870, and her husband died July, 1872. Laura Hamilton, their fourth daughter, was born June 16th, 1846. She removed to the United States.

William, the third son of William and Louisa Hamilton, was born November 17th, 1803. He was married to Martha Prestley, June 1st, 1834. Emeline, their daughter, was born May 29th, 1835. He was married again to Mary Irwin, widow of the late Duncan Mc-Shanick, April, 1864. They have two sons and two daughters. He inherits a part of what was his father's farm in Brookfield, and goes by the name of Queer Bill. Louisa, the fourth daughter of William and Louisa Hamilton, was born July 20th, 1806. She was married to James Stevens, Esq., January 22nd, 1829. They had six sons and five daughters

Archibald Hamilton, their fourth son, was born February 17th, 1810. He was married to Ruth, daughter of Peter and Mehetabel Stevens, November 29th, 1830. He inherits the homestead and a part of what was his father's farm at Brookfield. Maria Hamilton, the eldest daughter of Archibald and Ruth Hamilton, was born May 30th, 1832. She was married to James Dinsmore. They had two sons and four daughters. Esther, their second daughter, was born August 5th, 1833. She removed to the United States, and was married there to George Edwards. They have one son. Alfred, their eldest son, was born June 16th, 1835. He was married to Rachel Wrath, October 27th, 1857. They have two sons and three daughters. Rhoda, their third daughter, was born June 24th, 1839. She was married to Mr. Hawes, of the United States, and had one daughter. Mr. Hawes died, and she was married again to Mr. Oliver, of the United States. They have one son. They now reside in Granville, N. S. David, their second son, was born August 1st, 1841. He removed to Kansas, U. S., and was married there to Dorah McLain, about the year 1865. Minerva, their fourth daughter, was born January, 1845. Harriett, their fifth daughter, was born March 31st, 1847. She removed to the United States, and was married there to Joseph Wilkens. They had one son and one daughter. William Augustus, their third son, was born July 1st, 1849. Thressa, their sixth daughter, was born August 30th, 1851. Sophia, their seventh daughter, was born May 6th, 1854.

Mary, the eldest daughter of Robert Hamilton, Sen., and Agnes Ferguson, was born in Ireland, January 21st, 1761. She was brought by her parents to Nova Scotia when ten years old. She was married to John, the eldest son of Thomas Archibald and Janet Orr, in the year 1784. They had four sons and four daughters, who appear among the Archibald families. She died at Brookfield, August 20th, 1847, aged 86 years; and her husband died at Upper Stewiacke, September 1st, 1832. Margaret, their second daughter, was born October 4th, 1763. She died unmarried.

Robert Hamilton, second son of Robert and Agnes Hamilton, was born in Ireland, February 16th, 1765. He was brought by his parents to Nova Scotia when six years old. He was married to Phebe Ann, the eldest daughter of David McCollum, Sen., and Margaret Moore, in November, 1794. They had one daughter. Her name was Nancy. She died when about ten years old. He settled on the farm that Charles Cox recently owned, on the interval south of the River in Upper Stewiacke, and he died there in December, 1815. His widow was married again to Robert Gammell, June 20th, 1816. She died April 8th, 1859, aged 82 years.

John Hamilton, the third son of Robert Hamilton, Sen., and Agnes Ferguson, was born in Ireland, July 31st, 1768. He was brought by his parents to Nova Scotia when three years old. He was married to Elizabeth, daughter of Thomas Archibald and Janet Orr, October 27th, 1796. He settled in Brookfield; and, in January, 1800, he was paralyzed. (And, on this occasion, the Rev. John Waddell visited him, and preached the first sermon that was ever preached in Brookfield. His text was Isaiah 35th chapter and 1st verse—"The wilderness and the solitary place shall be glad for them; and the desert shall rejoice, and blossom as the rose.") Shortly after this, he removed to Upper Stewiacke, and resided there for about eight or nine years, and then returned to Brookfield, where he spent the remainder of his days. He died July 1st, 1835, aged 67 years, having been for thirty-five years deprived of the use of his limbs. His wife died February 18th, 1831, aged 60 years. They were buried in the Truro Cemetery.

Thomas Hamilton, their eldest son, was born in Brookfield, October 29th, 1797. He was married to Agnes, daughter of William Carter and Agnes Cox, his wife, April 8th, 1830. They settled in Brookfield, where they reared their family. He died there July 14th, 1868, aged 71 years. His widow perished on the railroad, above William Murray's, in February, 1873. Elizabeth, the eldest daughter of Thomas and Agnes Hamilton, was born January 17th, 1831. She was married to George Risa in November, 1858. Eleanor, their second daughter, was born June 6th, 1832. She died when young. Charles Hamilton, their eldest son, was born November 2nd, 1834. He was married to Catherine McCulloch, of Pictou, November, 1857. They had four sons and one daughter. They reside in Truro. John Hamilton, their second son, was born August 20th, 1836. He was married to Sarah Jones, July 12th, 1862. They have three sons. Nancy, their third daughter, was born April 10th, 1837. She was married to Alexander Davies, October, 1864. They have three sons. George and Eleanor, twins, were born October 26th, 1841. Eleanor was married to George Bagleman, November 15th, 1859. They have five sons and one daughter.

Robert, the second son of John and Elizabeth Hamilton, was born September 23rd, 1799. He was married to Jane, the only daughter of William and Mary Soley, of the Lower Village of Truro, October 27th, 1825. He inherits a part of what was his father's farm in Brookfield. He has been a Justice of the Peace for about thirty years. John Hamilton, their eldest son, was born March 1st, 1827. He was married to Eleanor, daughter of William Moore and Alice Kennedy, January 30th, 1851. They now reside in the house with his parents. William Soley Hamilton, their second son, was born July 5th, 1831. He was married to Martha Ryan, May 1st, 1856. They have four sons and five daughters. He now carries on the blacksmith business in Brookfield. Mary, the eldest daughter of Robert and Jane Hamilton, was born September 16th, 1828. She died February 23rd, 1831. Mary Jane, their second daughter. was born March 8th, 1834. She was married to James Kennedy, February 14th, 1865. They have three sons. They now reside about two miles north of Brookfield. Samuel George Hamilton, their third son, was born April 5th, 1836. He died March 11th, 1842. James Hamilton, their fourth son, was born July 9th, 1838. Baxter Hamilton, their fifth son, was born November 11th, 1841. He was married to Lavinia Clark, August, 1864. They have three sons and two daughters.

Elizabeth and John Hamilton, twin daughter and son of John and Elizabeth Hamilton, were born in Stewiacke, September 23rd, 1803. Elizabeth was married to Edward Brinton, and had four sons and six daughters. John Hamilton was married to Martha, daughter of Moses Clarke and Elizabeth Fisher, his wife, December 20th, 1832. Martha Clarke was born December 31st, 1814. They now reside on the homestead that was his father's. Moses Clarke Hamilton, their eldest son, was born February 18th, 1834. He was married to Maria Jane Dinsmore, of Economy, January 28th, 1868. Timothy Hamilton, their second son, was born November 19th, 1839. He was married to Ellen Boomer, April 28th, 1866. They have one son and two daughters. Anne, the only daughter of John and Martha Hamilton, was born April 2nd, 1841. She was married to Dr. Charles H. Munro, of Pictou County, September, 1861. They have one son and three daughters.

William, the fourth son of John and Elizabeth Hamilton, was born in Stewiacke, January 24th, 1807. He died a bachelor, September 9th, 1868, aged 61 years. Hants Hamilton, their fifth son, was born in Stewiacke, May 10th, 1809. He was married to Phebe Ann, daughter of John Archibald and Mary Hamilton, December 27th, 1830. They had one son and two daughters. Mrs. Hamilton died August, 1837, and he was married again to Mary, daughter of Hants Hamilton and Jane, his wife, of Upper Stewiacke, November 27th, 1839. They had five sons and three daughters. He resided for some time in what was his father's old house, at Brookfield, and then removed to Pembroke, in Upper Stewiacke, where they now reside. Agnes, the second daughter of John and Elizabeth Hamilton, was born in Brookfield, August 21st, 1811. She was married to John Carter, November 29th, 1827. They had five sons and four daughters. She died June 13th, 1854, aged 43 years. Rachel Hamilton, their third daughter, was born April 16th, 1814. She was married to John Clarke, in 1833. They had three sons and two daughters. They now reside in Masstown, Londonderry.

Archibald, the fourth son of Robert Hamilton, Sen., and Agnes

Ferguson, was born March 19th, 1771, on the passage out. He died a bachelor.

George Hamilton, their fifth son, was born in Truro, January 5th, 1774. He was married to Eleanor Wilson Archibald, third daughter of Matthew and Janet Archibald, November 23rd, 1802. He built the house that Mr. George McLeod now resides in, on the north side of Salmon River, in which he resided. He carried on the shoe-making business in a shop that stood on the bank, where Mr. William Mc-Leod now resides. He then sold out in Truro, and removed to Upper Stewiacke, to the farm that Mr. Hugh Dunlap now resides upon, where he spent the remainder of his days. He died there September 13th, 1842, aged 68 years, and his wife died August 15th, 1857, aged 76 years.

Robert and Matthew Hamilton, their twin sons, were born in Truro, October 11th, 1803. Robert was married to Ann, the eldest daughter of David Hingley and Sarah Fulton, of Merigomish, July 27th, 1837. They had three sons and three daughters. They reside on the south side of Stewiacke River, Upper Settlement. Matthew, their other twin son, was married to Catherine Holdman in 1833. They had six sons and three daughters. Mrs. Hamilton died, and he was married again to Susan Dean, of Musquodoboit. They had three sons. He settled, and still resides in Musquodoboit. Nancy, the eldest daughter of George and Eleanor W. Hamilton, was born in Truro, September 19th, 1805. She was married to John Holdman, of Musquodoboit. They had seven sons and four daughters. She died some time ago. Janet Hamilton, their second daughter, was born March 17th, 1810. She was married to John G. D. Archibald, February 8th, 1838. They had three sons and three daughthrs.

Barry Hamilton, their third son, was born April 24th, 1812. He was married to Agnes Jane, second daughter of James M. McCurdy and Margaret Miller, March 17th, 1840. They had two sons and one daughter. Mrs. Hamilton died April 19th, 1846. He was married again to Susan Dunlap, widow of the late William Gammell, Esq., January 15th, 1850. They had two daughters. Mrs. Hamilton died December 29th, 1860, and he was married again to Alice Tupper, widow of the late James Creelman, Esq., January 2nd, 1862. Phebe Ann, the third daughter of George and Eleanor W. Hamilton, was born February, 1814. She was married to Alexander McDougall, of Musquodoboit, August, 1841. They had one son and one daughter. Mr. McDougall died January, 1848, and she was married again to

John Ogilvie, of Musquodoboit. They had two sons and two daughters. George, the fourth son of George and Eleanor W· Hamilton, was born in 1816. He was married to Margaret, daughter of William Fraser and Eleanor Archibald, of the Middle River of Pictou. They had two sons and three daughters. He settled in Pictou, where he spent the remainder of his life. He died there in September, 1860, aged 44 years. Elizabeth Hamilton their fourth daughter, was born in 1818. She was married to George Archibald, March 30th, 1839. They had five sons and one daughter. Sarah Hamilton, their fifth daughter, was born in 1820. She was married to Thomas Ellis Archibald, February, 1850. They had three sons and four daughters. These last two families have removed to the United States. Eleanor Hamilton, their sixth daughter, was born in 1822. She was married to David Fisher in 1849. They had two daughters. She died in 1860.

Agnes, the third daughter of Robert Hamilton, Sen., was born in Truro, April 26th, 1776. She died when young.

Hants, the sixth and youngest son of Robert Hamilton, Sen., and Agnes Ferguson, was born in Truro, January 1st, 1780. He was married to Jane, daughter of James Cottom, of Debert River, and Mary Wilson, November 14th, 1811. They settled in Upper Stewiacke, on the north side of the River, where they reared their family. He died there in 1856, aged 76 years, and his widow died in May, 1859, aged 66 years. She was born February 22nd, 1793. Agnes Hamilton, their eldest daughter, was born April 24th, 1813. She died January 6th, 1817, aged nearly four years. Mary, their second daughter, was born February 28th, 1815. She was married to Hants, son of John Hamilton, November 27th, 1839. They had five sons and three daughters. Robert, the eldest son of Hants and Jane Hamilton, was born January 27th, 1817. He died unmarried, February 16th, 1839, aged 22 years. Agnes, their third daughter, was born November 30th, 1818. She died November 12th, 1823, aged five years. James Hamilton, their second son, was born April 11th, 1821. He was married to Hannah H. Murray, of Musquodoboit, December 31st, 1841. They had one son and five daughters. He died April 6th, 1861, aged 40 years, and his widow was married again to William Deyarmond. Hants, the third son of Hants and Jane Hamilton, was born January 5th, 1823. He was married to Elizabeth, daughter of William Dunlap and Rachel Logan. They had three sons and five daughters. Mrs. Hamilton died June 30th, 1865, aged 37 years.

John Hamilton, their fourth son, was born February 22nd, 1825. He removed to the United States, and was married there to Hannah Lylia, and they have a family of children.   Jane, their third daughter, was born August 27th, 1827.   She was married to James Rutherford. They had two sons and one daughter.   She died in February, 1862, aged 35 years.   Susan, the fourth daughter of Hants and Jane Hamilton, was born March 1st, 1830.   She was married to Daniel Bently in 1849.   They had one son and four daughters.   Margaret, their fifth daughter, was born January 16th, 1832.   She was married to Thomas Croker in 1858.   Mr. Croker died April 22nd, 1871. They had two sons and two daughters.   William Alexander Hamilton, their fifth son, was born February 9th, 1834.   He was married to Martha, daughter of William Gammell, Esq., and Susan Dunlap, October 8th, 1863.   They have one son and one daughter.   He inherits what was his father's farm.   Rebecca Hamilton, their sixth daughter, was born February 22nd, 1837.   She was married to James Thompson, December 27th, 1866.   Robert Samuel Hamilton, their sixth and youngest son, was born March 15th, 1840.   He was married to Janet Proven, December 31st, 1870.

CHAPTER LX.

James Fulton was among the early settlers of Truro, but not a Grantee.   He was born in Ireland in the year 1726, and his wife, Ann Collwell, was born in the year 1728.   They were married about the year 1753, and removed to Halifax, Nova Scotia, in the year 1761. They settled at LaHave for about two years, and then removed to Cumberland in the spring of 1764, and remained there about twelve years.   As there was considerable difficulty in Cumberland at the time of the American war, they removed to Pictou, and continued there about four or five years ; then they removed again to the Lower Village of Truro.   In removing from Pictou to Truro they underwent great hardships.   They had then to travel through the woods without any road, and carry their stuff and their children on their backs. This journey occupied the whole of the week, although they had the assistance of several men— (the late James Kennedy was one who assisted them.)   While on their way there came on a snow storm, which caused them much suffering, as they had to stop in the woods five nights, and one night in particular, their fire works being damp, they could get no fire for some time, and were in great danger of perishing. When they arrived in Truro, they settled on the same place Mr. Charles Crow now resides, in the Lower Village, where Mr. Fulton spent the remainder of his days. He died about the year 1792, and his wife died March, 1812, aged 84 years.

John, their eldest son, was born in Ireland about the year 1754, and was brought by his parents to Nova Scotia when about seven years old. He was married to Mary Simpson in the year 1775. John Simpson Fulton, their eldest son, was born in 1776. He removed with his father to Ohio, U. S., about the year 1811. He died there in 1814. Ann, the eldest daughter of John Fulton and Mary Simpson, was born in the year 1778. She was married to Eddy Tupper, October 12th, 1798. They had three sons and five daughters, who appear among the Tupper families. Janet T., the second daughter of John and Mary Fulton, was born in 1780. She was married to Daniel Ross, of Pictou, 1799. They had two sons and five daughters. They removed to Ohio, U. S., in 1811, and died there. Mary, another daughter of John and Mary Fulton, was married to William Pollock. They removed to Ohio, U. S., and died there. Elizabeth, their fourth daughter, was married to John Crockett, of Pictou. They had nine sons and nine daughters. She died in Pictou in the year 1867. Sarah Fulton, their fifth daughter, was married to David Hingley in 1812. They had four sons and five daughters. They settled in Merigomish. Mr. Hingley is dead. William, the youngest son of John and Mary Fulton, was born in the year 1792. He was married to Janet, daughter of John Blackie, of Pictou, in 1826. They had one son and four daughters. He died in Stewiacke in 1840, aged 48 years. His wife died in the year 1857. John Fulton's first wife died, and he was married again to Christie second daughter of the Rev. Daniel Cock and widow of Mahew Tupper. They removed to Ohio, U. S., and died there.

William, the second son of James Fulton and Ann Collwell, was born in Ireland in the year 1757, and was brought by his parents to Nova Scotia when about four years old. He was married to Sarah, the eldest daughter of James Dunlap and Mary Johnson, in the year 1783. He was one of the eight who removed to Upper Stewiacke in the spring of the year 1784. He settled on the same place that his grandson, William Fulton, Esq., now resides, where he and his wife spent many happy days. He died there December 11th, 1812, aged

55 years, and his wife died September 20th, 1814, aged 49 years. John J. Fulton, their eldest son, was born in the year 1784. He was married to Sarah, the second daughter of Robert Corbett and Susannah Fletcher, of Londonderry, in the year 1808. He settled first at the South Branch of Stewiacke, and about the year 1818, he exchanged farms with Stephen Johnson, and removed to the Lower Village of Truro, to the same place that his grandfather lived and died. He built the house in which Mr. Charles Crowe now resides. He continued to reside in this house until some time after his first wife died. She died about the year 1838. He was married again to Janet, the eldest daughter of James and Agnes McCurdy, of Onslow, widow of the late John Kent. He died June, 1856, aged 72 years, and left no family. His widow died September 1st, 1870, aged 84 years. James Fulton, their second son, was born in Stewiacke in the year 1786. He was married to Margaret, the second daughter of James Kent, Esq., and Margaret Williams in the year 1810. He settled on the farm adjoining the east side of William Cox's farm, after the death of Mahew Tupper, who had occupied it until his death. He resided in the house that George Fulton, Esq., now occupies, where he kept an Inn until the time of his death. He died there suddenly, March 18th, 1829, aged 43 years, and left a widow, five sons and three daughters to mourn their loss. His widow died at Londonderry, February 1st, 1870, in the 83rd year of her age.

Joseph Fulton, the third son of William and Sarah Fulton, was born in Stewiacke in the year 1788, and it is said that he was the first child who was baptized in Upper Stewiacke. He was married to Eleanor, the third daughter of Robert Corbett and Susan Fletcher, of Londonderry, about the year 1812. They had four sons and five daughters. He inherited his father's property in Upper Stewiacke, where he resided and kept an Inn, where his son William recently resided. He was a Justice of the Peace for a number of years before his death. He died December 6th, 1842, aged 54 years, and his widow was married again to John Graham, of Hants Co. Mary, the eldest daughter of William and Sarah Fulton, was born in the year 1790. She was married to Major Alexander L. Archibald, December 13th, 1810. They had four sons and two daughters, who appear among the Archibalds. She died September 8th, 1828, aged 38 years, and her husband died February 12th, 1859, aged 71 years.

Samuel, the fourth son of William and Sarah Fulton, was born in the year 1792. He learned the tanning and shoemaking trade with his brother-in-law, Major A. L. Archibald, and then purchased a place and built the house in which Mr. Charles H. Blair now resides. Here he built a tannery and made preparations for carrying on an extensive business ; but being disappointed in securing the affections of a certain young lady, on whom he fancied his happiness depended, he suddenly deeded his property away, left his business unsettled, and emigrated to the United States in 1816, and never returned.

Adam, the fifth son of William and Sarah Fulton, was born in the year 1795. He was a very short man, and not very healthy. He lived a while with his brother John. in the Lower Village of Truro, where he died a bachelor, January 17th, 1820, aged 25 years. Jane, their second daughter, was born March, 1797. She was married to Jonathan Marsters, a Barrister, February 8th, 1821. Mr. Marsters purchased the house which was owned by the late Matthew Archibald, which is standing yet, near the bank of the River, on Bible Hill, and is owned by Rev. Dr. McCulloch. Here Mr. Marsters spent the remainder of his days.

Ebenezer, the sixth and youngest son of William and Sarah Fulton, was born December 27th, 1799. He was married to Jane, the youngest daughter of Robert Gammell and Margaret Kennedy March 25th, 1824. They had three sons and one daughter. Mrs. Fulton died November 30th, 1836, aged 32 years. He was married again to Sophia, widow of the late John Corbett, May 7th, 1840. They had four sons and two daughters. Mr. Fulton's second wife died March 27th, 1863, aged 51 years. He purchased the farm in Middle Stewiacke that John Corbett, senr., had owned for nearly twenty years. He still occupies it.

Rachel, the third daughter of William and Sarah Fulton, was born 1802. She was married to Ebenezer Munro, Esq., December 10th, 1832. (He is now Judge of Probate for the County of Colchester).

Ann, their fourth and youngest daughter, was born 1804. She was married to John Goudge, February 26th, 1825. They now reside in Halifax.

Samuel Fulton was another son of James Fulton, Senr., and Ann Collwell. He was married to Mary, the second daughter of James and Mary Dunlap. She died in Stewiacke not long after they were married. He was married again to Alice, the fourth daughter of Eliakim Tupper, Esq., and Elizabeth Newcomb. This is said to be the first marriage in Upper Stewiacke. It took place in the house of

Samuel Fisher, who was married to her eldest sister. They removed to Ohio, U. S. Their son, Eliakim, returned a few years ago and spent the winter in Stewiacke among his relatives.

Joshua was another son of James and Ann Fulton. He was married to Nancy Simson, the youngest sister of John Fulton's wife. He sympathized very much with the Americans during the time of their rebellion, and not long after they gained their independence he removed to New York, and we know nothing of him or any of his descendants. Ann, daughter of James and Ann Fulton, was born in Cumberland, in the year 1765. She was married to James, son of James and Elizabeth Johnson, December 10th, 1786. They had three sons and six daughters. She died at Stewiacke January 15th, 1824, aged 59 years, and her husband died October 11th, 1842, aged 84 years. Elizabeth, another daughter of James and Ann Fulton, was married to John Johnson. They had one son and two daughters. Mr. Johnson died at Stewiacke July 1st, 1799. She was married again to Robert Logan. They had one son and one daughter. She died February 20th, 1827, and her second husband died December 31st, 1833, aged 70 years, Jane, the youngest daughter of James and Ann Fulton, was married to Caleb Putnam, of, Maitland, in the year 1787. They had two sons and six daughters. She was Mr. Putnam's second wife. She and her husband both died some time ago. Mr. Putnam died September, 1838.

CHAPTER LXI.

Samuel Creelman was born in Ireland, about the year 1728. He was married to Isabell Flemming, about the year 1748. He was a cooper by trade. He removed with his wife and family to Nova Scotia, and arrived in Halifax in the fall of the year 1761. They went to Lunenburg that fall, where they spent a hard winter, subsisting mostly on the eels they caught. In the spring of the year 1762, they returned to Halifax, and he worked that summer at his trade; and, in the fall, he removed to Cumberland. When he was leaving Halifax, he raised his hands and voice exclaiming against the town, as the most wicked place that he ever beheld. He remained in Cumberland until the fall of the year 1771, or the spring of 1772, when he removed and settled at the Black Rock, on the west end of the Township of Truro. When he was removing with his family from Cumberland, he took passage in a vessel with Captain Lockard. When they arrived, they were landed on the point, on the east side of Shubenacadie River. This point is known by the name of Lockard's point ever since. He purchased a lot of land that was laid off for David Archibald, Esq., as five hundred acres, extending from the point before mentioned four miles up the Subenacadie, and fronting on the River. Also another lot, the same size, adjoining the first lot, and on the east side of it. On these lots he continued to reside the remainder of his days. He died at his son Matthew's house, which place is now called Princeport, about the year 1810. His wife died several years before. They were buried near the house of Mr. James Davis, about one mile from the Black Rock. It may here be observed that his forefathers names were Ashmore, and that some of them had a large contract for carrying provisions to a number of convicts, which they did in *Creels* carried across the horse's back, and by this the name was changed from Ashmore to *Creel*man. The name of Ashmore is still kept as a second name by some of the Creelmans.

Samuel, the eldest son of Samuel Creelman, Sen., and Isabell Flemming, was born in Ireland, in the year 1751, and was brought by his parents to Nova Scotia when he was ten years old. He was married to Mary Campbell, of Londonderry, about the year 1775. He removed to Upper Stewiacke in the year 1786, and settled on the farm that was afterwards owned by his three sons, William, John and Andrew. He built the first mill that was built on the brook on the south side of the River, on which the spinning machine now stands. He had his first house on the interval, near the River, and he built his next house on the same place where Mr. Daniel Webster now resides. Here he spent the remainder of his days. He died in October, 1835, aged 84 years, and his wife died August 20th, 1831.

Isabell, the eldest daughter of Samuel Creelman and Mary Campbell, was born in the year 1777. She was married to the Rev. Duncan Ross, of the West River of Pictou, in the year 1796. They had nine sons and six daughters. She died in May, 1845, aged 68 years, and her husband died October 25th, 1834, aged 65 years. Esther Creelman, their second daughter, was born in the year 1779. She was married to George, son of James Fulton, Esq., and Margaret Campbell, of Bass River, about the year 1797. They had six sons and three daughters. They settled on the farm that their son, John, now resides upon, on the south side of Stewiacke River. Here they spent the remainder of their lives. She died June 4th, 1821, aged 42 years. Mr. Fulton was married again to Ann, daughter of John and Mary Fulton, widow of the late Eddy Tupper, in the year 1822. Mr. Fulton died in February, 1858.

James, the eldest son of Samuel and Mary Creelman, was born November 2nd, 1781. He was married to Margaret Graham, of Pictou, in the year 1803. He settled on the farm that his son. Charles, now resides upon, near Springside Church, where he spent the remainder of his days. He died September 12th, 1863, aged 82 years. David, the eldest son of James and Margaret Creelman, was born September 16th, 1804. He was married to Agnes Graham, daughter of William and niece of Rev. Hugh Graham. They had five sons and three daughters. They now reside in Halifax. Mary Campbell Creelman, their eldest daughter, was born June 6th, 1806. She was married to Robison, son of Charles Cox and Agnes Thomson, in the year 1830. They had five sons and five daughters. Mr. Cox died in November 1871. Elspa Creelman, their second daughter, was born February 24th, 1808. She was married to William Brown. They had eight sons and two daughters. Samuel Creelman, their second son, was born July 12th, 1810. He was married to Janet Crocket, October, 1850. Mr. Creelman's first wife, Margaret, died January 25th, 1812, and he was married again to Margaret McGill, of the West River of Pictou, in June 1814. Elizabeth, their eldest daughter, was born March 8th, 1815. She died December 9th, 1823, in the 9th year of her age. John, their eldest son, was born September 23rd, 1816. He removed to California about the year 1845.

Esther, their second daughter, was born March 3rd, 1819. She died March 22nd, 1819. Mr. Creelman's second wife died November 22nd, 1820, and he was married again to Martha, daughter of Charles Cox and Agnes Thomson, February, 1822. Charles Creelman, their eldest son, was born October 18th, 1823. He was married to Agnes Johnson, April 24th, 1849. They had four sons and six daughters. He inherits what was his father's property, at Springside, Stewiacke. James Campbell Creelman, their second son, was born December 15th, 1825. He was married to Margaret, daughter of John Gammell and Sarah Tupper, in the year 1849. They had one son and one daughter. He removed to Australia, and from thence to the Fejee Islands. The natives of the Feejee Islands became troublesome to the white settlers. The war-ship "Challenge," of H. M. Australian fleet, under Commodore Lambert, was sent to chastise them. In an engagement between ninety men, who were sent on shore, and the natives, Mr. Creelman, acting as pilot at the request of the Commodore, received two gun shot wounds, from the effects of which he died in four days, August 3rd, 1868. His wife died December 3rd, 1852. Agnes, their eldest daughter, was born May 22nd, 1828. She was married to John Ellis in the year 1847. Mr. Ellis died, and she removed to the United States and was married there to Duncan Davis, and has four daughters. William Creelman, their third son, was born January 10th, 1831. He was married to Agnes, daughter of Archibald Cox and Mary Alexander, of Hants County, May 26th, 1859. They have two sons. Andrew Creelman, their fourth son, was born April 20th, 1833. He was married to Hetty Sterling, of Hants County, in the year 1863. They have three sons. They removed to the United States. Elizabeth, their second daughter, was born July 7th, 1835. She was married to Hugh G. Cox, third son of John and Margaret Cox, March 8th, 1861. They have one son and four daughters. Francis, their fifth son, was born February 15th, 1839. He died September 21st, 1852, aged 13 years. Hannah, their third and youngest daughter, was born August 12th, 1851. She died January 21st, 1860, in the ninth year of her age. Mr. Creelman's third wife died January 17th, 1856.

William, the second son of Samuel and Mary Creelman, was born April 17th, 1784, two years before they removed to Stewiacke. He was married to Hannah, the eldest daughter of Samuel Tupper, Esq., and Elizabeth Archibald, January 20th, 1808. He inherited a part of what was his father's farm, where he spent the remainder of his days. He died September 9th, 1857, aged 73 years, and his widow died September 27th, 1865, aged 78 years. Samuel, the eldest son of William and Hannah Creelman, was born November 19th, 1808. He was married to Elizabeth Elliott Ellis, February 11th, 1834. He represented the County of Colchester in the House of Assembly of this Province from the year 1847 until 1851, and from this time to the year 1855 he represented the South District of Colchester. In the year 1860 he was appointed a member of the Legislative Council of Nova Scotia, and still retains his seat. Eliakim, the second son of William and Hannah Creelman, was born September 25th, 1811. He was married to Grizell Ellis, December 19th, 1836. They had two sons and five daughters. Elizabeth, their eldest daughter, was born November 18th, 1813. She was married to David A., second son of William and Eleanor Fraser, of the Middle River of Pictou, February 11th, 1834. They now reside in Truro Village. Robert Creelman, their third son, was born January 12th, 1816. He was married to Susan, the fourth daughter of William and Susan Archibald, January 29th, 1841. They have four sons and three daughters, besides a number that died young. He carries on tanning. Mary Ann, their second daughter, was born June 5th, 1820. She was married to John Kelly, April, 1847. They now reside in Halifax. Rachel, their third daughter, was born October 7th, 1822. She was married to James D. Graham, youngest son of the Rev. Hugh Graham, March 4th, 1845. They had five sons and two daughters. Jane Creelman, their fourth daughter, was born April 13th, 1827. She was married to Adam McLeod, May 3rd, 1860. They have two daughters. William Creelman, their fourth and youngest son, was born July 13th, 1828. He was married to Sarah, daughter of Andrew Cox and Nancy Thomson, February, 1851. They had four sons and three daughters. He was one of the men who first started the Spinning Machine in Upper Stewiacke, in the year 1862.

Hannah, the third daughter of Samuel and Mary Creelman, was born in the year 1786. She was married to John McDonald, of Pictou, in the year 1803. They had six sons and three daughters. She died, and her husband died.

Samuel, the third son of Samuel and Mary Creelman, was born in the year 1788. He was married to Margaret, daughter of James Fulton, Esq., and Margaret Campbell, of Bass River, October, 1810. They settled on the farm that Barry Hamilton now lives upon. Mr. Creelman died October 11th, 1817, aged 29 years, and his widow was married again to John Rutherford, of Middle Stewiacke. She died February 10th, 1824, aged 31 years. James, the eldest son of Samuel and Margaret Creelman, was born July 17th, 1812. He was married to Alice, the fourth daughter of Eddy Tupper and Ann Fulton, December 5th, 1833. They had eight sons and one daughter. He inherited his father's homestead and a part of his farm. He was a Justice of the Peace for some time before he died. He died May 22nd, 1857, aged 44 years, and his widow was married again to Barry Hamilton, January 2nd, 1862. Samuel, the second son of Samuel and Margaret Creelman, was born in the year 1814. He was married to Sarah Tupper (sister of James' wife), November, 1834. They had three sons and four daughters. He inherited a part of his father's farm for a time, and afterwards removed three times to different places in

Stewiacke. He died January 3rd, 1866, aged 53 years, and his widow was married to Jonathan Campbell, April, 1868. George, the third son of Samuel and Margaret Creelman, was born in the year 1816. He was married to Hannah Jane, the fifth daughter of Thomas Crowe and Esther Fulton. They had three sons and two daughters. He died at Bass River, in the year 1859, aged 43 years, and his wife died. William, their fourth son, was born April, 1817. He died June, 1833, aged 16 years.

John, the fourth son of Samuel and Mary Creelman, was born August 30th, 1790. He was married to Margaret, daughter of James Rutherford and Elizabeth Johnson, December 8th, 1812. He inherited a part of his father's property, where he reared his numerous family. He died July 5th, 1855, aged 65 years. Duncan Ross Creelman, their eldest son, was born March 30th, 1814. He was married to Elizabeth, daughter of John Fletcher and Margaret Graham, of Masstown, October, 1836. They had two sons and four daughters. Elizabeth, the eldest daughter of John and Margaret Creelman, was born September 9th, 1815. She was married to James, son of James Kennedy and Janet Dickey, January, 1832. They had four sons and five daughters. Mr. Kennedy died September 7th, 1847, and she was married again to Robert Logan Johnson, March 20th, 1849. They had two sons and three daughters. Mary, the second daughter of John and Margaret Creelman, was born December 8th, 1817. She was married to Robert Frame in the year 1840. They had eight sons and four daughters. They reside at the South Branch of Stewiacke. James Creelman, their second son, was born April 16th, 1819. He was married to Isabell Patterson in the year 1843. They had six sons and six daughters. They removed to Canada some time ago. Samuel Ashmore Creelman, their third son, was born November 18th, 1820. He was married to Eleanor, the only daughter of Hugh G. Cox and Elizabeth Tupper, in the year 1845. They had one son and five daughters. He died at South Branch, May 4th, 1870, aged 50 years. Esther, their third daughter, was born July 23rd, 1822. She was married to John Kennedy. They had three sons and one daughter. Mr. Kennedy died October, 1867. Alexander Creelman, their fourth son, was born July 25th, 1824. He removed to the United States, and was married there to Martha Robertson. They had one son and four daughters. He died in the year 1868, aged 44 years. John Creelman, their fifth son, was born January 1st, 1826. He was married to Sarah Kaulback, of

Musquodoboit, December 23rd, 1852. They had one son and four daughters. It was he and William Creelman who first started the Spinning Machine in Stewiacke. He died April 14th, 1863, aged 35 years. Hannah Creelman, their fourth daughter, was born May 3rd, 1828. She was married to Samuel Tupper Dunlap, November, 1854. They had five daughters. She died November 12th, 1871, aged 43 years. Ann Creelman, their fifth daughter, was born September 21st, 1829. She was married to David Fraser, October, 1847. She died March 21st, 1862, aged 32 years. Margaret Rutherford, John Creelman's first wife, died June 3rd, 1830, and he was married again to Susan Johnson, of the Lower Village of Truro, April 12th, 1831. Margaret Rutherford Creelman, their eldest daughter, was born June 14th, 1832. She was married to Robert, third son of James Dunlap and Christiann Aikens, March 21st, 1861. They have two sons and four daughters. Catherine Creelman, their second daughter, was born October 23rd, 1833. She was married to Francis Cox, December 26th, 1859. They have six sons. Susan Creelman, their third daughter, was born April 26th, 1835. She died January 31st, 1836. Isabell Creelman, their fourth daughter, was born November 28th, 1836. She was married to John Christie Archibald, of Salmon River, May 9th, 1867. Jane Creelman, their fifth daughter, was born September 26th, 1838. She was married to George, third son of John Johnson and Janet Logan, January 1st, 1862. They have removed to the United States. Susan, their sixth daughter, was born June 11th, 1840. She was married to George Forbes, December 8th, 1859. They had one son and three daughters. Charlotte Creelman, their seventh daughter, was born November 29th, 1841. She was married to Rufus Wilson. They had one daughter. Mr. Wilson died March 17th, 1870, and she was married again to James W. Fulton, of Bass River, December 21st, 1870. Ebenezer Creelman, their only son, was born August 5th, 1843. He was married to Gertrude, daughter of David and Janet McNutt, of North River, January 31st, 1872. He inherits the homestead and a part of what was his father's farm. Martha Creelman, their eighth daughter, was born October 22nd, 1844. She died March 14th, 1855, aged 10 years.

Janet Creelman, the fourth daughter of Samuel Creelman, 2nd, and Mary Campbell, was born in the year 1792. She was married to Francis Fulton, of Bass River, October, 1810. They had three sons and four daughters. Mr. Fulton died in January, 1867.

Ann Creelman, their fifth daughter, was born in the year 1794.

She was married to James Fulton Johnson, November 18th, 1813, they had two sons and one daughter. Mr. Johnson died September 14th, 1818, and she was married again to James Roddick, lately from Scotland. They settled at the West River of Pictou, where they both died some time ago.

Mary Creelman, their sixth daughter, was born in the year 1796. She was married to John Dichman, of Musquodoboit, in the year 1815. They had six sons and six daughters. She died April 9th, 1865, aged 69 years, and her husband died May 1st, 1865.

Francis, the fifth son of Samuel Creelman, 2nd, and Mary Campbell, was born in the year 1798. He was married to Esther, daughter of John Fulton and Esther Crowe, of Bass River, November 25th, 1820. They settled at Bass River. Rebecca, the eldest daughter of Francis and Esther Creelman, was born July 10th, 1823. She was married to James William, son of Samuel Fulton and Rebecca O'Brien, February 25th, 1848. She died April 17th, 1870. He was married again to Charlotte Creelman, widow of the late Rufus Wilson, December 21st, 1870. Mary Jane Creelman, their second daughter, was born February 27th, 1825. She was married to John Logan Johnson, of Stewiacke, March 18th, 1855. Samuel Creelman, their eldest son, was born November 28th, 1827. He was married to Arabella O'Brien, November 18th, 1857. They had two sons and four daughters. John Creelman, their second son, was born on the 23rd December, 1829. He was married to Susan Davison, December, 1852. They had two sons and one daughter. Ann Creelman, their third daughter, was born December 29th, 1835. She was married to William Campbell, May, 1862. They had two sons and three daughters. Francis and Esther Creelman had three sons and one daughter that died young.

Andrew, the sixth and youngest son of Samuel and Mary Creelman, was born January 23rd, 1802. He was married to Susan, daughter of James and Ann Johnson, of Middle Stewiacke, December 28th, 1824. They settled on what was a part of his father's farm for a time, and then exchanged farms with Matthew Creelman, and removed to Otterbrook. Some time after this they removed to the Newton Mills, where they spent the remainder of their lives. He died July 15th, 1867, aged 65 years, and his wife died January 11th, 1863, aged 61 years. She was deprived of her sight a number of years before she died. James, their eldest son, was born October 31st, 1825. He was married to Elizabeth, daughter of Robert and Margaret

Archibald, of Truro, November 22nd, 1853. They had five sons and three daughters. They are settled at Newton Mills. Nancy Creelman, their eldest daughter, was born September 10th, 1827. She was married to James Thomas Dunlap, of Otterbrook, June 20th, 1848. They have five sons and five daughters. Samuel Flemming Creelman, their second son, was born November 10th, 1829. He was married to Jane, daughter of John Gammell and Sarah Tupper, July, 1860. They have two sons and four daughters. He is settled near Otterbrook. Mrs. Creelman died January 16th, 1873. Mary Creelman, their second daughter, was born December 10th, 1831. She was married to John Miller, of Pictou, December 27th, 1866. They had one son and one daughter. Ann Creelman, their third daughter, was born October 23rd, 1834. She died unmarried, March 7th, 1865, aged 30 years. Sarah Creelman, their fourth daughter, was born December 24th, 1836. She was married to Charles Chaplin, of Middle Stewiacke, December, 1861. They have three sons and three daughters. Duncan Ross Creelman, third son of Andrew and Susan Creelman, was born August 12th, 1839. He was married to Mary Kennedy, January 11th, 1864. They have one son and two daughters. Adam Creelman, their fourth son, was born February 15th, 1842. He died May, 1862, aged 20 years. John Creelman, their fifth son, was born September 11th, 1844. He was married to Rachel Brinton, November 9th, 1871.

Francis, the second son of Samuel and Isabell Creelman, was born in Ireland in the year 1759, and was brought by his parents to Nova Scotia in the year 1761. He was married to Esther Campbell, of Londonderry, about the year 1782. He continued to reside on the farm at the Black Rock until about the year 1792. He then exchanged farms with Robert Forbes, and removed across the Bay to Debert, and continued there until the year 1806, when he exchanged farms again, with James Johnson, Junr., and removed to Otterbrook, Stewiacke, and settled on the farm that James Thomas Dunlap now resides upon, where he spent the remainder of his days. He died July 23rd, 1836, aged 77 years, and Esther, his wife, died February 24th, 1833, aged 72 years.

Samuel, their eldest son, was born in Truro Township, October 31st, 1783. He was married to Mary, the second daughter of William Cox and Mary Smith, January, 1809. He inherited a part of what was his father's land, upon which he made improvements and built a house and barns, being the same on which his two grandsons,

Samuel and William Smith, now reside. He died there suddenly, October 11th, 1841, aged 58 years, and his first wife died December 28th, 1816, aged 26 years. He was married again to Rachel, daughter of Samuel B. Archibald. She died January 16th, 1865, aged 61 years. Esther, the only daughter of Samuel and Mary Creelman, was born September 17th, 1810. She was married to John Smith, Feby. 17th, 1829. They had five sons and four daughters, who appear among the Smiths.

James Campbell Creelman, the second son of Francis and Esther Creelman, was born in Truro, June 1st, 1785. He was married to Alison Jamison, the eldest daughter of Mahew Tupper and Christiann Cock, February 4th, 1808. They settled on the farm that John Smith, Esq,, now resides upon, where they reared their family, and lived together more than fifty years. Mrs. Creelman died there April 22nd, 1860, aged 75 years, and he removed to Halifax with his youngest son, John. He died there June 30th, 1869, aged 84 years, and his body was taken to Stewiacke and buried beside his wife. Isabell Creelman, their eldest daughter, was born October 10th, 1808. She was married to John Benvey, of Musquodoboit, October 8th, 1827. They had one son and six daughters. They removed to Sheet Harbour. She died there November, 1870, aged 62 years. Mr. Benvey died July, 1872. Christiann Creelman, their second daughter, was born October 19th, 1810. She was married to Jonathan Campbell, December 24th, 1831. They had seven sons and three daughters. She died May 25th, 1867, aged 57 years, and Mr. Campbell was married again to Sarah Tupper, widow of the late Samuel Creelman, sixth, April, 1868. Esther Creelman, their third daughter, was born February 18th, 1813. She was married to William Newcomb, March 27th, 1838. They had five sons and two daughters. They have resided in Halifax since the year 1848. Jane Creelman, their fourth daughter, was born July 5th, 1815. She was married to Henry Campbell, March 11th, 1835. She died April 19th, 1835, aged 20 years. Mary Creelman, their fifth daughter, was born September 22nd, 1817. She was married to James Ellis, March, 1839. They had three sons and four daughters. Samuel Creelman, their eldest son, was born October 22nd, 1819. He was married to Grizell Ellis, March, 1843. They had two sons and one daughter. They removed and now reside at Cape John, in the County of Pictou. Elizabeth Creelman, their sixth daughter, was born April 27th, 1822. She was married to Peter Suther Smith, March, 1842. They had one son and four daughters. She died February 17th, 1861, aged 39 years, and her husband died January 15th, 1859, aged 39 years. Mahew Tupper Creelman, their second son, was born April 30th, 1824. He was married to Sophia Hall, of Sheet Harbor. They have one daughter. John, the third and youngest son of James C. and and Alison J. Creelman, was born November 4th, 1826. He was married to Louina Bentley, July 15th, 1851. They have six sons and three daughters. He inherited the homestead and a part of his father's farm for a few years, and then removed to Halifax, where he still resides.

Matthew Creelman, the third son of Francis and Esther Creelman, was born at the Black Rock, October 6th, 1788. He was married to Sarah Webster, of King's County, October 15th, 1822. He inherited a part of what was his father's farm, for a time, and then he exchanged farms with Andrew Creelman, and removed up to the place where Daniel Webster now resides. He died July 20th, 1856, aged 67 years, and his wife died July 12th, 1851, aged 61 years. Mary, the eldest daughter of Francis and Esther Creelman, was born in Truro Township, August 16th, 1790. She was married to David McLellan, of Londonderry, in July, 1831. They had two daughters. Mr. McLellan died in 1859. Esther Creelman, their second daughter, was born September 23rd, 1796. She was married to Robert, son of Simeon Whidden and Dorothy Blair, of Middle Stewiacke, November 9th, 1813. They had five sons and five daughters. Mr. Whidden died April 1st, 1834, aged 46 years. Margaret Creelman, their third daughter, was born March 7th, 1798. She was married to John, second son of William and Mary Cox, December 25th, 1821. They had five sons and two daughters. Mr. Cox died April 24th, 1867, aged 71 years. William, the fourth and youngest son of Francis and Esther Creelman, was born November 30th, 1800. He was married to Abigail, fifth daughter of Eliakim and Lydia Tupper, January 27th, 1831. He inherited the homestead part of his father's farm at Otterbrook, until about the year 1856. He removed, and is now living on the south side of the River and interval, near the same place where Charles Cox settled when he first removed to Stewiacke. Mary Jane, their eldest daughter, was born August 12th, 1832. She was married to James Smith, second son of Eliakim Tupper, Esq., and Elizabeth Newcomb, July 27th, 1859. Eliakim Tupper Creelman, their oldest son, was born May 5th, 1834. He removed to the United States, and was married there to Mary Johnson, in June, 1864. They have one son. Frank, their second son, was born July 16th, 1836. Matthew Creelman, their third son, was born November 28th, 1838. He learned the harness-making trade in Truro, and removed to the United States. He was married there to Elizabeth, daughter of the late John Gammell and Sarah Tupper. William Putnam Creelman, their fourth son, was born March 28th, 1841. He settled on a new farm in the woods, and lived there alone, improving his farm. On the 2nd of April, 1870, he was found dead under a tree, which he had been cutting down. From several circumstances, it is believed that he had been in that situation from the 26th of March. During all this time, his cattle had been confined in the barn without food or water. Lydia Creelman, their third daughter, was born November 13th, 1843. She was married to George Chaplin, January 23rd, 1863. They have five sons. They removed to the United States. Charles Dickie Creelman, their fifth son, was born January 31st, 1848. He remains at home with his parents. Henry, their sixth son, was born April 28th, 1850. He has removed to the United States. Esther Margaret, their third and youngest daughter, was born on the 6th June, 1852.

Matthew, the third son of Samuel Creelman, Sen., and Isabell Flemming, was born in Cumberland, in December, 1762. He was married to Nancy Knox, of Londonderry, in the year 1791. They settled on a part of what was his father's land, about three miles up the Shubenacadie River, now called Prince Port. On this place they reared their family and spent the remainder of their days. He died there August 12th, 1835, aged 72 years, and his wife died March 18th, 1844.

Samuel, their eldest son, was born October 4th, 1794. He was married to Isabell, the fifth daughter of James Moore and Susan Teas, December 9th, 1821. They settled on a part of what was his father's farm, where they spent the remainder of their lives. James Creelman, their only son, was born December 18th, 1822. He is known by the name of Farmer Jimmey. He is a Justice of the Peace. He was married to Susan Messenger, November 13th, 1844. They have three sons and one daughter. Samuel Creelman's first wife died 1824, and he was married again to Martha Laughead, December 25th, 1832. She died April 21st, 1835. He was married again to Rebecca Smith, widow of the late Robert Alexander, December 20th, 1836. William Isaiah, their only son, was born August 3rd, 1840. He was married to Mary, the only daughter of John Sanderson and Mary Forbes,

June 12th, 1866. Isabell, the only daughter of Samuel and Rebecca Creelman, was born December 31st, 1837. She was married to Samuel C. Sanderson, October 13th, 1856. They had three sons and two daughters. Samuel Creelman died January 8th, 1867, aged 72 years, and Rebecca, his third wife died January 29th, 1867. Jane, the eldest daughter of Matthew and Nancy Creelman, was born October 10th, 1796. She was married to William Sanderson, January 22nd, 1823. They had six sons and one daughter. Mr. Sanderson died June 11th, 1868.

John, the second son of Matthew and Nancy Creelman, was born September 3rd, 1799. He was married to Eleanor McCollum, of Hants County, October, 1821. (She came from Scotland a short time before they were married.) He settled on the high land about one mile east of his father's place, where his three sons now reside ; on this place he spent the remainder of his life. He died there very suddenly on July 7th, 1863, aged 64 years, and his widow died February 7th, 1865. Abigail, their eldest daughter, was born April 23rd, 1822. She was married to James Hughes, July, 1846. They had five sons. James N. Creelman, eldest son of John and Eleanor, was born March 24th, 1828. He was married to Sarah, daughter of John Park and Rebecca Crowe, March 23rd, 1854. They have five sons and one daughter. Esther Creelman, their second daughter, was born June 27th, 1830. She was married to David Dart in 1850. They have three sons. Samuel Creelman, their second son, was born January 28th, 1834. He was married to Letitia Park, January, 1855. They have three sons and two daughters. William Creelman, their third son, was born October 27th, 1838. He was married to Catherine Wilson, November 10th, 1864. They have four sons. Jane, the third daughter of John and Eleanor Creelman, was born Sept. 11th, 1842. She was married to Martin Curtis, September 21st, 1865. They have two sons and one daughter.

William, the third son of Matthew and Nancy Creelman, was born March 17th, 1802. He was married to Susan, third daughter of James and Jane Laughead, of Clifton, December 9th, 1824. He inherited the homestead and a large part of what was his father's farm. He died February 13th, 1873, aged 71 years. Jane, their eldest daughter, was born July 30th, 1825. She was married to William, the only living son of James Philips and Margaret Moore. They had two sons and two daughters. Lucinda, their second daughter, was born July 6th, 1827. She was married to Harry

Hughes, October, 1843. Mr. Hughes was drowned out of a boat at Pitchbrook, while engaged carrying off an anchor from a vessel that he was then Captain of, April 5th, 1845. She was married again to Samuel Laughead, December, 1852. Mr. Laughead died July 9th, 1872, aged 45 years, and left no family. George, the eldest son of William and Susan Creelman, was born April 20th, 1829. He was married to Eleanor, daughter of George and Susan Yuill, of Clifton, October 3rd, 1856. They have three sons and two daughters. Nancy, their third daughter, was born May 24th, 1831. She was married to Matthew Sanderson, Esq., August 12th, 1854. They have four sons and four daughters. Martha, their fourth daughter, was born August 2nd, 1834. She was married to Matthew Frame, December 16th, 1858. They had one son. Mr. Frame died March 16th, 1869. Matthew, the second son of William and Susan Creelman, was born November 21st, 1836. He was married to Jane Cameron, of Hants County, August, 1858. They have two daughters. Mary, their fifth daughter, was born February 18th, 1839. She was married to Daniel Philips, December 15th, 1857. They have three sons and one daughter. Eliza, their sixth daughter, was born February 10th, 1841. She was married to Michael Ambrose, September, 1856. They had two sons. Mr. Ambrose died October 9th, 1869, aged 35 years. James Creelman, the third son of William and Susan Creelman, was born December 1st, 1843. He died May 8th, 1861, aged 17 years. Mehetabel, their seventh daughter, was born July 23rd, 1845. She was married to John Cook, October, 1861. They had one son and two daughters. She died July 21st, 1870, aged 25 years.

Isabell, the second daughter of Matthew and Nancy Creelman, was born December 9th, 1804. She was married to Captain James Norris, February 14th, 1828. They had three sons and three daughters. Mr. Norris died December 10th, 1866.

Margaret, the eldest daughter of Samuel Creelman, Senr., and Isabell, was born in Ireland in the year 1749, and was brought by her parents to Nova Scotia when she was twelve years old. She was married to Samuel Smith in 1791. Mr. Smith came from England a short time before they were married. They settled on the farm that George Taylor, Esq., now resides upon at Middle Stewiacke. She died at the house of Mr. James Norris, of Princeport, December, 1836, aged 87 years. She left no children. Mr. Smith died about the year 1840.

Nancy, the second daughter of Samuel Creelman, Senr., and Isabell Flemming, was born in Ireland, January, 1761, and was brought by her parents to Nova Scotia when but a few months old. She was married to William Pollock in the year 1781. They settled on the farm that Mr. John Teas now resides upon at Lower Stewiacke, where Mrs. Pollock died suddenly, August, 1786, when her only daughter was but three months old ; this daughter is now the widow of the late William Green, and is living at date (November 7th, 1872). She is in the 87th year of her age. Samuel, the only son of William and Nancy Pollock, was born in the year 1784. He was married and has a family of children. He settled and built a house on a part of what was his father's farm. In the spring of the year 1816 he and his father both sold their farms to Isaac Miller and his sons, and a few years after, he left Nova Scotia. William Pollock died January 18th, 1846.

Ann, the third daughter of Samuel and Isabell Creelman, was born in Cumberland in the year 1765. She was married to Robert Wilson, a Scotchman. They had one daughter ; her name was Isabell. She was married to Murdock Frame, of Middle Stewiacke, in 1808. They had six sons and two daughters. She died May 5th, 1866, aged 77 years. Mr. Frame died August, 1838, aged 58 years. Robert Wilson died, and his widow was married again to Joseph Marshal. They had four sons and one daughter. She died March, 1808, aged 43 years. Mr. Marshall died October, 1844. Mr. Marshall lived and reared his family on the lower farm in Middle Stewiacke, being the same that Mr. James Taylor now resides upon.

CHAPTER LXII.

Jacob Lynds was an early settler in Cobequid. He was born in Ireland, about the year 1720. He was married there to Mary Guild, being then the widow McNutt, in 1746. They removed to New England in 1756. They removed again to Nova Scotia in 1761. He settled for a time at Advocate, where he obtained a grant of one thousand five hundred acres of land, and remained there but a short time. He removed further up the Bay of Fundy. He settled on the farm that is now owned by the Messrs. Putnam at Fort Belcher,

where he spent the short remainder of his life. He died there
November 22nd, 1768. His body was taken up the Bay in a boat,
and buried in the Onslow Cemetery. This was the second body that
was buried on this Island. The first was Miss Mary McNutt,
daughter of William and Elizabeth McNutt, who died August 15th,
1765. After the death of Mr. Lynds, the farm at the Fort was sold
to Mr. Richard Upham, and the family removed and settled on the
farm that his eldest son, Thomas Lynds, and his son Thomas, lived
and died upon, at North River. His widow was married again to
James Whidden, of Truro. Mr. Whidden died December 13th,
1790. She was again left a widow. She returned again to the
house of her eldest son, Thomas, at the Fort, where she spent the
remainder of her life. She died there in 1810.

Thomas, the eldest son of Jacob and Mary Lynds, was born in
Ireland, in 1747. He was brought by his parents to America when
he was about nine years old, and to Onslow when he was twenty-five
years old. He was married to Rebecca, fifth daughter of Captain
William Blair and Jane Barns, January 27th, 1774. They reared
their family and lived together for sixty-three years. He died January
6th, 1839, aged 92 years. His wife died January 9th, 1838, aged 80
years. Benjamin and Simeon Lynds, their twin sons, were born
November 15th, 1774. Benjamin was married to Mary McNutt,
September 12th, 1793. They had six sons and four daughters. He
settled first on the top of the East Mountain of Onslow. After a
while he found it inconvenient to live on the top of the Mountain.
He built another house near the foot of it, where he spent the
remainder of his life, being the same house that his youngest son,
Benjamin, now resides in. He died there in October, 1858, aged 83
years. His wife died September 18th, 1853. Simeon Lynds, the
other twin son, was a wheel-wright. He died a bachelor, August
15th, 1857, aged 82 years. Susan Lynds, their eldest daughter, was
born September 2nd, 1776. She was married to Robert McCurdy,
in 1794. They had one son. Mr. McCurdy settled about two miles
up the old Tatamagouche Road, from the Onslow Church. He died
September 16th, 1863, aged 78 years. His wife died January 18th,
1862, aged 85 years. Lydia Lynds, their second daughter, was born
March 11th, 1778. She was married to Nathaniel Marsters, Esq.,
November 5th, 1798. She was Mr. Marsters' second wife. They
had two sons and one daughter. She died April 25th, 1830, aged 52
years. Mr. Marsters died July 19th, 1843, aged 85 years. Mr.

Marsters' first wife was Sarah Upham. She died November 29th, 1789. They had two sons. Jacob Lynds, their third son, was born in 1780. He died when young. David Barns Lynds, their fourth son, was born September 10th, 1781. He was married to Sarah, the second daughter of John and Nancy Blair, October, 1810. They had one daughter. He settled in Truro, on the place that was owned by William Logan, Sen. He practised as a Doctor until the infirmities of old age came upon him. He died June 9th, 1871. Elizabeth Lynds, their third daughter, was born September 22nd, 1783. She was married to Nathaniel Wiswell, in 1802. They had four sons and five daughters. She died in 1850, aged 67 years. Mr. Wiswell was killed by falling from a staging of a new house that he was working at in St. John, N. B., in the summer of 1841. Rebecca Lynds, their fourth daughter, was born September 24th, 1785. She was married to Philip Freeman, in 1805. They had two sons. They removed to the United States. She died there, and Mr. Freeman died there. James Lynds, their fifth son, was born October 23rd, 1787. He was married to Margaret Hall, November 9th, 1809. He settled on a part of his father's farm. He died there January 5th, 1852, aged 64 years. He left no children. Dorothy Lynds, their fifth daughter, was born in April, 1790. She died unmarried, October 12th, 1866, aged 76 years. Thomas Lynds, their sixth son, was born in March, 1792. He inherited the homestead and a large part of his father's property. He died a bachelor, March 28th, 1865, aged 73 years. Sarah Lynds, their sixth daughter, was born July 20th, 1795. She was married to Wren Johnson, May 15th, 1828. They had one daughter. Mr. Johnson died September 28th, 1862, aged 68 years.

Mary and Jacob, twins of Jacob Lynds, Sen., and Mary Guild, were born in 1752. Mary Lynds was married to Solomon Hoar, April 1st, 1773. They had two sons and six daughters. She died in 1815, aged 63 years. Mr. Hoar died in 1828.

Jacob Lynds was married to Martha Morrison, November 13th, 1786. He settled on the top of Onslow Mountain. He was known by the name of Whispering Jacob. He died December 23rd, 1833, aged 81 years. His wife died in March, 1829, aged 67 years. Mary Lynds, their eldest daughter, was born January 6th, 1788. She was married to Jacob Workman, February 4th, 1810. They had five sons and seven daughters. Mr. Workman died in Truro, May, 1867. Jane Lynds, their second daughter, was born April 26th, 1790. She was married to Gideon McNutt, November 23rd, 1806. They had six sons and six daughters. She died January 1st, 1873, aged 83 years. Martha Lynds, their third daughter, was born December 23rd, 1791. She was married to William Miller, of Newport, in December, 1809. They had six sons and three daughters. She died March 5th, 1873. Mr. Miller died in May, 1858. Jacob Lynds, their eldest son, was born March 10th, 1793. He drove the mail from Truro to Pictou from about the year 1815 to 1828. He is known by the name of Post Jacob. He settled on the old Pictou Road. He was married to Hannah Lockhart, of Newport, Oct. 14th, 1820. They had one daughter. Mrs. Lynds died May 8th, 1827. He was married again to Eleanor, the youngest daughter of David and Esther Archibald, March 12th, 1830. They had one son and four daughters. Ruth Lynds, their fourth daughter, was born February 4th, 1795. She was married to Hugh Tucker, April 6th, 1815. They had six sons and four daughters. He settled on Tatamagouche Mountain. He died at North River, July 1871, aged 78 years. Elizabeth Lynds, their fifth daughter, was born January 17th, 1800. She was married to Robert Nichol, December 5th, 1823. They had four sons and four daughters. She died December 26th, 1870, aged 71 years. Mr. Nichol died January 9th, 1871, aged 72 years. Robert Lynds, their second son, was born January 17th, 1798. He was married to Catherine Embree, of Wallace, in 1831. They had three sons and four daughters. He is living in Wallace. John Lynds, their third son, was born March 29th, 1804. He was married to Charlotte Embree, of Wallace, in 1831. They had one son and one daughter. He inherited his father's farm on Onslow Mountain. He died in January, 1835, aged 31 years. Sarah Lynds, their sixth daughter, was born February 4th, 1802. She was married to Samuel McNutt, in 1821. They had three sons and six daughters. They removed to the United States. She died there January 1st, 1867. Lavinia Lynds, their seventh daughter, was born June 26th, 1807. She was married to Ebenezer Harris, June, 1829. They had one son and three daughters. She died March 18th, 1869, aged 62 years.

Lydia, the second daughter of Jacob Lynds, Sen., and Mary Guild, was born in 1750. She was married to John Arnold, in 1780. They had one son and three daughters. She died at North River, February 17th, 1788. Ruth Lynds, their third daughter, was born in 1754. She was married to David Hoar, January 30th, 1779. They had four sons and five daughters. They removed, and settled at Shepody, where they both died some time ago.

John, the third son of Jacob and Mary Lynds, was born at Bunker's Hill, U. S., in 1760. He was brought by his parents to Nova Scotia when he was one year old. He was married to Eunice McNutt, in 1781. He settled on the farm that his grandson, John Lynds, now resides on, up the North River. He died there in August, 1838, aged 78 years. His wife died in March, 1835.

William Lynds, their eldest son, was born in 1782. He was married to Margaret McCollum, November, 1801. They had five sons and four daughters. He purchased what was Mr. McCollum's farm. David Lynds now resides upon it, He died there December 13th, 1848, aged 66 years. His wife died November 13th, 1847, aged 64 years. Jacob Lynds, their second son, was born May 24th, 1784. He was married to Eleanor, second daughter of Thomas Fletcher and Elizabeth Barnhill, November 1st, 1810. They had five sons and five daughters. He died May 27th, 1858, aged 74 years. His widow died January 17th, 1867, aged 78 years. Lucy Lynds, their eldest daughter, was born in 1786. She was married to William Polley, of Cumberland. They had four sons and five daughters. She died in Cumberland, in 1862, aged 76 years. Mr. Polley died some time ago. Thomas Lynds, their third son, was born November 11th, 1788. He was married to Elizabeth Clark, in 1813. They had three sons and four daughters. He settled on the south side of Salmon River, where Charles D. Upham now resides. He died there in November, 1848, aged 60 years. Hannah Lynds, their second daughter, was born in 1790. She was married to Peter Blackmore, November, 1809. They had five sons and five daughters. Mr. Blackmore died in October, 1864, aged 81 years. Barnabas Lynds, their fourth son, was born July 9th, 1792. He was married to Ruth Archibald, October 20th, 1818. They had three sons and five daughters. Mrs. Lynds died November 18th, 1853, aged 52 years. John Harris Lynds, their fifth son, was born February 28th, 1794. He was married to Abigail Workman, March, 1823. They had three sons and three daughters. Mary Lynds, their third daughter, was born February 16th, 1803. She was married to William Cutton, December 6th, 1822. They had two sons and one daughter. She died in August, 1838, aged 35 years. Sarah, the youngest daughter of Jacob Lynds, Sen., and Mary Guild, was born April 18th, 1768. She was married to John Wright, November 25th, 1788. They had four sons and eight daughters.

CHAPTER LXIII.

Charles Dickson removed from New England to Nova Scotia among the first settlers when he was young. He resided in Kings County until about the year 1771 ; he then removed up the Bay to Onslow, and purchased a large tract of land from William McNutt, at Onslow Parade, where he commenced and carried on a large business at farming, merchandize, building and sailing ships. He was an active man for business ; he was Registrar of Deeds for Colchester, and representative of Onslow in the House of Assembly, as before mentioned. On September 16th, 1780, he was appointed Justice of the Peace for what are now the counties of Colchester and Pictou. In 1796 he went to the West Indies in one of his vessels ; on his return he called at Halifax and took ill of yellow fever, and died there on September 3rd, 1796. His widow was married again to Joseph McLain. After his death his four sons carried on the business for a few years, under the firm of John Dickson & Co. He was married to Amelia Bishop in 1772. She died November, 1846.

John Dickson, their eldest son, was born in Onslow, June 7th, 1773. He was married to Lydia Hamilton, October 20th, 1796. They had four sons and five daughters. He followed the sea as Captain a considerable length of time. He was the Senior Justice of the Peace for the County several years. He died at Onslow, December, 1858, aged 85 years. His widow died March, 1866. Charles Dickson, their second son, was born April 6th, 1775. He was married to Rachel Todd Archibald, December 31st, 1799. They had five sons and six daughters. He was a carpenter by trade. He died March, 1821. Mrs. Dickson died in 1819. Robert Dickson, their third son, was born July 8th, 1777. He was married to Lavinia De Wolfe in 1798. They had seven sons and three daughters. He was a Justice of the Peace, Commissioner of Sewers, representative of Onslow, and Colonel of the Militia. He was an extensive farmer. He died November, 1836. His widow died July, 1854, aged 78 years. William Dickson, their fourth son, was born in 1779. He was married to Rebecca, second daughter of Colonel Thomas and Martha Pearson, of Truro, January 29th, 1801. They had six sons and six daughters. He represented Truro in the House of Assembly eight years. He died February 15th, 1834. Mrs. Dickson died June,

1833, aged 49 years. Abigail Dickson, their eldest daughter, was born in 1781. She was married to Andrew Wallace, of Halifax, February 27th, 1798. They had three sons and one daughter. Mr. Wallace died, and she was married again to Robert Lowden, of Merigomish. They had four sons and two daughters. She died in 1868. Sarah Dickson, their second daughter, was born in 1783. She died when young. Mary and Olivia Dickson, their twin daughters, were born in 1785. Mary was married to Dr. John Murray Upham, son of Judge Upham, of New Brunswick, in 1803. They had one son and two daughters. She died at Tatamagouche, December 6th, 1872. Olivia Dickson, was married to Colonel David Archibald, February 5th, 1801. She had five sons and five daughters. She died February 7th, 1872. Elizabeth Dickson, their fifth daughter, was born in 1786. She was married to S. G. W. Archibald, March 16th, 1802. They had eleven sons and four daughters. She died May 13th, 1830. Thomas Dickson, their fifth son, was born in 1788. He was married to Sarah Ann Patterson, of Pictou. They had one son and eight daughters. He studied law with S. G. W. Archibald. He died in Pictou town, about 1857. His wife died about 1850. Their children are all dead. Lavinia Dickson, their sixth daughter, was married to Rev. John Burnyatt, April 27th, 1823. They had two sons and one daughter. She died October, 1860. Mr. Burnyatt died April 7th, 1843, aged 59 years.

CONCLUSION.

A FEW HISTORICAL EVENTS WHICH TOOK PLACE IN TRURO AND ITS NEIGHBORHOOD FROM ITS EARLY SETTLEMENT UP TO THE PRESENT TIME.

William Fisher was the first Town Clerk who was in Truro. He acted from the year 1761 to 1771. Samuel Archibald, second, was Clerk from this time until 1779, the time of his death. His brother, Robert Archibald, was Clerk for the years 1780 and 1781. James Archibald, Esq., was Clerk for the year 1782. Dr. John Harris was Clerk until the end of 1790. Gavin Johnson was then Clerk until the end of 1798. Then David Archibald, seventh, acted four years; when he removed to Onslow. Alexander Miller was Clerk from the beginning of the year 1803, until the time of his death, in 1834. The first Court of Sessions was held in Onslow about the year 1769, in the house of Samuel Nichols, Senr., which stood then about forty rods west of the new Church. At one time the Grand Jury voted £15 to pay Mr. Nichols for the use of his house to hold Courts in, on condition that he would not sell any rum during the sitting of the Courts. The people of Pictou came to Onslow to attend Court up to the year 1790. Courts continued to be held in Onslow until 1800. A Court house was built on the top of the hill on the north side of Salmon River, front of the Metzler House, in 1799. The Courts were held there but a short time. In the year 1803 this house was taken down by the late Ebenezer Archibald, and hauled through the interval and River, and set up again on the parade in front of the present Court-house. It was used as a Court-house until the year 1844; it was removed after the present one was built. At the first settlement of the County, Cobequid had no Jail for a considerable number of years, excepting the cellar of David Archibald, Esq., which was occasionally used for that purpose. After some time, when Courts were held in Onslow, they had some kind of log Jail there. The first Jail that was in Truro was built in 1803; it stood on what is now the street in front of the Registrar of Deeds' office. There had been but little use for a Jail in Truro hitherto, but about this time and for a number of years after, imprisonment for debt was very common, much more so than at the present day. In May, 1817, this first Jail was burnt down. Beggs and Munro, two Scotch tailors, were suspected of setting it on fire. These two men were confined in Jail at the time, charged with burglary and stealing. In 1818 another Jail was built, and was used until 1865, when it was taken down, after the present Jail was erected. The first mail was carried from Halifax to Pictou in December, 1801, by the late Alexander Stewart (who kept an Inn on Mount Tom, at the same place that his daughter Nancy continued to keep while she lived). He travelled on foot, carrying the mail in his pocket or on his back, once a fortnight until about 1812.

Mr. Niles, of Cumberland, carried a mail from Halifax to Amherst during the year 1813, once a week, which it took him the six days of the week to perform. He did it himself, with the exception of one week, altogether on horseback. About this time Ezra Witter removed from the western part of the Province and settled on Bible Hill, where he carried on chaise building. He took the mail to carry from Halifax to Cumberland, which he did with a chaise drawn by one horse for a number of years. Richard Upham Marsters carried the mail from Truro to Pictou during the year 1813, on horseback. Eliakim Tupper carried it in 1814. Jacob Lynds drove the mail from Truro to Pictou from 1815 until 1828. Mr. Witter drove it from Halifax to Cumberland about the same time, with the assistance of Michael Summers and others. In 1828 there was a company formed to run a coach from Halifax to Pictou to carry the mail and passengers. In 1842 Hiram Hyde purchased these horses and coaches and drove until the cars commenced to run, in December, 1858. The first engine passed up Salmon River on the railroad on August 21st, 1866 ; it was engaged in ballasting the road. The same fall the railroad was opened for the conveyance of mail and passengers to Pictou. Charles B. Archibald carried the mail and passengers from Truro to Cumberland for more than twenty years, up to November, 1872, when the Intercolonial railroad was opened for traffic. William and Robert Watson drove from Truro to Cumberland for a number of years before Mr. Archibald commenced.

In the early part of the settlement of Nova Scotia, there were large amounts of labour lost in road-making, for want of having them properly laid out. If we had been placed in the same situation that our forefathers were, at the first settlement of the place, the probability is that we would have done no better. Their main object was to keep out of the swamps and wet land with their paths, or roads, through the woods. To attain this object, the highest land was passed over, and deep valleys crossed in their narrowest places. As it was, the travelling for man and beast was very laborious. This state of things continued until Sir James Kempt became Governor of Nova Scotia. We may give him the credit of being the originator of level roads in Nova Scotia. He was not long in Nova Scotia until he set to work to get rid of the travelling over the heavy hills. He obtained the assistance of Mr. George Whitman, and other scientific men, in carrying out this desirable object. The first part of the road between Halifax and Truro, on what is called the level system, was made about the year 1828, along the edge of the Grand Lake. In the year 1834, it was made from Truro to Brookfield. This work was carried on until the level road was completed from Halifax to Pictou, about the year 1840. When Mr. Whitman took surveys from Halifax to Truro, and reported to the Government that a line of road could be got that would have no greater rise in it than one foot in thirty, he was laughed at by many of the people.

At the first settlement of this country, and for a long time after, the wheat crop yielded an abundant harvest ; and there was no such thing then as the manufacture or use of oatmeal. In the year 1818, John Young, Esq., (father of Sir William Young, who is now Chief Justice of Nova Scotia), wrote a number of letters in, the *Acadian Recorder*, over the name of Agricola, upon agriculture, which stirred the people up to a new system of farming. One thing he recommended was the erection of mills to manufacture oatmeal. Upon this recommendation, Thomas Dickson, Esq., (who was his co-representative for the County of Sydney a few years after) fitted up a mill for that purpose, at the same place that the mills now stand in Truro. The first oatmeal that was manufactured in Colchester, (and, I think, in the Province), was done at this mill in 1820. Before this time, oatmeal was unknown by the natives of Nova Scotia. Not many years after the use of oatmeal commenced, the wheat crop began to fail. In this year, September 6th, the first cattle show was held in Halifax. Sir James Kempt took a lively interest in this. He was in attendance, and distributed the prizes. John Young, Esq., took a very active part in this business, as well as many others. The next fall, the first cattle show was held in Truro. About this time, ploughing matches commenced, and more interest was taken in agriculture and the improvement of stock.

On February 18th, 1826, a public meeting was held in Halifax, on the subject of the Shubenacadie Canal. The estimated cost of this Canal was £60,000. Messrs Jeffery and Cunard subscribed £1000 each. There were £13,000 subscribed at this meeting, a company was formed, and the House of Assembly granted £15,000. Charles Rufus Fairbanks took a very active part in the work. On Monday, July 24th, the ground was broken for the commencement of this great work by His Excellency the Earl of Dalhousie, in presence of Sir James Kempt, the Members of Council, and a large number of respectable citizens. The work went on for a number of years, a larger amount of money was expended than the estimate. This great work turned out to be all but a useless undertaking.

As before mentioned, Cobequid was directed to be included in the County of Halifax, in 1761. In 1765 Charles Morris, jr., was returned to represent the township of Truro in the House of Assembly, and James Brenton, Esq., for the township of Onslow. Mr. Morris being returned to represent Kings County at the same time; he accepted for Kings County, and Truro was unrepresented until 1766, when David Archibald, Esq. took his seat on June 5th. In 1770 William Fisher was returned to represent Truro, Joshua Lamb for Onslow, and Captain John Morrison, having removed from Truro to Londonderry in 1769, took his seat in 1770 to represent Londonderry, without opposition. Mr. Fisher being in a bad state of health, Samuel Archibald, (eldest son of David Archibald, Esq.), took his seat in the Assembly, June 27th, 1775. In 1777 Samuel Archibald was returned to represent Truro, which he continued to do until the time of his death, in 1779. Dr. John Harris represented Truro after the death of Mr. Archibald until 1785 without opposition. Charles Dickson represented Onslow from 1777, it being unrepresented for a few years before, on account of there being no pay for members at this time. John Morrison continued to represent Londonderry until 1778. Richard Cunningham was the representative for Londonderry until the end of the Long Parliament, which continued from 1770 to 1785. There were seventeen sessions during that time. In 1785, Matthew Archibald was returned to represent Truro, Charles Dickson for Onslow, and James Smith, (eldest son of Rev. David Smith), for Londonderry. Mr. Smith's seat was declared vacant, April 6th, 1789, Robert McElhenney was elected to represent Londonderry on Feby. 25th, 1790. In February, 1793, there was a general election in the Province, this being the first election for the County of Halifax in which a Poll was opened in Onslow. It closed there February 26th. Matthew Archibald was returned to represent Truro, Charles Dickson for Onslow, and Robert McElhenney for Londonderry. In 1799 Simon B. Robie, of Halifax, was returned to represent Truro, Daniel McCurdy for Onslow, and Samuel Chandler for Londonderry. Up to this date the County of Halifax was represented altogether by men residing within the Town of Halifax; at this election, as before mentioned, James Fulton, Esq., of Bass River, and Edward Mortimer, of Pictou, were the first who offered to represent the County, who did not reside in Halifax. A Poll was opened in Halifax, Onslow, and Pictou; it was closed in Pictou December 13th, being the first election held in Pictou, when Fulton, Mortimer, Tonge, and Morris were returned. November 18th, 1806, the new Assembly met, (9th general assembly, first session). Members returned for the County of Halifax, Edward Mortimer of Pictou, S. G. W. Archibald of Truro, Simon B. Robie and William Lawson of Halifax; Thomas Pearson for Truro, Nathaniel Marsters for Onslow, and Samuel Chandler for Londonderry. The tenth General Assembly of this Province was elected in 1811, (the first election within the recollection of the writer.) Mortimer, Archibald, Robie, and Lawson were again returned to represent the County of Halifax. James Kent for Truro, Nathaniel Marsters for Onslow, and James Flemming for Londonderry. In 1818 Mortimer, Archibald, Robie and Lawson were again returned for the County of Halifax. William Dickson for Truro, Robert Dickson for Onslow, and James Flemming for Londonderry. Mr. Mortimer died October 10th, 1819. George Smith of Pictou was returned without opposition to fill his place. In 1820 there was another general election in this Province, on account of the death of King George the III. At this election, Archibald, Smith, Robie and Lawson, were again returned to represent the County of Halifax; William Dickson for Truro; Robert Dickson, for Onslow; and James Flemming for Londonderry. In 1826, S. G. W. Archibald, George Smith, William Lawson, and Lawrence Hantshorne, were returned to represent the County of Halifax. There was a pretty sharp contest at this time between William Flemming and Charles Dickson Archibald (the eldest son of S. G. W. Archibald). At the close of the poll, Archibald had one of a majority; and at the last minute before closing the poll, Archibald had his own vote recorded for himself. Flemming attempted to do the same, but was too late, as the time had arrived for closing the poll. A scrutiny was demanded.

by Flemming. On March 8th, 1827, the committee which investi-
gated this contest, reported in favour of Archibald's retaining his seat
as representative of Truro. John Crowe was returned for Onslow,
and John Wier for Londonderry. At the meeting of the Assembly
on February 1st, 1827, S. G. W. Archibald was unanimously chosen
Speaker of the House. In 1830, the memorable election on the
brandy question (as before mentioned) was held. S. G. W. Archibald,
George Smith, William Lawson, and Jotham Blanchard, were returned
to represent the County of Halifax ; Alexander Lackie Archibald for
Truro ; Robert Dickson for Onslow, and John Wier for Londonderry.
Archibald continued Speaker. In 1836, the law went into operation
for dividing the County of Halifax into three Counties, viz. : Halifax,
Colchester and Pictou. At the election held in November, 1836,
S. G. W. Archibald was returned to represent Colchester County ;
Alexander L. Aichibald, for Truro ; Alexander McC. Upham, for
Onslow, and G. W. McLellan for Londonderry. Archibald continued
Speaker. In 1841, S. G. W. Archibald was appointed to the office
of Master of Rolls, and Thomas Dickson was elected to represent
Colchester. In 1843, John Ross was returned to represent Colchester ;
William Flemming, for Truro ; John Crowe, for Onslow, and G. W.
McLellan for Londonderry. In 1847, Samuel Creelman, of Stewiacke,
was returned to represent the County of Colchester ; Alexander L.
Archibald, for Truro ; John Crowe, for Onslow, and G. W. McLellan,
for Londonderry. In 1851, Adams G. Archibald and G. W. McLellan
were returned to represent the County of Colchester ; James Campbell,
of Tatamagouche, for the north District, and Samuel Creelman for
the south. In 1855, Adams G. Archibald and G. W. McLellan
were returned again to represent Colchester ; Thomas F. Morrison for
the north District, and Hiram Hyde for the south. During the
sitting of the Assembly in the early part of 1858, G. W. McLellan
died in Halifax. His son, A. W. McLellan, was returned without
opposition, to fill the vacant seat for one year. In the year 1859,
Adams G. Archibald and Alexander Campbell were returned to
represent the south District of Colchester, and Thomas F. Morrison
and A. W. McLellan for the north District. In the year 1863, A.
W. McLellan and William Blackwood, of Tatamagouche, were
returned to represent the north District of Colchester ; Adams G.
Archibald and Francis Parker for the south District. In the year
1867, A. W. McLellan was elected to represent the County of
Colchester in the House of Commons of Canada. Thomas F. Morrison

and Robert Chambers to represent Colchester in the Local Parliament of Nova Scotia. In the year 1869, Adams G. Archibald was elected to represent Colchester in the House of Commons of Canada, in the place of A. W. McLellan, who had accepted office. In 1870, Frederick M. Pearson was returned to represent Colchester in the House of Commons, in place of Adams G. Archibald, who had accepted office. In 1871, Thomas F. Morrison and Samuel Rettie were returned, without opposition, to represent Colchester in the House of Assembly of Nova Scotia. On August 15th, 1872, Frederick M. Pearson was elected, by a large majority of votes, to represent Colchester in the House of Commons of Canada.

It may here be mentioned, the critical situation the people of Cobequid were in at one time, when their friends and relations in the thirteen Provinces, or States, of New England rebelled against British rule or authority. They were strongly induced to join the States. In 1777, two Justices of the Peace were sent from Halifax to Truro, Onslow and Londonderry, to tender the oath of allegiance to the inhabitants, when there were but five found willing to take the oath. When their representatives went to the House of Assembly the next session, they were not allowed to take their seats, on account of the people being suspected of disloyalty. At one time, the people of Truro assembled at Eliakim Tupper's Inn, in the village, to consult about this matter,. James Wright (who had been in His Majesty's service at Fort Cumberland, when he was discharged, was allowed to retain his musket and uniform), when he got notice of this meeting, he put on his uniform, shouldered his musket, with fixed bayonet, and marched down and entered a crowded room in Mr. Tupper's house in great rage. He flourished his gun, and cried out, " Show me the man that will say anything against the rule of King George." He soon cleared the room, some escaping by the door, others by the windows, without any one being killed or wounded. No doubt but he was one of the five who took the oath of allegiance. They, soon after, made up their minds to remain loyal to the British Crown. During this rebellion, the British soldiers were dependent, to a certain extent, on the inhabitants, residing on the sides of the Bay of Fundy for provisions. On one occasion, a number of the soldiers came up the Bay in their boat or small vessel. They landed at Bass River, and went to the house of James Fulton, Esq., entered the house, and helped themselves to what they needed to eat, then laid themselves down for a night's rest. In the morning, they went to the bureau and took out what clean shirts they could get, and dressed themselves. They then went to the pasture and took a heifer three years old, butchered her, and took her away with them. The inhabitants dare not make the least resistance.

On the night of October 4th, 1869, the tide rose about four feet higher that it was ever known to rise before in the Bay of Fundy. It destroyed the dykes in Colchester, which laid open about one thousand acres of marsh. It cost about five thousand dollars to repair the dykes and fences. In the County of Cumberland. the damage was very great, carrying away barns, stacks of hay, dykes and fences. In 1770, a Registrar of Deeds was appointed for Colchester. The office was kept by Joshua Lamb, in Onslow, from the year 1770 to 1777. Charles Dickson, Esq., of Onslow, filled the office from that date until the time of his death, September 3rd, 1796. His third son, Robert Dickson, filled the office, which was kept in Onslow, until 1803. At that date, William Dickson was appointed, who had removed to Truro the year before. He continued to fill the office until 1825. Israel Allison was then appointed Registrar, and continued until 1831. George Dill was then appointed, and continued until the time of his death, January 4th, 1854. On February 21st, 1854, James K. Blair was appointed, and continues to fill the office at the present time, May 1873.

Matthew Harris died at Pictou December 9th, 1819, aged 88 years. He was among the early settlers of Pictou. He was brother of Dr. John Harris, and father of Thomas Harris, Land Surveyor. Thomas Harris surveyed and divided the back land of the Township of Truro, under the writ of partition, and made a plan of the same, which is still in use, and is dated August 12th, 1788.

The first settlers of Upper Stewiacke assembled regularly for Public Worship in the house of Samuel Fisher, from the year 1787 until 1793. They then erected a log Church on the north side of the river, on the opposite side of the road from where the church now stands, in the Village. In October, 1810, the frame of a new church was raised quite near the site of the present church. It was fifty feet long, by forty feet wide, and two storeys high. In 1853, owing to the rapid increase of the congregation, it became necessary to provide more church accommodation. In October, same year, a new frame was raised, forty-six feet, by seventy five, and partly covered in, but was blown down in December. In July of the following year the frame of the present church was raised, and the work progressed steadily until it was completed.

About the year 1780 the first church in Onslow was raised, but the inside was not finished until 1812. William McNutt, grand-father of the McNutts in Lower Village, and at North River, was the principal architect. In 1871 it was taken down, and a new one erected on the same site.

In 1872, the Baptists of Onslow erected a church near the same place. It has been asked, how the old Onslow church came to be owned and occupied by both Presbyterians and Baptists? At the time the church was built the inhabitants of Cobequid were all Presbyterians; but, in course of time, some of them changed, and joined the Baptists, and the house was occupied jointly by the two denominations as long as it stood. In June, 1856, a church was erected between Salmon River and Onslow Mountain, called the Union Church.